Doing
Comparative
Politics

DOING COMPARATIVE POLITICS

An Introduction to Approaches and Issues

Timothy C. Lim

LYNNE
RIENNER
PUBLISHERS

BOULDER
LONDON

Published in the United States of America in 2006 by
Lynne Rienner Publishers, Inc.
1800 30th Street, Boulder, Colorado 80301
www.rienner.com

and in the United Kingdom by
Lynne Rienner Publishers, Inc.
3 Henrietta Street, Covent Garden, London WC2E 8LU

Library of Congress Cataloging-in-Publication Data
Lim, Timothy C., 1960–
    Doing comparative politics : an introduction to approaches and issues / by
Timothy C. Lim.
        p. cm.
    Includes bibliographical references and index.
    ISBN 1-58826-320-7 (hardcover : alk. paper) — ISBN 1-58826-345-2 (pbk. :
alk. paper)
    1. Comparative government. I. Title.
JF51.L56 2005
320.3—dc22

                                                                    2005011303

British Cataloguing in Publication Data
A Cataloguing in Publication record for this book
is available from the British Library.

Printed and bound in the United States of America

The paper used in this publication meets the requirements
of the American National Standard for Permanence of
Paper for Printed Library Materials Z39.48-1992.

5 4 3 2 1

Contents

Figures

Preface

If you read the prefaces of many introductory textbooks, you will find a similar refrain. Invariably, the writers want to help students understand the subject better and believe that they offer an approach that will do just that. Sometimes, too, the writers are frustrated with the existing material—they simply cannot find materials that cover the subject in the ways they want or that do so in a manner that is accessible to most undergraduate students. I must admit to the same motivations. I was dissatisfied with the standard textbooks on comparative politics, many of which adopted a country-by-country approach or were too dense for the typical undergraduate student. Many existing textbooks are also very long, some as much as 900 pages. My basic goal, then, was to write a relatively brief, accessible book that would introduce students to the study of comparative politics in a systematic and rigorous manner. To me, "systematic and rigorous" meant focusing on the methodological and theoretical aspects of the field rather than providing a broad survey of five, ten, or even twenty different countries. At the same time, I wanted to make the study of comparative politics interesting, engaging, and relevant. As any textbook writer knows, this is not easy to do, for writing about, much less teaching, "theory and method" can put even the most bright-eyed student to sleep.

My solution to this problem was partly inspired by Mark Lichbach and Alan Zuckerman's 1997 book, *Comparative Politics: Rationality, Culture, and Structure,* in which the authors divided the study of comparative politics into three broad research traditions. I use these same three traditions—rationality, culture, and structure—as the central organizing principle for *Doing Comparative Politics.* Chapter 3 provides a primer on theory and on the three research traditions. More important, though, I connect each research tradition, and the theories each encompasses, to a series of important and interesting *questions* on poverty (Chapter 4), prosperity (Chapter 5), democracy (Chapter 6), terrorism/political violence (Chapter 7), and social movements (Chapter 8). My objective in these chapters is to help students learn to "think theoretically" about big issues and questions. Even more, my overarching goal is to help students learn how to think in a *critical* manner. I believe my basic approach does just that, as students are compelled to confront, in a systematic and rigorous manner, competing explanations of the same general phenomenon.

My approach to making the study of comparative politics interesting, engaging, and relevant was also inspired by a much less likely source, Michael Moore's 2002 film, *Bowling for Columbine*. In this film, Moore was interested in answering the question, why do so many people in the United States kill each other with guns? His primary approach to answering this question was, simply, to compare. He compared the United States, for example, to England, Germany, Japan, France, and Australia. He also compared, in a bit more depth, the United States to Canada. Although his comparative approach was hardly systematic and rigorous (which, to be fair, should not be expected in a general-audience film), he clearly demonstrated the relevance and utility of comparing. He also made comparing "fun" and interesting. It is for all these reasons that this book draws from Moore's film, although, I should emphasize, his film presents as many negative lessons (that is, lessons on what not to do) as it does positive lessons. I discuss these points, and the comparative method more generally, in Chapter 2. As with the chapter on theory, the principles and concepts covered in Chapter 2 are integrated throughout the book. The aim is to get students into the habit of thinking comparatively, which—together with thinking theoretically—is essential to doing comparative politics.

Chapters 1 and 9 provide important bookends for *Doing Comparative Politics*. Chapter 1 not only provides a thorough overview of the general approach used in this book, but even more important, it is designed to help students develop a clearer understanding of the field as a whole. This, I think, is a crucial but often neglected task. Many students simply never learn what the field of comparative politics is or how it differs from related fields, such as international relations. The book ends with a discussion, in Chapter 9, of globalization and its impact on the field. Arguably, this chapter would be better placed at the beginning of the book, for it raises issues that students should be focused on from the very beginning of their studies. At the same time, a discussion of globalization will undoubtedly make more sense to students after they develop a firm grasp of comparative politics.

As I noted at the outset, one of my more practical goals was to write a relatively brief introductory text, which should allow instructors to either pair this book with a range of other materials or have it serve as a stand-alone text. I have found, moreover, that many students—even those who have had coursework in comparative politics—are unfamiliar with or lack mastery of the core concepts, principles, and methods of comparative political analysis. For this reason, the book could serve as a crucial foundational text and valuable reference for more advanced students, including graduate students. I should also point out that, in writing this book, I assumed that the students would have no background or knowledge of specific countries, regions, or issues. Thus, I have provided basic information where I felt it was needed. I have also included a glossary (glossary entries are indicated by **bold type**). Still, to get the most from the book, it is likely that students will greatly benefit from doing additional research on their own or through assigned supplemental readings.

On a more general note, I would like to say that in writing and teaching from *Doing Comparative Politics,* I have learned a great deal. It has forced me to take seriously various approaches, arguments, and issues I had not thought much about previously or, even worse, had largely dismissed. I hope, then, that not only students but also my peers will learn something from this book. Of course, having my eyes opened to new ways of looking at comparative politics is no guarantee against making errors. I would, therefore, welcome feedback to improve the text.

This said, I want to express my deep appreciation to those who helped me start, develop, and finish this project. I have already mentioned two of these individuals, Mark Lichbach and Alan Zuckerman, without whose work I likely would never even have begun this project. Coincidentally, even the title of this book comes from another book written by Zuckerman, entitled *Doing Political Science* (I say "coincidentally" because I did not think up the title *Doing Comparative Politics;* this was the idea of Marilyn Grobschmidt, my editor at Lynne Rienner Publishers). There are, moreover, dozens of other scholars whose work I have drawn from both directly and indirectly. This is part and parcel of the academic enterprise, and as it would be unwieldy to mention everyone's name, suffice it to say that this book would not have been possible without their efforts and scholarship. Needless to say, I am entirely responsible for any misrepresentations.

I am also very grateful to students in my comparative politics courses at California State University, Los Angeles, both at the undergraduate and graduate levels. Many had to suffer through my early and sometimes confusing drafts, but they nevertheless provided me needed encouragement through their positive and enthusiastic comments. In fact, it is because of my students that I know the approach and material in this book can and does "work." My students, I am confident in saying, proved very capable of learning how to compare and how to theorize in a systematic, rigorous, and critical manner. With varying degrees of success, in short, all learned how to do comparative politics.

I would like to thank, too, the four anonymous reviewers of my first and second drafts, who all provided me with detailed, fair, and helpful suggestions and criticisms. One reviewer, in particular, agreed to review both drafts and provided not only incisive comments on both but also words of support that made the writing process much easier. Marilyn Grobschmidt also deserves special thanks. She responded with amazing alacrity to my initial proposal and has been an enthusiastic supporter of this book since then.

I am most thankful, however, to my wife, Atsuko Sato, who pushed me to complete this book after I had almost given up. Writing a textbook under the best of conditions is difficult, but it is even more difficult in an environment where institutional support is severely lacking. This was certainly true in my case. Writing the book, in fact, was almost exclusively a weekend and summer-break project. Atsuko gave me the support I needed to keep working and even agreed to write Chapter 8 (she also has a PhD in political science). Without Atsuko's support, encouragement, and direct intellectual contribution, I'm not sure I would have ever completed this project.

Finally, I would like to dedicate this book to my wonderful and loving mother, Sandye Lim. In the course of writing the book, I've had to miss or cut short many holidays with my family and forgo many family trips. These decisions were all the more difficult because it meant that my mother and my extended family have had very little time to spend with my now two-year-old daughter, Ailani Sato-Lim, and vice versa. Yet, my mother has always been understanding and has never complained about my schedule. Even though a few words in a preface cannot make up for lost time, they can, at least, memorialize my gratitude and love.

—*Timothy C. Lim*

DOING
COMPARATIVE
POLITICS

PART 1

The Basics

1

Introduction

Doing Comparative Politics

Let us begin this book with a few basic, but very big questions:

- Why are there so many gun-related homicides in the United States?
- Why do so many peoples and countries around the world remain mired in poverty and economic misery? Conversely, how have some peoples and countries been able to become "rich" and prosperous in only a generation or two?
- Can democracy be successfully imposed on Iraq and on other countries? Or are all such efforts doomed to failure?
- What are the causes of terrorism and other forms of political violence? Is anyone capable of becoming a terrorist, or are terrorists the product of a particular type of society and culture?
- How do social movements, such as the 1989 democracy movement in China, emerge and why do some succeed while others fail?

There are, of course, many answers to these questions. Some answers may sound very persuasive, whereas others may *seem* far less convincing, even absurd. On the first question, for example, Michael Moore argued in his Oscar-winning 2002 film *Bowling for Columbine* that the high level of gun violence in the United States is largely due to a "culture of fear" that has been created and constantly reproduced through policies and practices that exacerbate insecurity throughout US society. This culture of fear, Moore suggested, pushes Americans to resolve problems and interpersonal conflict through violence, a reaction that, in turn, creates a self-confirming cycle: fear begets violence, which begets more fear, which begets even more violence, and so on. A culture of fear may not explain everything we need to know about gun violence in the United States, but according to Moore, it is almost certainly a major element of any explanation that purports to tell us why Americans are so prone to shoot-

3

ing each other. Is Moore right? Or is his argument completely baseless? *How do we know?* Indeed, how do we know if any argument—especially one that deals with complex social, political, or economic phenomena—is valid or even plausible? This book is designed, in part, to help you answer this question. Learning how to evaluate arguments, however, is secondary to the overarching goal of this book, which is to enable you to better understand and explain social, political, or economic processes, events, and outcomes *on your own*.

So, what does all this have to do with comparative politics? The answer is fairly simple: comparative politics, as a field of study, provides us with a ready array of conceptual and analytical tools that we can use to address and answer a wide range of questions about the social world. I will talk about exactly what this means shortly; for now, though, let me just add that comparative politics provides a systematic, coherent, and *practical* way to understand and make better sense of the things that happen in the world around us. In a broader sense, moreover, comparative politics is relevant to almost anyone, even those not interested in "studying foreign countries." A "comparative politics approach" can be applied to a huge variety of problems, from the mundane to the sublime, in a wide variety of areas. Explaining gun violence is just one example, but there are many others. Consider the following potpourri of questions and issues: Can a national health care system work in the United States? Are fundamentalist religious beliefs and democracy compatible? Is vast economic inequality a necessary by-product of a capitalist system? What encourages people to save and invest? Are government bureaucracies necessarily inefficient? If marijuana use is legalized, will such use necessarily lead to the abuse of "harder" drugs? What are the most effective policies against drunk driving?

A comparative politics approach is well suited for addressing such questions. At this point, of course, the reasons are not at all clear, but they will become much clearer as we proceed. It is also important to say, at this early juncture, that comparative politics is not the only, nor is it always the best, approach one can use. Nonetheless, virtually any student or concerned citizen (not to mention scholar or policymaker) will benefit tremendously from cultivating and developing a "comparative politics approach." With all this in mind, the next important step we need to take is to clarify what the term "comparative politics" means and what it implies. As we will see, this is easier said than done.

■ What Is Comparative Politics?

Many textbooks on comparative politics provide a clear, seemingly simple answer to the question, what is comparative politics? Perhaps the simplest is this: comparative politics is the study of politics *in foreign* countries (emphasis added; Zahariadis 1997, p. 2). Few texts, though, stop here. Most also emphasize that comparative politics, in slightly more formal terms, involves both a *method* of study and a *subject* of study. As a method of study, comparative politics is—not surprisingly—premised on comparison. As a subject of study, comparative politics focuses on understanding and explaining political phenomena that take place within a **state, society, country,** or **political system.**[1] (See Figure 1.1 for a discussion of these various terms.) This slightly more detailed definition of the field gives us a better sense of what comparative politics is and how it may differ from other fields of inquiry, although, as I will discuss below, it is a definition that raises far more questions than it answers. Still, defining comparative politics as a method of study based on comparison and a subject of study based on an examination of political phenomena in a country (or other **"macrosocial"** unit) highlights several important points. First, it immediately tells us that the field is primarily concerned with *internal* or domestic dynamics, which helps to distinguish comparative politics from **international relations** (IR)—a field of study largely, though not exclusively, concerned with the "external" relations or foreign policies of states. Second, it tells us that comparative politics is, appropriately enough, concerned with "political" phenomena. Third, and perhaps most important, it tells us that the field is not only characterized but *defined* by a comparative method of analysis. I might also point out that this second definition does not automatically exclude the United States (as the first does) from the field of comparative politics: the United States is a state or country in exactly the same sense that France, Japan, India, Mexico, South Korea, Zimbabwe, or Russia is.[2]

As I already suggested, though, this second definition raises a number of other questions and issues. Can comparative politics, for example, focus only on what happens *inside* countries? In other words, is it possible to understand the internal politics of a place without understanding and accounting for the impact of external or transnational/international forces? This is a very important question, but there are several others: What is meant by *political* phenomena—or by politics more generally? Are economic, social, and cultural phenomena also political, or do they fall into a completely different category? Regarding the question of method, we might also ask: What does it mean to compare? Is comparison in comparative politics different from, say, comparison in sociology or any other field of study? Even more basically, *why* do we compare? That is, what's the point of making comparisons in the first place? And, last, *how* do we compare?

The Importance of Definitions

In asking so many questions, I realize that I also might have raised a question in *your* mind, namely, why can't we be satisfied with the relatively short and easy-to-understand definition first mentioned? One reason is clear: before we begin studying any field, we need to understand what the field is *really* about.

Figure 1.1   Some Key Concepts in Comparative Politics: State, Nation, Nation-State, Government, and Country

The terms "state," "**nation**," "**nation-state**," "**government**," and "country" are often used interchangeably, especially in the popular press and media. Although this practice is not entirely unwarranted, it is important to recognize that the terms are not synonymous. A state, for example, is a legal concept that is premised on a number of conditions: a permanent population, a defined territory, and a *national* government capable of maintaining effective control over its territory. In addition, many scholars (following **Max Weber**) argue that a state must have a monopoly of the legitimate use of physical force or violence within a given territory. Notice that the definition of state includes a reference to government, which can be defined as the agency or apparatus through which a body exercises authority and performs its functions. In this definition, governments need not be part of a state; moreover, multiple governments may exist within a single state. Indeed, we can find governments in all sorts of places—in a university or school (that is, the student government) or in sovereign "nations" (for example, a Native American tribal council)— and at many levels. Cities, counties, provinces, and whole regions (for example, the **European Union**) can also have their own separate governments.

The example of Native Americans is a useful way to differentiate a nation from a state. A nation, in the simplest terms, can be defined as a group of people who recognize each other as sharing a common identity. This common identity can be based on language, religion, culture, or a number of other *self-defined* criteria. This makes the concept of the nation inherently subjective or

(continues)

To do this, we typically start at the most basic level—with how people define the field. Unfortunately, even seemingly simple and straightforward definitions (or questions, such as what is comparative politics?) are often filled with complexities and subtleties, many of which are not immediately apparent. As students generally—and as students of comparative politics specifically—I want you to keep this firmly in mind. Moreover, I want you to understand that few (social, political, or economic) issues can be adequately understood or explained without taking the time for careful and serious reflection. A second related reason is this: *definitions are important.* Very important. This is partly because they tell us what is included in the field of study and what is left out. Definitions that leave very little out are often not very helpful. Consider the definition offered at the beginning of this section: "Comparative politics is the study of politics in foreign countries." By this definition, we might say that

---

Figure 1.1 continued

---

intersubjective. Nations do not require states or governments to exist, nor must nations exist within a single defined territory. One can speak, for example, of nations that transcend borders, such as the Nation of Islam. Combining the definitions of state and nation creates the concept of the nation-state. Technically speaking, a nation-state would only exist if nearly all the members of a single nation were organized in a single state, without any other distinct communities being present (Willets 1997, p. 289). From this perspective, despite its prevalent usage, many scholars argue that there are no true nation-states and that the concept should be entirely abandoned. But there are what we might call *national states*—states in which a common identity is forged around the concept of nationalism itself (for more on this issue, see Eley and Suny 1996). For example, people living in the United States may be divided by a wide range of religious, cultural, ethnic, linguistic, and other differences. Yet they all may share a common sense of "being American." Practically speaking, the term "national state" is often used as a synonym for nation-state. The notion of a national state, moreover, comes close to the more concrete concept of country, which may be defined as a distinct political system of people sharing common values and occupying a relatively fixed geographic space (Eley and Suny 1996). "Country" is the most generic of the terms referred to here.

---

comparative politics studies politics *in* foreign countries, whereas IR studies politics *between* or *of* foreign countries. Still, it is not clear what the difference is. A good definition should tell us. On the other hand, a good definition should also avoid making unnecessary or unjustified distinctions or exclusions. Unfortunately, comparative politics, or at least those who have helped shape the field, have been guilty of just this sin. Indeed, it would be fair to say that the early development and conceptualization of the field were profoundly influenced by the **ethnocentric** biases, values, and political domination of US scholars and leaders who saw the United States as the guiding light for the rest of the world.

To see this (and to see the danger of this type of influence), consider the character of comparative politics prior to World War II, when the field was almost entirely defined in terms of western European affairs. During this period, the vast majority of research by scholars in the United States was devoted to a handful of countries: Britain, France, and Germany (a little later, the Soviet Union and Japan were included). These were the countries considered most important in US eyes—they were, to put it more bluntly, the only countries that were deemed to matter. Predictably, then, issues that are now considered especially important to researchers in comparative politics and to other comparative social scientists ("comparativists" for short), such as economic development and democratization, were also largely ignored by early students of comparative politics in the United States. These issues were not considered pressing or worthy of study, because the West had already "solved" them. In other words, nondemocratic and economically "backward" countries were treated as aberrations or immature versions of the West and of the United States specifically, "rather than as political systems with distinct characteristics . . . worthy of examination on their own merits" (Zahariadis 1997, p. 7). The tendency for political scientists in the United States to ignore most of the rest of the world (even much of western Europe), moreover, rested on the immodest assumption that the United States simply had little or nothing to learn from anyone else. From this perspective, it is far easier to understand why comparative politics remained so narrowly defined for the first half of the twentieth century. "The reasons," as Wiarda (1991) nicely put it,

> go to the heart of the American experience, to the deeply held belief that the United States is different [from] and *superior* to European and all other nations, the widespread conviction at the popular level that the United States had little to learn from the rest of the world, the near-universal belief of Americans in the superiority of their institutions and their attitudes that the rest of the world must learn from the United States and never the other way around. Hence political science as it developed as a discipline in the United States was predominantly the study of American politics, for that is where the overwhelming emphasis and interest lay. . . . Those who studied and wrote about comparative politics were generally believed to have little to offer intellectually to other areas of the discipline. (emphasis added, p. 12)

The Changing Context of Comparative Politics

The relegation of comparative politics to the margins of political science changed dramatically, however, following the end of World War II—although it would be more accurate to say that the deepest changes began during the war, when US policymakers recognized an urgent need for area specialists, that is, people with a strong understanding of specific cultures, languages, societies, and political systems, and not just in Western Europe. What sparked this newfound interest in the rest of the world? The answer is easy to discern. Specifically, World War II brought home the importance of knowing about other countries so that the military-strategic interests of the United States could be better protected. Certainly, in terms of funding and official support, there is little doubt this was true. As Bruce Cumings (1997), a prominent area specialist on Korea, pointed out, the first effort to create a systematic base of knowledge about "foreign" countries (from the perspective of the United States) was carried out by the Office of Strategic Services (OSS), the forerunner of the Central Intelligence Agency (CIA). According to Cumings, in

1941, OSS director William "Wild Bill" Donovan established the rationale for employing the nation's best expertise to collect and analyze all information and data that might bear upon national security. Once this rationale became policy, the future of comparative and **area studies** in the United States brightened considerably.[3]

The war not only broadened the perspective of the United States with regard to the list of *countries* that mattered but also with regard to the *issues* that mattered. In particular, the rise of **fascism** and militarism in Germany, Japan, and Italy and the rise of **communism** (and **Stalinism**) in Russia and, later, China, had a profound impact on the field of comparative politics and political science as a whole (Wiarda 1991). For good reason, scholars, policymakers, and others wanted to understand these political phenomena, which differed so much from the democratic and capitalist paths followed by the United States and most Western European countries. They especially wanted to understand not only how and why fascist or **totalitarian** rule emerged and developed but also how and why it seemed to thrive in certain places (especially to the extent that it represented a serious and real threat to the democracies of the West). The question was how to best accomplish this understanding. For an increasing number of scholars and policymakers, the answer was to be found in a more sophisticated approach to comparative study. One of the leading advocates of this view was Roy Macridis (1955), who, in the mid-1950s, strongly criticized traditional comparative politics as being overly parochial (with its near-exclusive focus on Western Europe), too descriptive (as opposed to analytical), exceedingly formalistic, atheoretical, and even noncomparative. Macridis's critique helped lay the basis for a sea change in the field.

The Cold War and Comparative Politics

The impact of World War II on comparative politics, therefore, was immense; but it was the onset of the **Cold War** that ensured the longer-term prominence of the field. It was the conflict between the Soviet Union and the United States that compelled US policymakers to pay *sustained* and *systematic* attention to "lesser" countries and regions—especially to a huge number of former colonies, variously referred to as the "South," the "developing world," the "Third World," and even the "Majority World" (see Figure 1.2). The reason is clear enough: since these hitherto neglected countries were viewed, in strategic terms, as potentially important allies or enemies, it behooved US policymakers to know more about the peoples they would now have to treat as relatively independent players in world affairs. Significantly, it was not just any countries and regions that were included: "Japan got favored placement as a success story of development, and China got obsessive attention as a pathological example of abortive development" (Cumings 1997). Latin and South American countries also became important foci of attention for scholars and policymakers (starting in the

**Figure 1.2   Note on Terminology—What's in a Name?
The "Third World" and Other Terms**

The terms "South," "Third World," the "developing world" (or developing countries), and "less developed countries" (LDCs) are often used interchangeably to refer to those parts of the world except for Western Europe, North America (Canada and the United States), Australia, New Zealand, Japan, and the former communist "bloc." During the Cold War era, so-called Third World countries were distinguished from "Second World" countries largely based on political ideology and military power; thus, the Second World comprised the communist or socialist regimes, including the Soviet Union and its satellite states (it is not clear, however, whether other communist states—such as China, Vietnam, North Korea, and others—were included). Today, of course, the former Soviet Union and its erstwhile "satellites" no longer exist. They have been replaced by Russia and a plethora of newly independent states, located primarily in Eastern Europe and Central Asia. For this reason, the concept of the Second World has essentially disappeared (although, even during the Cold War era, the term was rarely used).

So where have these countries gone? Into the Third World, or someplace else? This is not a trivial question, for there is considerable debate over the issue of what terminology to use. For many researchers, the concept of the Third World has not only become an anachronism but was suspect from the very beginning in that it implied inferiority—as did the term "less developed countries." Instead, many preferred the more neutral term, "South." This term, too, is problematic, given that countries such as Australia and New Zealand are situated in the Southern Hemisphere, whereas most countries of Asia, many countries of Africa, and even some countries of South America are located in the Northern Hemisphere. More recently, others have proposed a whole new set of terms. Advocates of neoliberalism, for example, like the term "emerging markets"; not surprisingly, that term has not been embraced by everyone. One interesting alternative has been proposed by Titus Alexander (1996), who argued that the most appropriate term is "majority world." This term, noted Alexander, is descriptively accurate but does not imply any degree of homogeneity among the huge number of countries that compose the majority world—an important point considering the "huge social, economic and political differences within and between all countries" (p. ix). Moreover, "majority" world does not contain any connotation of inferiority, backwardness, or subordination.

1960s), as did South Korea, Taiwan, and a few other countries that showed "promise." Much of the research during this time, moreover, was driven by the desire to understand and challenge the appeal of and potential challenge posed by communism. In this regard, it is no coincidence that one of the most influential academic books of the 1950s and 1960s was W. W. Rostow's *The Stages of Economic Growth: A Non-Communist Manifesto* (1960). Although not strictly a work of comparative politics, Rostow's anticommunist sentiments were shared by the foremost scholars of comparative political development of the time, including the likes of Gabriel Almond, James Coleman, and Lucien Pye (Wiarda 1991, p. 14).

This bit of history, it is important to understand, is still relevant. For it tells us, quite clearly, that outwardly objective fields of study are not immune to a host of subjective, generally hidden social and political forces. And what is true of the past is almost assuredly true of the present. This means that we always need to be careful, and even a little skeptical, of the knowledge that is produced in any context. This does not mean that all of today's scholarship, even more, the scholarship of the 1940s and 1950s, is irredeemably tainted and illegitimate. It is not (although *some* parts may certainly be). Instead, it means that we should never assume it is entirely or even mostly "objective."

This said, since the 1960s, the field has continued to change. Definitions of the field, too, have changed. Today, in fact, the definition of comparative politics, except in a very broad or generic sense,[4] is characterized as much by divergence as by consensus. (For a sampling of current definitions of comparative politics, see Figure 1.3.) This is one reason why the bulk of this chapter is devoted to the question, what is comparative politics? Unless you can get an adequate grasp of this deceptively simple question, it will be exceedingly difficult to develop a grasp of the field as a whole. Given the lack of consensus, my intention is not to provide *the* definition of comparative politics in this chapter. Instead, my intention is, first, to help you understand the "complexities and subtleties" of defining the field and, second, to give you a basis for deciding how best to answer the question. One of the best ways to accomplish this is by asking the type of questions I posed above. Next, of course, we need to try to *answer* these questions, which is what we will endeavor to do in the remainder of this chapter.

■ Why Does Comparative Politics Focus on What Happens *Inside* Countries?

To answer the question upon which this section is based, it is extremely useful to recognize that comparative politics is not the only field in political science that focuses on countries or states as the primary **units of analysis**. Scholars in international relations, as I noted above, are also intimately concerned with

---

Figure 1.3   A Few Definitions of Comparative Politics

"Comparative politics involves the systematic study and comparison of the world's political systems. It seeks to explain differences between as well as similarities among countries. In contrast to journalistic reporting on a single country, comparative politics is particularly interested in exploring patterns, processes, and regularities among political systems" (Wiarda 2000, p. 7).

"Comparative politics involves both a subject of study—foreign countries—and a method of study—comparison" (Wilson 1996, p. 4).

"What is comparative politics? It is two things, first a world, second a discipline. As a 'world,' comparative politics encompasses political behavior and institutions in all parts of the earth. . . . The 'discipline' of comparative politics is a field of study that desperately tries to keep up with, to encompass, to understand, to explain, and perhaps to influence the fascinating and often riotous world of comparative politics" (Lane 1997, p. 2).

"Comparative politics . . . involves no more and no less than a comparative study of politics—a search for similarities and differences between and among political phenomena, including political institutions (such as legislatures, political parties, or political interest groups), political behavior (such as voting, demonstrating, or reading political pamphlets), or political ideas (such as liberalism, conservatism, or Marxism). Everything that politics studies, comparative politics studies; the latter just undertakes the study with an explicit comparative methodology in mind" (Mahler 2000, p. 3).

---

countries or, more accurately, states. But, as I also noted, international relations is typically more interested in relations between and among states—that is, with their *interactions* in an international system. Even though this has not precluded IR scholars from looking at what happens inside states or countries, a good deal of research in the field has tended to treat states as undifferentiated wholes, which is to say that IR scholars (especially those associated with the dominant research school in IR, **realism** or **neorealism**) assume that states are *functionally alike* when interacting with other states. This is a critical assumption, largely because it suggests that it is possible to explain the behavior of states or countries *without* a careful examination of their "internal workings." The reasoning behind this assumption stems from the belief that the international system is **anarchic**, so that each and every state is forced to behave in similar ways regardless of its internal makeup or its domestic politics. The logic here is both simple and compelling: in an anarchic (as opposed to **hierarchic**) system, states must compete with other states for security, power, and influence. They must do so precisely because there is no ultimate rule maker and rule enforcer for the system as a whole. Lacking an ultimate authority, individual states (or actors) are forced to take matters into their own hands, so to speak. Each state must, in other words, do those things that ensure its own long-term survival. This generally means, among other things, building a strong army, developing a network of mutually beneficial military-strategic alliances, maintaining a diplomatic corps, gathering intelligence, and engaging in military conflict when necessary.

In this view, the internal (political) makeup of a country is *relatively* unimportant in terms of explaining or predicting its external behavior. Thus, for example, a liberal democracy with a strong **presidential system** (such as the United States) would behave—with regard to its foreign policy decisions—in the same way that a single-party, **communist**-led dictatorship would.[5] In a similar vein, we would expect a state governed by an Islamic (or Christian) fundamentalist regime, say Iran, to act in essentially the same manner as any other state. A more salient consideration would be the size and military capacity of a country. That is, a large, militarily powerful country would behave differently from a small, militarily weak country. The foregoing discussion, I should stress, is highly simplified and stylized; in addition, it fails to account for wide and significant divergences within IR scholarship.[6] Nonetheless, it is a useful way to grasp a basic distinction between IR and comparative politics. This is necessary if only because so many people, including some political scientists, are largely oblivious to the differences between the two fields. Yet, for the most part, the two fields have developed along very different lines both theoretically and methodologically (as I will discuss shortly) and have only occasionally intersected in a significant and meaningful manner. This is reason enough to spend a lot of time defining comparative politics, for if we cannot even distinguish it from related fields, how can we reasonably talk about a "comparative politics approach"?

Given the strong focus on external (or interstate) relations in IR, comparative politics has, by default, tended to focus on the internal dynamics of countries. In this respect, we might say that, whereas IR is generally based on an "outside-in" approach, comparative politics is generally based on an "inside-out" approach. The different emphases of the two fields, in turn, have produced (at least in the past) a very clear-cut "division of labor." Thus, as Zahariadis (1997) pointed out:

> Comparative research tends to be geographic in orientation; that is comparativists generally describe themselves either as country specialists or as Europeanists, Africanists, Asianists, and so on. [Ironically, this has led many "comparativists," in practice, to eschew actually engaging in comparative research; instead, many have become narrowly, even exclusively, focused on their country of expertise.] In contrast, divisions in international relations are more thematic and involve issues such as international conflict or international political economy that transcend geographic boundaries. (p. 4)

Zahariadis is correct, but his observations do not go far enough. The division of labor between comparative politics and IR has resulted not only in different orientations and research interests but also in a belief that there is a real and fundamental difference between domestic and international politics.

Is It Possible to Understand the Internal Politics of a Place Without Understanding the Impact of External Forces?

All this brings us back to an integrally related issue, one raised earlier in the chapter, namely, is it possible to understand the internal politics of a place without understanding the impact of external forces? *My* answer to this question is an unequivocal "no." This, I think, has been true for a very long time (at least since the beginnings of colonialism in the fifteenth century) but is particularly true today. Processes such as **globalization** in all its various dimensions (a topic that I cover at length in Chapter 9), in particular, have made it nearly impossible to understand the internal dynamics of a country without looking at what happens on the "outside." In practice, virtually all comparativists clearly recognize this, although there is still a great deal of disagreement over the relative importance of internal versus external factors. Some scholars argue that "external" and, particularly, system-level factors—such as the **structure** of the world economy or particular relationships of **dependence** (see Figure 1.4) between poor and rich countries—are extremely and sometimes overwhelmingly important. Others argue that, although such

---

Figure 1.4   Structure and Dependence

When comparativists use the term "dependence," they are usually referring to the inability of poor and weak societies (or subordinate social classes) to control their own economic and political fates. They argue, instead, that the economic and political fate of poorer societies—primarily former colonies—is primarily determined by their relationship with more powerful economic actors, which itself is a reflection of the structure of the world economy. This structure, not surprisingly, is dominated by Western European countries, the United States, and Japan. In this structure, the rich countries (that is, the core) occupy privileged positions that allow them to dominate and exploit most other countries in the world (that is, the periphery). The structure itself is made up of myriad rules, practices, and ongoing relationships, all of which were institutionalized by the rich countries of the core and all of which are designed to virtually guarantee the status quo.

things matter, what matters most are the individual attributes of societies and their states. These individual attributes may derive from particular historical experiences, from culture, from language, from religion, and so on. The debate between these two sides is related to the main theoretical approaches in comparative politics, which we will cover in much more depth in subsequent chapters. For now, suffice it to say that although almost all comparativists recognize the peril of defining the field strictly in terms of what happens inside a country, state, or society, there is no consensus on exactly what this means.

Comparative Politics: The Interplay of Domestic and External Forces

Admitting that comparative politics cannot be limited to looking at what happens inside a country or other large social unit, I should stress, does not mean that we need to completely abandon any distinctions among fields of study, and especially between comparative politics and IR. We do need, however, to amend our definition of comparative politics. Thus, rather than defining comparative politics as a subject of study based on an examination of political phenomena *within* or *in* countries, we can say that *comparative politics examines the* interplay *of domestic and external forces on the politics of a given country, state, or society*. This amended definition, unfortunately, still does not tell us if it is legitimate to separate the study of politics from economics, society, culture, and so on. It is to this question that I will turn next.

■ What Is Politics?

Traditionally (that is, prior to World War II), comparative politics mainly involved *describing* the basic features of political systems. Most research in comparative politics, moreover, operated on the premise that politics referred exclusively to the *formal* political system, that is, to the concrete institutions of government (such as the parliament, the congress, and the bureaucracy) and to the constitutional and judicial rules that helped governments function. Accordingly, early studies tended to be little more than factual and generally superficial accounts of how particular institutions of government operated and were organized or how certain laws were written and then passed. Such accounts may be useful and even necessary, but they can only tell a small part of what we need to know about politics. Even those political processes and actors closely associated with the formal political system—such as political parties, elections, foreign and domestic decisionmaking—were left out of these early studies. Politics, in short, was conceived of in very narrow terms.

A Process-Oriented Definition of Politics

This narrowness began to change in the 1950s, when scholars laid a new foundation for the field of comparative politics and for political science more generally. There are several complex reasons for this, some of which I have already discussed (and some of which I will discuss later). For now, I would like to concentrate on how the traditional concern with the formal and legalistic definition of politics was challenged and ultimately cast aside in favor of a broader definition. An influential article by Roy Macridis (whom I mentioned above) and Richard Cox (1953) symbolized this change. The two authors argued that the preoccupation with formal political institutions and judicial rules was too close to the study of law and not close enough to the study of politics, "which [in contrast to the study of law] observed that relations between society and authority were governed by judicial but also by informal rules and sometimes by brute force" (cited in Zahariadis 1997, p. 7). Although Macridis and Cox (along with several other prominent scholars) succeeded in breaking the hold of **formalism/legalism** in comparative politics, they did so only to a limited extent. This was true for two basic reasons. First, although the move away from formalism/legalism opened the door to comparative study of a broader range of political institutions and processes, politics was still defined primarily if not solely in relation to activities that involved the state or the government. Second, the discipline of political science generally and comparative politics specifically remained tied to the idea that "politics"—as a subject of study—could be separated from economics, sociology, history, geography, anthropology, or any other field in the **social sciences** and **humanities**.

The limitations of this latter view become particularly clear, noted Adrian Leftwich (1983), "when one considers concrete problems in modern societies, such as unemployment in the industrial societies on the one hand, and rural poverty in the Third World on the other. The harder you think about these issues, the more difficult it is to identify them as strictly economic, social, or political in their causes or consequences" (p. 4). I agree, which is why in this book we will begin with a definition of politics that is broader than what is offered in many traditional textbooks. This alternative definition, what we might call a *process-oriented definition* (Stoker and Marsh 2002), sees politics as part and parcel of a larger *social process*. In this view, politics *"is about the uneven distribution of power in society [or between societies], how the struggle over power is conducted, and its impact on the creation and distribution of resources, life chances and well-being"* (emphasis added; p. 9). This process-oriented definition, as should be clear, makes it difficult if not impossible to maintain firm boundaries between disciplines. To see this, consider, for example, how uneven distributions of power in societies come about in the first place. Are these uneven power distributions the product of history? Or do contemporary economic forces play the determinative role? What about the effects of culture, religion, custom, or even geography? Is it possible to say that one type of factor always predominates, or is there an inextricable interaction among these different forces—be they economic, social, political, cultural, geographic, and so on? The answers to all these questions, I believe, are fairly clear, and boil down to the conclusion that "politics" is integrally and necessarily tied to history, culture, economics, geography, and a variety of other forces. In practice, most comparativists agree with this view of politics, which is why comparative political analysis today tends to be wide-ranging and inclusive.

In addition to transcending disciplinary boundaries, a process-oriented definition of politics has at least two other implications. First, it clearly takes politics out of the governmental arena and puts it into almost all domains of life. These other domains include virtually all social and civil institutions and actors, such as churches, factories, corporations, trade unions, political parties, think tanks, ethnic groups and organizations, women's groups, organized crime, and so on. Second, a process-oriented definition of politics reinforces our amended definition of comparative politics above (namely, "as a field that looks at the interplay of domestic and external forces on the politics of a given country, state, or society"). For it is clear that politics—as a struggle for power over the creation and distribution of resources, life chances, and well-being—is not something that can be easily compartmentalized into the domestic and international. This is because the activities that determine the distribution and use of resources (at least for the past few hundred years) are rarely confined to a single, clearly defined political territory; *thus, as all politics is local (according to one popular saying), all politics is also potentially international and global.*

Losing Focus?

There are, I should note, many political scientists who would disagree with this broad conception of politics. We are already familiar with the basic argument. To repeat: overly broad definitions force us to lose focus; that is, because there are no neat boundaries telling us what is and what is not included in the scope of the definition, we are studying both everything and nothing. Zahariadis (1997), for example, would like us to differentiate politics from "corporate decisions"; the latter, he asserted, "affect only a specific corporation" (p. 2). Yet, although there are certainly myriad decisions made within a corporation (or within a family, factory, church, or other social institution) with a very limited public or societal impact, it is also true that a vast number of "private" decisions have a clear and sometimes profound public dimension. By their very nature, in fact, many corporate decisions have a deep influence on how resources are obtained, used, produced, and distributed. Moreover, in an era of megacorporations—where the largest firms are bigger, and often immensely bigger, than many countries in terms of command over economic resources—the idea that corporate decisions do not have a far-reaching public impact is difficult to maintain. Consider, in this regard, Wal-Mart. In the 2004 fiscal year, Wal-Mart's total sales amounted to more than a quarter *trillion* dollars ($256.3 billion, to be exact), which was only slightly less than Saudi Arabia's **gross domestic product (GDP)** of $287.8 billion (2004 estimate) but vastly more than the GDP of most of the world's countries ("Wal-Mart 2004 Annual Report"). (See Figure 1.5 for additional comparisons.) Where, then, do we draw the line between public and private decisions? Is it even possible to do so? I would argue that the line, in some respects, has simply become too blurred to be of major significance today.

At the same time, it would be a mistake for politics to be defined as "everything-including-the-kitchen-sink." Indeed, as I discuss in subsequent chapters (and as I suggested earlier), it is often necessary to provide clear-cut,

Figure 1.5   Wal-Mart vs. the World

The table below provides some simple (maybe simplistic) comparisons of Wal-Mart, the world's largest company in terms of sales, and a number of selected countries. Traditional definitions of politics suggest that countries, no matter how small, have greater relevance to "politics" than corporate actors. These figures, although hardly definitive, suggest otherwise.

	Wal-Mart	Saudi Arabia	Bolivia	Haiti
Employees/ population	1.5 million	25.8 million	8.7 million	7.6 million
Sales/GDP-PPP (in billions US$)[a]	$256.3	$286.2	$20.8	$12.1
Per capita sales/GDP	$170,822	$11,800	$2,400	$1,600
Growth rate	12%	4.7%	2.1%	–1.0%
International sales/exports (in billions US$)	$47.5	$86.5	$1.49	$0.32
Imports (in billions US$)	N/A[b]	$30.4	$1.5	$1.0

Sources: Figures for Wal-Mart are all based on the 2004 fiscal year. International sales are included in overall sales figures ("Wal-Mart 2004 Annual Report," http://www.walmartstores. com/Files/annualreport_2004.pdf). Figures for Saudi Arabia, Bolivia, and Haiti are based on estimates from 2003 ("Infoplease Almanac," http://www.infoplease.com/almanacs.html).

Notes: a. GDP = gross domestic product; PPP = purchasing power parity.

b. The figure for imports was not available, but most analysts agree that a large proportion of goods sold at Wal-Mart stores is produced overseas and imported by Wal-Mart for sale in its retail stores in the United States.

precise definitions. This is especially true when trying to develop an argument or when trying to support a specific hypothesis or claim. After all, if you cannot precisely or adequately define what it is you are studying—say "democracy" or "terrorism"—how can you possibly claim to say anything meaningful about that subject? In defining an entire field of study, precision is less important, but not irrelevant. The trick, then, is to develop a definition that is neither too narrow nor too unfocused. One solution, albeit a pragmatic one, is to acknowledge that the politics about which comparativists (and other political scientists) are most concerned, according to Stoker and Marsh (2002), (1) is primarily *collective* as opposed to primarily interpersonal and (2) involves interaction *within the public arena*—that is, in the government or state—or *between* the public arena and social actors or institutions (p. 10). No doubt, this qualification will still be unsatisfactory to many political scientists, but it is also one upon which a large number of comparativists have chosen to base their research and analysis.

With all this in mind, let us now turn to the other major aspect of comparative politics, namely, comparing. To begin this discussion, let me pose a simple question: what does it mean to compare?

■ What Does It Mean to Compare? What Is a Comparativist?

In thinking about what it means to compare, let's first consider what one scholar has to say: "Thinking without comparison is unthinkable. And, in the absence of comparison, so is all scientific thought and scientific research" (Swanson 1971, p. 141; cited in Ragin 1987, p. 1). This scholar is telling us that in *all* social sciences, researchers, scholars, and students are invariably engaged in making some sort of comparison. If this is so (and it is fair to say that it is), then there is very little that sets comparative politics apart—on the surface, at least—from other fields of study. This is to say that the comparative strategies used by "comparativists" are not, *in principle,* different from the comparative strategies used by other political scientists, sociologists, economists, and so on. But it does not mean that no differences exist: arguably, one practice that sets comparative politics apart from other fields is the explicit and direct focus on the comparative method—as opposed to simply "comparing."[7]

The comparative method, as I will discuss in detail in the following chapter, is a distinctive mode of comparative analysis. According to Ragin (1987), it entails two main predispositions. First, it involves a bias toward (although certainly not an exclusive focus on) **qualitative analysis**, which means that comparativists tend to look at *cases as wholes* and to compare whole cases with each other. Thus the tendency for comparativists is to talk of comparing Germany to Japan or the United States to Canada. This may not seem to be an important point, but it has significant implications, one of which is that comparativists tend to eschew—or at least, put less priority on—**quantitative analysis**, also known as **statistical** or **variable**-centered **analysis** (Ragin 1987, pp. 2–3). In the social sciences, especially over the past few years, this orientation away from quantitative and toward qualitative analysis definitely sets comparativists apart from other social scientists. Even within comparative politics, however, this is beginning to change. The second predisposition among comparativists is to value *interpretation* and *context* (pp. 2–3). This means, in part, that comparativists (of all theoretical orientations, I might add) begin with the assumption that "history matters." Saying that history matters, I should caution, is much more than pointing out a few significant historical events or figures in an analysis; instead, it involves showing exactly how historical processes and practices, as well as long-established institutional arrangements, impact and shape the *contemporary* environment in which decisions are made, events unfold, and struggles for power occur. *It means, in other words, demonstrating a meaningful continuity between the past and the present.* This is not easy to do, but for a comparativist using "history," it is often an essential task.

Although understanding the predisposition of comparativists is important, this still doesn't tell us what it means to compare—a question that may seem easy to answer, but in fact is not. Just pointing out or describing differences and similarities between any two countries, for example, is not by any account the be-all and end-all of comparative analysis. Indeed, if you stay strictly at the level of superficial description—for example, China has a **Confucian** heritage, whereas the United States does not; both France and Russia experienced **social revolutions**—you will never genuinely engage in comparative *analysis,* no matter how accurate your observations may be. And you're even less likely to tell your audience anything meaningful or insightful about political phenomena. Comparing, then, involves much more than making observations about two or more entities. Just what else is involved in comparative analysis is the topic of our next chapter, so I will reserve the remainder of my discussion on this topic until then. In the meantime, we need to address another basic and essential question: why compare?

■ Why Compare?

To be good comparativists, we need to know *why* we compare. In other words, what is the purpose of comparing? On this question, Giovanni Sartori (1994) offered us a very simple answer, namely, we compare to **control**. By control, Sartori means to say—albeit in a very loose way—that we use comparisons as a way to check (verify or falsify) whether our claims or assertions about certain phenomena are valid by controlling for, or holding constant, certain variables. Take the statements, "poverty causes corruption" or, conversely, "corruption causes poverty"; "authoritarianism is more conducive to high levels of economic growth than democracy"; and "social revolutions are caused by relative deprivation." How do we know, Sartori asked, whether any of these statements is true, false, or something else? "We know," Sartori answered, "by looking around, that is, by *comparative checking"* (emphasis added; p. 16). It is important to understand that, in most comparative analyses, actual **control variables** are not used. This issue may not be very clear right now and, for our purposes, is not critical. The main point is this: different types of comparisons allow a researcher to treat a range of similarities or differences as if they are control variables. In so doing, the researcher can safely eliminate a whole range of potentially significant factors and, instead, concentrate on those variables he deems most important.

To make this point more understandable, let us return to an example I have already used, namely, the argument made by Michael Moore in *Bowling for Columbine*. Although largely implicit, a key methodological strategy used by Moore in this film was comparative checking, a strategy that he used effectively to dismiss a range of competing arguments about gun violence in the United States. Many people have argued, as Moore pointed out, that the high level of gun violence in the United States is due to the influence of "antisocial" rock music and to specific singers, most notably Marilyn Manson. Others have argued that the violent history of the United States is the main reason for the large number of gun-related homicides or that the country's racial and ethnic divisions are the key factor. Still others simply point to the high level of gun ownership in the United States. Through simple comparative checking, however, Moore was able to test and problematicize all of these claims. For example, Moore demonstrated that "Goth rock," a particularly virulent form of antisocial music according to some critics, is popular throughout the world, and especially in Germany (which is home to the world's largest modern gothic festival, the yearly Wave Gotik Treffen in Leipzig) Germany, however, has one of the lowest gun-related murder and overall homicide rates in the world. Gun ownership, too, does not always correspond to high levels of gun-related homicides. In Finland, to cite one clear-cut case (although not one Moore referred to in his film), the level of gun ownership is higher than in the United States, but the level of firearm homicides is roughly seven times lower (Cuiker 1998, Table 2). Comparative checking, in sum, allowed Moore to "control for" a number of potentially significant variables, which, in turn, enabled him to demonstrate that, by themselves, they could not account for or explain the extreme rate of gun violence in the United States.

Unfortunately, comparative checking usually cannot (indeed, can almost never) provide definitive answers. This is true, in part, because comparative checking is an imperfect mode of analysis, at least when comparing real-world cases. It is also true, in more substantive terms, because comparison—although one method of control—is clearly not the best, or even a particularly good one. There are much better methods of control, such as the **experimental method** and statistical control. "But," as Sartori also noted, "the experimental method has limited applicability in the social sciences, and the statistical one requires many cases" (1994, p. 16), something that research in comparative politics generally lacks (this is referred to as the **small-N** problem). Like it or not, therefore, comparison often represents only a "second-best" method of control in the social sciences and comparative politics.

Despite its second-best status, comparing to control is an undeniably important purpose of comparative analysis. Yet many comparativists, especially those with a strong predisposition toward qualitative and historical analysis, are not always, or even mostly, involved in "testing" theories or hypotheses through their comparisons (Ragin 1987, p. 11). Instead, as Ragin noted, "[many comparativists] . . . *apply* theory to cases in order to interpret them" (emphasis in original; p. 11). We will see examples of this in subsequent chapters, but what Ragin meant, in part, is that comparativists recognize that countries or other types of macrosocial units all, in important ways, have a unique story to tell. Ragin suggested, therefore, that some researchers are often most interested in using comparative analysis to get a better grasp of these *individual* "stories," rather than primarily using them as a way to verify or falsify bigger arguments. In other words, for these researchers, in-depth **understanding** is the goal of comparative analysis. Comparing to understand, to put it in slightly different terms, means that researchers use comparison to see what other cases can tell them about the specific case or country in which they have the most interest.

In a similar vein, some comparativists assume that the sheer complexity of real-world cases makes control a worthwhile but difficult, if not impossible, goal to achieve. Instead, they advocate a more pragmatic approach that attempts to build theoretical generalization—or **explanation**—through an accumulation of case-based knowledge (this is sometimes referred to as **analytical induction**). In this view, it is understood that no case, by itself, or no comparison of a small number of cases is sufficient to test a theory or general claim. This is largely because the overwhelming complexity of any given case makes any test problematic and highly contingent. Instead, each case or each small-N comparison provides comparativists another piece (albeit often a very complicated piece in and of itself) to work into a much larger puzzle. I will come back to this issue—and specifically the issue of complex causality—below.

Even though the foregoing discussion may be a little confusing, the key point is simply that, although researchers use comparisons for different reasons, doing comparative politics requires that you be aware of *your* reason and rationale for making a comparison. Figure 1.6 provides a summary of the three general purposes of comparing.

Figure 1.6   Three Purposes of Comparing: A Summary

| | *General Purpose* | | |
	Comparing to *Control*	Comparing to *Understand*	Comparing to *Explain*
Basic strategy or purpose	Comparative checking	Interpretation	Analytical induction
Logic or approach to comparative analysis	Researcher uses a range of cases as a way to "test" (verify or falsify) a specific claim, hypothesis, or theory.	Researcher is primarily interested in a single case and uses different cases or general theories as a way to learn more about the case he/she is studying.	Researcher uses cases as a way to build a stronger theoretical explanation. Cases are used in a "step-by-step" manner, with each case contributing to the development of a general theory.
Basic example	(1) *Begin with a claim:* "A high level of gun ownership will lead to a high level of gun-related homicide." (2) *"Test" the claim:* Researcher examines a range of countries in order to "control for" gun ownership; if countries with the highest rates of gun ownership have low rates of gun-related homicides (and vice versa), the claim is falsified and must be rejected.	(1) *Begin with a case (and issue):* The high level of homicides in South Africa (2) *Use existing theories and/or other cases to better understand case:* Researcher uses a range of theories on gun violence to better understand why South Africa is the most violent country in the world. Researcher also uses other cases to see what those cases can tell her about South Africa.	(1) *Begin with a general theory:* "Structural theory of democratization" (2) *Use various cases to strengthen the theory:* Researcher begins by looking at the democratization process in Mexico. This examination may lead researcher to "tweak" or revise elements of theory; he then looks at Taiwan, Poland, and Ukraine. Each case is used as a stepping-stone in developing or strengthening original theory.

■ What Is Comparable?

Another important question about comparing involves the issue of exactly what one can compare. What, to put it simply, is *comparable?* Again, the answer may seem obvious at first blush (especially in the context of comparative politics). For instance, it certainly seems reasonable to assert that countries, governments, societies, or similar entities are comparable. Yet, why should this be the case? What makes "countries" (or other units of analysis) comparable? One easy answer to this question is simply that all countries share at least some common attributes—for example, they all occupy a territory defined by political boundaries, they all represent the interests of a political community, they are all recognized (albeit not always "officially" as in the case of Taiwan) by other countries or states, and so on. At the same time, they each differ in some meaningful way. Indeed, differences are crucially important in any type of comparative analysis. After all, if all countries were *exactly alike,* there would be no reason to compare, because what we say about one case would necessarily be the same in any other case. In this respect, we might say that comparing apples to oranges generally makes more sense than comparing oranges to oranges or apples to apples.

Thus, to determine what we can compare, we can begin by saying that we can compare "entities whose attributes are in part shared (similar) and in part non-shared (and thus, we say, incomparable)" (Sartori 1994, p. 17). Saying this, however, still doesn't tell us all we need to know. Is it appropriate, for instance, to compare the United States, Côte d'Ivoire, Japan, Indonesia, Guinea-Bissau, and New Zealand? Well, the answer is, it depends. That is, it depends on what the researcher is hoping to accomplish, and it depends on the particular research design the researcher plans to use. This is an obvious point; still, it is one worth making because when phrased as a question—"on what does our comparison depend?"—it forces us to think more carefully about the design of our analyses. It forces us, as well, to *justify* the comparisons we ultimately end up making.

Comparing Cases

What we can compare, I should stress, is definitely not limited to countries (more on this in Chapter 2). Nor is it necessarily limited to comparable data from *two or more* countries. Such a restriction, for example, would automatically exclude comparatively oriented but single-country (or single-unit) **case studies**, including such classic comparative studies as Alexis de Tocqueville's *Democracy in America* ([1835] 1998) and Emile Durkheim's *Elementary Forms of the Religious Life* ([1915] 1961, both cited in Ragin [1987, p. 4]). As Ragin explained it, "Many area specialists [i.e., researchers who concentrate on a single country] are thoroughly comparative because they implicitly compare their chosen case to their own country or to an imaginary or theoretically decisive ideal-typic case" (p. 4). Others, including Sartori, would disagree, or at least would be quite skeptical of the claim that single-country case studies can be genuinely comparative. Sartori wrote, for example, "It is often held that comparisons can be 'implicit.' . . . I certainly grant that a scholar *can be* implicitly comparative without comparing, that is, provided that his one-country or one-unit study *is* embedded in a comparative context and that his concepts, his analytic tools, are *comparable*. But how often is this really the case?" (emphasis in original; 1994, p. 15).[8] Sartori made a good point, but so too did Ragin. My own view is that single-case studies can be unequivocally comparative, especially (but not only) if the researcher takes *time* into account. That is, looking at a single case over an appropriately long period of time (during which a significant change in the variable or variables under investigation occurs), logically speaking, is the same as looking at two **most similar systems**.[9] (Some comparativists call this a **within-case comparison**, which I will discuss briefly in Chapter 2; the concept of most similar systems will also be discussed in the following chapter.)

The Importance of Logic

We are not going to resolve the debate here. Suffice it to say, then, that doing comparative analysis requires far more than just looking at a "foreign country" or just randomly or arbitrarily picking two or more countries to study in the context of a single paper or study. It is, instead, based on a general "logic" and on particular strategies that guide (but do not necessarily) determine the comparative choices we make. *Understanding the logic of comparative analysis, in fact, is essential to doing comparative politics.* Needless to say, this will be an important topic of discussion in Chapter 2. To conclude our general discussion of comparing for now, however, it would be useful to consider some of the advantages of the comparative method (a number of disadvantages are discussed in Chapter 2).

■ What Are the Advantages of the Comparative Method?

Earlier I noted that comparativists tend to look at *cases as wholes* and to compare whole cases with each other. There are important advantages to this practice, the first and most important of which, perhaps, is that it enables researchers to deal with **complex causality** (or **causal complexity**). At one level, complex causality is an easy-to-grasp concept. After all, there is little doubt that much of what happens in the "real world" is an amalgam of economic, cultural, institutional, political, social, and even psychological processes and forces. Not only do all these processes and forces exist independently (at least to some extent), but they *interact* in complicated, difficult-to-discern, and sometimes unpredictable (or contingent) ways. Thus, in studying a particular phenomenon—say, political violence—it is likely that several or even dozens of factors are at play. Some factors may be primarily "economic," such as poverty, unemployment, and unequal income distribution. Other factors may be "cultural" (for example, specific religious values and practices), "political" (for example, lack of democracy or a skewed distribution of political power, which itself could be based on religious or ethnic differences), "socioeconomic" (for example, strong class-based divisions), and so on. An adequate understanding of political violence may have to take all these factors into account and will likely have to specify their interrelationship and interaction within certain contexts. Ragin (1987) provided a very useful, three-point summary of complex causality:

> First, rarely does an outcome of interest to social scientists have a single cause. The conditions conducive for strikes, for example, are many; there is no single condition that is universally capable of causing a strike. Second, *causes rarely operate in isolation.* Usually, it is *the combined effect* of various conditions, *their intersection in time and space,* that produces a certain outcome. *Thus, social causation is often both multiple and conjectural, involving different combinations of causal conditions.* Third, a specific cause may have opposite effects *depending on context.* For example, changes in living conditions may increase or decrease the probability of strikes, depending on other social and political conditions. . . . The fact that some conditions have contradictory effects depending on context further complicates the identification of empirical regularities because it may appear that a condition is irrelevant when in fact it is an essential part of several causal combinations in both its presence and absence state. (emphasis added; p. 27)

The point to remember is that other methods of inquiry (such as the experimental method and statistical analysis) cannot, in general, adequately deal with complex causality. Comparative (case-oriented) analysis, by contrast, is especially—perhaps uniquely—suited for dealing with the peculiar complexity of social phenomena (Rueschemeyer 1991). Why? Quite simply because comparative analysis, to repeat a point made above, can and often does deal with cases *as a whole*—meaning that a full range of factors can be considered at once within particular historical contexts (which themselves vary over time). This is especially apparent with regard to "deviant" or anomalous cases. Comparative analysis can help explain why, for example, some relatively poor countries—such as India, Mauritania, and Costa Rica—are democratic, when statistically based studies would predict just the opposite.[10] To account for such anomalous cases (as many comparativists might argue), we need to look very closely at the particular configuration of social and political forces in these individual countries and understand how, from a historical perspective, these configurations emerged and developed. We also need to understand how external forces and relationships interacted with the domestic environment to produce the specific results that they did. None of this is likely to be achieved, to repeat, without considering the whole context of each individual case.

A second, strongly related advantage is that comparative analysis (especially when carried out in a qualitative as opposed to quantitative manner) allows the researcher to better understand or explain the relationship between and among factors. Quantitative or statistical research, by contrast, does a very good job in showing that relationships *exist* (for example, that capitalist development is related to democratization) but does not generally do a good job at telling us what the nature or underlying dynamic of this relationship is. To use a metaphor from aviation, we might say that quantitative analysis shows a strong **correlation** between engine failure and plane crashes, but it typically does not tell us the exact reasons (or the chain of causal events leading to the crash—since not all engine problems, even very similar ones, lead to the same outcome, and vice versa). To find out the reasons planes crash, therefore, investigators almost always have to look inside the black box or flight data recorder (see Figure 1.7).[11] They have to analyze the myriad factors—some of which will undoubtedly be unique to individual flights—to determine the cause of any particular crash. Even this may not be enough: quite frequently, investigators have to literally reassemble the fragments of the destroyed plane to determine the chain of causal events. To be sure, the cause is sometimes obvious and does not require intensive investigation, but more

Figure 1.7   The Black Box of Explanation

Factor X ⟶   ⟶ **Outcome Y**

Example:
Capitalist
growth

Example:
Democracy

Statistical or quantitative analysis does a very good job of showing a correlation between *X* and *Y* but typically does not explain why this correlation exists in the first place. Getting inside the black box of explanation may be possible with statistical analysis, but qualitative analysis—and especially qualitative *comparative* analysis—is usually much better suited for this task.

often than not, the *incident as a whole* needs to be examined in order to develop a complete explanation.

◼ By Way of a Conclusion: Method and Theory in Comparative Politics

The metaphor of the black box is instructive, but we should be careful not to take it too far, for comparative analysis is more than just opening up the black box and analyzing its contents. It also involves—as might already be apparent from my discussion of the two types of comparative research strategies—a process of a priori conceptualization. At the most basic level, this simply means that the selection of cases to investigate should not be purely random or arbitrary but should be guided by certain criteria, some of which derive from the particular research design we choose. Yet before we even get to the research design, important choices have to be made regarding the factors (or variables) we consider significant in the first place. These choices are guided by **theory**. In Chapter 3, I talk much more about theory. For now, then, let me highlight one general point: theory has a bad reputation among students. Part of the blame, I think, falls on professors who do not help students understand why theory is not only important but is something none of us can do without (whether in an academic discipline or in everyday life). As I will make clear, we all theorize about the world, all the time. Yet just because we all theorize does not mean we all do it equally well—this is especially true for those of you who operate on the assumption that theories have nothing to do with the "real world," or that one can explain or understand anything simply by appealing to the "facts." One way to rectify this problem is to simply become more self-conscious and explicit about theory/theorizing; this has the added benefit, I might add, of helping you become a more disciplined, critical, and analytic thinker. Thinking theoretically about comparative politics, in this regard, has value well beyond the confines of this particular subfield. The same can be said about thinking comparatively, which is the topic of our next chapter.

To sum up, *doing comparative politics* requires, minimally, a clear-eyed understanding of what comparative politics is, of what it means to compare, and of the importance and necessity of theory. There is, of course, more to doing comparative politics than just these three requirements, but they constitute an essential foundation upon which everything else will stand.

◼ Notes

1. Terms that appear in boldface type are defined in the Glossary (see p. 291).

2. This seems an obvious point about which most scholars would agree. Yet the distinction between American and comparative politics still exists in the United States. There are, of course, plenty of reasons for this, one of which is that it is "natural" for people to see their own country or society as separate and distinct from other places. Nonetheless, there is no solid justification for the distinction. As Sigelman and Gadbois (1983) nicely put it, "the traditional distinction between American and comparative politics is . . . intellectually indefensible. . . . Comparison presupposes multiple objects of analysis . . . one compares something to or with something else" (cited in Sartori 1994, p. 14).

3. For an interesting discussion of the relationship between US government support and the development of area studies (specifically in relation to Asia) in the United States, see Selden (1997).

4. Most researchers in the field, I should emphasize, can probably agree on a basic, but very general, definition of comparative politics (such as the ones listed in Figure 1.3). There is far less agreement, however, on how the field should be constituted in terms of a particular theoretical or even methodological approach. In a wide-ranging discussion on the role of theory in comparative politics, for example, some of the leading names in comparative politics and comparative analysis fail to achieve a consensus on what is or should be the theoretical core of the field (see Kohli et al. 1995).

5. I should note, however, that there has never been unanimous agreement on this point. Indeed, one of the main areas of controversy in international relations theory today revolves around the "democratic peace thesis" (Doyle 1995). The crux of this argument is that liberal (or democratic) states do not go to war with other liberal states. In essence, advocates of the democratic peace thesis argue that there is something unique about the *internal* constitution of liberal states that changes their behavior in relation to other liberal states.

6. For obvious reasons, I cannot provide a detailed and nuanced discussion of international relations theory here. Fortunately, there are a number of very good introductory texts that do just this. See, for example, *The Globalization of World Politics: An Introduction to International Relations* (2005), edited by John Baylis and Steve Smith. Chapters 7 through 12 in that book cover both mainstream and alternative theories in some depth and detail. Another useful textbook is Jill Steans and Lloyd Pettiford's *International Relations: Perspectives and Themes* (2001).

7. Despite the fact that the field is defined in terms of particular method—that is, comparison—there are many scholars in the field of comparative politics who, according to Giovanni Sartori, "have no interest, no notion, no training, in comparing" (1994, 15). The reason, I might note, may have more to do with the ethnocentric way the field has been defined than with the scholars themselves. To understand this point, consider the fact that comparative politics (in the United States) has been defined, most simplistically, as "studying other countries." Thus, as Sartori put it, "a scholar who studies only American presidents is an Americanist, whereas a scholar who studies only French presidents is not" (Sartori 1994, p. 14). The US-based scholar who decides to study only France, in other words, is only classified as a comparativist by dint of his or her interest in a country other than the United States.

8. Later, Sartori (1994) stated his case more strongly. "I must insist," he contended, "that as a 'one-case' investigation the case study cannot be subsumed under the comparative *method* (though it may have comparative merit)" (p. 23).

9. One prominent comparativist, Dietrich Rueschemeyer (1991), seemed to agree with me on this point. As he put it, "Even in single-case studies comparative aware-

ness and especially a longer time span of investigation can—logically analogous to cross-country comparisons—make the structural conditions of different event sequences more visible" (p. 29).

10. Costa Rican democracy, especially, has been an issue of special interest to comparativists, since it constitutes, according to Rueschemeyer, Stephens, and Stephens (1992), "the real exception to the pattern [of authoritarianism] prevailing in Central America" (p. 234).

11. Rueschemeyer, Stephens, and Stephens (1992) made a very strong argument on this point. They noted that, although cross-national statistical work has shown an undeniable and very strong link (correlation) between capitalist development and democracy, this correlation, by itself (and no matter how many times it is replicated), "does not carry its own explanation." "It does not," they continued, "identify the causal sequences accounting for the persistent relation, not to mention the reason why many cases are at odds with it. Nor can it account for how the same end can be reached by different historical routes. The repeated statistical finding has a peculiar 'black box' character that can be overcome only by theoretically well grounded empirical analysis" (p. 4).

2

Comparing to Learn, Learning to Compare

An Introduction to Comparative Methods

With a few exceptions, most introductory textbooks on comparative politics spend very little time discussing the question of how to compare.[1] I am not sure why this is, but, as I noted in the preceding chapter, comparative politics is the only field in political science that is explicitly defined in terms of a particular method. For this reason alone it makes sense to devote serious attention to the issue of comparison. But there's another good reason: learning how to compare is an extremely useful and valuable skill— and not just in the context of comparative politics. Indeed, as one pair of comparativists put it, *"Comparison is the engine of knowledge"* (emphasis added; Dogan and Pelassy 1990, p. 8). French historian Fernand Braudel explained it this way: "Live in London for a year," he wrote, "and you will not get to know much about England. But through comparison, in the light of your surprise, you will suddenly come to understand some of the more profound and individual characteristics of France, which you did not previously understand because you knew them too well" (Braudel 1972, p. 24; cited in Logan and Pelassey 1990, p. 8). Comparing, in other words, can help open your eyes to the world—including or especially your *own* world—in a manner that simply would not be possible otherwise. Of course, a newfound "vision" does not come automatically. Many people can look at the world around them and see absolutely nothing new. Worse still, they may look around the world merely to confirm already closely held, but incorrect, beliefs.

Learning to compare, therefore, entails more than just a capacity to look at a "foreign" place. It also requires a willingness to *understand* and *evaluate* differences (as well as similarities) in an *open-minded* manner. Unfortunately, none of this is easily taught inside a classroom (in the same way, say, that a professor can teach you a simple math equation). This especially applies to open-minded-ness, for open-mindedness is an attribute that comes as much from the inside as it does from the outside. As a student and as a human being, in other words, you must make a commitment to this general principle, or else it is likely that you will not learn a great deal from this or any book. At the same time, just remind-ing yourself to be open-minded is not enough. Many of our most ingrained bi-ases, in fact, are those of which we are completely unaware—those that we do not consider biases at all, but simply natural or self-evident truths. Unfortu-nately, this tendency is not limited to students. As I discussed in Chapter 1, the development of comparative politics has been clearly influenced by the belief, on the part of US academics, that the economic and political systems of the United States were the standards by which all other countries should be judged. In retrospect, it is easy to blame US scholars for their **ethnocentrism** (see Fig-ure 2.1); yet it is important to note, as Dogan and Pelassy did, that one of the best ways to recognize and then avoid the trap of ethnocentrism is through compari-son. "Indeed," as they put it, "the very concept of ethnocentrism simply cannot exist without the comparative exercise. Only with exposure to other cultures does one become conscious of possible intellectual occlusion" (1990, p. 9).

■ Comparing and Critical Thinking

An important and clearly related aspect of open-mindedness is critical think-ing. By critical, I do not mean quick to judge (as in, "My mom was really crit-

---

Figure 2.1   Ethnocentrism

Ethnocentrism refers to the taken-for-granted belief that one's own cultural values and practices are the standard by which all other cultures or societies should be judged. Frequently, this leads to distrust of out-groups and to a sense of superiority. From the standpoint of the social sciences, ethnocentrism can create serious and often unrecognized problems of bias. For example, from the 1940s on, it is fair to say that many theories of political and economic devel-opment were influenced by the ethnocentric view that European and US the-ories, practices, and ideas represented the ideal. Implicit in this view, more-over, was the assumption that any deviation from the Western ideal was potentially dangerous and, therefore, unacceptable. Not surprisingly, then, al-ternatives to the Western model were not always treated in a detached, neutral, or "scientific" manner by Western social scientists. Instead, they were often vilified, debased, and condemned.

ical of my nose ring"). I mean just the opposite. That is, to be critical means to engage in a process of careful, well-considered, and reflective evaluation. Indeed, if you make comparisons in a superficial, haphazard, or unreflective manner, you might as well not bother. For you are not only unlikely to develop any meaningful insights, but you run the risk of constructing a dangerously distorted or entirely erroneous analysis. Unfortunately, as with open-minded-ness, thinking critically is not easy to teach. Professors can lecture all they want about the importance of and necessity for thinking critically, but you must first be willing to make the effort to discipline your mind to do so. This said, it would be useful to offer a few more words about critical thinking.

For this, let me turn to Daniel J. Kurland, who wrote in 1994 in *I Know What It Says . . . What Does It Mean*, "Broadly speaking, critical thinking is concerned with reason, intellectual honesty, and open-mindedness, as op-posed to emotionalism, intellectual laziness, and closed-mindedness" (cited in Fowler n.d.). This, in turn, involves a number of concrete practices, the most important of which are "following evidence where it leads; considering all possibilities; relying on reason rather than emotion; being precise; consider-ing a variety of possible viewpoints and explanations; weighing the effects of motives and biases . . . not rejecting unpopular views out of hand; being aware of [and self-reflective about] one's own prejudices and biases; and not allow-ing them to sway one's judgment" (cited in Fowler n.d.). Anyone who follows these guidelines will almost certainly become a better, stronger student of comparative politics and of life more generally. As I have already said, how-ever, none of this is easy to teach, much less learn. Fortunately, comparative analysis provides a useful path toward good critical thinking, since it encour-ages—and, if done right, forces—you to put into practice many of the points raised above. Indeed, I believe that comparative analysis is *the* ideal frame-work for critical thinking in the social sciences.

■ Strategies of Comparing

There is no one way—or even a best way—to do comparative analysis. In fact, as we'll see in the following sections, there are numerous methods or strategies one can use to carry out comparative analysis, all of which are equally valid. "Equally valid," though, does not mean that each type of com-parison is equally suited for different tasks, purposes, or questions. This is a key point. *For it is the questions you ask and the goal you wish to achieve that should determine the comparative framework you use, and not the other way around.* But you should already know this if you read the first chapter care-fully. Still, we will keep coming back to the point throughout this chapter. At the same time, this chapter also addresses questions of a more practical nature: What are the specific ways of comparing? How does one go about choosing

the cases used in comparative analysis (for example, what criteria should one use)? Once you have selected your case or cases for comparison, how many should be compared—one, two, three, a dozen, or perhaps the whole universe of countries that currently make up the world? What are the specific advantages and disadvantages of the different comparative strategies? We will address all of these questions in this chapter. We need to start, however, with a discussion of the general logic of comparing.

■ The Logic of Comparative Analysis

Comparative analysis, as I have already stressed, is an imperfect method. Still, done correctly, it is a valuable method of social scientific inquiry. To do comparative analysis correctly (and to do comparative politics) requires a basic understanding of the logic of comparative research design. Part of this logic is represented in two general comparative strategies known as the most similar systems (MSS) and the **most different systems (MDS)** designs. These are not the only general strategies of comparative analysis—many comparativists, for example, draw from John Stuart Mill's discussion of the **method of agreement, method of difference**, and **indirect method of difference**, which he includes in his seminal book, *A System of Logic: Ratiocinative and Inductive* ([1843] 1967). The MSS and MDS designs, however, are arguably the most common strategies of comparative analysis today. Moreover, and not coincidentally, both are based on the logic first articulated by Mill.

The Most Similar Systems Design

As the name implies, the most similar systems strategy is based on finding two or more very similar social systems, typically "countries." More specifically, it is based on matching up and then comparing two or more systems that share a whole range of similarities (political, social, demographic, economic, cultural, and so on) but also differ in at least a couple of important respects. Przeworski and Teune (1970)—whose book, *The Logic of Comparative Social Inquiry,* is considered by many to be the bible on comparative analysis in the social sciences—gave as an example the Scandinavian countries (Sweden, Norway, Finland) or the two-party systems of the Anglo-Saxon countries (that is, the United States and Britain), which are viewed as archetypical most similar systems "because these countries share many economic, cultural, and political characteristics . . ." (p. 32). In methodological terms, the important point is that the characteristics the systems share in principle can be held constant and can therefore be considered irrelevant in explaining a particular social or political phenomenon (the **dependent variable**) that occurs in one, but not both cases. Having "controlled for" a range of variables, the comparativist can focus on

finding a significant *dissimilarity* between the two systems, which can then be put forward as *the* causal factor or key **independent variable**. (See Figure 2.2 for further discussion of the independent and dependent variables.)

To help make this discussion clearer, consider a comparison of the United States and Canada, two "most similar systems." If we use these two cases to try to answer a research question—why is the homicide rate higher in the United States than in any other advanced, industrialized country?—we can immediately control for or hold constant a wide range of potentially significant variables. Again, this is precisely what Michael Moore did, at least in a very casual and implicit manner, in *Bowling for Columbine*. Specifically, be-

---

Figure 2.2   The Independent and Dependent Variables

In an *experimental* setting, the *independent variable* is the variable controlled or (intentionally) manipulated by the researcher in order to observe its effect. The *dependent variable*, on the other hand, is the phenomenon that is in some way affected by the independent variable. In comparative politics and other social scientific research, however, experimental designs, as we have learned, are generally not possible. This means that the "independent variable" cannot be manipulated but must instead be analyzed retrospectively or indirectly. For instance, a researcher studying presidential elections may argue that "when the unemployment rate exceeds 7.0 percent, incumbent presidents are not re-elected." In this example, the "dependent variable" is the reelection of incumbent presidents. The "independent variable" is the overall unemployment rate. To assess the relationship between the independent and dependent variables, a researcher could collect (historical) data on unemployment rates from several countries. If the researcher found that in every instance the unemployment rate was greater than 7 percent at the time of a presidential election that the incumbent lost, the initial hypothesis would be strengthened. In this case, to reiterate the main point, the independent variable was not manipulated by the researcher but was instead evaluated indirectly or retrospectively through the use of historical data. (The example used above is from "Writing Political Science," http://www.unc.edu/depts/wcweb/handouts/polisci.htm.)

To many researchers, it is, strictly speaking, erroneous to talk about independent and dependent variables in the type of analysis illustrated above. For our purposes, therefore, we need to be clear that the terms "independent variable" and "dependent variable" are used in a less formal but still clear-cut manner by most comparativists. *To repeat: the independent variable is the one that you think of as causal, and the dependent variable is the one that you think of as being affected by the independent variable.*

cause the United States and Canada share so many attributes—such as relatively high per capita gross domestic product (GDP), moderate levels of poverty and unemployment, high literacy rates, a relatively high level of ethnic and racial diversity, a Christian-based heritage and culture, a similar type of government and political system, similar levels of immigration, and so on—we can assume that no one of these similarities is responsible for the high rate of homicides in the United States or, conversely, for the relatively low rate of homicides in Canada. Instead, we can turn our attention to identifying significant differences between the United States and Canada. *It is this difference (or differences) that is key.* Figure 2.3 provides a summary, in tabular fashion, of the basic MSS design just described.

So what is the key difference between the two countries that might account for the high level of gun-related homicide in the United States? Although answering this question is beyond the scope of this chapter, some observers have pointed to the extremely high level of gun ownership in the United States (and the legal-institutional and historical factors that make the high levels of gun ownership possible). In fact, there are *thirty times* more firearms in the United States than in Canada, although on a per capita basis, the difference is not as dramatic: in the United States there is approximately one firearm for every 1.3 people, whereas in Canada there is one gun for every 4.2 people (Firearms Research Unit 1998). (See Figure 2.4 for comparative statistics.) In this view, one can make a plausible argument that the level of gun ownership is at least part of the explanation for the high homicide rate in the United States. Indeed, if we set up another MSS design, this time comparing the United States and Britain (where gun ownership is extremely limited), we might find even more support for the hypothesis that lower rates of gun ownership (the independent variable) lead to lower rates of gun-related homicides. On the other hand, a little more "comparative checking" will tell us that the issue is not so clear-cut. As I noted in Chapter 1, Finland (and Norway) have gun-ownership rates almost as high as that of the United States, yet their respective levels of gun-related homicides are much lower, even lower than Canada's. This does not mean we must reject the claim that gun ownership is a key factor, but we know that, by itself, it cannot explain the relatively high number of gun-related murders in the United States. There must be another factor that sets the United States apart. One possibility, discussed in Chapter 1, is Michael Moore's thesis, which revolves around the idea that gun violence in the United States is driven by a "culture of fear." We can assess this argument, too, by using an MSS design and other comparative strategies. (Rather than doing this for you, however, I encourage you to think about setting up your own research design to "test" Moore's argument.)

Limitations of the MSS design. It is important to understand that *no* comparison of the United States and Canada by itself will *prove* that gun owner-

Figure 2.3 A Simple MSS Design Using Canada and the United States

	System 1: Canada	System 2: United States	Similar or Different
Dependent variable			
• Level of gun-related homicides	very low	very high	different (i.e., variance)
Key differences (independent variable?)			
• Level of gun ownership	moderate	very high	different
• Public sense of fear and insecurity ("culture of fear")	very low	very high	different
• Level of social protection (health care, social welfare, public housing)	high	low	different
Other variables (examples)			
• Level of economic wealth	high	high	similar
• Level of poverty and unemployment	moderate	moderate	similar
• Educational levels and literacy	high	high	similar
• Exposure to "antisocial" and violent forms of entertainment	high	high	similar
• Level of racial and ethnic diversity	moderately high	high	similar

In this MSS design, the researcher compares Canada and the United States, which are considered "most similar systems." This means, in part, that the researcher expects to find a range of similarities between the two cases. At the same time, the logic of the MSS design dictates that there be at least two key differences or dissimilarities. Specifically, the dependent variable should be different between the two cases (it is), and there should be at least one significant difference with regard to the presumed independent variable. Identifying this key difference is often the major objective of the researcher.

Figure 2.4   Comparing Gun-Related Homicide Rates in the United States and Canada

According to the Canadian Firearms Centre, between 1987 and 1996 the *firearm* homicide rate was *8.1 times higher* in the United States than in Canada. During this period, the average firearm homicide rate was 5.7 per 100,000 in the United States, compared to 0.7 per 100,000 for Canada. More specifically, the *handgun* homicide rate was *15.3 times higher* in the United States than in Canada. For 1989–1995, the average handgun homicide rate was 4.8 per 100,000 in the United States, compared to 0.3 per 100,000 for Canada. Handguns were involved in more than half (52 percent) of the homicides in the United States, compared to 14 percent in Canada.

Source: Canadian Firearms Centre, "Firearms: Canada/United States Comparison" (June 1998), http://www.cfc-ccaf.gc.ca/en/research/other_docs/notes/canus/default.asp.

ship or a "culture of fear" or some other factor is *the* only possible cause of the high rate of gun-related homicides in the United States. There are two basic reasons for this. First, and most obvious, a comparison of only two cases does not and cannot provide a strong enough empirical basis for making "big" claims. A moment's reflection should help us understand why this is the case. With only a limited number of cases, there is no way to be sure that your findings are any more than coincidental or happenstance. In other words, all researchers need to be able to "replicate" (at least in a general manner) their findings to have any confidence that they are valid. Second, and far less obvious, it is important to understand that, even though the United States and Canada may be very similar systems, they are not exactly alike. Indeed, the closer we look, the more differences we are likely to find, to the point, some might argue, that the two countries no longer seem very similar at all, still less "most similar." In this sense, we should think of the term "most similar" as relative—that is, relative to other systems, the United States and Canada are most similar (certainly the United States shares many more similarities with Canada than it does with Nepal, Poland, Burkina Faso, or Angola). The main methodological point, however, is this: because there are so many differences between the United States and Canada, we cannot simply assume that the one difference we identify (for example, a high level of private gun ownership in the United States versus a lower level of private gun ownership in Canada or a "culture of fear" versus a "culture of security") is the only difference that matters. The MSS design, in this sense, suffers from an unavoidable and significant flaw. Simply put, no matter how similar two (or more) systems may seem, there are bound to be so many potentially relevant differences that it would be impossible, in strict methodological terms, to establish exactly which differences have causal significance and which do not (Hopkin 2002, p. 254).

I am not saying this to confuse or frustrate you but to emphasize the need for caution and restraint in using the MSS design. At best, the MSS design is useful (and sometimes indispensable) in giving added weight to certain explanations (or variables) over others. *But, to repeat, it cannot definitively eliminate all other possible causes.* There are, as one comparativist aptly put it, simply "too many variables, [and] too few countries" (Lijphart 1971) for this to be possible. The lesson, therefore, is clear: *do not exaggerate.* That is, do not claim that your findings from an MSS comparison are unequivocal proof of your argument.

The importance of differences in the MSS design. With this important caveat in mind, when using the MSS design it is also particularly important to understand that the differences between the systems are as important as the similarities. I have already made this point at least once, but it bears repeating. Indeed, you should etch this point into your brain: *differences are crucial to the logic of the MSS design.* The logic is straightforward: In a vast sea of similarities, there should be at least two meaningful differences between the systems. One of these differences should be among the many potential explanatory or independent variables. The other difference must be in the dependent variable. With regard to this latter point, in particular, comparativists like to say that the MSS design *requires variance in the dependent variable.*

To better understand why it is necessary to have different independent and dependent variables, let's look at another illustration of an MSS design (see Figure 2.5). The illustration shows a (very) simple—*and logically flawed*— representation of an MSS design using South Korea and Taiwan, two "most similar systems." The comparison is based on a popular argument (which we'll discuss in more detail in Chapter 5) that posits that the **developmental state** is responsible for the high rate of economic growth both countries experienced in the post–World War II period. Aside from the presence of a "developmental state" in Taiwan and South Korea, both systems share a broad range of other similarities. For example, both were former colonies of Japan, both were very poor following their liberation after World War II, both had authoritarian political systems (in the early postwar period), both lack natural resources, both had close political/economic ties with the United States (at least for part of the postwar period), both share some important cultural characteristics (that is, a Confucian heritage), both developed highly educated and skilled workforces, both implemented similar economic policies (for example, **export-oriented industrialization**), and so on. Significantly, both also achieved hitherto unprecedented rates of economic growth (the dependent variable). In sum, in both systems, there is *no* significant variance or difference with regard to the presumed independent *and* dependent variables, and there is no difference with

Figure 2.5　A Flawed MSS Design: Comparing South Korea and Taiwan

	System 1: South Korea	System 2: Taiwan	Similar or Different
Dependent variable (y)			
• Rate of national economic growth	very high	very high	similar (i.e., no variance)
Key differences (independent variable, x)			
• Type of state	developmental	developmental	similar
Other variables (examples)			
• Cultural heritage	Confucian	Confucian	similar
• Political systems	authoritarian	authoritarian	similar
• Importance of education	high	high	similar
• Workforce skills	high	high	similar
• Relationship with United States	strong	strong	similar
• National resource endowment	limited	limited	similar
• Geographic location	NE Asia	NE Asia	similar
• Economic policy	EOI/ISI[a]	EOI/ISI	similar

Note: a. EOI = export-oriented industrialization, ISI = import-substitution industrialization

The argument is that both cases experienced a "very high rate of economic growth" (dependent variable, y) and both have a "developmental state" (independent variable, x). Therefore, x is the cause of y.

But, how do we know that x is the key independent variable, or even a significant independent variable? What about *culture* or *skilled workforce* as the significant independent variable?

Based on MSS design with no variance on the dependent variable (y), we cannot say that other variables are insignificant. Therefore, we cannot determine the validity of the main argument.

regard to a range of other, ostensibly irrelevant variables (that is, the afore-mentioned similarities). This is a problem. *It is a problem because it is impossible to conclude that the presumed independent variable (the "development state") actually explains the high rate of economic growth in both South Korea and Taiwan.* How do we know that some other characteristic is not, in fact, responsible? After all, if both cases have a developmental state *and* close ties with the United States *and* a lack of natural resources *and* a "Confucian culture" *and* a similar economic strategy, how can we rule out any of these factors (or a host of other similarities)? The short answer is that we cannot. And we cannot because the design of this particular comparison violates the logic of the MSS design. In a MSS design, to repeat, it is crucial that both the dependent and presumed independent variables vary between the two systems.

Ironically, many well-seasoned comparativists ignore this logical rule in their own research and analysis—in fact, in Chapter 5, we will seemingly violate this rule ourselves (using the same examples discussed above, South Korea and Taiwan). Usually, there is some practical and even justifiable reason for doing so, but strictly speaking, the practice cannot be recommended *if* done in an unthinking or careless manner. Yet even when researchers are careful only to compare "most similar systems" in which there is variance on the presumed independent and dependent variables, the design is far from foolproof—for reasons I already discussed in some detail above. Accordingly, many comparative methodologists (most notably Przeworski and Teune) suggest not only that the MSS design be used with caution but that the alternative comparative strategy—the most different systems design—be used whenever feasible. This is a useful, albeit not sacrosanct, point to remember as we move to a discussion of the logic of the most different systems design.

The Most Different Systems Design

Not surprisingly, the logic of the most different systems design is largely the reverse of that of the MSS design. This is most evident in the general approach of the MDS design, which is to find two systems that are different in almost every respect, except for the variable(s) under investigation.[2] The basic idea, to state it in slightly different terms, is to find—in a vast sea of differences—key similarities between very dissimilar systems. Also, in contrast to the MSS design, variance on the dependent variable is *not* required. In fact, the dependent variable should be the same in all cases, for, in an MDS design, the researcher is attempting to show that the relationship between the presumed independent variable(s) and a dependent variable holds across a wide variety of vastly divergent settings. This means, in practical terms, that the comparativist will often select cases in terms of the dependent variable. If a researcher wants to study religious or ethnic conflict, for example, she will only look for cases in which such conflict was/is present. It is important to note, however, that not everyone agrees on the merit of this practice. As Peters (1998) pointed out, "there are disputes over the appropriateness of selecting cases on the dependent variable, with qualitative researchers arguing that this is essential, and quantitative researchers arguing that it invalidates most findings" (p. 67). We cannot resolve the debate here, except to say that comparativists, in general, put greater emphasis on qualitative analysis.

This said, Przeworski and Teune (1970) provided one hypothetical, but useful, example to illustrate the basic logic of the MDS design. Consider a comparison of the Zuni, the Swedes, and the Russians (prior to the collapse of the Soviet Union), three "most different" systems. Now suppose that the rates of suicide (the dependent variable) are the *same* in each of these societies. Based on this very simple design, we can conclude that the factors that distinguish Zuni, Swedish, and Russian societies are irrelevant for the explanation of suicide in each system. In other words, we can safely disregard a full range of (system-level) differences and instead focus on identifying a common factor or factors (the presumed independent variables) within each society that seem to explain the similar level of suicides across the three cases. On this point, it is useful to note that the MDS design, in general, presupposes that the similarities that exists between/among systems reside at a lower, or subsystemic, level. This means, as Peters (1998) explained it, "that often this strategy is looking at individual level behaviour, and attempting to explain relationships among variables in samples of individuals" (pp. 39–40). Thus, in our hypothetical example (see Figure 2.6), we might identify a high level of alcoholism in all three cases as the (proximate) cause of or reason for the relatively high levels of suicide.

Another, more pertinent, example is provided by Theda Skocpol (1979) in her influential book, *States and Social Revolutions*. In this book, Skocpol compared France, Russia, and China. It is interesting to note that Skocpol did not explicitly base her analysis on a most different systems design (instead, she referred to Mill's methods of agreement and difference), but it is fairly clear that this was the case. Consider her explanation for why she chose to focus on France, Russia, and China. To wit, she recognized that the three countries were very different in many ways (that is, they were clearly most different systems), yet they "exhibited important similarities in their Old Regimes and revolutionary processes and outcomes—similarities more than sufficient to warrant their treatment together as one pattern calling for a coherent causal explanation" (p. 41). In other words, the key reasons for comparing France, Russia, and China, according to Skocpol, derived, first, from the profound similarities each shared with regard to the dependent variable—which she defined as a social revolution characterized by the creation of a "centralized, bureaucratic, and mass-incorporating nation-state with enhanced great-power potential in the international arena" (p. 41). Second, and just as important, Skocpol argued that the causes of social revolutions in all three countries (that is, the independent variables) were essentially the same. In

Figure 2.6   A Simple MDS Design Using Russia, the Zuni, and Sweden

	System 1: Soviet Russia	System 2: Zuni	System 3: Sweden	Similar or Different
Dependent variable (*y*)				
• Rate of suicide	high	high	high	similar
Key similarities (independent variable, *x*)				
• Rate of alcoholism	high	high	high	similar
Other variables (examples)				
• Religious heritage	Russian orthodox	tribal	Lutheran	different
• Political system	communist, single-party	tribal	constitutional monarchy	different
• Climate	moderate	desert	subarctic	different
• Economic wealth	low	very low	very high	different

Using an MDS design, the researcher found three widely divergent cases (in general, the more divergent the cases, the better). Unlike an MSS design, however, the task is to find key similarities among the cases in a "vast sea of differences." One of these similarities should be the independent variable (or variables) and the other the dependent variable. It is also useful to note that, of the three cases, two are countries and one is a relatively small Indian tribe, which resides on the Arizona–New Mexico border, along the Zuni River. This sort of comparison is perfectly reasonable given the research issue.

short, her stated research design (at least the main part of her design) followed the logic of the MDS approach very closely, if not exactly.

Although the foregoing discussion might be a little difficult to follow, the *basic* logic of the most different systems design is really quite simple. Just remember that it is not merely a matter of finding very different systems (a fairly easy task), but of finding different systems in which there are key similarities on the independent and dependent variables. This said, like the MSS design, the MDS design is far from perfect. There is no guarantee, for example, that the findings from an MDS design will unequivocally, or even confidently, identify **causal relationships**, which are generally what social scientists are most interested in determining. To see this, let us reconsider the example of suicide among the Zuni, Swedes, and Russians. Assuming we found a common characteristic within all three societies—say, a high level of alcoholism—how do we know that alcoholism is the *root* cause? Indeed, it may be the case (and likely is) that alcoholism and suicide are the product of a third, still unidentified factor. (In this sense, "alcoholism" may be symptomatic rather than causal.) And it may be, moreover, that this third factor is different in all three societies. This raises a second, perhaps more serious problem with the MDS system design, namely, that it cannot adequately deal with **multiple causation** (Ragin 1987). In other words, there is no reason to presume that a certain phenomenon (such as social revolution or suicide) is necessarily the product of *one and only one* cause. Different causes may produce the same or similar results. Similarly, different *combinations of causes* may produce the same result. If a comparativist uses an MDS design without considering these possibilities, he may end up with distorted or completely unfounded conclusions.

The Logic of Comparing: A Brief Conclusion

In stressing the limitations of the MDS design, my intention, again, is not to confuse you, still less dissuade you from using either the MDS (or MSS) design in your own analysis. Rather, my intention is to emphasize the need, as I have already stated several times, for caution, care, and constraint. Too often students (and professional researchers, including professors) tend to jump to hard conclusions or to make big generalizations based on limited comparisons. This is not a good idea, and it is not intellectually or methodologically justifiable. The main lesson, therefore, is simply to understand the advantages *and* limitations of the methods of comparative analysis.

■ Concrete Strategies of Comparative Analysis

The most similar systems and the most different systems are useful frameworks for organizing comparative analysis. As Dogan and Pelassy (1990) pointed out, however, they do not provide a nuts-and-bolts sense of "the different possibilities offered to the researcher [and student] who has to delineate the area of analysis and choose the countries to be included in the comparison" (p. 111). Fortunately, Dogan and Pelassy (as well as a number of other scholars) helped to fill this gap. Specifically, the authors listed several specific strategies open to comparativists. These include, but are definitely not limited to: (1) the case study in comparative perspective, (2) **binary analysis** or a comparison of two units, (3) a multiunit comparison involving three or more units, and (4) a mixed design. With respect to the case study, I would also add two very closely related strategies: analytical induction and within-case comparison. In the remainder of this chapter, I will spend time discussing each of these strategies, albeit in fairly sketchy terms (with the exception of the case study). There are a couple of reasons why I do not provide in-depth, highly detailed discussions. First, it would probably do little good to overwhelm you with methodological "minutiae," much of which will not be fully understandable until you have a good chance to actually *do* some real comparative analysis on your own. Second, the strategies themselves are more like signposts than detailed blueprints; moreover, once the basic logic of comparative analysis is understood, the various strategies can be grasped with relative ease. With these points firmly in mind, let us begin with a look at the first strategy of comparative analysis, the case study in comparative perspective.

The Case Study in Comparative Perspective

In comparative politics, a case study is typically associated with an *in-depth* examination of a specific country or political system, as in the "Mexican case," the "Japanese case," or the "French case." But a case or case study, I should emphasize, need not be associated with a country at all. The Zuni, for example, are not a country but comprise a relatively small Indian tribe located on the border between Arizona and New Mexico. In fact, subnational "units"—for example, neighborhoods, cities, counties, provinces or states (such as California), even specific **institutions**, political regimes, or events—are frequently used as a basis for a case.[3] It is also important to understand that comparativists rarely, if ever, do a case study of a country in its own right (for example, they do not just study Mexico for the sake of learning more about Mexico). Nor do comparativists simply study the *entire* history, culture, or politics of a country. Instead, researchers are almost always interested in *linking* the study of a country's unique circumstances with a particular political, social, or economic phenomenon. Thus, a researcher may conduct a case study of postwar *Japanese industrialization*, or the *French* (or Chinese or Russian or American) *revolution*, or *Far Left terrorism in Italy* (or West Germany or Spain), or the American *civil rights movement* (or even *suicide* among the Zuni). Each of these examples, you should note, is based on (1) a specific issue or concern (terrorism, industrialization, revolution, a **social movement**), (2) a delimited geographic space (Japan, France, Italy, the United States), and (3) a certain period of time (although this is only implicit in the examples given). Taken together, these three characteristics give us a good foundation upon which to answer the question, what is a case? That is, if we select a *particular issue* or concern and study it within a *circumscribed* period of *time* and *space*, we have a case. Admittedly, this is a very simple and imperfect definition, but one that should suffice for the time being. (For further discussion, see Figure 2.7.)

Figure 2.7   What Is a Case? Some Considerations

The concept of the *case* is a basic feature of comparative analysis and of social science research more generally. Yet, as Ragin and Becker (1992) pointed out, there are many questions about (1) how a case should be defined, (2) how cases should be selected, and (3) what the criteria are for a good case or set of cases. These are all important issues, but for the sake of brevity (and simplicity), let me focus on the most basic one, namely, how a case should be defined. As with the question posed in Chapter 1, what is comparative politics?, the answer is not as clear-cut as you might think or hope. Is a case, for example, a generic category, such as a country, a society, a family, a community, or even an individual? Is it a historically or theoretically constituted category: for example, an "authoritarian personality"? Or is a case a specific event, such as an anticolonial revolution? The simple response is that all these various examples represent—or *can* represent—cases. I emphasize "can," because, as Ragin and Becker pointed out, a "case is not inherently one thing or another, but a way station in the process of producing social science. Cases are multiple in most research efforts because *ideas and evidence may be linked in many different ways*" (emphasis added; p. 225). What these two scholars are saying is that cases are not self-evident. Indeed, researchers often only determine what an appropriate case is in the course of their research. Thus, according to Ragin and Becker, "Cases often must be found because they cannot be specified beforehand" (p. 220). Although I realize this discussion may be more confusing than enlightening, the point to remember is that you cannot simply pick a case out of thin air. Rather, you need to understand that selecting a case—or deciding what a case is—requires a great deal of thought and constant evaluation.

Is a case study comparative? For our purposes, the more salient issue is *how to do* a case study in comparative analysis. Before addressing this question, though, it would be useful to return (very briefly) to a question I first raised in Chapter 1, namely, can a single case study even be comparative? We should not gloss over this question, for, if a single case study *cannot* be comparative, then we really have no business discussing it here. As I pointed out, some scholars, such as Giovanni Sartori, are highly skeptical of the idea that single-unit case studies can be genuinely comparative. Sartori raised a legitimate concern. After all, there are many scholars (especially area studies specialists) who treat their cases as unique or literally incomparable and, therefore, *noncomparable*. There is some justification for this, as the case study approach assumes that the particular historical, political, cultural, and social *context* surrounding an issue or concern always creates a distinctive or original sequence of events. At the same time, when the researcher is even partly concerned with understanding or explaining more general political, social, or economic phenomena (such as Far Left terrorism, rapid capitalist industrialization, or social revolution), comparative analysis is extremely difficult to avoid, even if one wants to do so. Consider the issue of *rapid* capitalist industrialization: how can we judge what is rapid or what is slow without comparing cases? Although this is an admittedly trite example, it is not difficult to raise more substantive, deeper questions. For instance, how can we even speak of capitalist development in one place and time without recognizing that capitalism is a general process that profoundly impacts all cases, albeit with differential results (thus setting the stage for more meaningful comparative analysis)? The answer to both questions is easy: we cannot. That is, in trying to explain or understand broader political, social, or economic phenomena in a single place, we are compelled to think in a comparative manner. As I noted in Chapter 1, moreover, single case studies can be unequivocally comparative when *time* is taken into account. That is, looking at a single case over an appropriately long period of time—during which a significant change in the variable or variables under investigation occurs—is logically speaking the same as looking at two most similar systems. Comparativists call this a within-case comparison (Collier 1997).

Case studies and the within-case comparison: A few words. Typically, within-case comparisons are done in a tacit or unstated manner; sometimes the researcher himself does not even realize what he is doing. But the logic is usually quite clear. To wit, in a great many single-unit case studies, the researcher will often divide the study into at least two separate time periods, with the intention of explaining a significant change (in the dependent variable) between the two periods. In addition, in this research design, it is presumed that all other variables remain the same from the first period to the second, with the exception of the variable that caused or brought about the change in the dependent variable. In short, within-case comparisons follow the logic of an MSS design exactly. Indeed, one might argue that a within case comparison is the nearest one can get to setting up a perfect MSS design.

How to Do a Case Study in Comparative Perspective: Basic Guidelines

Recognizing that case studies can and sometimes must be comparative, unfortunately, does not tell us *how to use* a case in comparative analysis. Even more unfortunate, at least for beginning comparativists, is that there is no single, step-by-step procedure for doing so. The discussion that follows, then, is meant to be a loose (and extremely simple) guide, rather than a strict set of instructions, on how to do a case study in comparative perspective.

With the above caveat in mind, the first general "rule" of doing a case study in comparative perspective is to see your case *in relation* to others. This requires you to be *familiar with both similar and dissimilar cases,* even if you do not explicitly or systematically incorporate these other cases into your analysis. If you are doing a case study of "ethnoreligious conflict" in Yugoslavia (in 2003, Yugoslavia was divided into a loose federation of two republics called Serbia and Montenegro), for example, you would be well advised to read about ethnic conflict in Sri Lanka, Northern Ireland, Rwanda, Indonesia, Sudan, and other relevant places. Doing so allows you to see more clearly how distinctive the Yugoslavian case really is and how representative it is of the broader problem of ethnoreligious conflict. Indeed, you *cannot* make a conclusion about the distinctive or representative nature of ethnic conflict in Yugoslavia (or anywhere else) without knowing something about comparable cases.

Examining your case in relation to others also provides you a cursory but still important method of control for any claims you make about your case. *Indeed, many a case study has been ruined by the writer's blithe ignorance of other relevant cases.* After examining the Yugoslavian case in depth, for example, a researcher might find evidence of deep-seated religious differences. Further analysis may show that ethnic violence in Yugoslavia has revolved around these differences. This observation, in turn, could easily lead the researcher to make a strong causal connection between ethnoreligious conflict (a dependent variable) and religious differences (an independent variable). More specifically, the researcher might conclude that the "deep" difference in religious beliefs among two groups in Yugoslavia led to or caused ethnic violence. In a similar vein, the researcher might put forward the following hypothesis: the stronger the degree of religious difference within a society, the more likely it is that ethnic conflict will break out. Without being aware of or considering other cases—using either an MSS or MDS design, or both—it would be easy to be satisfied with such a conclusion, especially since "religious differences" are no doubt an element in many cases of ethnic violence. But a good comparativist will also ask: Are there cases in which age-old and deep-seated religious differences exist *without* ethnic violence? If so, what might these cases tell us about the causal relationship between religious differences and ethnic violence? Perhaps they tell us that the mere existence of religious differences is not enough—that something else *must* exist as well for the differences to matter. Or perhaps they tell us that ethnoreligious differences as a specific phenomenon are not important. One scholar, for example, argued that ethnoreligious differences are just one of many possible "ordering devices" that can be used to spark and sustain widespread political violence (Mueller 2000). In this view, ethnoreligious differences by themselves are not particularly important, since virtually any difference that can be used to distinguish one group from another would suffice—even loyalty to a particular soccer team. Whatever the answer, however, the researcher cannot know unless she is careful to examine her case in relation to other "comparable" cases.

("Comparable," it is important to remember, may mean cases that are either similar or dissimilar to the main case, both in terms of the independent and dependent variables.)

Dogan and Pelassy (1990) gave us a second, strongly related rule for doing a case study in comparative perspective. As they put it, a case study in comparative perspective is one that "aims at generalization" (p. 122). This takes us a step further than just examining a case in relation to others. For what Dogan and Pelassy were telling us is that we need to self-consciously fit our case into the bigger (theoretical) picture. They explained it this way:

> To view Morocco in the perspective of the Arab world, to consider the Nazi experience within the framework of the totalitarian model, or to study recent Turkish history in the light of problems raised by development means including the monograph in a series of comparative studies. Sometimes the general perspective is clearly stated [that is, is explicit], and sometimes it is implicit. *But it must be present for the monograph to become a real* [comparatively oriented] *case study.* (emphasis added; p. 122)

Let's consider Dogan and Pelassy's rule in light of the example I used above, ethnoreligious conflict in Yugoslavia. Aiming at generalization with this case means, among other things, consciously attempting to discern where the Yugoslavian case fits in with regard to existing theories of ethnic conflict. Is the Yugoslavian case representative of a general pattern or model of ethnic conflict? If so, which one and why? Or is Yugoslavia a truly unique case, theoretically speaking? Even, or especially, if the researcher decides that Yugoslavia is a unique case, it is important to understand that this, too, has broader implications for theories about ethnic conflict. Simply put, it tells us that general theories about ethnic conflict are necessarily limited in that they *do not* account for the Yugoslavian case. And if these theories cannot adequately account for the Yugoslavian case, maybe they do not adequately account for other cases as well. In this sense, "aiming at generalization" does not mean that the researcher will always achieve the goal of generalization—sometimes just the opposite may happen. Still, regardless of the outcome, "aiming at generalization" requires that the researcher be constantly focused on examining her case in light of larger theoretical or conceptual concerns.

This last point is important to remember, but difficult to put into practice, especially for the novice comparativist. After all, most students not only are unfamiliar with the history and complexities of specific cases, but also are struggling to make sense of the myriad theories that purport to explain a particular political, social, or economic phenomenon. Just consider the numerous theories purporting to account for or explain ethnic mobilization and conflict. According to Taras and Ganguly (2002), there are at least ten distinct theories on these issues (see Figure 2.8); this is a lot to digest even for an expert, much less a beginning student. Regrettably, there is no quick and easy solution to this "problem." Instead, doing a case study in comparative perspective—doing it well, at least—means that the student must not only conduct *intensive* (that is, highly focused) research on the primary case but must also carry out *extensive* (that is, broad-based) research on a range of other relevant cases. Moreover, she must read and be familiar with as much of the relevant theoretical literature as possible. This is not something that most students want to hear—understandably (but mistakenly), many students decide to do a case study precisely because it *seems* to entail less work than explicitly comparative analysis. But knowing about other cases and about the theoretical literature, even for a single case study, is a difficult-to-avoid fact of life in doing comparative politics.

Figure 2.8　Theories of Ethnic Political Mobilization

1. Indirect Theories
   A. Negative Theories of Integration
      - *Mobilization–Assimilation Gap Explanation* (K. Deutsch)
      - *Rising Expectation–Rising Frustration Explanation* (S. Huntington, D. Lerner)
      - *Strain Theory* (C. Geertz)
   B. Negative Theories of Cohesion
      - *Plural Society Approach/Incompatibility Theory* (J. S. Furnivall, M. G. Smith)
      - *Consociationalism* (A. Lijphart)
      - *Theory of Hegemonic Exchange* (D. Rothchild)
   C. Indirect Theories of Disintegration
      - *Theory of Relative Deprivation* (T. Gurr)
2. Direct Theories
   A. Primordialist Theories
      - *Ethnic Identity/Consciousness* (N. Glazer, D. Moynihan, C. Enloe, D. Horowitz, and others)
   B. Instrumentalists
      - *Internal Colonialism/Reactive Ethnicity* (M. Hechter)
      - *Communalists/Ethnic Competition* (P. Brass)

Theories of ethnic political mobilization are classified according to different basic principles, but even within a single category there may be several competing explanations. Above are listed a few of the major explanations along with the names of significant proponents of each view.

Source: Adapted from Ray Taras and Rajat Ganguly, *Understanding Ethnic Conflict*, 2nd ed. (New York: Longman, 2002), p. 11.

Think comparatively but deeply and systematically. The two general "rules" introduced above provide a very simple, but nonetheless important, foundation for carrying out a case study in comparative perspective—or, really, almost any type of comparative analysis, including the other ones discussed in this chapter. Certainly, it would be possible to provide a much longer list of ever more complex or sophisticated rules, but this would probably—and unnecessarily—serve more to confuse than to enlighten you. For the key to doing a "good" case study in comparative perspective is quite basic: *think comparatively but deeply and systematically.* This maxim applies equally to cases that are original or representative (and everything in between). Indeed, as I suggested earlier, a researcher cannot say with any confidence that a case is original unless she first compares it to a range of other cases. This said, doing a single case study in comparative perspective is not without its pitfalls. And, as students, it is vital that you recognize both the advantages and pitfalls of a particular method of analysis, which is the topic of our next section.

Analytical induction and the case study: Some advantages and pitfalls. The case study, it is important to understand, represents a significant trade-off. On the one hand, limiting an analysis to a single country or unit has the advantage of allowing the researcher to study a subject in great depth and detail. This allows the researcher, in turn, to achieve a degree of understanding about the case that generally cannot be matched by other comparative strategies. On the other hand, depth of understanding invariably comes at the expense of explanation. Thus, although a comparatively oriented case study may aim at generalization, as I suggested above, it can *never* "hit the bull's-eye." To many scholars, this is a serious if not fatal limitation. That is, if a single case study can never establish general "truths" or explanatory "laws" about the social world, then it will always remain of dubious "scientific" value. There is no denying this point. Still, in the messy real world of political, social, and economic phenomena, a case study sometimes serves as an *indispensable* complement to building more comprehensive or encompassing theories. In this regard, individual case studies might best be seen as empirical/theoretical stepping-stones. Some of you may recall this is the same idea behind analytical induction, which, as I noted in the beginning of this section, can be considered a separate, although strongly related, comparative strategy.

Consider a study that makes a general claim about, say, the significance of the middle class in bringing about stable democracy. At first glance, this claim may seem to hold water—if one looks at a broad range of cases, it would be easy to find numerous situations in which the emergence and development of a strong middle class coincided with long-lived democracy. But what if a researcher wanted to "test" this theoretical claim more thoroughly? How might this be done? Well, one way would be to do a study in which the selected case appears to reflect strongly the main premises of the theory. If an in-depth examination of the case—keeping the existing theory firmly in mind—reveals no inconsistencies, then the case has helped to support (but has not proved) the validity of the theory in question. The case, in short, is one of many useful stepping-stones. If, on the other hand, the researcher identifies, or thinks she has identified, a significant inconsistency or exceptional circumstance in her case, this could lead to—even require—a revision or further refinement of the theory (Dogan and Pelassy 1990).

In fact, this latter situation is far more likely; that is, in-depth single case studies (especially those based on a strategy of analytical induction) often bring to light hitherto neglected factors or variables while simultaneously problematizing already-identified causal factors. At the least, they usually provide a more nuanced understanding of these factors and variables than comparative analysis involving multiple cases. In studies of democratization in Latin America, for example, many scholars, to draw from another common argument, contend that divisions within the "ruling elite"—between hard-liners and soft-liners—are a major reason for the breakdown of authoritarian regimes, but this was certainly not true in every single case. In other words, there are a few "deviant" cases (especially outside of Latin America) in which divisions within the ruling elite did not play a significant role in the democratization process. And although a researcher may be tempted to discount or ignore exceptional or deviant cases, such cases can often make or break a theory. In this regard, it is useful to note that deviant cases can also play a theoretically important role of **falsification** (see Figure 2.9). As Peters (1998) explained it, "The basic argument [regarding falsification] is that science progresses by eliminating possible causes for observed phenomena rather than by finding positive relationships . . . there is no shortage of positive correlations in the social sciences; what there is sometimes a shortage of [is] research that dismisses one or another plausible cause for that phenomenon" (p. 40). Individual case studies, to put it more simply, often send researchers back to the (theoretical) drawing board. (This, by the way, is a practical strategy to use if you disagree with a particular theory—that is, try to falsify the theory by doing a case study!) In this situation, too, an individual case is an important stepping-stone, but one that might lead us down a slightly different path. Whatever the situation, however, individual case studies are helping researchers to advance toward stronger and more coherent explanations, which represents, to repeat, the basic strategy of analytical induction.

Peters (1998) also provided us with another situation in which a case study can serve an indispensable role in the construction of theory. As he wrote, "The second reason for using a single case is that the case may be the hardest one, so that if the theory appears to work in this setting it should work in all others" (p. 64). The particular strategy for this situation is more or less the converse of the one above; that is, instead of choosing a case that appears

---

Figure 2.9   Falsification

Falsification is based on the simple idea that a single nonsupporting occurrence can refute or invalidate a **hypothesis**. For example, a single black swan refutes the general hypothesis that "all swans are white." The idea of falsification is important because, in practice, it is generally impossible to verify a theoretical generalization about the social world with absolute finality. That is, even if a researcher finds case after case that confirms her claims, there is always a possibility that new and potentially refuting evidence will surface. Unfortunately, like most concepts in the social sciences, the idea of falsification is not without its critics. Critics argue, for instance, that a single refutation is rarely, if ever, enough to summarily reject a theory or general hypothesis. Indeed, some critics assert that if science strictly followed the rules of falsification, science would most likely be crippled (Jary and Jary 1991, pp. 165–166).

---

to reflect strongly the main features of the archetypal case, you choose one that seems to contradict the archetypal case in as many ways as possible. Scholars who want to test theories about political phenomena in Western democracies, for instance, will often choose Japan because of its particularly distinctive political and social system (at least compared to major Western countries): if the theory works for Japan, the thinking goes, the theory itself must have general validity (Peters 1998, p. 64)—at least researchers can have greater confidence in the theory. This approach, however, is incremental, since a single case study can only lend additional support to a theory but, again, cannot "prove" it correct.

In sum, despite its undeniable limitations (and trade-offs), the single case study will likely always remain an important and legitimate research strategy in the field of comparative politics. This said, to reiterate a point made above, budding comparativists should not choose this strategy only because it appears easier, more convenient, or more manageable to do than a multiunit comparative study. In certain situations, a multiunit study may be a far better choice; it may even be necessary for the purposes of the research project. In the next few sections, therefore, we will take a look at multiunit comparative analysis, beginning with the simplest: the two-unit or binary comparison.

Comparing Two Cases (Two-Unit or Binary Comparison)

I will not say much about the two-unit or binary comparison, since (1) the logic that underlies this specific strategy is exactly the same logic as that of the MSS or MDS design, and (2) the rules that apply to the single-unit case study apply equally to the binary comparison. Thus, if you follow the suggestions and guidelines from the last few sections, you will already have a good foundation both for understanding and for doing a binary comparison. Still, it is worth reiterating that, in setting up a binary comparison, the selection of cases is an extremely important consideration. It should not be done in an arbitrary or essentially impulsive manner. Of course, this is true of all comparative strategies, but a binary comparison is particularly sensitive to "overdetermination" (of the dependent variable) if the cases are not selected carefully. Overdetermination is simply a type of bias in which the researcher chooses cases that are most likely to support or validate the argument he is trying to "test." The problem with overdetermination should be obvious; namely, if you only choose cases that are likely to support your argument, you are, to be blunt, cheating. In more formal terms, you are predetermining the results. This is usually not intentional, and it is frequently unavoidable in a binary comparison, but it is nonetheless a potentially serious methodological problem. In this regard, the most important "rule" to keep in mind is to understand that you can rarely, if ever, make strong theoretical conclusions *solely* based on a two-unit comparative analysis.

So, how *should* the cases for a binary comparison be selected? Unfortunately, there's no easy or uniform answer. One general principle, though, is to be aware that case selection is governed not always by methodological logic alone but also by theory. Since we will discuss theory in depth in the following chapter, at this point I will only say that "good" theories often tell us which (independent) variables to focus on in the first place. In so doing, *theory also guides our selection of cases*. For example, a researcher who believes that states with a high degree of "transformative capacity" (the independent variable) are essential in bringing about and sustaining industrial transformation will naturally select cases in which this "transformative capacity" exists or does not. Of course, in so doing, the researcher must be able to specify in advance what the elements of transformative capacity are and then must decide which basic strategy—MSS or MDS—to use. In this case, an MSS design would make more sense, since the presumed independent variable is not located at the level of the individual but is instead a "system-level" variable. Choosing an MSS design, in turn, means that the cases should show variance on the dependent variable. With all this in mind, a good contemporary two-unit comparison might be between Russia and China: the former is undergoing an extremely rocky transition (from communism to capitalism), and the latter is growing at a remarkably fast and sustained rate. This may not be a perfect binary, MSS design (in fact, it isn't). Still, the example should give you a sense of how to select cases in a two-unit comparison.

"Bigger N's": Comparing Three or More Cases

The next step beyond the two-unit comparison is a comparison of three or more units. Not surprisingly, the same logic that applies to a case study and binary comparisons applies equally to a comparison of three or more units. Generally speaking, though, when a comparison is extended to three, four, five, or even a dozen cases, the prospects for theory building improve, if only because the claims the researcher makes are based on a "bigger N," which ostensibly gives more control over the variables of interest. At the same time, as the number of units increases, the level of abstraction and generality increases, too. For many qualitatively oriented comparativists, this is a major (even unacceptable) trade-off if taken too far, since countries become mere "data points" rather than real places with their own histories, cultures, and political/social systems. In practical terms, moreover, when more than a handful of cases is incorporated into a (qualitatively oriented) research design, the analysis becomes empirically unmanageable, especially for an individual researcher. This is because there is simply too much material—too much information and potential evidence—to absorb, organize, and evaluate.

There is, I must emphasize, an obvious and important exception to what I've just said, namely, statistical or quantitative analysis. This type of analysis typically aims at "global comparisons"; that is, it is designed to include *all* relevant cases in the same analytical framework. In comparative politics research, this might (but does not necessarily) mean the inclusion of all 192 countries in the world (as of July 2002). Remember, too, that a case need not refer to a single country. For example, in a study by Barbara Geddes (1999), which I discuss in some detail in Chapter 6, the author defined a case in terms of political "regimes." To Geddes, each time an authoritarian regime breaks down, it constitutes a separate case. Thus, in a given country, there may be multiple "cases" (in fact, in her study Geddes identified 163 individual regime changes or cases). Statistical (or "big N") analysis, however, is distinct from the type of comparative ("small N") analysis we've been discussing thus far. And although the distinction certainly warrants further discussion, I will not cover it here, if only because most political science departments in the United States devote considerable and special attention to this method of analysis.[4] There is, therefore, no need to discuss this extremely well-covered ground in this book. Instead, let's return to the main issue of this section by asking the following question: if there are advantages to having more cases, but disadvantages to having *too many* cases, exactly how many cases is optimum for comparative research?

If you have been paying attention, the answer should be clear to you already: *it depends*. In other words, it is not possible to prespecify an optimum number of cases for comparative research, because each situation will be different. But, even if we know the specifics of a situation, we probably still could not specify the most appropriate number of cases to examine, because there simply are no standard criteria for doing so. Suffice it to say, therefore, that you should consider both what is practical and what is minimally necessary given the theoretical scope and ambition of your argument. So what does this mean? For most purposes and for most researchers, this probably means from three to five cases, but a few particularly ambitious researchers have incorporated dozens of cases into their analyses. In subsequent chapters, I give several examples of this. But first another caveat: as with the other forms of comparative analysis, careful case selection based on the logic of comparative analysis is important. Fortunately, with more cases, the problems of selection bias and "overdetermination" of the dependent variable are reduced (although not entirely eliminated). Moreover, with more cases, the researcher has greater flexibility with regard to the comparative logic she employs. Instead of having to rely exclusively on an MSS or MDS design, as is the case in a binary comparison, the researcher can use a mixed design, one that incorporates both logics into the same general framework.

The "Mixed Design"

In practice, comparativists frequently use a mixed design, and, in general, it is a very useful approach to take. A big reason for this is that a mixed design helps to mitigate the limitations of using only an MSS or MDS design. In principle, a mixed strategy may be necessary to fully develop an argument when a researcher finds that either an MSS or MDS strategy, by itself, is clearly inconclusive (which is, not surprisingly, often the case). A mixed design, in short, may not be a perfect solution, but it should be used whenever possible, practicable, and feasible. This said, setting up a comparative strategy based on a mixed design—as with all comparative strategies—requires forethought, planning, and a lot of research. Consider the example used above, Theda Skocpol's comparison of France, Russia, and China. You should recall that the primary logic of this comparison was based on the MDS design. At the same time, Skocpol was very much aware of the need to buttress her primary strategy with other comparative strategies. Here is how Skocpol explained her overall strategy:

> France, Russia, and China will serve as three positive cases of successful social revolution, and I shall argue that these cases reveal similar causal patterns despite their many other differences. In addition, I shall invoke negative cases for the purpose of validating various particular parts of the causal argument. In so doing, I shall always construct contrasts that maximize the similarities of the negative case(s) to the positive case(s) in every apparently relevant respect. . . . Thus, for example, the abortive Russian Revolution of 1905 will be contrasted with the successful Revolution of 1917 in order to validate arguments about the crucial contribution to social-revolutionary success in Russia of war-related processes that led to the breakdown of state repressive capacities. Moreover, selected aspects of English, Japanese, and German history will be used in various places to strengthen arguments about the causes of revolutionary political crises and peasant revolts in France,

> Russia, and China. These cases are suitable as contrasts because they were comparable countries that underwent non-revolutionary political crises and transformations in broadly similar terms and circumstances to France, Russia, and China. (1979, p. 37)

The specific details of Skocpol's argument are not important for our purposes. What is important is her rationale for the comparisons she makes. Note, for instance, that Skocpol planned a within-case comparison using Russia. Logically, as you now know, this is an MSS design, which helps to support her original argument by showing that a key change (in the independent variable) occurred between the 1905 and the 1917 revolutions. Although I have already said a little about the within-case comparisons, let me add that, because it allows the comparativist to increase the "N" without having to analyze a completely different country, within-case comparisons almost always help to strengthen causal analysis. Even more, the within-case comparison reduces the problem of **selection bias** because it introduces variance on the dependent variable (Collier 1997).

Skocpol also used three additional cases—England, Japan, and Germany (née Prussia)—to further buttress her argument. In her research design, England, Japan, and Germany (Prussia) were "negative cases" (that is, cases in which a successful social revolution did *not* occur). Although it is difficult to classify the selection of these cases as unequivocally based on an MDS or MSS design, Skocpol's objective is clear. She wanted to show that, in three "comparable" cases, the *absence* of the key independent variable or set of conditions that was *present* in France, Russia, and China (the three positive cases) resulted in a different outcome. In Figure 2.10, we can get a sense of how Skocpol's comparisons of the three primary and four secondary cases, in a mixed design, supported her overall argument and conclusions.

Skocpol's research design, of course, is not the only way to set up a mixed strategy, but it is a very instructive "real-world" example. For the sake of clarity, though, let's go through her design one more time. First, she began with a basic MDS design, using three primary cases. Second, she singled out one of these cases—Russia—and used a within-case comparison, in which there is variance on both the presumed independent and dependent variables, to validate her initial hypothesis. Third, she introduced three secondary and specifically "negative" cases. It is important to note that these three "negative" cases also differ from the primary cases with regard to the presumed independent and dependent variables. The comparison, therefore, further helps to support her initial hypothesis/thesis. Finally, in a fourth step not mentioned above, Skocpol returned to a deeper empirical examination of her three main cases in an effort (1) to highlight the key similarities and (2) to account for any significant differences that could weaken her overall argument. This reflects, at least partly,

Figure 2.10   Summary of Skocpol's Comparative Research Design

	Social Revolution	No Social Revolution
Conditions present (independent variables)	Russia (1917) France China *(Box 1)*	— *(Box 2)*
Conditions absent	— *(Box 3)*	Japan England Prussia (Germany) Russia (1905) *(Box 4)*

From the table, we can see that in those cases where the independent variables assumed to create the basis for "social revolution" (the dependent variable) were present, a social revolution occurred (Box 1). By contrast, there were no cases of a social revolution occurring in which the presumed independent variables were absent (Box 3). Skocpol's basic research design, therefore, seems to offer strong support for her argument.

The limitation, however, is the small-N: Skocpol examined "only" seven cases (which, from a qualitative perspective, is a significant number). Still, for other comparativists, the next question would be, are there any cases that would contradict Skocpol's findings?

the incorporation of a case study and analytical induction into her overall analysis. In sum, Skocpol incorporated the following comparative strategies into a *single framework:*

1. MDS design using three primary cases;
2. MSS design/within-case comparison using Russia;
3. Multiple-unit comparison (three or more units), using secondary cases;
4. Individual case studies/analytical induction.

Admittedly, Skocpol's research design and analysis may seem daunting for the beginning comparativist. Still, a basic mixed design strategy is in the grasp of even the most inexperienced comparativist. It really involves little more than a willingness and commitment to "think comparatively." Even if used in a relatively clumsy and cursory manner (which is almost unavoidable in the beginning), a mixed design encourages inexperienced comparativists to adopt a systematic and critical attitude in their analyses, the importance of which should not be underestimated.

A Methodological Exercise

As an exercise, it might be very useful to try setting up your own mixed-design strategy based on the issue of gun violence or overall homicide rates in the United States (or any other issue of interest). To get you started, remember that we already discussed at least one example of a binary comparison, based on an MSS design, using Canada and the United States (and also the United States and Britain). We also discussed Norway and Finland. You should recall that, even though the rate of private gun ownership (a potentially important independent variable) is very high in both countries, their gun-related homicides rates are among the lowest in the world. What type of comparison could we make using these cases, and what might a comparison tell us? Norway and Finland, of course, are not the only "comparable" cases. For example, it might make sense to think about countries with gun-related (or overall) homicides rates higher than the United States. Colombia, South Africa, and Brazil, for example, are the three deadliest places on earth in terms of gun-related murders. Significantly, all might also be classified as most different systems relative to the United States and relative to each other (at least for South Africa and Brazil/Colombia). Perhaps an even more pertinent case is the Philippines, which has a homicide rate essentially equal to that of the United States. (You must be careful, however, not to base your selection of cases solely on the dependent variable, or else you may be guilty of selection basis and overdetermination.) Another important possibility is a within-case comparison, whether at the national or subnational level. On this point, it is worth considering the issue of *time;* specifically, in the United States, the murder rate in general declined dramatically during the 1990s after a steady increase from the 1960s.

You should also remember that not all cases are countries, and vice versa. For an issue such as gun violence, in fact, it would be extremely useful, even necessary, to make subnational comparisons. In the United States, in particular, there are huge variations among cities, even among the largest cities such as New York, Chicago, Los Angeles, and Washington, D.C. What might a comparison of these cities (and others) tell us? What type of comparative strategy could be used to compare large, urban cities? Would it be legitimate or reasonable to include a comparison of smaller cities or towns? Finally, you should think about comparing specific institutions, including, most saliently, the police and the courts (but one should not presume that these are the only institutions that matter with regard to the issue of gun violence and homicide; social welfare institutions may also be extremely important). Institutions, it is important to note, can be compared cross-nationally and at the subnational level.

Thus, it would be possible to compare the police and judicial systems (or social welfare systems) in various countries as a whole, on the one hand, and the police and judicial systems in various US cities, on the other hand. Figure 2.11

Figure 2.11   An Example of a Mixed Design Strategy to Evaluate the Causes of the High Level of Gun-Related and Overall Homicide Rates in the United States

Cases	Basic Strategy	Variance on Dependent Variable	Goal
United States Canada	MSS	Yes	Identify key differences between two cases.
United States Norway Finland	MDS[a]	Yes[b]	Show that the level of gun ownership per se (a potential independent variable) does not automatically lead to high level of gun violence.
United States Philippines	MDS	No	US-Philippines comparison can help to identify potential important similarity; no variance on dependent variable is an advantage.
United States, 1960–1990 United States, 1991–2004	Within-case (MSS)	Yes[c]	Identify key changes between the two periods. These changes, or differences, may be regarded as potential independent variables.
New York City Washington, D.C.	Subnational, MSS	Yes[d]	Find significant differences (potential independent variables), if any, between two cities.
Washington, D.C., Pretoria, South Africa New York City Vilnius, Lithuania	Subnational, MDS	No[e]	Find key similarities, if any, in the two sets of cities. (Do the similarities match potential independent variables discovered in other comparisons?)

(continues)

Figure 2.11 continued

Cases	Basic Strategy	Variance on Dependent Variable	Goal
Institutional comparisons: police, judicial, social welfare systems	—	—	Institutional differences or similarities may reflect the results of other comparisons; more in-depth analysis may identify important institutional practices, relationships, or arrangements.

Notes: a. Some cases are difficult to classify as either MDS or MSS, but it is important to remember that the concept of most similar or most different systems is relative. In this regard, Norway and Finland might be considered "most different systems" when compared to the United States, although Norway and Finland themselves are most similar systems.

b. In 2001, the percentage of households with firearms in Finland was 50 percent, in the United States 41 percent, and in Norway 32 percent. The respective homicide rates by gun were 0.87, 6.24, and 0.32 percent per 100,000. *Source:* http://www.guncontrol.ca/Content/international.html.

c. In 1960, the (overall) homicide rate in the United States was 5.1 per 100,000; over the next 20 years, the rate doubled to 10.2. Beginning in the early 1990s, however, the rate slowly declined, reaching a rate of 5.5 in 2000. *Source:* FBI, Uniform Crime Reports, 1950–2000.

d. Although both cities have relatively high (overall) homicide rates, that of Washington, D.C., is exceptional. In 1996, the homicide rate in Washington, D.C., was 73.11, whereas in New York, the rate was 13.39. By 2000, the respective rates had dropped to 41.78 and 8.69 (Barclay and Tavares 2002, p. 10).

e. Washington, D.C., and Pretoria, South Africa, have two of the highest (overall) homicide rates in the world; the 1997 figures were 56.89 and 43.0 respectively. New York City and Vilnius, Lithuania, had almost identical (overall) homicide rates between 1996 and 2000 and also experienced comparable declines in homicides during that same period (Barclay and Tavares 2002, p. 10).

provides a basic summary of some, but not all, of the potential comparisons we just discussed.

In an actual comparative analysis, I should emphasize, it is impractical to carry out each of the comparisons mentioned, but the key point to remember is that using overlapping strategies—a mixed research design—will almost always help to develop a stronger, more sophisticated argument. More basically, thinking about how to set up a comprehensive, multilevel comparative research design is a useful and very important step in doing comparative politics. It isn't easy, but it isn't immensely difficult either, as, I hope, the exercise in this section demonstrates. And, although gun violence is not typically a subject of study for comparativists, the logic and procedures of setting up a mixed comparative design for this issue are the same as for any more traditional subject of study in comparative politics. Moreover, I think that focusing on a subject of "everyday" relevance helps to show that comparative politics is, in fact, a practical and very useful field of study.

I should end this section with one last caveat. It is important to remember the concept of complex causality. A mixed design strategy of the type we just outlined will almost undoubtedly identify a range of potentially significant factors. Moreover, it will likely show that the relationship between the potential independent variable or variables and the dependent variable is not necessarily or always clear-cut. *This is to be expected.* At the same time, complex causality does not mean that we cannot or should not try to focus on the significance of a single variable or set of variables, as, for example, in Michael Moore's argument. A "culture of fear" may not explain everything, but the fact that other factors are at play does not mean this argument is totally without merit. "Culture" may, indeed, be an integral part of any explanation about gun-related homicide in the United States.

■ Conclusion

Comparative analysis is a second-best strategy, but it is often the only viable strategy open to comparativists. This is especially true of qualitatively oriented researchers who take history seriously. Comparative analysis is also an extremely imperfect strategy, with many limitations and flaws. For this reason, *all* comparativists need to exercise care in their research design and restraint in the conclusions and claims they derive from their research design. This is a simple lesson, but one that is frequently forgotten or ignored. At the same time, comparison is, as I noted in the beginning of this chapter, *"the engine of knowledge."* If we want to better understand the world in which we live, if we want to explain social, political, and economic phenomena, we need to compare. But we need to compare in a logical, systematic, and well-informed manner. If we fail to do this, our "comparisons" may be worthless or, even worse, an engine for distortion, misunderstanding, and falsehood.

■ Notes

1. I cite a few of these exceptions extensively in this chapter. These include Dogan and Pelassy (1990) and Dogan and Kazancigil (1994). Another useful book focused on comparative analysis is B. Guy Peters's *Comparative Politics: Theory and Method* (1998).

2. Przeworski and Teune (1970) pointed out, though, that the most different systems design generally starts off with a variation of observed behavior below the level of the system (or society as a whole). "Most often," they noted, "this will be the level of individual actors, but it can be the level of groups, local communities, social classes,

or occupation. . . . [S]ystemic factors are not given any special place among the possible predictors of behavior" (p. 34).

3. Among comparativists, however, there is still a tendency to associate subnational units with the particular country in which they are located. For example, a researcher doing a study of conditions of poverty in Mexico City, Taipei, or Cape Town will generally link his or her research to the country as a whole: Mexico, Taiwan, or South Africa respectively.

4. Statistical or quantitative analysis is a major research method used in political science and the social sciences more generally. Indeed, in the United States, the large majority of social science departments require their students to take at least one and sometimes several courses dealing with quantitative methods and statistics (or scope and method). Largely for this reason—and also because there are dozens of good undergraduate textbooks covering quantitative analysis in the social sciences but very few covering *qualitative* analysis—I do not discuss statistical analysis in this chapter. It is important to understand, however, that many researchers in comparative politics do use quantitative analysis or cross-national comparisons and that quantitative analysis is clearly an important part of the research methodology in comparative politics.

3

Thinking Theoretically in Comparative Politics

An Introduction

In the social sciences, theory plays an absolutely essential role, although it is not always clear exactly what this role is. Indeed, one of the criticisms leveled at the field (from both within and without) is that there is no single or even dominant theoretical approach to distinguish comparative politics. Instead, there has been a proliferation of approaches (especially since the 1970s) "to the point," as one prominent comparativist put it, "where both graduate students and some professional practitioners in the field have at times seen the diversity as anarchy" (Verba 1991, p. 38). Others, like Peter Evans, see the theoretical eclecticism of the field in a more positive light, arguing that it gives comparativists the freedom "to draw on a mélange of theoretical traditions in hopes of gaining greater purchase on the cases they care about" (Kohli et al. 1995, p. 4). Theory, in this view, is pragmatic: it provides the tools to help frame and explain empirical puzzles, and comparative researchers are "opportunists" who use whatever works (Kohli et al. 1995, p. 46).

■ Why Study Theory?

The debate over the "proper" role of theory is important, but one that need not occupy us here. For now, it is better to focus on how and why theory is important in comparative politics (and in the social sciences generally). Let me first say that, in keeping with its bad reputation, I realize students are often intimidated by the word "theory." It not only sounds abstract and therefore difficult to understand, but it also sounds like something only professors, philosophers, or other "intellectuals" would be interested in studying. Thus, as I noted in Chapter 1, you might be surprised to learn that we all (including *you*) use theory, every day. We have to. I will come back to this issue shortly, but let me make one more general comment, which is the flip side of the first. Instead of being intimidated by theory, some students tend to think of it as useless, impractical, and therefore irrelevant. They equate theory with unsubstantiated and mostly subjective opinion—as in, "It's just a theory"—or worse still, consider it no more than an abstruse word unrelated to the real world. Theory, in this sense, is considered to be the opposite of or completely separate from fact or, as some might say, the "truth." Although somewhat understandable (in that the term "theory" is often used in a very casual and imprecise manner), this view is misguided and fundamentally misinformed. Indeed, it is important to understand that theory and fact are inextricably connected. To some scholars— those we might label **positivists**—theory, at least good theory, is an explanation of how "reality works." Positivists believe not only that good theories identify the underlying processes and forces that shape reality but also that, once we identify these processes and forces, we will be able to make predictions and develop "laws" about the social world (in much the same way that natural scientists develop laws about the physical world). To other scholars—in particular, those who embrace the principles of **post-positivism** or **reflectivism**—theory and reality are seen as *mutually constitutive*. Put in very simple terms, post-positivists believe that how we think about the world actually helps to *construct* or make the world in which we live. This particular view of theory, I should note, is especially prevalent among contemporary cultural theorists (whom we will discuss later in this chapter).

The disagreement between positivists and post-positivists (that is, between scholars who believe in **objectivity** and those who believe in subjectivity) is another important but complex debate. And although it deserves very serious attention, I will not say anything more on this subject. The main point to remember is that all scholars agree that there is no way to explain *or* understand reality without a firm grasp of theory. "Facts" and theory are inseparable. With this in mind, we can now return to a more general discussion of how and why theory is important and necessary.

How We All Theorize

Earlier I said we all use theory, all the time. There are several ways to interpret this statement. Most generally, if we understand theory as some kind of *simplifying device* that allows us to "see" which facts matter and which do not, then "it is at the very point when one starts selecting the relevant details that one begins to theorize" (Rosenau and Durfee 2000, p. 2). Theory, in this case, is clearly not optional. As Steve Smith and John Baylis (1997) nicely put it, "It is not as if you can say that you do not want to bother with a theory, all you want to do is to look at the 'facts.' We believe that this is simply impossible, since the only way in which you can decide which of the millions of possible facts to look at is by adhering to some simplifying device which tells you which ones matter the most" (p. 3). Their point should be clear, but an example might help. Consider the question (one that I devote a whole chapter to later in this book), why are some countries poor? A few quick responses might include the following: "Poor countries are poor because the people are uneducated and lack appropriate skills, are lazy), and have no sense of personal responsibility"; "Poor countries are poor because they lack natural resources or have too few resources given their population size"; "Global poverty exists because the world economic system is inherently unequal and exploitative"; "Corrupt governments are the reason some countries are poor."

Each of these responses highlights certain *facts*—a generally low level of education and poorly developed skills, limited resources, overpopulation, large technological and economic disparities, high levels of corruption. Yet, by choosing to highlight some facts while ignoring (or dismissing) others, you are unavoidably engaged in a theoretical process. Specifically, you are making judgments about what is and is not relevant or important in terms of explaining poverty; you are identifying, albeit implicitly, a specific **level of analysis** and unit of analysis; you are making assumptions about **power**, structure, and **agency**; and you are connecting certain facts with specific outcomes. You are, in short, theorizing. In an important sense, then, you're also doing what any trained researcher or scholar in comparative politics does. A key difference, however, is that most students are generally not aware of the theoretical assumptions they make when stating their answers to certain questions. Students may even assume that their interpretation is the only legitimate one—that is, that the facts they have chosen to focus on "speak for themselves." But, as one scholar forcefully put it, *facts never speak for themselves:* "they only take on meaning as we select some of them as important and dismiss others as trivial" (Rosenau and Durfee 2000, p. 3).

The ways in which researchers select and look at (or evaluate) facts give us another useful way to think about theory. As a number of scholars have explained it, working with theories is like looking through different pairs of sunglasses or, better yet, using different photographic lenses. Different types of "lenses" provide different ways to "see" reality. In our example above, one lens brings into focus *individual* attributes of a person or people—their specific levels of education, technical skills, motivation, ambition, etc. Another lens may focus on a different set of geographic, demographic, or political attributes, such as a country's natural resource endowment, its climate (in terms of its suitability for agricultural production), or its political and economic systems. Some lenses (for example, an infrared lens) may even bring to light otherwise "invisible" elements of reality, such as the "structures of global capitalism" or "relationships of dependence." The possibilities are virtually endless. Some researchers, of course, may feel their lenses—and pictures of reality—are more appropriate, more reliable, or simply truer than others. Researchers using different lenses/theories, in short, do not generally agree on who (or what "lens") is right. This is an important point to keep in mind, for students are often confused about the existence of multiple competing theories. We can understand this situation, at least partly, when we recognize that different lenses allow us to focus on different aspects of the same larger reality.

"Good" and "Bad" Theorizing

Theoretical disagreements are not only very common but also, at times, seemingly impossible to resolve; this does not mean, however, that all theories of the world are equally valid. This point is even more obvious when we acknowledge the fact that we all theorize, from the most erudite scholar to the greenest student, from the most abstruse pundit to the most hardheaded pragmatist. *Yet, just because we all theorize does not mean we are equally adept at it,* especially when we theorize about broader political, social, and economic phenomena. Some of us, for example, theorize in an extremely superficial or arbitrary manner. We jump to conclusions; we ignore or dismiss "facts" that don't fit into or don't jibe with our understanding of the world; we fail to see or acknowledge logical contradictions in our thinking; we confuse "observation" or correlation with **causation** (see Figure 3.1 for a brief discussion of these two terms); we never (ever) think about the assumptions upon which our views are based; or, worst of all, we regard our theories or theorizing about the world as self-evidently true (meaning we do not need to "prove" or support them with empirical evidence or logic). Each of these tendencies will likely result in inconsistent, problematic, and, quite possibly, completely erroneous understandings about the world. In this regard, even bad theorizing is relevant, for it can help justify, reproduce, and encourage harmful practices and views. Unfortunately, "bad theorizing" is probably more the rule than the exception, especially outside of academia. Turn on virtually any politically oriented talk show in the United States, in fact, and you're likely to hear empirically unsupportable, logically inconsistent, and methodologically suspect theories about all aspects of US political and social life. This tendency, moreover, is not limited to one side of the political spectrum: *Bad theorizing is an equal opportunity vice.*

So how can bad theorizing be avoided? The easy answer is to avoid all the pitfalls I listed in the preceding paragraph. Of course, this is easier said than done, since, for many people, it is difficult to know where or how to begin. More practically, then, a crucial first step toward "good theorizing" is simply to become much more aware and self-critical of how you think about the world. Think carefully about what informs your views—why you think the way you do in the first place. Do not presume that your views are correct, much less unassailable; instead, assume that you always have something new to learn. Similarly, listen carefully to what others have to say. If you disagree, try to identify

Figure 3.1   Correlation and Causation

It may rain whenever I wash my car, but washing my car is not the cause of the rain. The relationship between the two events, in other words, is not based on causation but correlation. *Correlation*, to be clear, describes a relationship or an association between two (or more) different variables. Correlation may be positive or negative, but it can also be spurious, as in the example. In a spurious correlation, it is sometimes the case that a third unidentified variable is actually the deciding influence. Thus, in the example, washing my car may (of course) have nothing to do with the occurrence of rain. Because I wash my car only on cloudy, humid days, however, there might very well be a positive (and nonspurious) correlation between "cloudy, humid days" and rain. Still, the positive correlation between "cloudy, humid days" and rain does not necessarily signify causation. To establish causality requires a stronger demonstration of a *cause-and-effect* relationship. To do this, other variables need to be eliminated from consideration, which, in turn, requires a proper research design and adequate empirical support. Establishing causation, in short, normally requires systematic observation, analysis, and "testing."

Let's consider a more realistic example—the correlation between television viewing and attention deficit hyperactivity disorder (ADHD). Many studies have confirmed that an association between these two variables exists and, from this, assert that excessive television viewing *causes* or at least contributes to the development of ADHD in very young children. But the researchers may be jumping to conclusions. After all, it *might* very well be the case that children prone to ADHD are drawn to television. In this case, television viewing is not the cause but is merely symptomatic of a still unidentified cause. Or the causality could be completely reversed; that is, it may be that ADHD causes excessive television viewing. This is just speculation, however. To determine whether a causal relationship exists or what the direction of causality is requires a proper research design, observation, and analysis.

clearly the key weakness in the competing view. Obviously, these are basic suggestions, all of which correspond to the dictates of critical thinking we discussed in Chapter 1. Good theorizing, however, requires more than critical thinking. You also need to develop a clear understanding (1) of what theory is in general and (2) of what the principles of "good theory" are, especially within the context of comparative politics. We will be addressing the "rules" of or principles for good theory for most of the remainder of this chapter (and throughout this entire book), so I will not say any more on this point here. As for what theory is, perhaps the best place to start is with a basic definition.

Defining Theory

I define theory in the following way: *theory is a simplified representation of "reality"* and *a framework within which facts are not only selected but also interpreted, organized, and fitted together so that they create a coherent whole*. Embedded within this simple definition are the following key points:

- *Theory* necessarily simplifies reality but is not separate from reality (even more, theory and reality may be mutually constitutive).
- *Theory* helps us to determine what facts are important, meaningful, and relevant; that is, theory helps us *select* facts.
- *Theory* guides our *interpretation* of the facts (what do the facts "mean"?).
- *Theory* tells us how to *organize* the facts: How do different facts relate to one another? Which are primary and which are secondary?
- *Theory* allows us to develop "whole" arguments, that is, arguments that stick together firmly from beginning to end.

We have already discussed the key elements of this basic definition, but it is worth underscoring a key point, namely, that all theories necessarily involve simplification or abstraction. *Theories are not reality*. They cannot be. On this point, it may be helpful to consider another analogy: theory as a map (Woods 1996). Maps, as you know, are graphical representations of physical reality. They are also extremely simplified versions of that reality. Despite this, almost everyone agrees that maps are valuable and indispensable "tools" (which, by the way, does not necessarily mean that maps are entirely **objective**: maps can and do reflect the biases and subjective perceptions of those who make them). Using the analogy of the map, we can see that, in the social sciences, theory/theorizing represents an effort to simplify the social world by identifying and then interpreting the *key* forces and/or processes. This is crucial. As we will see in the following sections, the different research traditions in comparative politics can be classified largely in terms of the key forces/processes on which each centers. Moreover, we can "draw" our conceptual maps of the world in many different ways and for many different purposes. Some maps may help us find our friend's house in an unfamiliar city, whereas other maps may help a seismologist locate fault lines. Whatever the shape or purpose of the map, however, it is always an abstraction of a far more complex physical reality.

■ Theory in Comparative Politics

So far we have discussed theory in very general, essentially generic terms. In this section, I would like to turn to a more concrete but still general discussion of theory in relation to comparative politics. As I noted earlier, there is a diversity of theoretical approaches in comparative politics and, except for very short periods, no one theoretical perspective has dominated the field (in the same way, for example, that realism has dominated international relations [IR] since the end of World War II). The theoretical diversity that characterizes the field, however, does not mean that the field is completely rudderless. On this point, one fairly recent volume on theory in comparative politics (Lichbach and Zuckerman 1997) argued that, despite the lack of a single unifying theory, the field is dominated by three strong and well-developed research traditions based on the principles of *rationality*, *culture*, and *structure*. I will discuss each of these in more detail below—in fact, this chapter and the remainder of this book are largely organized around these three approaches. But first, let's engage in a simple yet instructive exercise.

Thinking About Violent Crime: A Basic Exercise in Theorizing

Consider the following two questions, which, by now, are quite familiar to you: *Why do people commit violent crimes? Why are some societies more violent than others?* How would you answer these two related questions? As an exercise, before you finish reading this paragraph, do just this. That is, write down your answer by listing the reasons—the factors, or independent variables— people commit acts of violence and why some societies are more violent than others. Thinking about the question of violent crime, a significant social and political issue, is a good way to grasp some of the theoretical issues with which most students, researchers, and scholars in comparative politics must deal all the time. Now that you have written down (or at least thought out your response), consider the following three arguments.

• *Argument No. 1.* A major source of violent crime lies in predictable human behavior. In places where the risks of getting caught are minimal—where, for example, the police presence is limited and ineffective—and where the potential rewards are high, individuals are likely to commit more crimes in general. This is especially true in poorer communities, where people may have limited access to jobs, education, and skills training. Violent crime specifically is more likely (1) when the use of violence is a particularly efficient or necessary "tool," (2) where the use of violence to achieve one's ends entails relatively limited risk compared to the alternatives, and (3) where the alternatives to a "life of crime" are limited. All of this is clearly demonstrated in the United States, where violent crime is disproportionately concentrated in the inner cities. In the inner cities, law enforcement is relatively weak and ineffectual, poverty is high, and the use of violence is not only necessary given the general availability of firearms but is also relatively free of risk.

• *Argument No. 2.* Capitalism causes violence—the violence of one individual against another. The violence is not caused directly, but through an unrelenting process that divides societies into the "haves" and "have-nots" and that glorifies competition and efficiency while reducing individuals to abstractions—to anonymous buyers and sellers whose claims on each other are determined solely by their capacity to pay. In this way, capitalism alienates people from each other, their families, and their communities, thus setting the stage for antisocial, increasingly violent behavior among ordinary people, against ordinary people. Violence is a response to the "soullessness" and hopelessness engendered by an inherently exploitative economic system. Of course, violence is not unique to capitalism, nor are all capitalist societies equally violent. Where the most destructive, alienating, and exploitative aspects of the capitalist process are mitigated, intrasocietal violence is lessened. But where the forces of capitalism are unleashed and where vast segments of society are left unprotected, violence thrives.

• *Argument No. 3.* People and societies are responsible for their own actions and decisions, but they do not exist or act in a social vacuum. Their behavior, in other words, is partly determined by the "environment" in which they live. This environment, which we might call "culture," may encourage certain practices and values that encourage criminally violent behavior among certain groups of people. More specifically, in some places, a "culture of violence" has been created. In this culture of violence, members of the community learn to resolve problems and conflicts primarily through the use of violence. Violence, in other words, becomes a dominant and largely accepted **norm** within the community. It is important to note that cultures of violence are partly a response to objective conditions, such as a lack of jobs or economic opportunities, pervasive institutional discrimination, and so on. Over time, however, these responses become deeply embedded within a community, taking on a life of their own. Thus, even if objective conditions change, the use of violence may not diminish.

Although the foregoing arguments are admittedly very general and highly stylized, they are fairly representative of the type of arguments you will find in the scholarly literature. Indeed, you may even find one or all three to be quite persuasive. If you read each of the arguments above carefully, moreover, you'll note several key differences (you'll also notice some similarities). These differences can be categorized in a number of ways. For example, Argument No. 1 focuses on what some comparativists call *microlevel* factors, whereas the second argument focuses on *macrolevel* factors. Argument No. 3, by contrast, fits somewhere in the middle; appropriately, therefore, we can say it concentrates on *mesolevel* factors (meso-, as a prefix, simply means "in the middle"). In a similar vein, we can also use the concepts of structure and agency to divide the arguments (see Figure 3.2 for a discussion of these two terms). Argument No. 2, for example, strongly emphasizes structure, as it claims that crime is primarily a function of the larger socioeconomic system

---

Figure 3.2 Agency and Structure

Agency is the capacity of actors to operate independently of externally imposed constraints. Put more simply, agency is the power of human beings to make choices and to impose those choices on the world, rather than the other way around. In this regard, agency implies that the lives we live are primarily of our own making; our lives and choices, in short, are determined *by* us, not *for* us. Certain theories and approaches in comparative politics consider agency primary, whereas others assume just the opposite. Mainstream economic theory, rational choice, and public choice (a variant of rational choice), for example, tend to be agent centered, whereas Marxist theories tend to be structure centered. *Structure*, in the latter case, refers to an overarching context or framework within which choices are made and actions taken. The existence of a (social) structure implies that human action or agency is not completely undetermined. Indeed, structuralists tend to argue that our choices and actions are often severely constrained, shaped, or otherwise determined by structural factors. It is important to understand, however, that most contemporary researchers reject a completely dichotomous view of agency and structure. Instead, both in theory and practice, they have embraced an approach that gives weight to both structure and agency. Not only this, but most contemporary researchers understand that structure and agency are interrelated, meaning simply that agency affects structure and vice versa.

---

over which individuals have little control. The first argument, by contrast, suggests that individuals make their *own* decisions and that they make these decisions in an intentional and purposeful manner. "Structural" factors may matter, but they do not ultimately determine the behavior or decisions made by free-thinking individuals. The third argument, again, falls somewhere in between the first two—that is, Argument No. 3 assumes that individuals make purposeful decisions, but it also assumes that these decisions are strongly, even powerfully, influenced by environmental conditions in such a way that certain decisions or patterns of behavior become very difficult to change.

Theoretical Divisions: Rationality, Structure, and Culture

Although the foregoing categories are useful, I believe it is more practical to divide the arguments above based on the analytically distinct classification of rationality, structure, and culture. This threefold classification has a number of advantages. Most important, perhaps, it more closely reflects the principal theoretical divisions in comparative politics (in a way that the micro/meso/macro or the twofold agency/structure divisions do not). At the same time, using a limited number of analytical categories has the distinct advantage of simplifying what would otherwise be an extremely complicated mélange of theoretical approaches. If you recall, I noted that comparative politics is a field that is characterized by tremendous theoretical diversity. Indeed, there are scores of specific theories used by comparativists, the sheer number of which can easily overwhelm even the brightest student (see Figure 3.3 for a partial list of theories in comparative politics). In this regard, a threefold classification provides a very manageable—yet meaningful—set of analytical frameworks for both the beginning researcher and the more seasoned comparativist.

A three-part division, however, is still arbitrary. Certainly, I could include one, two, or even more additional categories. One particularly salient nominee would be **institutionalism**, which can be considered an intermediate, but distinct, analytical/theoretical category. (I will briefly discuss institutionalism later in this chapter.) Primarily for reasons of space and simplicity, but also because institutionalist approaches not only fit within but have also been explicitly incorporated into the other research traditions, I have opted to stick with a threefold classification.[1] With this important caveat in mind, let's turn to a discussion of the three research traditions in comparative politics, beginning with rationality. These discussions, I should note, will be brief and quite general. The reason, in case it is not already clear, is simple: the remaining chapters in this book will examine concrete issues in comparative politics

---

Figure 3.3   A Sampling of Theories in Comparative Politics

- Bureaucratic authoritarianism
- Corporatism
- Critical development theory
- Dependency
- Elite theory
- Feminism (several variants)
- Imperialism (and new imperialism)
- Instrumentalism
- Marxism (several variants)
- Marxist rational choice
- Modernization
- New dependency

- New institutionalism
- New social movement theory
- Pluralism
- Political culture
- Political systems
- Postimperialism
- Poststructuralism
- Rational choice (several variants)
- Resource mobilization theory
- State-society relations
- Structural-functionalism
- World-systems theory

Suggested Reading: Students interested in exploring the various theories of comparative politics in more depth should see Ronald Chilcote's *Theories of Comparative Politics: The Search for a Paradigm Reconsidered* (1994) and his related text, *Theories of Comparative Political Economy* (2000).

using each of the three research traditions as a general framework of analysis. The main objective in the discussion that follows, therefore, is to give you a basic and purposefully *nontechnical* sense of what each research tradition is, how they differ, and how they overlap.

■ Rationality: A Nontechnical Introduction

Comparativists and other political scientists who use rationality as a basis for their research believe that politics—and therefore political analysis—should focus on the behavior of human beings themselves. In other words, the key unit (and level) of analysis is the *individual.* To focus political analysis at the level of the individual, however, requires certain simplifying assumptions about human beings and their motivations. The reason is fairly clear: without the ability to make certain clear-cut assumptions about human behavior, *which must be regarded as generally true for all individuals,* it would be nearly impossible to develop powerful generalizations and ultimately predictions about larger-scale or collective political outcomes, which is typically the intent of comparativists who use a rational choice approach. Simplifying assumptions, it is important to understand, allow the researcher to use **deductive logic** (see Figure 3.4), which is ostensibly the hallmark of good science.[2] So what is the crucial assumption in theories based on rationality and rational choice? Simply put, it is that people are rational maximizers of self-interest "who calculate the value of alternative goals and act efficiently to obtain what they want" (Zuckerman 1991, p. 45). Steven Brams stated it in slightly simpler terms: "To act

---

Figure 3.4   Deductive Logic

Deduction is the process of reasoning that moves from the general to the particular. For example, from the general proposition that all trees have leaves and the further proposition that oaks are trees, one may draw the deductive inference that oaks have leaves (this example is taken from *The Concise Oxford Dictionary of Linguistics*). In comparative politics, deductive analysis is most apparent in the rational choice research school. Here the general principle is the assumption of rational action. From this general and very abstract principle, many general propositions are derived about all sorts of issues of interest, from political violence, to mass-based movements, to political change, to economic transformation, and so on. These general propositions are then used to develop explanatory accounts, and, finally, specific cases are examined to demonstrate the validity of the deductive model.

rationally means . . . to choose *better* alternatives over worse ones" (emphasis added; Brams 1992, p. 313).

From these two statements, it is clear that the concepts of rationality (or rational action) and self-interest are strongly, even integrally, connected. It must be emphasized, however, that rational choice does not absolutely require the assumption that individuals are self-interested. Instead, as Margaret Levi (1997) and others have pointed out, as long as people *act consistently in relation to their preferences*, it is possible to use a rational choice approach (this is a type of **utility maximization**). In this regard, it is perfectly feasible for rational choice scholars to incorporate *nonegoistic* considerations (for example, altruism) or motivational norms, such as community standards or fairness or religious convictions, into their analysis. Doing so, however, increases the complexity and difficulty of the analysis, which is something that many rational choice theorists are reluctant to do. It is for this reason that the assumption of self-interested (that is, egoistic) behavior is generally used.

This said, it is also important to understand that "self-interest" itself is an ambiguous concept. Indeed, what constitutes self-interest will vary depending on the general context or environment in which decisions are being made. For example, if the context is a stable market economy, where actors are engaged in buying and selling, it is reasonable to assume that self-interest will be defined in terms of maximizing wealth. If the context is a high-risk environment in a poor rural area with no social safety net, self-interest could be defined in terms of maximizing personal survival (Levi 1997). Or if the context is a political system in which the main actors are politicians and government officials, self-interest would likely be defined in terms of staying in office. There are many other possibilities, but the important point is that the interest (or preference) be defined, first, as a general principle, and second, *ex ante*—that is, expected or intended *before* the event occurs—for a particular application (Levi 1997). To put it simply, you need to state *in advance* what motivates people's decisions and actions in a particular setting. This is a crucial *initial* step in analyzing any issue using a rational choice framework. Once this is done, the real work of **deduction** begins. Thus, if we begin with the assumption that individuals rationally pursue their self-interests (whether it be wealth maximization or something else), we can come up with a range of testable **hypotheses** (general claims about political, social, or economic behavior subject to empirical falsification), which can then be used to help explain and predict specific outcomes given a certain set of conditions. Consider the example of crime. If we assume that criminals are rational maximizers of self-interest, several hypotheses are possible. A researcher might say, for instance, that policies that rely *solely* on deterrence (for example, more police on the street, a "three-strikes" law, the death penalty, and so on) will not significantly reduce crime. Why? Because in deciding whether or not to commit crimes, individuals respond not just to potential costs, such as being apprehended and punished, but also to "benefits" and a range of perceived alternatives. If viable job opportunities are extremely limited, to take the most salient example, individuals may commit criminal acts even if the prospects of being caught and severely punished are extremely high. Thus, a researcher might also hypothesize that the most effective way to reduce crime is to combine policies of deterrence with meaningful job-creation programs. This is a simplistic example, but one that should at least give you a broad sense of how rational choice analysis "works" in practice.

Rationality, Calculation, and Uncertainty

In the foregoing example, we can see that self-interest itself is manifested through a process by which individual actors weigh the *cost and benefits* of their decisions. This process is referred to as *strategic calculation*. This adds yet another complicating factor to the determination of self-interest or preferences. Indeed, in the real world, strategic calculation is often part of an interactive or interdependent process, involving at least two "players." When more than one player is involved, the decisionmaking process becomes more complex or uncertain. The concept of uncertainty, in fact, is a central element in the rational choice framework. And it is easy to see why this is the case. After all, if all decisions were made with complete foresight of the consequences or of the trade-offs, there would not be very many interesting—and important—real-world puzzles to solve. But there are. Why, for example, have many societies been wracked by profound and debilitating political violence, as in Rwanda, Sudan, and Bosnia? Why do elites agree to democratize when democracy threatens their economic and political interests? Why do some political leaders—Saddam Hussein, to cite a particularly conspicuous example—go to war against an overwhelmingly superior opponent? Part of the answers to these and other questions lies in the uncertainty of not knowing what other players in the "game" will do.

Uncertainty, however, results not just from not knowing how others will act or respond to your decisions but also from a more general lack of information. For instance, a student faced with a decision of whether to attend graduate school or to accept a low-level entry position in a Fortune 500 company will not have all the information necessary to know for certain what the best choice is. Given an inability to know "all the facts" in advance, the student may make a bad choice. The fact that people can and do make bad choices, however, does not mean that rational choice is wrong. Indeed, "bad choices," or less-than-optimal decisions, are part and parcel of the rational choice framework. Part of the researcher's job is to figure out why and even under what circumstances actors are likely to make bad decisions. The key, to repeat, is understanding that uncertainty adds an element of complexity to the decisionmaking process. It is up to the researcher to take this into account when analyzing political, social, or economic phenomena. In other words, the researcher must consider the capacity of actors to assess the risks they face, to gauge the potential benefits of their behavior, and to understand the effects their actions are likely to have on other actors (and vice versa).

The Importance of Constraints

Rational choice theory generally takes self-interest or individual preferences as *causes* of the actions people take (Little 1991; cited in Ward 2002, p. 70). At the same time, most comparativists using a rational choice framework understand that self-interest and individual preferences do not take shape in a social, political, or economic vacuum. In other words, rational choice comparativists reject, even if only implicitly, the principle of **methodological individualism** and instead assume that individual behavior is shaped by a range of *constraints*, which can be economic, social, institutional, and even cultural. Indeed, Levi (1997) argued that the "real action" in rational choice comes from constraints on individual behavior (p. 25). The two most important sources of constraints, according to Levi, are *economic* and *institutional*. Economic constraints have to do with scarcity. Because we do not live in a world of unlimited resources, individuals must "maximize with the confines of available resources" (p. 25). If, for example, you have only $10 to spend in a day, your range of choices is extremely limited compared to someone with $1,000.

Institutional constraints are less obvious, but no less important. As Levi explained it, "Institutions are sets of rules (and sanctions) that structure social interaction and whose existence and applicability are commonly known within a community. Institutions, so defined, *structure the individual choices of strategic actors* so as to produce equilibrium outcomes, that is outcomes that no one has an incentive to alter" (emphasis added; Levi 1997, p. 25). Institutions can be formal or informal; they can be political, economic, cultural/religious, or social; they can be limited to a specific community or place; or they can be national, international, or global in scope. In a broad sense, we might simply say that institutions constitute the *decisionmaking environment*. For the comparativist using a rational choice framework, it is essential to understand the environment in which decisions are made and to specify how environmental factors influence or constrain the behavior of strategic actors. Failure to do so will likely make one's analysis overly simplistic and even vacuous.

Rationality and Comparative Politics

The deductive logic and simplifying assumptions of rational choice mean that it cannot explain everything, nor, as Levi (1997) pointed out, "does it unravel all puzzles equally well, but it can illuminate and advance the explanation of a wide range of phenomena in a larger variety of countries and time periods" (p. 33). This makes rational choice a valuable and useful approach even for those researchers who are uncomfortable reducing social and political life to "self-interest" or utility maximization—uncomfortable because doing so ignores the complexity of the world in which we live. The critics, to a certain extent, are correct. But remember a point we made earlier: *all* theories are necessarily simplifications—abstractions—of a more complex reality. So the question to consider is not whether the assumption of rationality is a simplification (of course it is!), but whether it is an appropriate and useful one. Since this is still a question of intense debate,[3] I will only say that it is a potentially useful assumption in comparative politics, especially if we use the "thick variant" of rationality, which accepts the premise that rationality can be institutionally, culturally, or socially conditioned or defined.[4]

In subsequent chapters, we will address other important aspects of rationality. For now, just remember that rationality is much, much more than simply asserting that people "act rationally." To rational choice scholars, this is a truism. Far more important is how we can use this basic assumption to better explain the social world. Rationalists believe that the simple concept of rational action can, in fact, explain a great deal, including behavior that, on the surface, appears completely irrational. Indeed, one of the strengths of this research tradition, many scholars argue, is its capacity to provide rational explanations for irrational outcomes, especially at the collective—as opposed to the individual—level. Of course, not all comparativists agree that rationality provides the best answers. Some of the strongest critics are those who are associated with the structural tradition, the subject of our next section.

■ The Structural Tradition

A structural argument is concerned with *relationships*, which themselves exist within a broader framework or system of action. This means that in attempting to understand or explain any social phenomena, it is never enough to look only or even primarily at individual attributes or the behavior of an individual actor. Instead, one must examine the "networks, linkages, interdependencies, and interactions among the parts of some system" (Lichbach 1997, p. 247). Thus, where rationalists begin political analysis at the level of the individual, structuralists begin at a more abstract level—for example, the historical system, the international system, the social system. The logic behind this practice is not all that difficult to understand: structuralists believe that human action and behavior are fundamentally shaped by the larger environment, which, in turn, is the product of dominant economic, political, and social arrangements. We already talked about one of these arrangements—that is, the international system. The realist idea that the anarchic international system forces every nation-state to behave in similar ways regardless of its internal makeup or its domestic politics is a structural argument par excellence. It is the structure (or political arrangements) of the international system, in other words, that *determines* the behavior of individual states.[5]

All structuralists, however, are not the same. "Structural realism" (or neorealism) in IR is premised on the notion that the primary structural force governing international relations is *political* and *timeless* (that is, it is defined by a struggle for power and will forever remain the same). In comparative politics, by contrast, most but not all structural arguments are *historical,* which means, in part, that the structures themselves are capable of changing or transforming into something quite different (it also means that historical structures, like capitalism, are unique, albeit long-lasting).[6] Historical structures, in other words, are contingent rather than permanent. The idea that structures—and the specific relationships they entail—can and do change is an important point to keep in mind. It is also important to understand why and how structural change can occur. One reason, according to Cardoso and Faletto (1979)—famous for their work on **dependency** in Latin America—is that historical structures, although enduring, are the product of humankind's collective behavior. This implies a mutually dependent relationship between structures and agents. That is, although structures "impose limits on social processes and reiterate established forms of behavior" (p. xi), the **reproduction** of structures requires human agency. Moreover, many structuralists also contend that structures, by their very nature, generate **contradictions** and social tensions, "thus opening the possibilities for social movements and ideologies of change" (p. xi).

Admittedly, this is a lot to digest. It might help, however, to think of structures as deeply embedded games, which are governed by a set of unyielding rules and conventions. Significantly, these rules and conventions, like structural forces, define the roles for each player or part of the game: they tell us what the various parts or pieces of the game can and cannot do; they tell us the position that each occupies in the game; and they define how much power individual pieces have. In chess, for instance, the pawn is the lowest-ranking chess piece and may only move forward one square at a time (or two squares in the first move). Pawns do not have much independent power (or agency), and their main purpose is to serve as fodder for the more powerful pieces. The queen, by contrast, has a great deal of power and can move in any direction on the board. And yet, the queen's movements are still governed, not only by the rules and conventions of the game—that is, the queen can only move in a straight line—but also by the limits of the board itself. The chess board, in this sense, is the basic structure within which the entire game *must* be played. (Figure 3.5 provides an illustrated depiction of the relationship between chess and structure.) Moreover, even though some games, such as chess, remain virtually unchanged for long periods of time, other games undergo significant changes. Football in the United States today, for instance, is certainly different from football as it was played a century ago. Other games may die out altogether, to be replaced by something entirely new. In this very basic sense, then, games

Figure 3.5 Comparing Chess and the Structural Approach in Comparative Politics

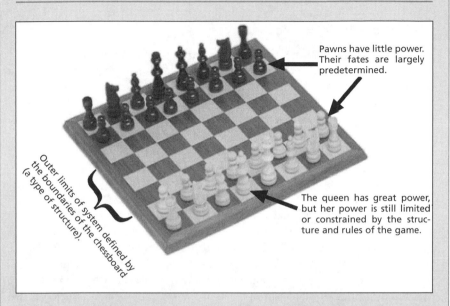

Pawns have little power. Their fates are largely predetermined.

The queen has great power, but her power is still limited or constrained by the structure and rules of the game.

Outer limits of system defined by the boundaries of the chessboard (a type of structure).

The chessboard defines the outer limits of the system (or overarching structure) in which the game is played. The "rules of the game," in turn, define the roles, starting positions, and power of each playing piece or "actor" within the system. The rules, in other words, tell us what each actor can and cannot do. In chess, the pawns have the least power, and queens have the most power. The rules allow pawns to transform themselves into queens, although the possibility of this happening is very low. Together, the structure and rules of the game shape and largely determine the fate of each actor on the chessboard.

are analogous to, although certainly not the same as, complex social structures. With this caveat in mind, the ways to understand a game and a social structure are generally similar. For both, you need to understand the structure or framework within which the "game" itself is played; you need to identify the "rules of the game"; and you need to understand how the game plays out and changes. Although rationalists are also concerned about the rules of the game, structuralists generally see these rules as far more powerful and enduring. In addition, for the comparativist, it is vital to assess the impact of the "game's" operation on the lives of ordinary people and whole societies or countries.

None of this, I should note, needs to be done from scratch. Over the years, scholars have spelled out many different aspects of the "games" or larger social structures that shape and govern the modern world. In comparative politics, the historical structuralist position is dominant, so it would be useful to focus on this perspective.

History, the Economy, and Marx

Historical structuralists are generally concerned with *economic* (or *material*) as opposed to political forces. Indeed, many see political processes as essentially a reflection of economic forces. **Karl Marx** (1818–1883)—upon whose writings most historical structuralist arguments are ultimately based—is perhaps the most famous proponent of this view. Marx argued, for example, that the preeminent political institution in capitalism—that is, the state—is nothing more than an instrument or tool of the dominant economic class. (This view, however, has been subject to a great deal of criticism; today, in fact, even most Marxists agree that the state has relative autonomy or the capacity to act independently of the interests of the capitalist class.[7])

The emphasis on economic forces has other implications as well. One of the most important of these is that societies do not consist *just* of individuals but of individuals who occupy certain economically determined categories or **social classes**. In historical structural analysis, it is the particular category that an individual occupies that is important, not the individual per se. In the **feudal** world (the era just prior to capitalism in western Europe), for example, society was organized around a predominantly agricultural mode of production. This meant, among other things, that those who owned or controlled agricultural land—the landlords—necessarily occupied a privileged position in society, whereas those who actually worked the land—peasants or serfs—were in a far different and clearly subordinate position (to use the analogy from chess, we might say that the peasants were pawns and the landlords knights or rooks). *The nature of the relationship between these two categories was all-important.* Clearly, occupying one or the other category had a fundamental impact on what an individual could or could not do. The opportunities available to peasants, in particular, were extremely limited if not predestined. **Feudalism**, of course, is not the only historical structure. Today, the historical structure of capitalism is quite different, which helps explain why the relationship between peasant and lord no longer even exists. Yet, make no mistake, capitalism also imposes strong, essentially inescapable constraints on human action, although for most of us, these constraints are not always obvious.

The focus on economic forces also implies that significant social change is not likely to come about *purely* through individual action or agency. This does not mean that structuralists discount agency; instead, they understand that historical structures necessarily shape the possibilities for change. As Marx famously put it, "Men make their own history, but they do not make it just as they please; they do not make it under circumstances chosen by themselves, but under circumstances directly encountered, given and transmitted from the past" (Marx [1869] 1994, p. 15). In this view, feudalism did not end because peasants became fed up with being oppressed and decided to do something about it; rather, it ended because broader changes in the economic structure *allowed* or enabled movements against feudalism to succeed.[8] We can make the same sort of argument for social revolutions of all types. Theda Skocpol, well-known for her structural interpretation of social revolutions (an issue of strong interest to comparativists), provided a useful perspective.[9] She argued that, if one wants to understand why social revolutions succeed, it is necessary to examine patterns of relationships among groups and societies (both domestically and transnationally), for this shows us that revolutionary situations are not "made" but that they "emerge" (Skocpol 1979). What Skocpol meant by this is that successful revolutionary movements never begin merely with a revolutionary intention— that is, a group of people getting together and deciding to overthrow the existing system. Rather, revolutionaries must first wait for the "emergence of politico-military crises of state and class domination" (p. 17); it is only within these crisis situations that the possibilities for revolution can be realized.

It is clear from the foregoing discussion that structural approaches and history are closely connected. Indeed, by definition, historical structuralist approaches are historically grounded. At the most basic level this means, to repeat a point I made in Chapter 1, that "history matters" a great deal. It matters in the sense that the structural relationships that exist in the world today are products of history. It also matters in that structural forces, although they exert similar pressures in all societies, do not always create the same outcome. Indeed, the same structural forces can sometimes create seemingly contradictory outcomes, say, communist revolution in one country and capitalist transformation in another. In this regard, structuralists like to say that historical sequence matters, too (Rueschemeyer, Stephens, and Stephens 1992). For instance, different sequences of industrialization—for example, whether a country began the process of industrialization in the early 1800s, in the late 1800s, or post-1945—may give a very different character to internal changes in what would otherwise be a similar set of countries. The task of the structuralist, in part, is to identify and explain the typical paths of development and change and to discern the causal patterns that underlie these different paths. Structuralists, therefore, very often do *comparative histories* in an effort to discover the "historical laws" of structural development (Lichbach 1997).

The Broad Scope of the Structural Tradition

The structural tradition is a broad one. Within it there are "hard structuralists" who see our actions as tightly constrained and almost predetermined as well as "soft structuralists" who see a much closer, mutually constitutive interaction between structures and agents. There are also historical structuralists and struc-

turalists who eschew historical analysis altogether. In addition, there are structuralists who focus their analytical attention on an individual society or state as
the primary unit of analysis, and there are others who believe the main unit of
analysis is the system as a whole (for example, **world-systems theory**, a perspective discussed in Chapter 4, argues that the basic unit of analysis should be
the historical system, such as the capitalist world-system). In practice, moreover, many comparativists tend to slide back and forth between different positions within the structural tradition. The "structural tradition," in short, can be
terribly complicated and confusing, especially for the beginning comparativist.
It is, nonetheless, a research tradition that cannot be ignored. Structuralists
have told us a lot about the world and have given us many valuable conceptual
and intellectual "tools." Even those of you who are uncomfortable with the
basic assumptions of structuralism need to understand its utility and value for
comparative and social scientific analysis.

Final Note: Comparing Structural
Approaches and Institutionalism

Before moving on to a discussion of the third major research tradition, it is important to clarify the distinction between the structural tradition and institutionalism. The two are often confused, especially by beginning comparativists.
The basic reason for the confusion lies in the fact that contemporary or "new"
institutional approaches clearly contain structural elements (see Figure 3.6 for
a "primer" on institutionalism); that is, institutions are said to influence the behavior of actors, either directly (according to a stronger version of institutionalism based on **normative theory**) or indirectly (according to the weaker, rational choice version of institutionalism). The difference derives primarily from
the question, where do institutions come from, and how do they change? For
historical structuralists, especially, institutions are primarily the products of underlying structural forces. Therefore, institutions are of secondary, as opposed
to primary, importance. Institutions, in short, have no power independent of the
structure in which they are embedded. Changes to institutions, therefore, will
be due more to macrostructural dynamics than to agency. This position contrasts quite sharply with rational choice institutionalism, which is premised on
the assumption that institutions can be "undone" or changed when they no
longer serve actors' interests. In this sense, institutions provide only short-term
and essentially voluntary constraints on individuals' behavior (Peters 1999, p.
148; cited in Lowndes 2002, p. 105). The contrast with normative institutionalism is not nearly as sharp, but is still pertinent. Thus, although normative institutionalists agree that institutions reflect distributions of advantage and social
power and are embedded in society (as a structuralist would argue), they also
consider institutions to have a *structurally independent* influence on political,
social, and economic events and processes. Structuralists would not necessar-

Figure 3.6   A Brief Primer on New Institutionalism

The term "new institutionalism" was coined by March and Olsen (1984), partly in response to the gradual decline, since the 1960s, of "traditional" institutional approaches within the discipline of political science. Traditional approaches tended to adopt a very restricted and descriptive view of institutions—the major focus was on the institutions of government and on formal rules and arrangements. March and Olsen, however, were also responding to the tendency by mainstream and even radical scholars to dismiss institutions as mere reflections of individual behavior (or underlying structures), rather than as "autonomous political actors in their own right" (p. 738). This assertion by March and Olsen is, to a certain extent, the crux of new institutionalist approaches. To repeat: new institutionalism is based on the premise that institutions matter. They matter because, once created, they are not simply *arenas* within which contending social forces struggle for power; they are also "collections of standard operating procedures and structures that *define and defend interests*" (emphasis added; p. 738). The new institutional approach is also new in the sense that proponents have generally adopted a more much expansive definition of what institutions are. Thus, political institutions are no longer equated with governmental agencies or organizations; instead, the term "institution" is understood more broadly to refer to a "stable, recurring pattern of behaviour" (Goodin 1996, p. 12; quoted in Lowndes 2002, p. 91). A crucial point, too, according to Lowndes, is that "new institutionalists concern themselves not just with the impact of institutions upon individuals, but with the interaction between institutions and individuals" (p. 91).

This said, the new institutional approach is quite varied. (For instance, Peters [1999] identified seven separate varieties of institutionalism: normative, rational choice, historical, empirical, international, sociological, and network.) Still, as Lowndes pointed out, there is one basic cleavage within new institutionalist thinking between "normative" approaches and those inspired by a version of rational choice theory. *Normative institutionalism* is based on the idea that institutions *directly* influence the behavior of actors by shaping their values, norms, interests, identities, and beliefs. Normative institutionalism, therefore, considers **norms** and values as explanatory **variables** in their own right (p. 95). A simple example might help to illuminate this point. Consider the so-called code of silence prevalent among police officers. The code of silence is a norm that helps to define or determine "appropriate" behavior among members of the police force. It is not codified but is, instead, an "unwritten" rule that everyone understands. In contrast, rational choice institutionalism is based on

(continues)

Figure 3.6   continued

---

the assumption that, although institutions matter, they do not independently determine the interests and behavior of actors. Instead, institutions are said to influence behavior by affecting the environment in which decisionmaking occurs; that is, institutions affect **strategic interaction** by providing information about the likely behavior of other actors and about the incentives and disincentives attached to different courses of action (Ostrom 1982, pp. 5–7; cited in Lowndes 2002, p. 95). Thus, unlike normative institutionalism, rational choice institutionalists would argue that the code of silence does not directly determine the behavior of individuals but, instead, provides information about the consequences of a particular course of action.

New institutionalism, of course, is much more complicated than this brief discussion and few basic examples indicate. If you are interested in finding out more, I strongly encourage you to read the entire chapter by Lowndes (2002). She also suggested the following additional sources: Goodin (1996), March and Olsen (1989), and Peters (1999).

---

ily or entirely dismiss this argument but would still emphasize the overriding priority of deeper structural forces over institutions and institutional dynamics.

■ The Cultural Tradition

For students, the cultural tradition often makes the most intuitive sense, but it is generally the most misunderstood and misused of the three research traditions. There are good reasons for this, not the least of which is that the concept of culture itself is extremely nebulous. In addition, in popular usage and even among some prominent scholars, culture is most typically portrayed in a simplistic manner. On this point, consider a January 25, 2004, editorial by a columnist for the *St. Petersburg Times* (Florida). In discussing the prospects for democracy in Iraq (and the Arab world more generally), the author wrote: "There is a reason political pluralism, individual liberty and self-rule do not exist in any of the 16 Arab nations in the Middle East. Cultural traditions there tend toward anti-intellectualism, religious zealotry and patriarchy, values which provide little fertile ground for progressive thinking."

This type of argument is common and may even be "right" in a certain, very limited way. Nonetheless, it is seriously misinformed, intellectually crude, and unequivocally ethnocentric. There are three basic reasons for this: first, the argument is based on the mistaken assumption that culture is essentially *static;* second, it is based on an equally erroneous assumption that culture is *monolithic* or *univocal* (that is, "speaks" with a single voice); third, it falsely presumes that the effects of culture are *one-directional* (for example, culture serves either as an obstacle to or as an open path toward certain political, economic, or social developments). The argument, in short, ignores the complex and fluid nature of culture.

More concretely, to see the folly of this type of thinking—or bad theorizing—consider how many of the same charges the author levels against Islamic counties could have been, and still could be, leveled against the United States. After all, in US culture, there is a very strong anti-intellectual element—Americans are supposed to be pragmatic "doers," not pointy-headed, ivory tower intellectuals. There is also a great deal of religious zealotry in the United States. In fact, surveys tell us that the United States is one of the most religious countries in the world, and it is fairly clear that Christian fundamentalism occupies a prominent role in US culture and politics. Last, the United States was a profoundly patriarchal society when originally founded; for evidence, one need only recall that women were not allowed to vote until 1920. Despite all this, the United States is a democracy. My point, however, is not to prove that the United States and the Arab countries of the Middle East are cultural clones—they decidedly are not—but to emphasize the importance of thinking of culture in an open-minded and sophisticated manner. The first step toward doing this is to understand what "culture" is.

What Is Culture?

To understand the significance of culture, it is crucial to know what culture is. One basic definition is offered by Marc Ross (1997), who defined culture as a "worldview that explains why and how individuals and groups behave as they do, and includes both cognitive and affective [that is, emotional] beliefs about social reality and assumptions about when, where, and how people in one's culture and those in other cultures are likely to act in particular ways" (p. 45). To put it more simply, Ross asserted that culture marks a "distinctive way of life" that members of the culture *share* and upon which they forge a *common* and *unique identity* (p. 45). Embedded in this definition is the understanding that culture is inherently subjective or, more accurately, intersubjective. That is, culture is about what people believe and about how these beliefs—*when widely shared*—bind a people together in a meaningful way. The inherent intersubjectivity of culture, however, means that it is never completely fixed—there is no absolute, unchanging meaning to any culture. This is partly because culture must be learned and constantly reproduced. The "reproduction" of culture, in particular, makes cultural change inevitable. For human beings are not copy machines; when broad systems of meanings (that is, cultures) are reproduced, variations—whether unintentional or not, whether small or large—are virtually impossible to avoid. Moreover, in a world of multiple cultures, diffusion (or the passing of specific cultural practices, beliefs, and meanings from one society to another) makes the process of reproduction even less "perfect." This, by the way, is one reason why thinking of culture as static is such a big mistake.

The Significance of Culture

Despite its inherently subjective nature, most culturalists agree that culture does have objective *effects*—simply put, culture shapes the behavior and actions of people, both at the individual and collective levels. This is what makes culture especially relevant in an analysis of political, social, or economic phenomena. On the surface, the claim that culture shapes the behavior and actions of people does not sound much different from the argument we just criticized. There is, however, a crucial difference. In the argument above, you will recall that culture is portrayed as essentially static, univocal, and one-directional. Most culturalists today, as I already suggested, regard these assumptions as irredeemably flawed. Instead, they argue that culture must be understood as an inherently fluid system of meaning, with multiple "voices" and a complex influence on social, political, or economic processes. What all this means will become clear in subsequent chapters. For now, suffice it to say that the manner in which culture shapes behavior is ambiguous, rarely straightforward, and often contradictory. In this regard, it is also important to understand that most contemporary cultural theorists believe that culture is often cause and effect (we will return to this issue shortly), whereby cultural forces rarely, if ever, can be understood without examining them within specific contexts. Thus, it is more appropriate to see culture as *intersecting* with political, social, and economic forces to produce specific outcomes in specific places and time periods.

With all this in mind, one key to understanding the significance of culture is to recognize that *culture has power.* It not only has the power to shape individual perceptions and behavior but also has the power to unify and mobilize entire societies, sometimes across borders. It is important to note that this is well recognized by those people who wish to harness the power of culture. For this reason, the "reproduction" of culture is not always or even generally—as common sense might suggest—a neutral or apolitical affair. Indeed, the reproduction of culture is a profoundly political process. Moreover, the power to define culture has become a major source of conflict and political struggle in and across societies throughout the world. This is true even (or especially) in the United States, where the "culture war" has become a centerpiece of the US political and social landscape. It is important to understand, in case this point is not already clear, that "culture wars"—whether in the United States, Western Europe, the Middle East, Asia, or any other part of the world—are primarily about power. For culture is not *merely* a worldview or set of widely shared beliefs about social reality but also a political resource that can be used to achieve political, social, or economic goals. Part of understanding and assessing the impact of culture, in fact, requires an analysis of how culture is appropriated and manipulated by various groups within society. In Chapter 7, we will focus on this particular aspect of cultural analysis as we examine the phenomenon of political violence and terrorism.

At the same time, it is important to recognize and remember that culture is more than a political resource. One reason for this is obvious: culture is not tangible. It cannot be simply picked up or stored. In addition, culture is, by definition, "public." Everyone has access to culture, unlike other types of material resources. Last, despite its intersubjective and malleable nature, there is an enduring or historical substance to almost any culture. Cultures cannot simply be created out of whole cloth. For all these reasons, a comparativist must avoid reducing culture to a mere resource or asset.

Culture as "Cause and Effect"

Earlier, I suggested that the causal power of culture is ambiguous. There are several ways to interpret this statement. First, one can argue that culture is a reflection or product of more significant social forces (as a historical structuralist might argue). In this view, culture need not be taken seriously, since it has no *independent* causal power. Second, one can argue that culture, although important, acts only indirectly. That is, it influences behavior by affecting the structure of a situation, which may entail providing information about others' likely behavior (as a rational choice theorist might argue). Here, too, the causal significance of culture is suspect, since the behavior of actors is not strictly determined by cultural forces. Third, one can argue that culture is both cause and effect. In this view, culture *is* understood as a product of underlying social, economic, or political forces, but once established, certain cultural practices and beliefs tend to perpetuate themselves from generation to generation, even if objective conditions change or the practices themselves become "irrational." In this sense, culture begins to take on a "life of its own" and begins to operate as a semiautonomous force. Yet, even in this view, culture is not a causal power per se, something to which social events, behaviors, institutions, or processes can causally be attributed (Geertz 1973). This is partly because culture, to return to our earlier discussion, is intangible. It is this latter view that many, albeit not all, culturalists adopt.

A Few Final Words on the Cultural Approach

Culture is complex. It is malleable, and its effects are not always obvious or straightforward. Culture has power, but it is not always or necessarily a causal power. This may all sound very confusing, but it need not be. The key is to avoid treating culture as an unambiguous set of unchanging values, norms, and beliefs that define and unproblematically shape—even determine—the social, political, and economic fate of individuals, societies, and countries. Instead, recognize that culture is contested, profoundly political, and inherently fluid. Obviously, this is easy to say but not so easy to do. Fortunately, the next five chapters will provide examples of how to apply the basic principles of the cultural tradition to an examination of real-world problems and issues.

■ Separation or Synthesis?

My summary of the three research traditions is just that, a summary. It is not intended to be comprehensive or definitive (it certainly is not); rather, I intended to give you a general sense of what each is about—not only to help orient you to the field of comparative politics but also to allow you to figure out which research tradition best encompasses your *current* views (for it is no doubt the case that you already hold a number of theoretical assumptions). At the same time, I also intended to give you a general sense of how the traditions differ. On this point, though, it is vital that you understand that their differences are not just skin-deep. That is, it is not only a matter of the cultural, rational, and structural traditions having a different emphasis. This is obvious. But each also is premised on fundamentally different assumptions about "reality," about knowledge, and about what it means to do comparative analysis (these are difficult issues requiring far more discussion than can be provided here). It is for this reason that one cannot *merely* combine elements of the three traditions—as many students are invariably tempted to do. The reasons are clear enough. A culturalist, for example, *cannot* accept a version of rationality that posits invariant interests (for example, maximization of wealth, security, or power). For to do so would be to admit that culture has no real significance, that history has no meaning. At the same time, a rationalist must be very careful about incorporating culture into her analysis: although she can accept the notion that interests are culturally conditioned, she must draw the line somewhere. If she does not do so, then rationality accounts will themselves become highly particularistic, which is exactly the opposite of what rationalists hope to achieve. Moreover, if a rationalist accepts that culture shapes or determines behavior, then the core assumption of self-interest and individual preferences becomes almost meaningless. By the same token, structuralists cannot give too much weight to cultural factors (or to the concept of rationality) without risk of abandoning their core tenet, namely, that structures are "real" and have *primary* causal powers.

None of this is to say, however, that a synthesis or integration of the three traditions is out of the question; as I noted at the outset of this section, there are some comparativists who believe such a task is not only possible, but necessary. Lichbach (1997), Levi (1997), and McAdam, Tarrow, and Tilly (1997) are some of the more prominent proponents of this view. The latter three, in fact, propose an explicitly integrative approach in their study of social movements (which I cover in Chapter 8). For this reason, a detailed summary of their argument is not appropriate here; still, a few very general points are worth making. First, it is important to point out, as the authors did, that simply aggregating variables from the three perspectives will not do (p. 160). Instead, they argued that an integrative approach must show how different variables are *linked together* as part of a coherent *process*. Second, and in a closely related vein, the search for an integrative approach should avoid analyzing each set of cultural, structural, or rationality variables in isolation from one another. In their own analysis of the civil rights movement in the United States, McAdam, Tarrow, and Tilly showed that the effects of these variables were *mutually reinforcing* at each stage of the civil rights cycle. As they put it, "There is no substitute for relating all phases of a movement cycle to the three broad classes of [cultural, structural and rationality] factors . . ." (p. 163). At the same time, at certain stages one or another set of factors may be more or less prominent. It is up to the researcher to be aware of and extremely sensitive to the changing significance of culture, structure, or rationality. Third, integration, however accomplished, will not be easy. It takes a great deal of careful, well-considered thought to "blend" the three traditions together, and even then, the blendings will undoubtedly be far from perfect or free of contention (p. 159).

■ Conclusion: Bringing Everything Together

Comparative politics, as you have learned, is far more than "studying foreign countries." Nor is it simply about "comparing." Instead, it is an extremely diverse field that requires you to grasp a range of—sometimes conflicting, if not contradictory—methodological and theoretical concepts and issues. My main objective in this chapter was to help you to both focus and organize your thoughts for the tasks ahead. This is necessary because understanding what comparative politics is and what it is all about—still less "doing comparative politics"—is *not* easy. To acquire this understanding requires a more disciplined and broader style of thinking than most students are accustomed to doing. It also requires you to digest, as you have seen, a broad range of abstract concepts and methods and apply them to "real-world" cases—which themselves are chock-full of (empirical) complexities and subtleties as well as millions of potentially relevant facts. At the same time, nothing discussed in this chapter is beyond the reach of any student.

Before moving on to the next chapter, it would be worthwhile summing up, from our readings thus far, a few key points about becoming a good comparativist.

- First, in the most general sense, becoming a good comparativist (and doing comparative politics) means knowing how to use comparisons in conjunction with the use of theory. Theory and the comparative method are necessarily used together to develop and support larger arguments and explanations about the world.

- Second, becoming a good comparativist means knowing what the limitations of comparative analysis are. This may sound contradictory, but it is critical to recognize both what we can do with comparative analysis *and* what we cannot do.
- Third, becoming a good comparativist means being aware of and self-critical about your own theoretical understanding of the world; it also means being able to understand and apply theoretical principles in a consistent, coherent, and informed manner.
- Fourth, becoming a good comparativist means knowing how to support your position with adequate, sufficient, and reliable empirical evidence (that is, "the facts").

In short, becoming a good comparativist and doing comparative politics requires the effective integration of method, theory, and evidence. (Figure 3.7 provides a simple graphic representation of this requirement.) Obviously, as I have already emphasized, this cannot be learned all at once. It takes time, en-

Figure 3.7   Three Legs of Comparative Analysis: Theory, Method, and Evidence

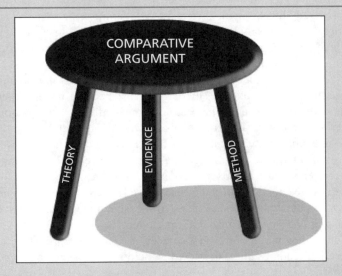

The key to understanding this figure is simple: comparative analysis cannot stand if any one of the essential elements is missing or weak. Doing comparative politics, in other words, requires an effective integration of theory, method, *and* evidence.

ergy, and a genuine commitment. It can be a daunting task, but one that I believe is well worth the effort.

■ Notes

1. For example, a variant of rational choice is rational choice institutionalism, which argues that institutions, as systems of rules and inducements, influence the environment within which individuals attempt to maximize their utilities. Normative institutionalism falls broadly into the cultural tradition and is based on the idea that institutional **norms** and values shape the behavior of individuals. The institutions themselves, however, are embedded in specific cultural and historical contexts. I discuss these issues later in the chapter.

2. The use of deductive logic contrasts with qualitative research in comparative politics, which is generally inductive. Induction, as Brams (1992) explained it, "involves searching for patterns or regularities directly in the empirical data at hand rather than using data to *test consequences* derived from a model" (emphasis added; p. 314). The problem with induction is that, although it may provide a strong explanation of the particular political phenomenon under investigation, it does not explain why some alternatives were selected over others. To resolve this problem, continued Brams, "Some prior assumptions are generally helpful and sometimes necessary for sorting out and making sense of the confusions and contradictions of political life, especially in trying to account for the choices political actors make that appear to violate common sense" (p. 314).

3. One famous and highly influential economist, Milton Friedman (1953), in fact, argued that assumptions need not have anything to do with "reality." Friedman claimed that as long as the assumptions undergirding a theoretical model lead to accurate predictions, the reality of the assumptions is irrelevant.

4. Students who are interested in exploring rational choice theory in more depth might begin with Jon Elster's *Nuts and Bolts for the Social Sciences* (1989) and *Ulysses and the Sirens: Studies in Rationality and Irrationality* (1984).

5. Although neorealist scholars are clearly structuralists, they also fully embrace the concept of rationality in their analyses. Specifically, they assume that individual states are "rational actors" who respond to the imperatives of the international system in generally predictable ways. In the neorealist framework, though, it is clear that structural forces take precedence, for it is assumed that the actors within the system have no capacity to alter the fundamental dynamics of the system or to otherwise escape from the "logic of anarchy."

6. Another meaning of "historical" derives from the belief, put forward by Marx, that human societies are embedded in their own past (Abrams 1982), such that what happened before necessarily impacts what happens today.

7. The state's relationship to society is another area of deep concern to comparativists. One of the best introductions to this subject is the edited book by Evans, Rueschemeyer, and Skocpol, *Bringing the State Back In* (1985). Another useful and more recent book is *State Power and Social Forces,* edited by Migdal, Kohli, and Shue (1994).

8. I am purposefully being vague on reasons for the breakdown in feudalism, since my intention is not to expound a particular argument, only to give a sense of what a structural argument would be at a very general level.

9. She explored this issue in depth in her 1979 book *States and Social Revolutions.*

PART 2

The Questions

4

Why Are Poor Countries Poor?

Explaining Economic Underdevelopment

Why are some countries poor? I asked this question in the preceding chapter to help illustrate how most of us (all of us) already theorize about basic issues in comparative politics. In this chapter, I would like to explore this question in much greater depth, this time paying closer attention to how researchers representing the three major traditions in comparative politics—rationalist, culturalist, and structuralist—deal with or approach the issue of poverty and "underdevelopment." There is, as I have already suggested, deep disagreement among scholars on the issue. But, I must emphasize, it is not an issue limited to the ivory tower. Poverty, whether domestic or international, concerns all of us—and not just in an abstract way. How we think (or theorize) about poverty, in other words, has far-reaching and quite practical implications. If, for example, you believe the poor are poor because of their own (rational) decisions or their own personal attributes (or lack thereof), this means that they should be left largely on their own to solve the problem of poverty. That is, the poor themselves must create the conditions for their own transformation, which means, in turn, that any efforts by others to help the poor—especially through state policies or government programs—may exacerbate situations of poverty rather than improve them. This is the argument made today by conservative Republicans and even by many liberal Democratic Party politicians in the United States against domestic welfare programs. These programs, it is argued, make it *irrational* for poor people to do those things that would allow them to break the cycle of poverty that typifies their lives. In this regard, such critics contend that welfare programs for the poor create a perverse system of incentives—that is, they "reward" poor people who do *not* work full-time, attend college or trade school, have fewer children (or no children) at all, or do anything that might help them achieve financial independence and prosperity. This line of theorizing, in short, essentially "blames the victims" (perhaps justifiably) for their situation's poverty.

There are, however, other perspectives—other ways of theorizing about poverty. One of these stresses the *structural* conditions that create and help reproduce poverty. These structural conditions, at a very general level, are based on the existence of and *need* for unequal and highly exploitative relationships between the rich and the poor, be they individuals, ethnic groups, or whole societies. In this view, the cause of poverty is not to be found primarily in the decisions that the poor make (or their lack of skills, education, or willingness to work hard), but in the positions they occupy within the broader economic structure at both the national and international levels. A popular variant of the structural argument is, not surprisingly, that the poor are "victims" of a system that essentially locks them into their positions. This does not mean that no people (or countries) will ever escape from poverty—there are always a few—but these cases represent exceptions to an otherwise ironclad rule. Indeed, if the exceptions actually became the rule, then we would be witnessing a breakdown or collapse of the existing structure. It is for this reason that structuralists, generally speaking, see the collapse of the existing structures of capitalism as a *good* thing; for it is only through the collapse of capitalism (at both the national and international levels) that genuine equality and social justice can be achieved for the majority of the world's population. Of course, this is what Karl Marx predicted would happen a long time ago. The perception that capitalism only seems to be getting stronger, however, has led many people to conclude not only that Marx was wrong about the eventual demise of capitalism but that his entire argument was off base. We will see, in the discussion that follows, that this is a difficult argument to sustain. For now, however, let's return to the basic question underlying this chapter, namely, why are poor countries poor?

We will address the question from a rational choice, cultural, and structural perspective respectively. Before we begin, though, let me make two points. First, it is important to understand that the discussions that follow are not meant to be comprehensive. I can only present "slices" of each research tradition, since all three are not only broad but extremely diverse. In other words, there is no single explanation of poverty using the principles of rational choice, nor is there just one cultural or structural interpretation of poverty. To give each research tradition full justice, this chapter would have to be much longer than it already is. At the same time, the discussion that follows is, I believe, representative of each research tradition. When necessary, too, I have included several "slices" from the various research traditions, to give you a better sense of important disagreements and debates.

Second, it is necessary to say something about the concept of poverty itself. At first glance, "poverty" seems like a clear-cut concept, but as with many concepts in the social sciences, appearances can be deceiving. Consider, for example, the following definition offered by the **World Bank**:

Poverty is hunger. Poverty is lack of shelter. Poverty is being sick and not being able to see a doctor. Poverty is not having access to school and not knowing how to read. Poverty is not having a job, is fear for the future, living one day at a time. Poverty is losing a child to illness brought about by unclean water. Poverty is powerlessness, lack of representation and freedom. . . . Most often, poverty is a situation people want to escape. So poverty is a call to action—for the poor and the wealthy alike—a call to change the world so that many more may have enough to eat, adequate shelter, access to education and health, protection from violence, and a voice in what happens in their communities. (World Bank n.d.)

The first part of the definition is straightforward, but the second part is more complicated and controversial. Even more, it is difficult to measure. How, for instance, does one measure "powerlessness" or "fear for the future"? Significantly, the World Bank does not try to do this in its own calculations of poverty. Instead, like most institutions and scholars concerned with national and global poverty, the World Bank relies on basic economic indicators, the most important of which is the percentage of people living on less than one or two dollars per day (adjusted to account for differences in purchasing power parity, or PPP, across countries). (Figure 4.1 provides a summary of the World Bank's statistics.) Although imperfect, such statistics provide a reasonable sense of the seriousness and scope of "poverty" in the world.[1] More to the point, such statistics provide a way to specify or **operationalize** the key subject—or dependent variable—around which this chapter is organized. As I have stressed several times, this is a critical task for a comparativist, for it is impossible to study a phenomenon adequately if the phenomenon itself is not clearly defined. With all this in mind, let's begin with a discussion of national poverty from the rational choice perspective.

■ Individual Choice, Collective Outcomes, and Poverty: A Rational Choice Perspective

People do not choose to be poor.[2] Nonetheless, there are hundreds of millions, even billions, of poor people and, by extension, dozens of poor countries and societies. The question, then, is why does this happen? Why, despite an unarguable interest in becoming more prosperous, do people (and their societies) remain mired in poverty over long stretches of time? Even more to the point, why are so many societies poor when the route to economic prosperity is well-known and well trodden (for example, why do poor countries not simply do the same things that now-rich countries did when they first started to become wealthier)? There is no one answer to these questions, but, from a rational choice perspective, there are a couple of general, and generally accepted, explanations. One of

Figure 4.1　Statistics on Global Poverty (by Region)

	Number of People Living on $1 per Day[a] (in millions)			Number of People Living on $2 per Day[b] (in millions)		
	1981	1990	2001	1981	1990	2001
East Asia	795.6	472.2	271.3	1,169.8	1,116.3	864.3
China[c]	*633.7*	*374.8*	*211.6*	*875.8*	*824.6*	*593.6*
Europe and Central Asia	3.1	2.3	17.6	20.2	22.9	93.5
Latin America and the Caribbean	35.6	49.3	49.8	98.6	124.6	128.2
Middle East and North Africa	9.1	5.5	7.1	51.9	50.9	69.8
South Asia	474.8	462.3	428.4	821.1	957.5	1063.7
India[c]	*382.4*	*357.4*	*358.6*	*630.0*	*731.4*	*826.0*
Sub-Saharan Africa	163.6	226.8	315.8	287.9	381.6	516.0
Total	1,481.8	1,218.5	1,092.7	2,450.0	2,653.8	2,735.6

Source: The World Bank Group, "Monitoring Global Poverty," http://www.worldbank.org/research/povmonitor/index.htm.

Notes: a. $1.08/day at 1993 purchasing power parity.

b. $2.15/day at 1993 purchasing power parity.

c. The figures for China and India are included in totals for East Asia and South Asia respectively.

the simplest is this: poverty is the result of decisions made by people who, while acting in an individually intentional and rational manner, generate an *unintended* and *socially irrational* outcome at a collective level (that is, national poverty). To this we can add the closely related claim that poor countries are poor because they are unable to overcome the problem of creating the **collective** (or **public**) **goods** (see Figure 4.2 for a definition of this concept) that would make economic development on a larger or a national scale possible.

Poverty and Constraints

To fully appreciate the logic of this (admittedly still broad) explanation, it is important to recognize, as I noted in the preceding chapter, that individual action does not depend entirely on the internal considerations of individual actors but also depends on *constraints* on their behavior. You should recall that constraints have two major sources. The first is scarcity: "[I]ndividuals maximize within the confines of available resources" (Levi 1997, p. 25). Someone without money or surplus income, for example, cannot generally make the invest-

---

Figure 4.2 Collective or Public Goods

Collective goods are any "goods" that, once created, are available to everyone, regardless of their individual contribution. National security or defense, law enforcement, public roads, and clean air are examples of collective or public goods. Notice that each of these examples is important, even critical, to the proper functioning of most, if not all, countries in the world. Law enforcement (which includes the system of property rights and contract enforcement in capitalist societies), for example, ensures that markets can operate efficiently and smoothly. Yet, as a collective good, individuals have little incentive to contribute *voluntarily* to the creation and maintenance of a system of law enforcement. The "collective goods problem" arises from the fact that voluntary contributions to the creation of collective goods are irrational, since rational actors will simply choose to consume the good for "free" once it is created (also known as the "free-rider problem"). The most effective way to overcome this problem, some (but not all) scholars argue, is to make contribution to public goods *involuntary*. Typically, it is the state, with its coercive power, that is best situated to enforce contributions to public goods.

---

ments that would lead to personal wealth. This has particular relevance in extremely poor societies, where day-to-day survival is often the rule and where "surplus" income is more dream than reality. The other important type of constraint, you should also remember, is institutional or organizational. As Levi defined it, "Institutions are the set of rules (and sanctions) that structure social interactions and whose existence and applicability are commonly known within the relevant community," whereas organizations are, simply put, "collective actors" that often serve the same basic function as an institution (p. 25). Together, material and institutional/organizational constraints play a crucial role in structuring the "incentives in human exchange, whether political, social or economic" (North 1990, p. 3). Material and institutional constraints, to put it in simpler terms, help to determine what choices are rational for the individual and what choices are not. The aggregation of myriad rational choices made by individuals, in turn, may either promote national development or retard it, may either create national prosperity or perpetuate national misery.

Unintended Consequences: Individual Rationality, Collective Irrationality

To explain national poverty in more concrete terms, rationalists often begin with the assumption that a critical *disjuncture* exists between what is socially good and what is individually advantageous (Bates 1988b). The key question, therefore, is why this disjuncture exists. The answer, to some rationalists, is fairly simple. Samuel Popkin (1988), for instance, suggested that it lies in the fact that, in poor countries, certain economic activities carry a very high risk, especially to those individuals with little or no margin for error. Most individuals (in his study, Popkin focused on peasants engaged in agricultural production) in these countries will therefore engage in practices that minimize their risk of failure but that may also result in relatively low levels of productivity. The main point, to reiterate, is that although this sort of behavior is rational and efficient from an individual standpoint, it is typically inefficient from the standpoint of the village (and larger economy). A good example, noted Popkin, is "the widespread practice of scattering plots [which is] . . . viewed by many economists as irrational. In fact, the scattering of plots substantially reduces the maximum damage that small local disasters or climatic variations can cause in a given season: mildew or rot in one area of the village, an errant herd, exceptionally light or heavy rains, and similar mini-disasters will be less likely to wipe out a peasant's entire crop when fields are scattered." At the same time, Popkin continued, "scattering also cuts the maximum yield per farmer and for the village as a whole" (p. 248). In other words, the practice of scattering plots represents a trade-off: greater personal security versus lower productivity and less accumulated wealth. In the context of poor agricultural communities with little or no safety net, however, the rational choice will almost always be greater personal security.

The practice of scattering plots (or similar practices), it is important to emphasize, is only one way in which rational individual choices can lead to irrational, or less than optimal, collective outcomes. Even more important, perhaps, are the decisions affecting the creation of public goods, such as irrigation facilities, dams, bridges, communication systems, roads, and so on. Here all societies (not just poor ones) face the classic **free-rider problem** that, simply put, happens whenever a collective project will benefit an individual whether or not she contributes to its creation. Thus, individuals will seek to free ride on the efforts and contribution of others whenever they believe they can "consume" the public good without contributing to the costs of its formation; this is rational behavior. For poor countries, this is an especially big problem. And again, according to Popkin and other rationalists, the reason is clear to see: free-rider problems are most pervasive and debilitating in those places where people and their societies are poorly organized, and it is generally in poor countries where such organization is lacking. To put it bluntly, unless organizations exist that can "force" individuals to contribute to the creation of public goods, such goods will not be created. And without certain public goods, especially infrastructural goods, the economy as a whole will tend to grow very slowly, if at all.

It is a fairly short step from Popkin's focus on organizations (and the political leadership needed to create organizations) to a focus on public, or nonmarket, institutions—especially those institutions associated with the government or state. Indeed, a number of other rationalists have focused explicitly on the role of the national government in promoting (or retarding) economic development (I will have much more to say on this point in the following chapter). The logic is simple. National governments are the preeminent public institution; as such, they have the capacity to secure the greatest contribution to the formation of public goods—in large part because national governments (or, more accurately, states) can make, implement, and *enforce* laws either universally or selectively.

The State as Solution or Problem?

It is worth highlighting that what *some* rationalists are saying about national poverty flies in the face of **neoliberalism** and another variant of the rationalist approach called **public choice**, both of which generally posit that the problem in most underdeveloped or poor countries is too little reliance on the market mechanism. Put another way, conservative economists (and many others) argue that national poverty is the result of *excessive* government or state interference in the market. Rationalists (and specifically rational choice institutionalists), however, suggest that just the opposite is true, at least to a certain extent. In other words, the logic of the rationalist argument, in this context, is that markets alone do not guarantee the development of the public goods necessary for national development. What is needed, therefore, is political leadership, organization, and the structuring of *coercion* through the creation of public institutions: this set of political elements represents integral parts of the development process (Bates 1988b, p. 242). Strong and effective public institutions, in this regard, provide the basis for overcoming the problems of creating the collective goods needed for economic development at a national level.

Poverty and Corruption: A Rationalist Perspective

At the same time, the people who command or aspire to command public institutions do not always act in the interests of their country as a whole. Indeed, many literally rob their countries of scarce and extremely valuable resources. Robert Bates (1988a) made this point very clearly in his analysis of agricultural policies in Africa, where political corruption has been a pervasive problem (see Figure 4.3 for a brief discussion of corruption in Africa). Bates argued that governments in Africa are driven to spend in ways that are politically rational but that often impose economic costs of "sufficient magnitude to retard development" (Bates 1988b, p. 244). As Bates explained it:

> A major reason why politically rational choices are not economically optimal is that expenditures that represent economic costs might well be re-

---

Figure 4.3 Public Corruption, Capital Flight, and Poverty in Sub-Saharan Africa

---

According to an estimate by Boyce and Ndikumana (2000), cumulative **capital flight** (a major indicator of public corruption) from twenty-five sub-Saharan African countries totaled *$193 billion* between 1970 and 1996 and more than *$285 billion* if imputed interest is included. To fully appreciate the magnitude of these amounts, consider that $193 billion was more than the total external debt of all twenty-five countries combined in 1996 (the combined debt was $178 billion; by 2004, this figure had climbed to about $300 billion). Despite pervasive national poverty, moreover, many individual African leaders are billionaires. Mobutu Sese Seko, the former leader of Zaire (formerly the Congo), was said to have accumulated $4 billion by the mid-1980s, and General Sani Abacha, the former leader of Nigeria, had a reported $2 billion in Swiss bank accounts. Although most observers would not reduce all of Africa's economic woes to illicit capital flight, it is an obvious and major problem on the continent. It not only reduces the amount of capital invested in the African economies but also raises the costs of goods, creates economic inefficiency, and undermines political and social stability.

---

garded by politicians as political benefits. Thus price distortions may create opportunities for rationing; although it is economically inefficient, rationing allows commodities to be targeted to the politically faithful. And government regulation may transform markets into political organizations, ones in which too few transactions take place at too high a cost but ones that can be used to build organizations supportive of those in power. (p. 244)

Bates and others provide an even stronger explanation for why national development (or why escaping from national poverty) is so hard to achieve, despite the fact that most individuals in poor countries—from peasants, to small-scale merchants, to the political elite—would *all* benefit from living in a richer country. To wit, those individuals who have the power to implement public policies that can promote national development simply have no incentive to do so. In fact, pursuing socially beneficial goals is irrational, since it is likely to mean an erosion or complete loss of political power. (This also helps to explain why mainstream economists believe that government intervention is bad for economic development.) This is not so much an issue of corruption as it is a case of doing what is necessary and reasonable (that is, rational) within a specific "opportunity structure," which itself represents a situation of **equilibrium** (in a situation of equilibrium, no one—or at least no one with the capacity to meaningfully impact policy decisions—has an incentive to change her choice).

Poverty and Path Dependence

Earlier I said that many rationalists employ history in their analyses. In the examples here, we can see some evidence of this. Neither Popkin nor Bates, for instance, operates on a purely abstract level. Instead, both are "thick rationalists" who take institutions (and organizations) seriously. Institutions (and organizations), however, do not arise out of thin air: they are either directly created, as was the Constitution of the United States, or they may evolve over time, such as conventions and codes of behavior (North 1990). In either case, they are products of specific historical circumstances, which the researcher must take into account in order to develop a more complete (although less "parsimonious") explanation for why some countries are poor and some are prosperous. For the rationalist, however, history matters in a specific manner: it matters in the sense that events in the distant past can initiate particular chains of causation that have effects in the present (Levi 1997, p. 28). Rationalists use the term **"path dependence"** to represent this idea.

How does path dependence affect the development of national economies? Most generally, it puts them on a particular (institutional) track that, over time, becomes very difficult to get off, even when it would be in the best interests of the country to do so. To illustrate this position, Douglass North (1990) provided the example of Spain, which at one point in history (circa the sixteenth century) was the most powerful nation in the Western world. As North explained it, Spain's polity consisted of a centralized but highly personalistic bureaucracy, in which "[e]very detail of the economy as well as the polity was structured with the objective of furthering the interests of the crown in the creation of the most powerful empire since Rome" (p. 114). A series of external shocks (for example, revolt of the Netherlands, decline in the inflow of New World treasure, and development of new technologies), however, put fiscal demands on Spain that "far outstripped revenue, and the result was bankruptcy, increased internal taxation, confiscations, and insecure property rights" (p. 114). Despite these severe problems, North noted that the crown and bureaucracy were completely unable "to alter the direction of the Spanish path in spite of their awareness of the decay and decline overcoming the country" (p. 115).

Spain, of course, is (and was) not a poverty-stricken country; the main point, however, is that once the country started down a particular institutional track, it became very difficult to alter or reverse course, even when it was clear that a reversal (or stepping onto an alternative path) was necessary to keep the country from declining. In the same way, we might say that most (all?) poor countries today are stuck on particular (inefficient or nonoptimal) paths leading toward the perpetuation of poverty. The problem, however, is not in recognizing that alternative paths exists, but in finding ways to overcome the obstacles to positive change.

■ Cultural Explanations of Poverty

Cultural explanations of poverty begin with the assumption that culture is more than just a reflection of economic or political forces. This is a significant assumption, for *if* culture is merely derivative of other, more basic forces, then there would be little reason to begin with or base any analysis on culture itself. This would be somewhat akin to studying a shadow rather than the real person or—to use the imagery already suggested—like studying a person's reflection in a mirror: reflections are not only two-dimensional and superficial, but they can easily be distorted, often without the observer even knowing (for example, some mirrors in clothing shops make a person appear slimmer than is actually the case). Assuming that culture is more than derivative, however, does not mean that it needs to be considered completely autonomous; few, if any, culturalists would go this far. Instead, cultural theorists tend to posit a highly interactive or mutually constitutive relationship among culture, politics, and economy. Max Weber, for example, adopted this position, at least tacitly, when he argued that culture was a significant—*but not the only*—factor in the rise of western Europe as the world's first center of capitalism. On this point, you should recall that Weber surmised that Europeans, notably Protestants, had a particular affinity for capitalism, which was represented in his idea of the "Protestant ethic." (See Figure 4.4 for a discussion of Weber's argument.)

Modernization: A Traditional "Cultural Approach"

Not coincidentally, Weber's treatment of culture had a major impact on early studies of economic development, especially among US scholars. Beginning in the 1950s, in fact, US academics generated a wealth of literature about the cultural roots of "underdevelopment" or of continuing poverty throughout the world. Although other factors, such as a lack of capital, inadequate technology, or low educational levels, were certainly not ignored, studies during this period zeroed in on the cultural (and also institutional and organizational) shortcomings of poorer countries. Thus, according to early **modernization theorists** (as they were generally called) the answer to the question why are poor countries poor? was clear-cut: *poor countries are poor because they lack the appropriate cultural values and practices that make sustained economic development possible*. It is important to recognize that this explanation was premised on an even more fundamental assumption about the nature of economic (and political) development. Namely, US scholars in the 1950s and 1960s took for granted that development is an *evolutionary, progressive,* and *phased* process (Comte 1964; Coleman 1968; and Rostow 1960) that is characterized by a progression from a primitive or lower stage of development to an advanced or "modern" stage of development (thus the term "modernization").[3] Needless to say, western Europe and the United States represented the

Figure 4.4   Max Weber, the Protestant Ethic, and the Rise of Capitalism

Weber argued that the relatively rapid development of capitalism in western Europe was due, in no small measure, to the relatively autonomous emergence of Protestantism and rational bureaucratic organization. Specifically, Weber argued (in his well-known work, *The Protestant Ethic and the Spirit of Capitalism,* [1930] 1958) that the tenets of Protestantism played an instrumental role in (1) legitimating individualistic profit seeking by making it a duty willed by God, (2) justifying capitalist exploitation and work discipline by making conscientious labor a sacred duty, and (3) creating a cultural climate in which poverty was seen as a result of individual failing. More generally, Weber suggested that Protestantism contributed to capitalist development by making a "new man"—rational, ordered, diligent, and productive (Landes 2000, p. 12). Weber, I should emphasize, was not saying that Protestantism was *necessary* for capitalism to survive and thrive, only that there was a particularly strong and mutually constitutive relationship—or affinity—between the two forces. In this view, history is obviously quite important, crucial even. For Weber clearly saw the particular social, political, and cultural context of western Europe as integral to an explanation of why capitalism originated and thrived there before it did anywhere else in the world. (Here, too, we can see how comparing Europe as a region to other regions of the world would be necessary to support this argument.)

most advanced stage (Tipps 1976), and most of the rest of the world represented varying levels of "primitiveness." (See Figure 4.5 for a summary of the evolutionary assumptions underlying classical modernization research.) If you detect a hint of ethnocentrism in this claim, you are certainly in good company. Indeed, many of the basic tenets of early **modernization theory** have been largely discredited precisely because of their ethnocentric bias, although it is still not difficult to find similar arguments today. To understand the criticisms of modernization theory, however, it is important that we spend a little more time discussing the logic of the argument, particularly as it pertains to the role of culture.

Modernization theory and cultural obstacles. Saying that a lack of appropriate cultural values and practices makes sustained economic development impossible raises an obvious question: what cultural values represent the greatest obstacles to development and why? To answer this question, early modernization researchers essentially divided cultural values into two categories: *modern* and *traditional*. Almost by definition, modern values are those associated

---

Figure 4.5 Evolutionary Assumptions Underlying the Modernization School

---

Classical modernization research draws many of its concepts from European evolutionary theory. According to Alvin So (1990), this latter theory sees social (including economic) change as unidirectional, progressive, and gradual. That is, the process of social change irreversibly moves societies from a primitive stage to an advanced stage, all the while making societies more like one another as they proceed along the path of evolution (this is called convergence). Early modernization researchers used these premises to inform their own theories, most of which are based on the following assumptions:

1. Modernization is a *phased* process (that is, it moves from one stage to the next, following virtually the same path laid out by the most advanced societies).
2. Modernization is a *homogenizing* process.
3. Modernization is the same as *Europeanization* or *Americanization* (which logically follows from the first two assumptions).
4. Modernization is an *irreversible* process (once started it cannot be stopped).
5. Modernization is a *progressive* process (modernization is not only inevitable but desirable, since it necessarily makes societies better off).
6. Modernization is a *lengthy* process (it is evolutionary, rather than revolutionary).

---

with economic achievement and prosperity, whereas traditional values are not. "Modern" cultural values include such traits as a commitment to rationality and science (over emotionalism and superstition), universalism, independence, and personal achievement. These values are said to contribute to economic—and especially capitalist—development because they make it possible for people to accept risk, to act in their own self-interest, to engage in long-range planning, to honor commitments to people outside their family (now referred to as "trust" or social capital), and so on. Traditional values, on the other hand, are generally thought to discourage the type of thought and action necessary for capitalism to thrive. Religious values that condemn individualism, exploitation, or competition, for example, are (as many have argued) hardly conducive to demands and imperatives of a capitalist economy.

Modernization's sterile view of culture. Ironically, the division of culture into two very broad categories had the effect of "dehistoricizing" culture. To early modernization researchers, in other words, the individual histories of specific societies were largely irrelevant—in essence, all traditional societies were the same. The only thing that mattered was where these societies were in terms of their "evolutionary" progress; whether they were more or less primitive, more or less traditional, or more or less modern. In this sense, early modernization researchers were not really culturalists at all, since they were interested not in individual cultures per se but in generalizing across cultures; culture, in this framework, was a highly abstract and basically generic category. The effort to overgeneralize, moreover, created some rather large holes in early research. Critics of classical modernization, for example, noted that once you looked carefully at some individual societies, the assumption that traditional cultural values are antithetical to capitalist development just did not hold much water. One of the best examples, in this regard, is Japan, where (later research seemed to indicate) supposedly dsyfunctional "traditional" values seemed to have contributed to that country's rapid ascent as a capitalist power, first in the period before World War II, but especially in the postwar period. (I will return to this issue below.)

The ahistorical and generic character of early modernization studies was, it is important to understand, a reflection of a flawed methodological approach. To put it simply, early modernization theorists adopted a variable-oriented and highly quantitative approach, when a more nuanced, qualitative, and case-based approach was needed. As Alvin So (1990) noted, most modernization researchers simply "adopt [a] cross-national method. They assume [for example] that twentieth-century China is like eighteenth-century Great Britain" (p. 57). Not surprisingly, this research method was an exceedingly heavy-handed and ultimately misguided way to deal with the complexity of real-world cultures and societies. Despite these and other criticisms,[4] modernization researchers did not abandon their basic argument. They did, however, take the main criticisms to heart. Accordingly, in a new wave of modernization studies, the most dubious assumptions of the "old school" were eliminated, and a significantly revamped framework of analysis was gradually developed. Significantly, one of the most important changes occurred in the method of analysis: the old and ahistorical distinction between traditional and modern was largely abandoned and replaced with a renewed focus on concrete, historically specific *case studies*. History, as So (p. 61) pointed out, was brought in to show specific patterns of development in particular countries. In-depth case studies, moreover, were often supplemented by comparisons with other cases or countries.

A new methodology for modernization theory. The introduction of historically informed case studies and comparative analysis reinforced the validity of earlier criticisms. For as modernization researchers relied more and more on comparative-historical analysis (both single-unit case studies and multiple-unit comparisons), it became clearer that the relationship between economic prosperity and culture was highly *contingent* (that is, depending on the specific context, certain cultural values may either promote, block, or even have a contradictory effect on economic growth). In short, newer studies based on comparative analysis unequivocally demonstrated that the simplistic distinction between "traditional" and "modern" cultures was profoundly misguided. This insight fits in well with the basic precepts of the cultural tradition introduced in Chapter 3.

The contingent nature of culture's relationship to national poverty was best exemplified, as I suggested a little earlier, in numerous studies of East Asian economic development, which is the main topic of discussion in the next chapter. Suffice it to say, for now, that early modernization researchers viewed East Asia's traditional values—primarily derived from **Confucianism**[5]—as the main source of that region's economic "backwardness" in the eighteenth and nineteenth centuries. East Asia's paternalistic values were said to have thwarted the development of the market because they promoted nepotism and rigid hierarchy, discouraged individual effort and creativity, blocked the development of rational business practices, and inhibited the emergence of universalistic norms. On closer examination, however, researchers in the "new" modernization school discovered that the later success of the East Asian economies could be attributed to these very same values. Paternalism and "groupism," for example, became an important, even crucial, attribute in a context where rapid capitalist development required discipline, self-sacrifice, and hard work. In addition, one well-known author credited Japan's traditional cultural values not only for helping to make the country's economic and political institutions highly—and *uniquely*—effective but also for enabling that country to avoid the corruption and **rent-seeking** so prevalent in the developing world (Fukuyama 2001). Cultural factors, therefore, seemed to play a role in economic development, but not in the sort of "black and white," "good and bad" way portrayed in earlier studies.

Despite such advances, modernization theory continues to be subject to a great deal of criticism, especially by contemporary cultural theorists. A large part of the problem is that researchers in the "new" modernization school still treat culture as essentially static and monolithic. Moreover, there is little sense of how culture is "produced" in the first place and how it is reproduced and/or changes over time. In other words, both old and new modernization studies tend to take culture as a given. Interestingly, it is not only contemporary cultural theorists (especially those identified with the **postmodern** school) who feel this way, but it has also been true of others who worked contemporaneously with modernization theorists—most notably those using an anthropological approach. One of the most prominent of these early cultural theorists is Oscar Lewis ([1968] 2000), whose work on "slum cultures"—or cultures of poverty—in Puerto Rico and Mexico provides an interesting and still very useful perspective on the relationship between culture and poverty. It is to Lewis's work that we will turn next.

Oscar Lewis's Cultures of Poverty

It has often been observed that the values and practices of poor people—especially of the poor within a larger society—are different from those who are well off or prosperous. Poor people around the world, as Lewis explained it, are often (although not universally) characterized as apathetic, fatalistic, hedonistic (that is, "pleasure-seeking"), present-time oriented, irresponsible, impulsive, provincial, unreliable, suspicious, ill educated, and so on. In addition, there is a tendency for poor people to have a critical attitude toward and even fear of the institutions of mainstream society, especially the police, court system, and the government in general. The poor also are distrustful of banks and related private-sector institutions, preferring instead to borrow from local moneylenders, pawnshops, friends, or family. The poor, in other words, are characterized by a lack of effective participation and integration into the major institutions of the larger society. This translates, too, into an unwillingness to take part in or to support collective activities; the poor generally do not join unions or voluntary organizations or participate in social movements of any kind. Lewis was careful to point out that none of these traits by themselves are distinctive of a culture—or more accurately, a *subculture*—of poverty; instead, it is their conjunction, their function, and their patterning that define the subculture.

Although Lewis primarily focused on poor communities (that is, "slums") within a larger society—thus his emphasis on the subculture of poverty—he also understood that a culture of poverty could, in fact, represent a very large segment of society. This is true in the developing world, and especially in those countries that were colonized or otherwise dominated by outside powers. In these situations, the imperial countries destroyed traditional social, political, and economic arrangements and replaced these with structures designed to ensure the servility, inferiority, and powerlessness of the indigenous population. At the same time, the imperial powers often introduced their own cultural values and practices (for example, Catholicism), but in a perverse manner meant to reinforce the subordination of the "natives" and to legitimize the rule and dominance of the invaders. Under such conditions, it is no wonder that many poor countries today continue to be plagued by overarching cultures of poverty. Indeed, Lewis suggested that the culture of poverty is endemic to colonialism.

Recognizing the existence of a culture of poverty, however, is not the same as saying that such cultures fully explain, still less *cause,* poverty. Indeed, Lewis ([1968] 2000) argued that the "culture of poverty is both an *adaptation* and a *reaction* of the poor to their marginal position in a class-stratified, highly individuated, capitalist society" (emphasis added, p. 111). In this regard, a culture of poverty "represents an effort to cope with feelings of hopelessness and despair that develop from the realization of the improbability of achieving success in terms of the values and goals of the large society" (p. 111). In this view, it is clear that a culture of poverty is *produced* as a response or in relation to dominant social, political, and economic forces. *Lewis, in other words, characterized culture as inherently malleable, as opposed to static.* At the same time, he argued that culture is not only an adaptation to a set of objective conditions and forces, for "[o]nce it comes into existence, it tends to perpetuate itself from generation to generation because of its effect on children" (p. 111). The perpetuation (or reproduction) of these values, in turn, means that poor people may continue to engage in practices that keep them poor, even if the "objective conditions" of their poverty change. That is, even if the poor have viable opportunities to increase their wealth and productive powers, they may continue to be poor because their values and beliefs systematically lead them to make the "wrong" decisions. *Culture, therefore, is both cause and effect.*

To give a somewhat simplistic but still meaningful example to illustrate this point, consider a poor person who wins $50,000 by gambling. This money could be used for a wide range of wealth-producing purposes: it could, for example, be invested in real estate or the stock market; it could be put into the bank; it could be used to start a small business; or it could be used to obtain a better education or vocational skills. Instead, the money is spent on expensive cars and knickknacks, more gambling, drugs, vacations, lavish gifts, and other nonproductive, or non–wealth producing, activities. After a year, the money is all gone, and the "winner" is, once again, poor. Culturalists suggest that, to fully understand this behavior, we need to take account of the cultural milieu in which the individual exists. For it is not just a matter of the person engaging in utility-maximizing behavior, as a rationalist might argue, but of the impact of cultural forces on the individual's understanding of and behavior in the world. This cultural milieu, to repeat, *explains* why the individual would rather consume than invest, but the milieu itself is the product—or an effect—of broader forces in society and the world.

Comparing Two Cultural Accounts

From the discussion above, the differences between Lewis's approach and the modernization approach (both old and new) should be readily apparent. In general, Lewis treated culture in a much more nuanced manner. He understood, for example, that culture is not static, and he understood that, even in a single society, there may be multiple cultures existing side by side. From a methodological perspective, moreover, Lewis also took history and especially *historical particularity* more seriously than modernization theorists. Thus, although he acknowledged that the "culture of poverty" is an abstract, highly generalized concept (which is similar to the modernization view), Lewis was careful to note that the "profiles of the subculture of poverty will probably differ in systematic ways with the difference in the national cultural contexts of which they are a part" ([1968] 2000, p. 114). In other words, not all "slum cultures" are alike, and sometimes the differences are significant. In a similar vein, Lewis was careful to distinguish between poverty itself and the culture of poverty. "In making this distinction," as he explained it:

> I have tried to document the broader generalization; namely, that it is a serious mistake to lump all poor people together, because the cause, the meaning, and the consequences of poverty vary considerably in different sociocultural contexts. There is nothing in the concept that puts the onus of poverty on the character of the poor. Nor does the concept in any way play down the exploitation and neglect suffered by the poor. Indeed, the subculture of poverty is part of the larger culture of capitalism, whose social and economic system channels wealth into the hands of a relatively small group and thereby makes for the growth of sharp class distinctions. (emphasis added; p. 117)

The distinction Lewis made between poverty and the culture of poverty is a critical one. For, within modernization theory, there is an unstated but still strong bias for "blaming the victim" (that is, either a pre-existing culture can adapt to capitalism or it cannot); there is also a strong tendency for losing sight of the broader historical and socioeconomic context within which national poverty exists. Lewis told us, however, that the persistence of national poverty in a system of global capitalism is not originally or primarily a product of "culture." At the same time, he told us that certain cultures may contribute to the perpetuation of poverty. The key is understanding the difference and the interaction between the objective conditions that create poverty and the culture of poverty.

■ Keeping the Poor Down?
Structural Explanations of Poverty

Rationalists, as we saw earlier, focus primarily on explaining poverty as a product of individual decisions made within a framework of institutional and material *constraints*, which themselves are historically determined. In this sense, rationalist arguments are not entirely nonstructural, as many critics claim. In fact, Keith Dowding and Andrew Hindmoor (1997) argued that rational choice explanation is as structural as it is individualistic. What they meant by this is that rational choice models *functionally define actors in terms of the roles they play;* actors, for example, are "voters," "capitalists," "workers," and so on. Structuralists are also very concerned with constraints—some might even say they are obsessed with them. Unlike rationalists, however, structuralists believe the most severe constraints are *externally* imposed. This is an important distinction, and one that has extremely important implications in explanations of national poverty. For example, you should recall from our discussion above that, in rationalist explanations of poverty, it is generally assumed that the rational actions of the poor produce an irrational (or suboptimal) outcome at the collective level. If the framework of incentives at the individual level is altered, therefore, such that people living in poverty no longer reproduce the conditions of their own poverty through their own purposeful decisions, it is possible to achieve a more optimal collective outcome (that is, societal prosperity). At least, this is the clear logic of the rationalist position.

Structural explanations of poverty, by contrast, might argue that it simply does not matter what most of the world's poor do. They are still going to be poor. Thus, a poor person can save money for the future, learn new and valuable skills, invest wisely, and even contribute to the development of public goods, yet none of this will guarantee a better, more prosperous life—especially at the collective level. Why? Because the fate of individuals and of individual countries is primarily determined by forces and factors beyond their control. This is not to say, as I pointed out earlier, that structural explanations rule out the possibility of a few "exceptions to the rule." Certainly, through dint of hard work, wise and prudent decisions, and maybe a little luck, some individuals (or even some countries) mired in poverty can achieve economic success and long-term prosperity. But—and this is a key assumption in structural analysis—what is true for the part is not necessarily true for the whole; what one individual (or country) can achieve *cannot* be achieved by all at the same time. This is, in admittedly simplistic terms, the crux of the structuralist argument about poverty.

Poverty and Dependency

Structural explanations of national poverty began, for the most part, with the emergence of a school of thought known simply as dependency (see Figure 4.6 for a discussion of dependency). Early dependency researchers were particularly skeptical of modernization theory, especially its assumptions about the evolutionary and Eurocentric character of economic development. Indeed, most argued that it was precisely because of Europe that Latin America, Asia, Africa, and other parts of the world were poor. In 1957, for example, Paul Baran (1957) argued that the economic "backwardness" of India was caused by the "elaborate, ruthless, systematic despoilation of India by British capital from the very onset of British rule" (p. 145). According to Baran, India's postcolonial poverty was due not only to Britain's plundering of the land but also to the destruction of India's native industrial base, the long-term distortion of its economy (for example, toward reliance on imported British goods, many of which were once produced more efficiently in India), and the disastrous reordering of Indian society. It is this last factor that is perhaps the most important. For, even though the other factors could be overcome (albeit with difficulty) once British rule ended, the creation of a new social and political order that was purposefully

---

Figure 4.6　What Is Dependence?

Theotonio Dos Santos, one of the leading scholars in the dependency school, defined dependence as "a situation in which the economy of certain countries is conditioned by the development and expansion of another economy to which the former is subjected" ([1970] 1996, p. 166). According to Dos Santos, dependence typically results in a condition of exploitation, but this does not mean that dependence necessitates a complete lack of economic growth or industrialization in the subordinate country. Continuing, he explained the situation this way: "The relation of interdependence between two or more economies, and between these and world trade, assumes the form of dependence when some countries (the dominant ones) can expand and be self-sustaining, while other countries (the dependent ones) can do this only as a reflection of that expansion, which can have either a positive or a negative effect on their immediate development" (p. 166). In sum, then, dependence represents a clear and unequivocal constraint on "subordinate" countries, but it does not imply absolute or permanent destitution.

---

based on dividing Indian society—essentially pitting different groups against one another in a zero-sum game—was a legacy that has proven to be extraordinarily difficult to root out. The result, according to Jawaharlal Nehru (cited by Baran, p. 149), has been that "nearly all [of India's] . . . major problems have grown up during British rule: . . . the princes; the minority problem; various vested interests, foreign and Indian; the lack of industry and the neglect of agriculture; the extreme backwardness in the social services; and, above all, the tragic poverty of the people."

Baran's argument, I might point out, is compatible with rational choice explanations: that is, given the framework of incentives imposed on India by British colonial rule, the actions of individuals in different competing groups were eminently rational. In principle, then, India's postcolonial problems were amenable to internal changes. This obviously contradicts the point I made above. Baran's argument, however, was one of the first studies in a now vast literature on dependency; it also tended to focus on the *enduring* significance of past colonial practices, which the modernization literature largely dismissed (if anything, modernization researchers saw colonialism as a "good" thing, since it exposed "primitive" societies to modern values). For this reason alone, Baran's study was an essential, but far from adequate, corrective. It was up to later dependency researchers to show that, just because formal colonialism was abandoned, the old structures of exploitation did not necessarily disappear. One of the most influential writers, in this regard, is André Gunder Frank. Frank ([1966] 1988) argued that the past *and* current "development" of the West was and is premised on the underdevelopment of the Third World—which he summarized quite nicely in his pithy concept, "the development of underdevelopment." Like Baran, Frank focused on the historical significance of colonialism, but he pointed out that, *from an economic perspective, it never really ended.* For after the French, the British, the Spanish, and so on had withdrawn their governors, administrators, and soldiers, the transfer of national wealth from the former colonies to their erstwhile oppressors continued unabated through a constellation of what Frank called metropolis-satellite relationships. These metropolis-satellite relationships, it is important to note, exist not just between poor and rich countries at the international level but within the poor countries themselves, at the national, regional, and local levels. (In this sense, dependency theorists did not lay all the blame for underdevelopment on external factors alone; clearly, the local elite played a critical role in perpetuating general poverty in their own countries while getting rich themselves.)

The main function of these relationships was to *extract* economic surplus from the poorer, less powerful areas to the richer, more powerful areas. The highest level—that is, the Western countries—retains the largest share of surplus, and the lowest retains just enough to survive. Because the relationship between the metropolis and the satellite is inherently unequal and exploitative, moreover, there was little chance, in this framework, that the poorer areas would become more prosperous through a "trickle-down" process. Instead, just the opposite is the case, since the longer the relationship persisted, the more the basis for autonomous economic growth in satellite regions was degraded. Frank's concept of the metropolis and satellite was later supplanted by the similar notions of core and periphery, which are the terms used most frequently today. Although the terminology has changed, the basic argument remains the same.

Other dependency scholars, however, continued to work on and refine the concept of dependency. Among these was Theotonio Dos Santos ([1970] 1996), who argued that there are at least three distinct historical types of dependence: (1) colonial dependence, (2) financial-industrial dependence, and (3) technological-industrial dependence. According to Dos Santos, it is the third type of dependence (which he also simply called the "new dependence") that exemplifies the period after World War II, when many former colonies experienced a degree of industrial development. To modernization researchers, of course, the incipient industrialization of former colonies signified the beginning of a process toward full modernization and eventual parity with the West. To scholars like Dos Santos, however, it signified a change in the dynamics and underlying nature of dependence but not of dependence itself. Consider, for example, what is necessary to industrialize: poor countries require industrial machinery or capital goods, which are only produced in the advanced capitalist economies. To purchase these goods, however, poor countries need "hard currency" (typically US dollars). Significantly, though, there are only two ways to get it: to borrow from Western financial institutions and to export. But it is not just a matter of rich countries controlling the purse strings, for the world trading system is also dominated by the advanced capitalist economies. This means, among other things, that "[t]rade relations take place in a highly monopolized international market, which tends to lower the price of raw materials [the primary export of developing countries] and to raise the prices of industrial products, particularly inputs [controlled by the richer countries]" (Dos Santos [1970] 1996, p. 169). Add to this the tendency "in modern technology to replace various primary products with synthetic raw materials" (p. 169), and developing countries typically find themselves with a highly unfavorable balance of trade. Over time, a persistently unfavorable balance in trade leads to large national deficits, which makes it necessary for developing countries to borrow foreign currency not just to purchase new capital goods but also to finance their growing deficits. Needless to say, this process only reinforces, through a constantly repeating cycle, the dependence of poor countries on the core.

Although this is a highly simplified account (I strongly recommend that students read Dos Santos's original argument), the basic point should be clear: poor countries are structurally disadvantaged in the world economy such that there are strict limits on the level of economic autonomy and prosperity they can achieve. The solution, therefore, is not to follow the same path as industrialized countries but to forge a completely independent, noncapitalistic path. At least this was the view of early dependency scholars, since their assessment of capitalist development essentially foreclosed the possibility of autonomous economic development in the periphery. This conclusion, however, turned out to be far too pessimistic, as the experience of the East Asian **newly industrializing countries (NICs)** (South Korea, Taiwan, Singapore, and Hong Kong) soon revealed. Indeed, the fact that the East Asian NICs achieved their success precisely by integrating themselves more closely into world capitalism created a seemingly irresolvable contradiction in **dependency theory**.

The problem, however, was less theoretical than it was methodological. The failure to recognize the possibility that rapid and fairly autonomous industrialization could occur in the periphery was basically the same error made by modernization theorists. To state the problem simply, dependency scholars attempted to overgeneralize, to say that their analyses of particular countries during particular periods were true for all times and all places. In this sense, early dependency studies were also, to a certain degree, ahistorical, despite the fact that they seemed to take history very seriously. This ironic situation occurred because early dependency scholars forgot an important caveat of comparative-historical analysis, namely, the experience of any country (or a whole region) is always, in a meaningful sense and to some degree, *unique*. A researcher who ignores the specificity of historical circumstances by making near-universal conclusions based on an analysis of only a handful of cases is, not surprisingly, likely to run into trouble. This, I might note, offers a good but very basic lesson for the beginning comparativist—that is, "talking about history" may make your analysis historical, but *comparing* cases both spatially and temporally is necessary if you aspire to develop a more generalizable explanation.

The Rise of "New" Dependency Studies

The experiences of East Asia and even of many Latin American countries, however, did not kill dependency theory, as many critics claimed.[6] Instead, like modernization, the experiences of East Asian economies pushed scholars to strengthen and refine, but by no means abandon, their arguments. Thus, dependency scholars sought to account for the possibility of relatively strong, even autonomous, industrialization in the periphery while still arguing that there were clear structural limits. One of the first to successfully take on this challenge (even before East Asian development became a significant issue) was Fernando H. Cardoso (a onetime sociologist, political activist, and former president of Brazil, 1995 to 2002). Cardoso (1973) introduced the concept of "associated-dependent development," which was based on the argument that, under certain conditions and to some extent, it is in the interest of core countries and their corporations to promote economic development in the periphery. These conditions, moreover, are not the same across time and space. Some countries in the periphery are better positioned—for a variety of historical and political reasons—than others to achieve a degree of associated-dependent development. Newer dependency studies also helped correct the tendency of classical dependency scholars to portray states and other actors in the periphery as little more than pawns, completely unable to exercise any meaningful degree of agency. In this regard, the newer studies argued that, although it is true that the agency of many state leaders and other local actors is structurally limited, it is never entirely absent. This is most apparent in studies on East Asian capitalism, which (as I mentioned above) is the subject of the following chapter.

Overall, the "new dependency" perspective directly addresses the basic problems in classical dependency research, including (1) its abstract and generally ahistorical tendencies, (2) its neglect of internal and sociopolitical activities, and (3) the inability to explain the possibilities of relatively independent and dynamic development in the periphery. With these three improvements, the new dependency perspective provides a more nuanced explanation of national poverty. Poverty, in this view, is still the product of a world order that privileges the already developed economies, but it is not a fixed condition. In other words, structure still is the primary determinant of national poverty, since poor countries face a daunting array of economic and political mechanisms designed (whether intentionally or not) to keep them poor. Structural obstacles, however, are not insurmountable. Given the right set of internal and external circumstances—for example, a strong, developmentally oriented state; an advantageous geopolitical position; a strategically valuable economic relationship with a core country; a domestic social structure conducive to export-oriented industrialization; and so on—development is a clear possibility. Of course, for those countries that manage to develop, it will still be a highly *dependent* development because the means of production (technology) and finance will remain concentrated in the advanced capitalist economies. On this point, just consider recent events in Asia, where the vulnerability of South Korea—one of the supposed models of East Asian capitalism—was starkly exposed by a financial crisis that threatened to ruin the economy. It was only through a massive US-led bailout that South Korea's economy survived, but only after the country's leaders kowtowed (some might argue) before the Western financial community.[7] Most poor countries, however, will never even manage dependent development, since not only is it difficult to create the "right set" of circumstances, but also to engineer a successful path to development once the circumstances are created is itself an extremely problematic process.

Poverty and the Capitalist World-System: An Alternative Structural Approach

The dependency approach, therefore, continues to be a relevant and valuable way to understand and explain national poverty. But it is not the only structuralist approach. It is not even the most influential. Instead, that honor belongs to a perspective called world-systems theory. World-systems theory is a complex perspective that shares many features with dependency but is also a critique of and response to the supposedly weaker aspects of dependency theory. The most salient similarity between the two approaches is the focus on the structural causes of poverty. Unlike dependency, though, the world-systems perspective takes the emphasis off the unequal and exploitative relationship between rich and poor *countries* and puts it on the *world-system as a whole*. This is a significant difference for many reasons, not the least of which is that it practically forecloses the possibility of noncapitalist paths to economic development in the present era. The reason for this stems directly from the logic of world-systems analysis, which posits that, within a given world-system, there is *one and only one* underlying set of processes to which *all* economies are subject. (On this point, I should note that it is possible for multiple "world" systems, each with its own governing logic, to exist simultaneously; however, today there is only one world-system, which encompasses the entire globe: the capitalist world-system.) Individual nation-states may attempt to delink from the world-system—as the Soviet Union, China, and a host of smaller states attempted to do in the twentieth century—but this is ultimately a doomed strategy, since these states must still operate within the confines of the capitalist world economy.

The *holistic* framework of the world-systems perspective also differs from dependency in that it provides a more comprehensive and dynamic (and even more structural) explanation of economic development in the world economy. This is largely because world-systems analysis is premised on the assumption of constant movement. The capitalist world economy, in other words, is not static, but is shaped by (1) an ongoing series of relatively short-term "cyclical rhythms" of expansion and contraction and (2) longer-term, or secular, trends of systemic growth or decline (Hobden and Jones 1997). It is the up-and-down, boom-and-bust nature of the capitalist world economy that helps *determine* the fate of poor countries. During periods of contraction, for example, the core tends to weaken its control over the periphery *as a whole* (in part because of the need to refocus on internal needs), which gives the periphery a limited chance to pursue autonomous development, usually through a self-reliant strategy of **import-substitution industrialization (ISI)** (see Figure 4.7). Only a very few poor countries are likely to be in a position to take advantage of these limited openings, however (for example, those with strong and very aggressive states—in this regard, like new dependency theory, world-systems allows some room for agency). During periods of expansion, on the other hand, the

---

Figure 4.7   Import-Substitution

Import-substitution is a strategy for economic development in which domestic manufacturers are encouraged—generally via government incentives, **subsidies**, and protectionist policies—to replace imported manufactured products with domestically produced goods. For example, to eliminate reliance on steel imports from Japan and the United States, the South Korean state, under President Park Chung Hee, developed its own domestic steel factory in the 1960s. The idea behind the import-substitution strategy (which can be limited to a few key industries or extended throughout the economy) is not only to reduce imports of manufactured goods (especially of consumer goods or "luxury" items) but also to save foreign exchange and create "economies of scope." Domestically produced steel, for example, could be used to subsidize the production of domestically produced ships and automobiles, two actual strategies of the South Korean government. It is significant that the import-substitution policies were heavily promoted and implemented beginning in the 1960s, but most efforts—throughout Central America and South America, in India, and elsewhere—were not successful. South Korea represented one of the few "success" stories, and even in this case, many observers argue that import-substitution industrialization only succeeded in South Korea because the state simultaneously implemented a policy of export-oriented industrialization.

situation reverses itself: the core attempts to regain control over the periphery in order to dominate the world market. During this expansionary period, development in the periphery becomes far more difficult, although certainly not impossible. But, unlike the situation during periods of contraction, poor countries that manage to "develop" in an expansionary cycle usually do so via a process that relies heavily on direct foreign investment by core capitalists. In this sense, a few select countries are *invited* to develop because they provide an internal environment highly "conducive" to investment (for example, a skilled but highly oppressed labor force, lax environmental regulations, extremely low tax rates on industrial activity, and so on). Most poor countries, of course, cannot even hope to "make the cut," so their chances for development along these lines will remain almost nonexistent.

The inability of most countries to break out of the periphery, I should stress, is no accident. In the world-systems framework, in fact, the existence of the periphery is a *necessary* and *permanent* feature of the capitalist world economy. This is similar to dependency theory, but world-systems adds another integral layer: the semiperiphery. The semiperiphery (which includes such countries as Brazil, Israel, Ireland, South Korea, Taiwan, and South Africa) is, as the term implies, an intermediate zone. Indeed, its main "function" in the capitalist world economy is to act as an intermediary, helping to smooth the process of exploitation—in both economic and political terms. Economically, the semiperiphery provides an essential outlet for the core. When, for example, hitherto leading industries in the core begin to decline, there must be places—the semiperiphery—to which capital can be transferred in order to avoid a sudden collapse of profits. The semiperiphery also provides a source of labor that counteracts upward pressure on wages in the core (consider how millions of factory jobs, once strictly limited to the core, have gradually moved to offshore locations). Politically, the existence of the semiperiphery acts as a sort of safety valve. With only two zones—one very small in terms of population, but extremely rich; the other very large in terms of population, but poor—the system would be highly unstable because of the stark polarization. The semiperiphery, therefore, not only helps to moderate this polarization by creating a middle-class sector but also provides an *actual* opportunity for upward mobility in the world capitalist economy.

More generally, the division of the world-system into three zones seemingly rectified the main problem with dependency theory (even the newer variants), for it provides a more consistent or coherent explanation for the complexities of economic development. On the one hand, world-systems researchers largely concur with dependency theorists on the inherently exploitative nature of capitalism, in which wealth (or surplus economic value) is extracted from the periphery through a system of unequal exchange, direct or subtle repression, and the control of marketing and the high-value ends of **commodity chains** (Roberts and Hite 2000, p. 15). On the other hand, the world-systems perspective tells us that exploitation itself is neither a static nor a uniform process: some areas are more exploited than others, and, under the right (albeit rare) conditions, exploitative and unequal relationships can be reversed (as when a former semiperipheral country moves into the core; real-world examples include the United States, Germany, Japan, and the former Soviet Union). Moreover, in the world-systems framework it is possible for certain hitherto core countries to experience downward mobility; that is, to move from the core to the semiperiphery. This is a prospect that is not even considered in dependency theory (or, I might note, in modernization, which portrays economic development as unidirectional). It is important to remember, though, that despite all this potential and actual movement, the tri-modal structure of the capitalist world economy must remain intact. This means that when one country (or region) moves up, another will necessarily move down, although not in lockstep fashion. It is not possible, in other words, for all countries (or the majority of the world's population) to achieve core status, given the logic of global capitalism. In order for such general prosperity to occur, a different logic—meaning a dramatically different historical system— would need to take the place of the capitalist world-system. Until this happens, poverty will be an unchanging fact of life.

■ Conclusion

In this chapter we have looked at several ways in which the three major research traditions of comparative politics approach the question of development and underdevelopment in the world today. I have tried to treat each tradition fairly (albeit not comprehensively), so that you can decide for yourself which provides the "best" explanation or understanding of world poverty. Of course, it is not necessarily the case that you must choose one tradition over the others. Each, as you have seen, has its own strengths and weaknesses. As a beginning student of comparative politics, in fact, I hope that you keep as open a mind as possible. It is almost certain that you can learn more by *taking seriously* what culturalists, rationalists, and structuralists all have to say about the issue of world poverty (and other questions of interest to comparativists). After all, each of these traditions represents the work of a great many very intelligent, very insightful individuals over many decades; it is therefore unlikely that any one of the traditions is completely or even mostly wrong. Even in those situations where the initial assumptions and methods of analysis turned out to be flawed, as in classic modernization and dependency theories, the original insights were often quite important (as in the idea that national poverty is not purely a product of internal processes but also of external relationships). In such cases, it would not only be imprudent to "throw the baby out with the bathwater" but downright unscientific.

Before ending this chapter, let me make one final note. Except for a few brief comments, I did not talk explicitly about methods of comparison in discussing the research on development and underdevelopment. One reason for this was just practical: this is already a lengthy chapter, so to have included separate discussions on methods would have been too much. But another reason is less obvious, namely, I want *you* to make the connection between theory and method on your own. When thinking about the problems in modernization and dependency theory, for example, did you consider what sort of comparisons would have helped researchers avoid making unwarranted conclusions? In a similar vein, did you ask yourself how a world-systems researcher would go about setting up a comparative research design, if in fact this is even possible (given the holistic approach of the theory)? If these sorts of questions did not cross your mind, you would do well to consider them now. Put yourself in the shoes of a researcher representing one of these traditions, and ask yourself: If I want to emphasize the role of culture, rationality, or structure, what should I compare? How should I compare? What conclusions can I legitimately draw from the comparisons I make? If you do all this, you'll be well on the way toward becoming a good comparativist and to doing comparative politics.

■ Notes

1. There is, the World Bank noted, a great deal of debate about how to properly and adequately measure poverty. Part of the debate hinges on the underlying definition or understanding of poverty, which may involve both qualitative (for example, happiness, a sense of purpose, and fulfillment) and quantitative or measurable elements. Another part of the debate has to do with questions of methodology. As the World Bank explained it, "in terms of methodology, global poverty estimates will vary according to the type of data sources used (national accounts data or household survey data); on the variable being measured (income and/or consumption); on the price adjustments used across time and space (use of purchasing power parities, PPPs); on the unit of analysis (individual or household); on the treatment of missing and zero incomes and of income misreporting" (World Bank n.d.). The World Bank's "Global Poverty Numbers Debate" Web page (World Bank n.d.) contains links to a number of useful articles on this issue, including a nontechnical commentary by Martin Ravallion (n.d.).

2. The perspective portrayed in this section, I should stress, represents the "thicker" variant of rational choice—one that gives much greater prominence to the institutional context in which rational action takes place. This "thicker" variant is generally referred to as rational choice institutionalism that, itself, is part of a broader trend in institutional approaches simply called "new institutionalism."

3. Samuel Huntington (1971), one of the most prominent modernization theorists of the time and still an influential figure today, added that modernization is an evolutionary process that changes societies in a revolutionary manner (cited in Roberts and Hite 2000, p. 9).

4. Alvin So (1990, pp. 53–59) provided a nice summary of the main criticisms against early modernization studies. Critics, for example, also challenged moderniza-

tion's (1) evolutionary assumption of unidirectional development, (2) assumption that traditional and modern values are mutually exclusive, (3) implicit justification of US intervention in the Third World, and (4) neglect of the issue of foreign domination.

5. I use the term "Confucianism" advisedly, since many casual observers of Asia have operated on the assumption that Confucianism is a coherent, largely static school of thought and values. As many scholars have pointed out, however, this is not at all the case.

6. Lawrence Harrison (2000), for example, asserted that "neither colonialism nor dependency has much credibility today" (p. xx). According to Harrison, "the statute of limitations on colonialism as an explanation for underdevelopment lapsed long ago. . . . Dependency is rarely mentioned today, not even in American universities where it was, not many years ago, a conventional wisdom that brooked no dissent" (p. xx). Harrison is only partly right. *Classic* dependency theory has largely disappeared, but so too has classic modernization theory. (Harrison, by the way, demonstrated an extremely strong bias in asserting that dependency "brooked no dissent"; remember, modernization theory was also a very powerful school of thought that itself "brooked no dissent" in many university departments.) The basic point is simply that offshoots of classic dependency, especially world-systems theory, have taken strong root in the intellectual community today. In this sense, dependency is by no means a moribund tradition. Harrison, too, evinced a basic misunderstanding of historical analysis in claiming that the "statute of limitations on colonialism as an explanation for underdevelopment lapsed long ago."

7. Admittedly, I'm exaggerating the situation, but only to make the point that, despite South Korea's impressive economic growth since the mid-1960s, the country is still far from "independent" economically or politically. To obtain the funds needed to bail out its economy, for example, South Korean leaders had to agree to a laundry list of conditions, which many ordinary Korean citizens and workers found humiliating.

5

Why Is East Asia Rich?

Explaining Capitalist Development in Japan, South Korea, and Taiwan

In the preceding chapter, I asked the question, why are some countries poor? This deceptively simple question, we discovered, can be answered in a number of different ways. It should come as no surprise, then, that the question, why is East Asia rich? can also be answered in a number of divergent ways. Indeed, the economic success of East Asia (see Figure 5.1 for a discussion of economic development in East Asia)—notwithstanding the region's recent economic difficulties—has been the subject of intense debate for some time now. There are those who, like David Henderson (2000), argue that the success of East Asia's main capitalist economies—Japan, South Korea, Taiwan, Singapore, and Hong Kong—has been based on close adherence to market principles in general and to "low government intervention or to reductions in government intervention" more specifically (p. 74). There are others who claim just the opposite, namely, that the state has played a central and pervasive role in first creating and then promoting, through carefully conceived and efficiently implemented economic strategies, rapid capitalist growth. Still others argue that economic (and political) development in East Asia has been primarily governed by external linkages and the broader systemic forces of world capitalism, over which individual governments or societies have little control. To this mix, we can also add culture-based arguments, many of which focus on the region's "Confucian heritage" or other aspects of East Asian culture.

In this chapter, we will look closely at a few of the more prominent arguments concerning East Asia's economic success. And, as I did in Chapter 4, I will divide these arguments roughly along rationalist, culturalist, and structuralist lines. At the same time, I should emphasize, not all of the explanations that follow fit easily into a single research tradition. But this is not necessarily a bad thing, since it gives you an opportunity to think seriously about how researchers must draw from different research traditions in order to construct

Figure 5.1   How "Rich" Is East Asia?

"Since 1960 Asia," noted **International Monetary Fund (IMF)** economist Michael Sarel (1996, n.p.), "the largest and most populous of the continents, has become richer faster than any other region of the world." Much of Asia's economic growth, however, has been concentrated in just a few countries located in the eastern part of Asia, with Japan leading the pack. Japan's early postwar economic growth, in fact, has been extraordinary by almost any measure—or as Burks (1981) described it, "in bald figures, the results were almost unbelievable" (p. 157). In the case of Japan, Burks noted, the country's "gross national product in current prices actually increased 1.9 times in a five-year period (1955–1960), jumped another 2.1 times in the next five-year period (1960–1965), and increased another 2.5 times in the succeeding five-year period (1965–1970)" (p. 157). In concrete terms, this meant that Japan's per capita income increased from $200 in the early 1950s to almost $2,000 by 1971, which made Japan the fifth-richest country in the world in terms of per capita income and third richest in terms of gross national product (GNP) (pp. 157–158). In the ensuing years, Japan's economic growth was even more impressive. Indeed, by 1998, Japan's per capita gross domestic product (GDP) had reached $42,081 (United Nations Development Programme 2000), placing it well in front of all the other Group of Eight (G-8) economies: the United States, France, Germany, Italy, Canada, the United Kingdom, and Russia. Although per capita GDP is, by itself, only a rough measure of prosperity, Japan also fared quite well in terms of other indicators. In terms of Purchasing Power Parity (PPP), for example, Japan ranked eighth in the world in 1998, and it ranked ninth on the **Human Development Index (HDI)** of the United Nations Development Programme (UNDP). You can find more updated figures (for 2003) in Figure 5.3.

In South Korea, Taiwan, Hong Kong, and Singapore (known collectively as the Four Tigers), the economic performance has been almost as impressive.

(continues)

their arguments. In this sense, the discussion that follows will also give you an opportunity to think seriously about the question of theoretical synthesis. Remember, though, theoretical synthesis is easier said than done, for it is not simply a matter of combining seemingly compatible aspects of different explanatory accounts. This may seem fine on the surface, but if the underlying assumptions of the various arguments contradict one another, then your synthesis will likely be unable to stand on its own.

Before beginning our discussion of the different explanatory accounts of East Asia's economic success, it would be useful to first provide a brief his-

Figure 5.1　continued

According to Sarel (1996), "The Tigers have had annual growth rates of output per person well in excess of 6 percent. These growth rates, sustained over a 30-year period, are simply amazing. While the average resident of a non-Asian country in 1990 was 72 percent richer than his parents were in 1960, the corresponding figure for the average Korean [for example] is no less than 638 percent" (n.p.). In raw figures, Taiwan's per capita income increased from $50 in 1970 to $2,500 in 1984, and in South Korea (which started its accelerated economic growth a little later), the comparable figures were $87 in 1962 and $1,709 in 1983 (all figures cited in Hamilton and Biggart 1997, p. 115). By 1998, in terms of PPP, per capita income in Taiwan and South Korea was $16,500 and $12,600 respectively. Moreover, despite a serious economic downturn, especially in South Korea following the Asian financial crisis in the late 1990s, by 2003 per capita income in PPP terms had increased significantly to $23,400 in Taiwan and $17,930 in South Korea. This put both countries a step or two behind the richest countries in the world, but well ahead of most of the so-called developing world. In terms of HDI, for example, South Korea ranked twenty-eighth in 2002 and was firmly ensconced in the category of "high human development." (Taiwan, because it is not a member of the United Nations, is not included in the UNDP's HDI calculations but would likely be ranked higher than South Korea.)

In sum, then, there is little doubt that East Asia not only has become a relatively rich region but also has achieved this status in relatively little time. Questions remain, however, on just how this prosperity was achieved and on just how replicable it is. As Sarel (1996) correctly noted, "Everyone agrees that the economies of East Asia, and particularly the Four Tigers, have grown spectacularly over the past generation, but nobody seems to agree on why. The debate over why they have grown so well in the past raises difficult questions about regional growth in the future and about the aspiration of countries elsewhere to replicate the East Asian success" (n.p.).

torical and comparative overview of economic development in the region, focusing on Japan, South Korea, and Taiwan. Providing a historical/comparative overview reflects an already-stated bias in this book that "history matters." But rather than attempting to tell you exactly how history matters in explaining the postwar economic prosperity of East Asia, my intention is to provide a general account that introduces you to a number of historical aspects of East Asian capitalist development, all of which are generally accepted as significant (a task that is unfortunately much easier said than done). In other words, I wish to avoid making a particular historical argument. This overview will also include a number of admittedly cursory demographic, geographic, and political comparisons among the three cases.

One last point before we begin in earnest: this chapter will focus on and compare, albeit not exclusively or always directly, three generally similar cases, all of which show no variance on the dependent variable. As I pointed out in Chapter 2, however, this is clearly problematic from a methodological point of view. A most similar systems (MSS) design, you should remember, requires or at least logically calls for variance on the dependent variable among at least two of the cases. Despite this, there has been a strong tendency in the literature on East Asian development to ignore the logical inconsistency of basing causal arguments on comparisons of this sort. This said, a focus on three most similar systems is not always what it appears to be. Many times, in fact, Japan, South Korea, and Taiwan are simply treated as single-unit case studies, where the other cases are used in a strictly secondary capacity (that is, a case study in comparative perspective). Less frequently, comparativists who focus exclusively on one, two, or all three of the major East Asian cases may use, although often only tacitly, within-case comparisons to complement their arguments. Done correctly, as I also noted in Chapter 2, within-case comparisons reduce, but do not resolve, the problem of selection bias precisely because they introduce variance on the dependent variable.

Whatever the situation, however, it is crucial for the beginning comparativist to cultivate a clear-eyed understanding of and appreciation for proper research design. With this in mind, as you read the various explanations of East Asian prosperity put forth in this chapter, think carefully about the strengths and weaknesses of the comparisons being made. In particular, consider what additional types of comparisons would help support the argument. What specific cases would you choose? Why? Constantly asking and reflecting on such questions will help you develop the mindset for doing comparative politics and becoming a good comparativist. I should emphasize that I will not leave you completely to your own devices; throughout the chapter (including in the conclusion), I will highlight important methodological points to assist you in the process of developing your comparative analytical skills.

■ The Context of Capitalist Development in Japan, South Korea, and Taiwan

The Importance of Colonialism

In comparing the *capitalist* development of Japan, South Korea, and Taiwan (see Figure 5.2 for a map of the region), one of the first things to note is that all three countries are so-called late industrializers; in this regard, all share a common historical context in terms of the *timing* of their capitalist development. Specifically, all three East Asian countries began to industrialize during

Figure 5.2 Map of East Asia with Japan, South Korea, and Taiwan

the period of Western colonial expansion. Western **colonialism** was a deliberate state policy whereby industrially and militarily weak territories in Asia, Africa, and the Americas were essentially made into economic and political appendages of the major European powers and of the United States (eventually, Japan also became a colonial power). Typically, subjugation of a territory involved the projection of military force, followed by the creation of a colonial structure that institutionalized—and "naturalized"—an unequal and highly exploitative relationship between the colonial "master" and the native population. It was not unusual, however, for the colonial power to **co-opt** local elite and other members of the native population once the colonial structure had been created.

Colonialism, most comparativists would agree, has been a major force in shaping the political and economic character of the modern world. This was almost certainly the case in East Asia, where the threat of colonial subjugation, for example, spurred Japan to adopt capitalism in the first place. The relative weakness of Japan vis-à-vis the West in the mid-1800s, in other words, motivated Japanese leaders to imitate Western economic and political practices in hopes of avoiding the fate of so many other non-Western countries. Fortunately for Japan, this strategy worked: not only did Japan avoid colonial subjugation, but it became an industrial—and colonial—power in its own right. On this point, it is important to note that Japan was not only the first of the three East Asian countries to imitate and adopt the economic patterns of Western development but was directly responsible for "introducing" capitalism to Korea (before its division into two countries) and Taiwan. The introduction of capitalism to these two countries, however, was accomplished through force, for (as I mentioned above) Japan imitated not only the economic practices of Western capitalism but also the political practices of Western colonialism.

The Historical Origins of the "Strong State" in East Asia

To *some* comparativists, the forceful imposition of capitalism in and political subjugation of Korea and Taiwan is another significant aspect of the historical context of East Asian capitalism. It is significant because, in dominating Korea and Taiwan, the Japanese imposed a *common* (albeit not identical) set of economic, political, and social institutions and arrangements that, to a significant extent, came to characterize *postwar* capitalist development in all three countries. One of the most important of these institutions was a highly articulated, disciplined, and penetrating bureaucracy (Cumings 1987) that constituted the core of the so-called strong state in Japan's colonial empire. Many comparativists, including rational choice comparativists, consider the strong state to be the key institution of late capitalist development. Of course, not everyone agrees (a point to which we will return shortly). Yet whatever one's view on the causal significance of the strong state, it is clear that the characteristics of the state structure in Japan, Korea, and Taiwan not only converged during the colonial period but remained largely intact following the end of World War II, when the era of Japanese colonial control ended. For this reason alone, some attention must be paid to the particular type of state structure that characterizes the three East Asian cases.

Historical Origins of State Economic Policies

In addition to the strong state, Japan introduced a particular model of state-directed economic development (Woo 1991). This model (which, again, was common to all three countries) was designed to mobilize, in a top-down fashion, the entire population for the purpose of achieving rapid industrialization. The model, moreover, was a highly intrusive and repressive one: to ensure compliance with state goals, it was necessary for the state to maintain strict control over the economic activities of workers, ordinary citizens, and capitalists. For workers and citizens, this involved ideological indoctrination, surveillance, and, when necessary, violent repression. For capitalists, control was exercised through less direct means. One of the most effective of these was the creation of a sophisticated but tightly controlled financial structure, which required capitalists to come to the state for any major investment project. A second source of control, or at least influence, was the subsidy (Amsden 1989), which the state used to promote specific or "targeted" industries. These two tools of state control, I should note, also laid the foundation for another distinctive aspect of the Japanese development model: a close, generally collusive, and highly exclusionary alliance between the state and business (Woo 1991). This is reflected in the oft-used terms "Japan, Inc." and "Korea, Inc." (it is significant, perhaps, that the same term is generally not used for Taiwan).

The period of Japanese colonialism, in sum, established strong political and institutional similarities among the three East Asian countries. These "colonial legacies," however, are not the only similarities that Japan, (South) Korea, and Taiwan share. Hamilton and Biggart (1997) provided a nice summary of and perspective on other important similarities: "All three countries," they noted, "have few natural, especially mineral resources." Thus,

> [t]heir success cannot be explained by the discovery of oil reserves, as in some comparably successful developing nations in the Middle East. Nor is land the source of their wealth. Taiwan, South Korea, and Japan are among the most populated countries in the world in relation to cultivable land. . . . Clearly, these are nations dependent on industry for wealth. They received economic aid and direction from the United States to repair and restart their economies [after World War II], but the aid alone, which was given to other countries as well, cannot explain the rapid development there. (p. 115)

The Cold War and East Asia's "Special Relationship" with the United States

The geographic and demographic similarities mentioned by Hamilton and Biggart may or may not be causally significant in terms of explaining East Asia's prosperity. Certainly, few (if any) researchers consider them to be of overriding import. But the same cannot be said about the significance of US military "aid and direction" specifically and of East Asia's "special" relationship with the United States more generally. Indeed, nearly all observers would agree that the three East Asian countries benefited tremendously from US aid and support, although there is less consensus, as is evident in the passage above, on whether this aid was essential. I cannot resolve this issue here; suffice it to say, then, that in assessing different explanatory accounts of East Asian prosperity, paying serious attention to the similar positions Japan, South Korea, and Taiwan occupied in the structure of Cold War politics is advisable.

Here, too, it is important to recognize that Japan, South Korea, and Taiwan all played key roles as bastions of anticommunism (and pro-Americanism) in Asia during their periods of rapid economic growth. As bastions of anticommunism, Japan, South Korea, and Taiwan not only received aid and direction from the United States but were given broad and generally one-way access to US markets. In other words, they were allowed to export their products (especially consumer goods) to the United States but were not compelled, at least until the 1970s and into the 1980s, to open their markets to US goods. Even in 2005, the domestic markets in Japan, South Korea, and Taiwan remain relatively closed to certain US and foreign products. Indeed, walking along the streets of Seoul or Tokyo, one would be hard put to find more than a handful of US or European automobiles (in South Korea, moreover, there are relatively few Japanese cars and vice versa). The ability to engage in highly uneven "trade" with the United States is, perhaps, one of the main reasons why all three East Asian countries share another significant feature, namely, a strong, even distorted, reliance on export-oriented industrialization, or EOI.

East Asia's shared reliance on export-led growth is sometimes held up as evidence of the benefits of "free trade." As should already be apparent, however, none of the three East Asian economies can be appropriately described as an exemplar of neoliberalism. If anything, just the opposite is true: all three countries followed a strategy of neomercantilism throughout the postwar period. To put it very simply, this meant that in Japan, South Korea, and Taiwan the state played an instrumental role in protecting, nurturing, and promoting domestic industries. This was done through the erection of high tariff and, particularly, nontariff barriers; the promotion of undervalued exchange rates; the tight regulation of foreign capital (especially "hard currency"); the imposition of restrictions and regulations on foreign direct investment; and the creation of other obstacles to foreign trade and entry. In addition to their trade policies, the states in Japan, South Korea, and Taiwan pursued similar financial and **industrial policies**, including (1) the targeting of specific industrial sectors and a general policy of import-substitution industrialization (which, in a counterintuitive sense, generally took place at the same time as export-oriented industrialization) and (2) the exercise of strong controls over the financial system.

Looking Closer: Key Differences Among the East Asian Cases

To comparativists, all these similarities are at least *potentially* significant. At the same time, it is important *not* to obscure the sometimes distinctly different roles the state played in each of these economies. Hamilton and Biggart (1997) noted, for example, that even though the Taiwanese state is no weakling, its intervention in the domestic economy has relied far less on coercion than has been the case in South Korea or Japan. Instead, state planning and intervention "is done in a 'loose, noncommand style,' is 'unsupported by controls,' has no credibility in its economic projections, and has 'no importance' in determining economic behavior" (p. 138, citing Little 1979, p. 487). Although this description may be exaggerated, the point is fairly clear: despite compelling similarities, it would be a mistake to assume that Japan, South Korea, and Taiwan are identical in all respects.

In fact, it is fairly easy to find other potentially significant differences among the three countries. One of the more obvious dissimilarities lies in the realm of **industrial organization** (Hamilton and Biggart 1997; Fields 1995). In South Korea, for instance, a relative handful of huge family-owned conglomerates (called *chaebol*) dominate the economy. The sheer size of these enterprises—the largest of which are now household names in the United States and Europe, including Hyundai, Samsung, and LG—gives them a capacity to influence almost every significant development in South Korea's political-economic landscape. In Taiwan, by contrast, the family firm (*jiazuqiye*) and business group (*jituanquiye*) are the main organizational forms (Fields 1995). Unlike the situation in South Korea, these firms are usually small or medium-sized and are characterized by relatively low levels of vertical and horizontal integration (Hamilton and Biggart 1997, p. 119). In Japan, yet another form of industrial organization exists, which is characterized by various types of networks—or enterprise groups. As Ronald Dore (1987) noted, enterprise groups are not conglomerates, nor are they cartels. Instead, they are "networks of preferential, stable, obligated bilateral trading relationships, networks of relational contracting" (p. 178).

There are, of course, many other potentially significant differences (and similarities) I could discuss. The point of this section is not to overwhelm you with detail, however, but to give you a sense of what is involved in almost any comparative-historical analysis. (See Figure 5.3 for a comparative summary of several *very* basic facts about the three countries.) As a budding comparativist, it is your duty to examine, assess, and explain the actual (as opposed to potential) significance of the similarities and differences you identify in a comparison of "similar countries." This is not an easy task. It is an especially difficult task if you begin your comparative analyses without a strong sense of how you can use the various theoretical or explanatory approaches available to you, which is why this chapter is organized in the manner it is. With this in mind, let us now proceed to an examination of the various explanatory accounts of East Asian prosperity from a rationalist, culturalist, and structuralist perspective.

■ Rationality, the Strong State, and Rapid Economic Growth in East Asia

In the preceding chapter, I introduced a simple but fundamental contention in the rational choice tradition regarding national poverty: poor countries are

Figure 5.3   A Summary of Basic Facts About Japan, South Korea, and Taiwan

	Japan	South Korea	Taiwan
Basic Statistics (data for 2004 except where indicated)			
Area	145,882 sq. miles	38,023 sq. miles	13,892 sq. miles
Arable land	12%	17%	24%
Natural resources	negligible	limited	limited
Population	127,333,002	48,598,175	22,749,838
Birthrate (per 1,000)	9.6	12.3	12.7
Infant mortality (per 1,000 live births)	3.3	7.2	6.5
Life expectancy at birth	81.0	75.6	77.1
Literacy rate	99%	98%	86%
HDI rank (2002)[a]	9	28	n/a
Gini index[b]	24.9 (1993)	31.6 (1993)	32.6 (2000)
Economic Indicators (data for 2003)			
GDP/PPP[c]	$3.567 trillion	$855.3 billion	$528.6 billion
GDP per capita (in PPP $)	$28,620	$17,930	$23,400
Population living below $1 per day, 1990–2002	0.0%	< 2.0%	n.a.
Unemployment rate	5.3%	3.4%	5.1%
Exports (free on board)	$447.1 billion	$201.3 billion	$143.0 billion
Imports	$346.6 billion	$175.6 billion	$119.6 billion
Other Information			
Political system	Constitutional monarchy; democracy since 1945	Democracy (under military authoritarian rule from 1961 to 1987)	Democracy (under authoritarian rule from 1949 to 1987 and one-party rule, 1987–1991)
Military spending (% of GDP) (2002)[d]	1.0	2.7	2.7
Significant security threats	—	North Korea	China

(continues)

Figure 5.3   continued

	Japan	South Korea	Taiwan
Major strategic ally	United States	United States	United States (since 1979, US-Taiwan relations "unofficial")
Public expenditure on education as % of GDP	3.6 (1999–2001)	3.6 (1999–2001)	n.a.
Religious affiliation	Shinto/Buddhist: 84% Christian: 0.7%	Christian: 26–35%[e] Buddhist: 26% Confucian: 1%	Buddhist, Confucian, Taoist: 93% Christian: 4.5%

Sources: Figures for all countries compiled from various online sources, including United Nations Development Programme, *Human Development Reports, 2004* (http://hdr.undp.org/reports/); "Wikipedia, The Free Encyclopedia" (http://en.wikipedia.org/); *The World Factbook 2003* (http://www.bartleby.com/151/); and "Military Factory: An Online Reference" (http://www.militaryfactory.com).

Notes: a. HDI = Human Development Index (see Glossary for definition).

b. The Gini index is a measure of economic inequality; a lower figure represents less inequality.

c. GDP = gross domestic product; PPP = purchasing power parity (see Glossary for definitions).

d. Military spending in South Korea and Taiwan was generally higher prior to the 1990s; in Japan, 1 percent of GDP has served as an unofficial limit for the entire postwar period.

e. Various sources provide significantly different figures for the percentage of Christians in South Korea; this is partly due to the tendency of many Koreans to indicate more than one religious affiliation.

poor because they are unable to overcome the problem of creating the public or collective goods that would make economic development on a larger or national scale possible. It would make sense, therefore, to argue that the reason for the relative prosperity of East Asia's economies—from a rational choice perspective—must be their ability to overcome the problem of creating collective goods. In a general sense, this is exactly what (some) rational choice scholars argue. Robert Bates, for example, was clear on this point. In his edited book, *Toward a Political Economy of Development: A Rational Choice Perspective* (1988b), he pointed to the critical importance of the state, as the preeminent public institution, in the development process. He suggested, in fact, that the efficient allocation of resources often requires less market and more state (intervention). The emphasis on the state is important, if you recall, because a major obstacle to achieving national prosperity—according to some, but not all, rational choice theorists—is the inability of poor societies to overcome the free-rider problem. To reiterate, people, when behaving as rational individuals, generally will fail to contribute to the costs of building roads, dams, bridges, and other public goods. They will instead attempt to free ride on the contributions of others *unless* a public institution (for example, the state) exists that can compel their participation (Bates 1988b, p. 242).

The existence of a strong state, though, is only part of the rational choice equation for economic prosperity. The other part of the equation centers on the following questions, also raised by Bates (1988b): What makes it in the private interests of those in power to implement policies designed to secure public goods? Even more to the point, what makes it in the political interests of the holders of power to adopt policies that promote economic development? (p. 243). According to Bates, the answers to both questions are linked to a number of factors, which may include (1) political ideology, (2) the economic interests of the political elite, and (3) the political elite's need for public revenues (p. 243). Bates gave some credence to all three factors—especially to the role of ideology (p. 244)—but he focused on a simpler position, namely, that *holders of power are likely to adopt policies that promote economic development when doing so allows them to retain political power* (Bates 1988a). The problem, of course, is that, in most poor countries, the conditions under which the pursuit of power by the political elite leads to socially beneficial outcomes are not at all common.

Based on the foregoing discussion, the core principles underlying the rational choice explanation for East Asia's economic prosperity should be clear. In case they are not, let me recapitulate. First, the existence of a strong public institution capable of overcoming collective action (that is, free-rider) problems is a necessary, though not sufficient, factor for national economic development. Second, there must be, among those who control the state apparatus, a clear private incentive (for example, maintaining political office or power) for acting in a socially beneficial manner. In comparing the main economies of East Asia—Japan, South Korea, and Taiwan—both of these core principles, starting with the first, seem to have empirical validation. From Chapter 2, however, we know that "validation" is relatively easy and, therefore, inconclusive from a strict methodological standpoint. Still, at a minimum, it provides an essential building block in the construction of theory in the social sciences. This said, let us now examine each element of the rational choice argument presented above in a little more detail.

The State's Role in Overcoming Collective Action Problems

As I discussed in the preceding section, all three countries (Japan, South Korea, and Taiwan) are characterized by strong, highly interventionist states. And although an in-depth comparative analysis of these three states would no doubt reveal important differences (as I already suggested), it would be difficult, if not impossible, to reject the basic proposition that they have all served to overcome collective action problems in their respective societies. On this point, it is important to understand that, following the end of World War II, the basis for state strength in all three countries remained extremely solid. A major reason for this stemmed from the role played by the US government: following the end of World War II, leftist or radical influence was strong throughout East Asia. The US government, therefore, decided to work with and strongly support the more conservative (that is, anticommunist and pro-American) governments in South Korea, Japan, and (a little later) Taiwan. This had the effect of ensuring that the basic structures of the "strong state" would remain intact and *in operation* in all three countries.

Indeed, in all three countries, there is (at least on the surface) a remarkable similarity in the role the state played in terms of economic policy. There is not enough space in this chapter to cover this issue in any depth, so let me just make two general but important points. First, it is fair to say that in Japan, South Korea, and Taiwan, the state possessed the capacity (or power) to compel private actors to contribute to national economic goals. In Japan, this power was manifested in a range of industrial policy instruments designed to overcome collective goods problems—tax incentives, research and production subsidies, **infant industry** and home market protection, government financing, export promotion, and **administrative guidance** (Okimoto 1989). In South Korea and Taiwan, the same policy instruments were generally used, although the Korean state tended to rely on coercion to ensure cooperation (when necessary), whereas the Taiwanese state relied more strongly on economic incentives (Cumings 1987). Second, and in a strongly related vein, the state has frequently played a leadership role in industrial development and planning in all three economies—this has led some scholars to describe industrial development in East Asia as "bureaucratic capitalism" or some variant thereof (Amsden 1988; Cumings 1999).

Constraints on Corruption and Rent-Seeking in East Asia: The Japanese Case

As for the incentive to pursue national economic goals, the evidence is not as clear-cut. Still, it is not difficult to support the rational choice claim that the actions of political leaders in East Asia were governed primarily by the desire to maintain political power. To see this, one must understand that, in the particular context of postwar East Asia, the power to rule and political legitimacy were both intimately, if not inextricably, tied to national economic development. There are many reasons for this, but one almost certainly has to do with the profound sense of national vulnerability found in all three countries. In Japan, this vulnerability was first set into motion during the late nineteenth century with the continuing thrust of Western imperialism. The almost certain threat of foreign domination, in this regard, provided the "rational" impetus for Japanese political leaders to pursue policies designed to bring about rapid industrialization and national economic development. It was only by "strengthening the nation" as a whole that they could hope to maintain their positions of power.

Following the war, the threat of colonial domination disappeared, but national economic development remained an important goal toward which (conservative) postwar political leaders—now entrenched in a US-imposed democratic system—were obliged to strive. One reason for this was that the policies and tactics used to repress the Left (which included a significant segment of Japan's population) required a quid pro quo: in return for electoral support, the conservative political leadership was required to formulate and effectively implement policies that would enable Japan to "catch up" with the industrialized West (Pempel 1982, p. 51). In other words, the authority to govern and national economic development had become strongly and unequivocally connected in the context of the Japanese political economy.[1] Of course, failure to achieve the goal of national development would have resulted in, at worst, electoral defeat rather than in national subjugation. Yet from a rational choice perspective, either outcome would still have meant a loss of political power.

In the cases of South Korea and Taiwan, colonialism also contributed (for obvious reasons) to a profound sense of national vulnerability. By itself, however, the experience with colonialism does not provide a sufficient explanation for why South Korean and Taiwanese political leaders pursued policies that generally promoted national development in the years following World War II. After all, plenty of former colonies continue to wallow in economic misery. For the first fifteen years following liberation, in fact, South Korean political leaders seemed to follow this same pattern of "politically rational" but economically destructive practices common to so many other poor countries. And there is good reason for this, particularly from a rational choice perspective: namely, the political and social environment of postliberation South Korea made certain political choices almost necessary for those who wished to retain power.

The South Korean Case: A Within-Case Comparison

Since this is not the place for an in-depth discussion of the sociopolitical dynamics of postliberation South Korea, suffice it to say that in the years following the end of Japanese colonialism, there was an intense struggle for power in South Korean society among a number of hostile factions. The main targets for each of these competing factions were the institutions and agencies of the state, which were understandably perceived as the key to political and social power. In this environment, gaining and keeping control of the state led to the use of economically "irrational" tactics and policies. These included financial policies that created negative real interest rates (that is, interest rates below 0.0 percent with inflation factored in), high levels of government spending (especially for the police and military forces), extremely biased lending practices (to supposed allies of the government), and so on.[2]

Over time, the less than optimal nature of South Korea's postliberation economic policies had predictable results: By 1960, the economy was close to collapse. Between 1955 and 1960, for example, per capita gross national product (GNP) had increased from $79 to only $86 (cited in Woo 1991, p. 58), and the per capita rate of GNP growth was a mere 1.5 percent between 1953 and 1962 (Mason et al. 1980, p. 187). But even this figure was exaggerated by the fact that South Korea had been receiving high levels of foreign aid from the United States—according to one estimate, it is likely that per capita GNP would have *decreased* by as much as 1.6 percent per year in the absence of US aid (Mason et al. 1980, p. 187). All of this raises an obvious, and fundamentally comparative, question: What changed? That is, what happened within South Korea that created the basis for rapid economic growth?

The short answer is simply this: a new, very strong leadership took over. It is important to understand, however, *why* this new leadership pushed national development, whereas the former regime did not. From a rational choice perspective, we would expect the answer to be found in a changed decisionmaking environment that compelled the new leaders to equate national economic development with their chances for political survival. And this is largely what happened. For just as the previous regime lost the legitimacy to rule because of the lack of economic development, the new regime could only establish legitimacy if it effectively and efficiently reversed the economic direction in which the country headed. In addition, it is important to note another critical contextual factor that helps account for the overriding importance the South Korean populace placed on a strong national economy. Simply put, it was the existence of a hostile and militarily powerful enemy situated right next to South Korea—the Democratic People's Republic of Korea, or North Korea. The threat posed by North Korea could not be ignored, particularly since the two countries had already engaged in a vicious and highly destructive war between 1950 and 1953 (even today, South and North Korea exist in a technical state of war). Given this ever-present and very real threat, a government that failed to build a strong national economy—one that could provide a material foundation sufficient to counter the North Korean threat—could hardly expect to stay in power. And while it is true that the previous regime(s) also faced the same external threat, internal rivalries for political power were much greater and more pervasive in the 1950s than in the 1960s after the military coup. In this respect, the military coup itself had a material affect on the decisionmaking environment within South Korea.

The Taiwanese Case

Taiwan, it is important to note, faced a quite similar, if not immensely more formidable, threat: China. The relationship between Taiwan and China is quite different from the relationship between North and South Korea, but the impact on domestic politics (a rationalist might argue) has been similar. It has been similar in that the political leaders in Taiwan after 1949—all of whom fled main-land China after engaging the Chinese Communist Party in a long-running civil war—have been faced with the constant threat of external domination. Indeed, to this day, the communist Chinese leadership considers Taiwan to be a "rene-gade province" rather than a sovereign country. Unlike South Korea's first gov-ernment, though, the initial group of Taiwanese political leaders *immediately* launched an ambitious industrialization plan. One prominent scholar, Robert Wade (1990), suggested that the motivation for rapid industrialization was less self-preservation than a desire to "recapture" the Chinese mainland. But, as Wade put it, "Recapturing the mainland—which remained a central preoccupa-tion of the government through the 1950s—required the development of some upstream industries" (p. 77). Whatever the case, the motivation of Taiwan's early political leadership clearly fit within a rational choice framework.

Rational Choice and East Asian Development: Conclusion and a Caveat

The foregoing analysis is, I readily admit, quite broad and even superficial. Certainly, it is not sufficient to clearly establish the empirical (much less the-oretical) validity of the rational choice perspective. But this decidedly is not my intention. Instead, my intention is simply to provide you—as a student new to the study of comparative politics—a general sense of how the basic principles and concepts of rational choice could fruitfully be used to analyze capitalist development in East Asia. I hope I achieved this goal. At the least, you should understand how a core assumption of the rational choice school—that is, that people are rational maximizers of self-interest (or utility maxi-mizers)—can provide a plausible account or explanation of how the three East Asian economies became prosperous. If you are interested in further explor-ing this issue, however, it is up to you to develop a more systematic, more rig-orous, and deeper plan of action. The same can be said for the alternative the-oretical analyses that follow.

An Alternative View of the State

Before we move on to other theoretical perspectives, though, it is necessary to re-emphasize that the rational choice account just offered is only one of sev-eral versions. Some rational choice variants, in fact, utterly reject the *general* premise that a strong, highly interventionist, and developmentally oriented state is needed to overcome collective goods problems in capitalist economies. Instead, they argue that *limited* state intervention is required only in situations of widespread market failure or imperfection. State intervention in the market must be limited because any interference in the market process tends to inhibit economic efficiency (and growth). This happens because state policies invariably create barriers or other obstacles to the free flow of goods, capital, labor, and information (all of which are needed to maximize economic gains through rational or self-interested action on the part of economic agents). Thus, from a mainstream economic perspective, the success of East Asia can be directly traced to minimal or very selective state intervention based on reducing market "imperfections." One set of economists, for example, has argued that the key to East Asian economic success was the adoption of "outward-looking development strategies," or EOI. This involves (1) a market- or private-sector-oriented approach, where business activities are mainly left to the private sector and "the allocation of resources is basically left to the market"; (2) the correction of price distortions (that is, bringing prices in line with market forces); (3) cautious financial management; (4) state support for education and human resource development; and (5) flexibility (James, Naya, and Meier 1989, pp. 17–21). The logical conclusion of this explanation, I should emphasize, is that once market imperfections are corrected, even limited state intervention will no longer be necessary.

Although we should not discount this mainstream economic argument, it is important to understand that it is based on a **deductive**, highly abstract, and noncomparative method of analysis. In contrast, the (institutional) rational choice explanation we discussed above, although also deductive, adopts a much more historically grounded, concrete, and comparative method. In other words, rational choice institutionalists examine how public institutions, such as the state, *actually* behave and interact with markets. In this regard, they explicitly link theory, method, and evidence together to support their arguments as opposed to putting forth axiomatic claims that, in essence, have little or no comparative-historical and empirical foundation. This said, other comparativists might argue that the rational choice perspective is still too general, that it does not look closely enough at the specific histories and cultures of particular societies. This criticism is particularly evident in the cultural approach, to which we will turn next.

■ Culture and Capitalist Development in East Asia

There are few, if any, scholars who argue that cultural factors *alone* can explain the economic rise of East Asia. There are, however, an increasing number of scholars who assert that completely ignoring or dismissing cultural factors is equally misguided. This latter view, generally speaking, is based on the belief that economic activity (and the institutions that sustain it) does not and cannot occur in a historical and cultural vacuum. With this as a starting point, some scholars argue that culture helps to shape the *specific* patterns and modes of economic activity and organization that differentiate one country (region or location) from another. This, in turn, can have a very large effect on how a national economy develops. Under certain conditions, moreover, specific types of cultural practices or patterns of cultural activity may, in fact, lead to rapid economic growth. In Japan, for example, some culturalists argue that the widely held Japanese belief in *wa,* or harmony (see, for example, Abegglen and Stalk 1985; and Benedict 1946, cited in Biggart 1997, p. 12), has led to a highly efficient but culturally specific form of cooperative economic behavior. In Taiwan, by contrast, some scholars argue that the Taiwanese business environment is "inspired by the heterodoxy of **Taoism**," which has led to an entrepreneurial class dominated by "rebels" and "bandits," figuratively speaking. It is this spirit of rebellion, the authors suggest, that has led to Taiwan's economic success. I will discuss this and other culture-specific views in more detail below. Before doing so, though, it is very important to say a few words about the most common cultural approach to capitalist development in East Asia, namely, the idea that Confucianism is a common ingredient in *all* East Asian societies and is, therefore, a central factor explaining the region's economic success. *Students should view this type of approach with extreme caution.* I will explain why below; for now, though, let me state the basic problem: those who use a Confucian argument typically commit the sin of dehistoricizing and decontextualizing culture; that is, of removing culture from its specific historical, social, and political context and then, worse still, assuming that a broad range of societies can be classified, in essence, as cultural clones. This type of "cultural" analysis will almost always lead to superficial and distorted conclusions, since treating culture as a generalized, even generic, variable is almost always a fundamental mistake.

Still, viewing the Confucian argument (and similar approaches) with skepticism does not mean that we should abandon all culture-based interpretations of East Asian capitalism. Nor does it mean that Confucianism is irrelevant in any account of East Asian capitalism. This is decidedly not the case. For, as I suggested above, there *are* valuable and valid interpretations of East Asian capitalism using a cultural approach, which we will discuss shortly. It might be useful, however, to first take a quick look at the Confucian argument as an exemplar of "bad" cultural analysis. The point of doing so, however, is not to belittle a particular cultural approach (and the scholars who still use it) but to help you understand what to avoid in your own cultural analysis.

The Confucian Argument: A Traditional View

Most arguments based on East Asia's shared cultural heritage claim that a "Confucian ethic" is the key to understanding the region's economic success. Some scholars argue, for example, that core values of Confucianism—which are usually identified as respect for authority, faith, loyalty, filial piety (that is, deference to and respect of elders), harmony, and intellectualism—have been instrumental in promoting economic development in East Asia. The impact of these values on capitalist development, though, is not necessarily direct. Instead, Confucian ethics are said to help build those institutions (for example, the state) and relationships (for example, state-business, state-labor, and business-labor) that are important for rapid industrialization. In this view, therefore, the prominent role of East Asian governments can be traced to the importance Asians place on respect for authority or obedience to superiors. This explains, for instance, why East Asian business leaders have generally deferred to government officials—that is, because government officials are, by definition, superior in a Confucian society, their authority to lead is not subject to challenge. The same pattern of patriarchal deference can be found in business-labor relationships. Workers are supposedly willing to give up personal gains because of their strong culturally rooted sense of self-sacrifice, loyalty, and discipline. One scholar explained it this way: "The Confucian cultural inheritance meant that the authority and benevolence of a business leader could be anticipated on the basis of authority and benevolence traditionally expected of the head of a family. Similarly, cultural expectations anticipated that employees would perform their jobs at the direction of their superiors without question or debate" (Park 1999, p. 131). This clearly defined and respected hierarchy, so the argument goes, has allowed the East Asian countries to function as a single, strongly focused, tightly disciplined, and highly efficient economic unit. Hence, the terms "Japan, Inc." and "Korea, Inc." have often been used to suggest that each of East Asia's economies is essentially a single, but massive, corporation, with the government as chief executive officer, the companies as departments or divisions, and the citizens as loyal employees. The capacity to act as a monolithic economic unit, according to advocates of this view, has given East Asian countries a critical competitive edge in international competition.

Variants of the Confucian argument see a more direct cause-and-effect relationship. Some writers, for instance, see Confucianism as a substitute for the "Protestant ethic," which supposedly unleashed the forces of capitalism in the West. The Protestant ethic, you should recall from Chapter 4, is based on the idea that capitalism thrived in the West when economic acquisition became solidly linked, as happened with the rise of **Puritanism** (in the sixteenth century), with the idea of salvation and service to God. In the Confucian version of the Protestant ethic, it is not believed that hard work and self-sacrifice will bring salvation in the afterlife but that core values of Confucianism encourage East Asians to behave in ways that have proven to be extremely helpful to rapid capitalist development in the postwar era. For instance, Confucianism preaches thriftiness. Thus, Asians are more prone to save than, say, Latin Americans (and increased national savings leads to a greater availability of investable and cheap financial capital, which is necessary for rapid economic growth). Self-sacrifice is another Confucian value; thus, Asians are supposedly more willing to give up personal gains if this means contributing to a broader, collective good. Perhaps the most important Confucian value, many argue, is education. In East Asia, as one proponent of this view clearly put it, there is "enormous prestige of education, with the concomitant motivation to provide the best education for one's children. . . . [There are also] severe (some would say, brutally severe) meritocratic norms and institutions, which, while egalitarian in design, serve to select out elites when they are at an early age" (Berger 1998, p. 5; cited in Chan 1993, p. 40). This "enormous" emphasis on educational achievement not only has given East Asian societies a huge advantage over less educated and less skilled societies but also has allowed East Asia to catch up with the West much more quickly than would otherwise have been the case.

On the surface, the Confucian argument, in all its various forms, makes sense, which is one reason why the argument remains popular today. If we look under the surface, however, a number of problems immediately pop up. The basic problem, to reiterate, is this: advocates of the Confucian argument assume that Confucianism has played an essentially similar role throughout East Asia generally, but as even the most cursory *comparative analysis* will show, this just is not true. Thus, although most critics of the Confucian argument agree that Japan, South Korea, and Taiwan share a Confucian (and, to a lesser extent, **Buddhist**) heritage, it is equally clear that this has not created a bunch of cultural or economic and political clones. Quite the contrary. In Japan, South Korea, and Taiwan (not to mention China, Singapore, Hong Kong, and other so-called Confucian societies), Confucianism not only is understood in very different ways but also occupies dramatically different positions with each respective society. Some of these differences will become clear below. The main point, however, is not to say that Confucianism is irrelevant in defining East Asian culture. It is not. Rather, the point is that Confucian values do not have the same impact or influence in every country or society. These values, for example, may be more or less accepted by the general population, or they may be accepted by only the economic or political elite of that society. Confucian values may also be modified or dramatically transformed (usually by the elite) in order to fit in with or to legitimize other dominant social, economic, or political arrangements. By the same token, the imposition of Confucian values may spur active resistance within society and encourage the development of strong and dynamic *countercultures*. Confucian values, too, generally must coexist with other strong cultural systems. In South Korea, for example, Christianity is a strong, if not dominant, religion: almost one-third of South Koreans say they are Christian. Contrast this with Japan, where a mere 0.7 percent of the population is Christian. What, if anything, does this difference mean? Indeed, once we recognize these possibilities and differences, we must admit that an *all-encompassing* Confucian argument cannot adequately explain the economic success of Japan, South Korea, and Taiwan.

Confucianism in Context: An Updated View

In place of an all-encompassing Confucian argument are approaches that examine the relationship between culture and economy with careful regard to *specific* contexts. This is what the better studies using a culturalist perspective do. A good example of this is the work of Gregory Ornatowski (1996), who argued that, although Confucianism was an important part of Japan's economic rise (both prewar and postwar), it was *transformed* and *selectively shaped* by the particular context of Japan's late development and its economic and military competition with the Western powers. This context of late development and competition, for example, encouraged Japanese government and industrial leaders to intentionally "identify Confucian values with Japan's national polity and nationalist ideology" (n.p.). Capitalist development, therefore, was *made* into both a patriotic and a moral duty (that is, it was not just a natural affinity). In this regard, Confucian values were used by those in power to promote rapid industrial development by encouraging sacrifice toward national goals as well as obedience to superiors within the workplace.

It is significant that Ornatowski also argued that in prewar Japan, the use of Confucian values "also limited innovation by tending to focus moral effort upon upholding company traditions and respecting the thinking of older generations rather than looking for innovative responses to new economic circumstances" (n.p.). As a result, continued Ornatowski,

> this approach stifled what might have been the development of more creative responses to the economic problems that Japan faced in the 1920s and 1930s, such as growing labor disputes, widening gaps between the rich and poor and the plight of the tenant farmer class. From the Confucian point of view, all of these problems were defined as moral problems and therefore required moral solutions rather than economic ones. Such a moral mindset, however, partly contributed to the growth of nationalistic answers to such problems. *This was possible because from the 1920s onward Confucian morality and nationalism were increasingly synthesized into a common kokutai* ["national essence"] *ideology.* Therefore when economic problems were defined as moral problems resulting from the influx of materialistic ideas from the West (individualism and socialism), the solution could easily become a re-assertion of Japan's and Asia's moral traditions through Japanese expansionism abroad in Asia. (emphasis added; n.p.)

In the prewar period, then, Confucianism both helped and hindered capitalist development in Japan. It helped by compelling self-sacrificing behavior, especially on the part of workers and ordinary citizens, but it hindered capitalist development by wrapping Japanese capitalism in a moral and highly nationalistic straitjacket. The two-edged aspect of Confucianism is important to highlight, for it illustrates a key point about contemporary culturalist approaches, which is that "culture" is complex and often has multiple, and unanticipated, effects in society. In this regard, culture is always more than just a political resource.

In the postwar period, Confucian values continued to play an important and very similar role. Yet changes in Japan's political and social context led to significant modifications in the moral code that governed Japanese capitalism. This was most apparent in the clear linkage that developed between the traditional Confucian values of educational achievement, loyalty, harmony (called *wa* in Japanese), and respect for hierarchy (or authority) and the concept of *fairness*. Indeed, some scholars, including Ornatowski, consider this linkage a key to understanding the dynamism of postwar Japanese capitalism. One of the strongest advocates of this position, however, is Ronald Dore, who has written extensively on the relationship between culture and capitalist development in Japan. Specifically, Dore argued that Japanese economic and social arrangements—which are a reflection of both cultural (primarily Confucian) influences *and* rational responses to market pressures—have generated a sense of fairness in Japan that enables people to work "cooperatively, conscientiously and with a will" (1987, p. 18). This sense of fairness, in Dore's view, not only makes Japan unique but is a large part of what gives the country its competitive edge in the international economy.

Finding Differences: Taiwan in Comparative Perspective

From the perspective of Ornatowski and Dore, one can say that Confucian values were effectively integrated into the social and economic arrangements of Japan. It is easy to see, then, why so many scholars have been keen to embrace a "Confucian argument," not just for Japan but for all of East Asia. After all, if Confucianism helped Japan develop, the thinking goes, then it must have helped South Korea and Taiwan develop, since both these countries draw even more deeply from a Confucian heritage. But this is precisely why in-depth, historically based comparative analysis is so important. For when we look below the surface, it is usually not very difficult to find important differences or dissimilarities (this is often a goal among scholars who use a cultural approach). Consider the case of Taiwan. In Taiwan, as Lam and Paltiel (1994) pointed out, Confucian orthodoxy *is* the dominant culture. But it is not the only, or necessarily the most important, dimension of culture in Taiwan. There is also a diverse and dynamic heterodox culture, which includes **Taoist**, Buddhist, and other subcultures or countercultures. Indeed, in Taiwan's case, Lam and Paltiel argued that it is the very dominance of Confucianism—which is premised on stifling restrictions and on stereotyped behavior—that has spurred the development of Taiwan's strong and long-standing underground counterculture. More important, Lam and Paltiel contend that it is this counterculture that defines and governs Taiwanese capitalism and not the dominant

Confucian culture. If they are right, then the Taiwanese case, *by itself,* would be enough to put to rest the grander and even not-so-grand claims made by advocates of the Confucian argument.

So, are they right? Lam and Paltiel made a compelling case. They began by pointing out an "indisputable fact," namely, that small- to medium-scale enterprises (SMSEs) have played a major role in Taiwan's economy. Although it would be incorrect to say that SMSEs are unimportant in Japan (or South Korea), it is clear that their role in Taiwan is far more significant. On this point, for example, Lam and Paltiel noted that firms with 200 employees or fewer account for 50 to 70 percent of Taiwan's exports. In Japan and South Korea, by contrast, superlarge firms utterly dominate the export market. The authors argued that this difference is due, in no small measure, to the particular political and social context of Taiwan (especially compared to Japan or South Korea). As they put it, "One factor that has engendered the proliferation of small-scale enterprise and reinforced its heterodox character in Taiwan is the social distance between the majority Taiwanese and the minority mainlanders who monopolized state power through the KMT [Kuomintang, the dominant political party in Taiwan]" (n.p.). The interaction between politics and culture, in other words, has helped to create unique economic arrangements in Taiwan. You will remember that the same could be said of Japan.

Unlike the situation in Japan, however, the glorification of Confucian values did not encourage cooperation and social harmony, much less provide the basis for rapid economic growth. Rather, in the context of Taiwan's postwar society, the attempt by the elite to inculcate a Confucian orthodoxy in the "hearts and minds" of the Taiwanese people led to widespread contempt and distrust of impersonal and patriarchal authority. In other words, it led to the growth of an *anti*-Confucian attitude in the general population. Indeed, as Lam and Paltiel argued, to fully understand the prevalence of SMSEs in Taiwan, one must take account of the strong anti-Confucian bias among entrepreneurs and ordinary citizens. As they explained it:

> As a firm begins to expand beyond the family, hires more distantly related persons, and forms partnerships with friends and even "outsiders," tensions and cracks begin to appear in the organizational structure of the firm. The classical Confucian reaction to these tensions is for the firm's "patriarch" to begin to act much like the Emperor in the state by replacing strictly personal, face-to-face loyalty with the more abstract loyalty of orthodoxy and punishing "unorthodox" or innovative behavior within the firm as "disloyalty," especially where it involves nonfamily members. Patriarchal behavior in the firm typically exacerbates underlying factional tensions and leads talented and innovative individuals to vote with their feet and form their own firms. . . . The tendency for talented individuals to exit larger firms as the firms' competitiveness declines partially explains why there is a large number of small-scale enterprises in Taiwan (n.p.).

More than encouraging the growth of SMSEs, Taiwan's strongly anti-Confucian bias helped to create a freewheeling, hypercompetitive domestic market that has imbued the Taiwanese economy with dynamism and resiliency. The underlying strength of the Taiwanese economy, the reason for the country's prosperity, to reiterate, is not Confucianism but the opposite: the *rejection* of Confucian values, combined with the embrace of heterodox, primarily Taoist, values. Lam and Paltiel went even farther than this. They claimed that where Confucianism is strongest in Taiwan's economy—in the largest, often state-owned firms—dynamism and entrepreneurism are weakest. In sum, *they argued that, in Taiwan, Confucianism has been a largely dysfunctional ideology insofar as capitalist development is concerned.*

Revealing the anti-Confucian foundation of the Taiwanese economy, however, is not enough to account for the country's economic success. There must also be, from a cultural perspective, something that creates a positive (economic) dynamic. According to Lam and Paltiel, this is not difficult to find. Simply put, it is the complex webs or networks of tightly integrated but independent firms. These are a product of anti-Confucianism generally but, more specifically, are a reflection of *guanxi,* or personal connections. Lam and Paltiel argued that Taiwanese firms have put great effort into establishing "close personal ties of *guanxi* between people as a way of subverting the orthodox Confucian order. Because of the unique relationships between firms in Taiwan, networks are created that facilitate challenges to the orthodoxy" (n.p.). On this point, it is important to understand that these networks do far more than facilitate "challenges to the orthodoxy"; they also have allowed Taiwan's SMSEs to create a functional substitute for large, hierarchically organized firms that, despite their drawbacks, provide a critical economic advantage, namely, economies of scale. Indeed, in international competition, "size" often is the key advantage to defeating rivals and dominating markets. Taiwan's SMSEs have been able to overcome their size disadvantage, however, precisely because they are part of a large but highly flexible network of firms. In fact, Lam and Paltiel argued that these networks, in many cases, are better thought of as constituting "group corporations" (*jituan gong*). If one wants to understand the reasons for Taiwan's prosperity, then the place to look most carefully is in the structure and dynamics of the country's business networks and group corporations. The key point to remember, though, is that these structures have a unique cultural foundation.

Culture and Capitalist Development: A Few Methodological Issues

From this brief summary of two cultural accounts, one thing should be clear: Confucian values have played very different roles in East Asian capitalism. Nor should this be a surprise. After all, to a culturalist, it is natural to expect societies—even those that seemingly share many traits—to differ in substantial and pervasive ways. This does not mean that we should automatically ignore or gloss over similarities between societies. Rather, it means that we should be extremely wary of efforts to generalize across cases, particularly without engaging in very careful, in-depth comparative-historical research. Indeed, in the cases of Japan and Taiwan, just a little careful (comparative) checking allowed us to see that Confucianism, *as a general concept,* explains little, if anything, about the nature of capitalist development in the two countries. That is, just knowing that Japan and Taiwan are "Confucian societies" does not tell us if Confucian values contributed to or undermined capitalist development in both countries. It certainly does not tell us *how* Confucian values impacted capitalist development (whether positively or negatively), even at the most general level. Instead, we learned that understanding the *context* of Confucianism is critical for a meaningful culture-based argument. In this regard, it is never enough to say that "Confucianism matters" or, more broadly, that "culture matters." Instead, it is crucial to examine, in as much depth and specificity as possible, the relationship between cultural factors and the broader political economy. Failing to do this will likely result in a vacuous argument. This is, I hope, a simple lesson you will keep in mind. At the same time, although cultural theorists tell us to avoid overgeneralizing, structuralists adopt, as you already know, a strongly contrasting approach. We will look at this research tradition next.

■ Global Capitalism and the Rise of East Asia

In general, structural accounts of East Asian capitalism do not completely reject the arguments made by scholars using different theoretical approaches. Indeed, as So and Chiu (1995) stated, each of the various perspectives (rationalist—or statist—and cultural) has "made a significant contribution to our understanding of the East Asian economic phenomenon" (p. 21). A major problem, however, is that these perspectives are unidisciplinary, by which So and Chiu mean that they tend to focus too heavily on one factor (or set of factors), and they tend to talk past one another. "What is missing . . . is a comprehensive meta-perspective that examines the complex interactions among economic, political, cultural forces in shaping East Asian development" (p. 21). So and Chiu also listed a number of other problems, the most serious of which is that none of the conventional perspectives properly accounts for the "big picture," so to speak. That is, they disregard or pay too little attention to the *system-wide dynamics of global capitalism* (pp. 21–22), which the authors suggest are far more determinative of national economic success than culture, strong states, or a "rational" domestic economic environment.

It is this last point upon which I will focus in this section, for it is the attention given to systemic dynamics that most clearly separates contemporary structural approaches from the others we have already discussed. In this regard, I should note at the outset that the structuralist account presented here is based primarily on the world-systems framework, which is only one of many structurally oriented perspectives. It is, however, an increasingly influential one, and this is the major reason for my focus on the world-system perspective in this section (and in the previous chapter).

East Asia in the World-System

Bruce Cumings, to whom I referred in Chapter 1, provided one of the first and most influential analyses of capitalist development in East Asia using (but not entirely adhering to) a world-systems approach. Drawing from a core premise of world-systems theory, Cumings began his analysis by declaring that any effort to portray capitalist development in East Asia as primarily a *national* phenomenon is fundamentally misguided. This is true, in large part, because national- or state-level analyses cannot account for the simultaneous and remarkably similar trajectories of South Korea and Taiwan—two countries that (in his comparative view) exhibit more differences than similarities in terms of culture, language, history, and ethnic makeup. In place of discrete, country-by-country analyses, Cumings suggested (demanded, even) that we adopt a dramatically different methodological approach, one "that posits the systemic interaction of each country with the others, and of the region with the world at large" (Cumings 1987, p. 47). In more concrete terms, this meant placing East Asian capitalism "within the context of two hegemonic systems: the Japanese imperium to 1945, and intense, if diffuse, American hegemony since the late 1940s" (p. 47). It only through considerations of this **hegemonic** context, Cumings argued, that one "can account for the similarities in the Taiwanese and South Korean political economies" (p. 47).

The importance of hegemony. Cumings used the term **hegemony** in a specific way. As he put it, "by hegemony [I mean] the demarcation of outer limits in economics, politics, and international security relationships, the transgression of which carries grave risks for any nonhegemonic nation" (Cumings 1987, p. 49). Translated into layperson's terms, Cumings was simply saying that hegemony determines what certain countries can and cannot do. In this perspective, the hegemonic country obviously occupies the top rung of a global or international hierarchy, but this does not mean that it is free to act in any manner it sees fit. This is because the hegemon, like all countries, is structurally embedded in a global (or world) system that creates its own pressures or demands. These pressures or demands create both opportunities and constraints; they also shape and, to a certain extent, determine the courses of action open to individual countries, from the strongest and wealthiest to the weakest and poorest. Such was the case in East Asia. In the case of Japan, for example, its relative lack of industrialization (in the mid-1800s) left open few possibilities. Indeed, one can argue that Japan had little choice but to try mimicking and beating the West at its own "game." This meant adopting capitalist practices and jumping into the competition for colonial possessions.

Capitalist development and "flying geese." Fortunately for Japan, it already had the internal capacity not only to play in the Western game but to do exceptionally well. What was fortunate for Japan, however, was not so fortunate—at least at the time—for Korea and Taiwan, both of which (as I discussed earlier) became colonial possessions. Yet, as Cumings argued, the colonial subjugation of Korea and Taiwan was not all bad (from the standpoint of capitalist development), for it was the forced integration of the three economies that created the basis for regional prosperity in the postcolonial (or postwar) period. Indeed, as Cumings put it, "However much it may pain the majority of Korean nationalists and the minority of Taiwanese nationalists, the place to begin in comprehending the region's economic dynamism is with the advent of Japanese imperialism" (Cumings 1987, p. 51). Cumings's reasoning here was largely (albeit not entirely) based on what is known as the product cycle or "flying geese" model of industrial development (see Figure 5.4). To put it very simply, this model is characterized by a particular pattern of industrial development, whereby a dominant economy (Japan) first masters a particular industrial sector (for example, textiles, steel, automobiles, light electronics, semiconductors) and then, when profit margins begin to decline owing to increased labor or other costs, transfers production (in whole or in part) to designated "follower" countries (Taiwan and South Korea).

Over the past century, Cumings noted, this pattern has characterized the economic relationship among Japan, South Korea, and Taiwan in almost textbook fashion. During the colonial period, of course, the benefits to Korea and Taiwan were minimal, but in the postwar period, things have obviously changed quite a bit. The reasons for this are varied, but it is not difficult to surmise that changes in the international system and in the dynamics of the world system have played a decisive role.

Making the world safe for capitalism. One of the biggest changes was the emergence of a new hegemony, which was premised on the simple but profound assumption that postwar stability could best (and perhaps only) be achieved by "making the world safe for capitalism." Although this may have been a largely self-serving belief on the part of Americans, it accurately reflected the systemic demands of a world economy premised on the unremitting accumulation of capital. From the perspective of world-systems theory, this goes a long way toward explaining the postwar prosperity of East Asia as a whole, and South Korea and Taiwan specifically. The logic is clear: capitalism *requires* large and growing markets, yet because of the emergence of

Figure 5.4   Flying Geese Model

Proponents of the "flying geese" model point to the fact that Japan moved from importing textile technology from England to producing its own textiles and then "upgraded" to the manufacture and export of cars and high-tech electronic products. At a certain point in the "product cycle" for each of these industries, Japanese firms then invested in Taiwan and South Korea, aiding their "economic miracles." Next came Indonesia, Thailand, and others, forming what is said to be a third tier of "geese." We can add China and Vietnam as the fourth tier.

international communism led by the Soviet Union, large parts of the world were cut off from capitalist expansion. This situation created a strong imperative on the part of the leading capitalist power, the United States, to establish or re-establish strong centers of capitalism everywhere the opportunity existed.[3] Japan was *selected* to be the center of capitalism in East Asia, and South Korea and Taiwan were eventually (and literally) *selected* to be Japan's hinterland or periphery.[4] Once this decision was made, the same general model of economic integration imposed during the colonial period was re-established among the three East Asian economies.

East Asian capitalism: Development by invitation. The difference this time around, however, was that the new hegemony was much less restrictive than the previous version. Indeed, it was not only less restrictive but seemingly altruistic in that the United States poured in a massive amount of economic and military aid, provided military protection, and opened its markets to all three East Asian countries.[5] (Of course, the "altruism" of the United States was based on broader geopolitical concerns and not on any generalized desire to help poor countries develop.) Whatever the case, US support allowed South Korea and Taiwan to turn their status as receptacles for declining Japanese industries into springboards into the massive US market, *and this is what created the basis for prosperity in East Asia as a whole.* Indeed, in the parlance of world-systems theory, we can say that all three East Asian countries were "invited" to develop.

It is fairly easy to see, at this point, that the interpretation of East Asian prosperity from the perspective of world-systems theory gives very little credit to the countries themselves. If anything, the economic rise of Japan, South Korea, and Taiwan is portrayed as almost entirely a function of forces beyond the control of strong states, capable entrepreneurs, visionary political leaders, hardworking (and well-educated) populations, or any other domestically based factor. And this is precisely the point that world-systems analysts such as Cumings wish to make.

World-systems and agency: The role of the East Asian states. At the same time, Cumings and others do not discount domestic factors completely; they suggest that, to take the best advantage of the opportunities presented (or the invitations extended), for example, strong and capable states do matter. So do particular social relationships, institutional arrangements, economic policies, and so on. This is the main reason why, despite almost identical positions in the regional and world-systems, Taiwan and South Korea followed divergent paths of development during the postwar period. Today, for instance, a handful of South Korean conglomerates have entered the ranks of the global business elite, whereas Taiwan's major private-sector companies remain, by comparison, quite small. Differences are also apparent in labor-business relations, in the pattern of democratization, in the role of civil society, in economic strategies, and so on. These differences, to reiterate, cannot be explained by reference to world-systemic dynamics *alone;* instead, it is necessary to examine the complex interaction among a number of world-systemic, regional, and domestic factors on the one hand and social, political, economic, and cultural factors on the other hand. This represents the holistic methodological approach upon which world-systems theory and other structuralist approaches are based.

The macrodynamics of the world-system, it is also worth noting, cannot fully account for the rise of Japan as a viable competitor to the United States.

That is, although world-systemic dynamics tell us why Japan pursued the path it did in the mid- to late 1800s (that is, to avoid being incorporated into the world capitalist system as a peripheral territory) and why Japan was "chosen" to develop after the end of World War II (that is, to further the geopolitical goals of the United States), they do not tell us—except in a very general manner—how Japan achieved its status as a global economic "superpower." Again, to answer this question, we must turn to an analysis of regional- and domestic-level factors, such as Japan's industrial and financial policies, its unique business structure (for example, networks of vertically or horizontally linked companies known as *keiretsu*), its culturally based pattern of industrial relations, and its "strategic deployment" of foreign investment throughout Asia.[6] To be sure, in assessing the importance of regional and domestic factors, it is critical to do so with a keen appreciation of how broader systemic and geopolitical forces helped or hindered Japan's economic ascendancy. But again, this is the strength of the world-systems framework.

■ Conclusion

It should be apparent that there is no easy answer to the question, why is East Asia rich? Saying this, however, does not mean that the question is unanswerable. Far from it. Indeed, one can argue that there are a number of plausible, even compelling, explanations for East Asian prosperity. Certainly, each of the major research traditions provides valuable insights into the process of "successful" capitalist development, although perhaps none provides a fully satisfactory account. This is not uncommon, nor is it necessarily surprising. For real-world capitalist development is a complex and—many would argue—highly contingent phenomenon, which is something you would be well advised to keep in mind. That is, the lack of a single, overarching explanation for capitalist development in all places, for all times, may be due to the possibility that no such explanation exists. There may be, to put it in slightly different terms, multiple explanations and multiple truths about the process of capitalist development.

At the same time, students must recognize that not all explanations are equally valid. The better theories of capitalist development need to be supported by an appropriate method and by evidence. In this regard, as I noted at the outset of this chapter, a comparison of *only* Japan, South Korea, and Taiwan is problematic. This is especially true if the researcher is not even aware of the logical pitfalls of comparing three "most similar systems" that do not vary on the dependent variable. One way to mitigate this problem, as I also noted, is to use within-case comparisons. In principle, this is an excellent strategy to use in conjunction with an MSS design in which the choice of cases is extremely limited. Unfortunately, this strategy is not always available. Of the three cases, for instance, South Korea is the only one in which a within-case comparison is unequivocally appropriate, since there is a clear demarcation between two periods: (1) a period of stagnant and declining economic development (dependent variable X_1) and (2) a period of rapid economic development (dependent variable X_2). In addition, between the two periods, there was also a major change in the political regime (an independent variable) while a range of other factors remained essentially the same.

Even when within-case comparisons are possible, however, a good research design will also incorporate other, completely separate cases, even if only on a secondary level. To "test" or further buttress the structural argument, for example, a researcher might find other cases that seem to have the same geopolitical advantages of the Japanese, South Korean, and Taiwanese cases. In this view, the Philippines might be a good candidate, since it was also a bastion of anticommunism, with a "special relationship" with the United States. In addition, the Philippines also had a "strong state," composed of highly trained and well-educated bureaucrats (often called technocrats). Unlike South Korea and Taiwan, however, the Philippines—which otherwise might be classified as a "most different system"—did not experience a comparable period of rapid industrialization, nor was its economy integrated into a regional economy led by Japan. Perhaps this was the critical difference. Or not. Only additional research and investigation can tell us the answer. We could use the Philippines, too, to test the rational choice argument, which focuses more heavily on the state itself. The key question here might be how and why did the Filipino state significantly differ from the East Asian states? Even a culturalist might have something to add, since the cultural foundation of the Philippines and its historical experience are very different from those of Japan, South Korea, and Taiwan. (Admittedly, using the Philippines also raises methodological issues, since, as a most different system, it would be better if the dependent variable did not differ from Japan, South Korea, and Taiwan. On this point, however, we are faced with the practical problem of simply not having enough cases to fulfill the strict requirements of our research design—that is, the small-N problem.)

The Philippines, of course, is just one possible example. North Korea and China, to consider two other candidates, might also be a good case for comparative analysis. Both are communist countries, but although North Korea has been mired in economic stagnation for several decades, China has become the fastest-growing economy in the world over the past several years. Notably, this did not happen until China embraced capitalism. Yet politically the country remains "communist," which has had profound implications in terms of its social, cultural, and political development since 1949. The same is true of North Korea. In this regard, China and North Korea can easily be considered most different systems compared to Japan, South Korea, and Taiwan, but compared to each other, the two communist countries are most similar systems. Comparing the five countries, then, would allow us to use a mixed research strategy, which would help us assess not only the various theoretical explanations offered in this chapter but also any argument about capitalist development. There are, moreover, many other viable candidates for comparison, both in and outside Asia. A "good comparativist" will keep her eyes open to all the possibilities.

■ Notes

1. One can argue that this basic context remained unchanged for the roughly twenty-year period between the early 1950s and early 1970s. But, in the early 1970s, as one well-regarded scholar noted, things began to change. "Public readiness to sacrifice present for future economic rewards turned to insistence upon a reexamination of priorities. Individual and collective demands for improved living conditions, even at the expense of lower growth rates, recurred constantly. The opposition parties were outspoken in their challenges to the policies of high growth. As a result of all these changes in the context of economic policy, a substantial shift took place in both the agenda and the process of Japanese economic policy" (Pempel 1982, p. 52).

2. For further discussion, see Woo (1991), especially chap. 3.

3. This particular argument was articulated in much greater depth and detail by Thomas McCormick in his book *America's Half-Century* (1989).

4. In his article, Cumings argued that US policymakers originally designated Southeast Asia as the "preferred candidate for Japan's hinterland" (Cumings 1987, p. 62). The idea was that Southeast Asia would provide markets for Japan's textiles and light industrial exports, and Japan would have access to badly needed raw materials. "The problem," however, "was that France and Britain sought to hold the countries in the region exclusively, and nationalist movements resisted both the Europeans and a reintroduction of the Japanese" (p. 62).

5. From 1945 to 1978, South Korea received about $13 billion in US military and economic aid, and Taiwan received about $5.6 billion (on a per capita basis, the amounts are much closer: $600 and $425 for South Korea and Taiwan respectively). Although by today's standards these amounts may not seem like much, the truth is that they represent a staggering amount in comparative terms. Consider, for example, that the amount of grants and loans received by South Korea alone from 1946 to 1978 equaled almost 90 percent of aid received by all African countries combined during the same period and about 40 percent of total economic aid to Latin America (Cumings 1987, p. 67).

6. Walter Hatch and Kozo Yamamura (1996) argued that Japanese investment in Asia is based on a strategic deployment of technology designed to build an expanded and potentially exclusive production zone that will essentially amount to an extension of Japan's domestic industrial base. Students who are interested in further exploring Japan's regional role in Asia should read Peter Katzenstein and Takashi Shiraishi's *Network Power* (1997), which examines the effects of Japan's dominance on the politics, economics, and culture throughout the region.

6

What Makes a Democracy?

Explaining Democratic Transition and the Breakdown of Authoritarian Rule

As recently as the early 1990s, but especially since the mid-1970s—the so-called Third World was still dominated by military governments, one-party regimes, and personal dictatorships (Pinkney 2003). Today, however, the situation has changed dramatically. Indeed, as Pinkney described it,

> virtually all the governments of Latin America . . . [are now] chosen by means of competitive elections. Asia, South Korea, Bangladesh, Thailand, Nepal, the Philippines, and Indonesia, have all emerged from authoritarian, military, or personal rule, and single party domination in Taiwan has ended with the main opposition party winning a free election. In sub-Saharan Africa the vast majority of countries have held competitive elections since 1990, even though many authoritarian tendencies persist and political violence continues. (p. 1)

To this list, we can also add much, but by no means all, of Eastern Europe: Croatia, the Czech Republic, Estonia, Hungary, Latvia, Lithuania, Poland, Slovakia, Bulgaria, and Romania (and at least nine other "partial democracies").[1] The main exceptions to this general trend—or the latest "wave" of democratization[2]—are most of North Africa, the Middle East, and parts of Asia, including China, which is a major exception all by itself. Impressive as the most recent wave of democratization is, it is still important to recognize that many countries have been or are in constant danger of being pulled back out to sea, so to speak. That is, even though a good number of countries seemed to have achieved a more or less permanent democratic transformation (often referred to as "consolidated democracy"), many others continue to struggle in the transitional stage. In fact, according to Barbara Geddes (1999), of eighty-five countries that underwent a transition from authoritarian rule to democracy between 1974 and 1999, fully fifty-five suffered a serious setback: nine lasted only a very short time before being overthrown; eight had elections and leadership changes but are otherwise very unstable; four descended into "warlordism"; and thirty-four reverted back to **authoritarianism**.

■ Explaining Democracy: Methodological Promise, Theoretical Shortfalls

Such figures suggest that democracy is a complex and problematic process. And it is, both in the "real world" and in the world of academic analysis. With regard to the academic world, scholars and comparativists, so far, have been unsuccessful in developing a *universal* explanation about the process(es) of democratic transition and consolidation. Indeed, there are dozens of competing, sometimes contradictory explanations. Of course, this should not surprise you. We have already seen that comparativists disagree strongly about the reasons for the seemingly intractable problem of poverty throughout the world or, conversely, about the factors that lead to national prosperity. Unlike the issues of poverty and prosperity, however, there appears to be a much firmer methodological (especially comparative) basis for explaining transitions to or consolidations of democracy.

In the transition from communism in Europe and in the former Soviet Union, for example, dramatic regime change (toward both democracy *and* authoritarianism) occurred in some two dozen roughly similar countries virtually simultaneously. As McFaul (2002) explained it, this has provided "the perfect data set for testing extant theories and developing new hypotheses about regime change" (p. 212). Moreover, McFaul continued, "[c]lear variation on the dependent variable with a finite set of independent variables would seem to offer a unique laboratory to isolate causal patterns" (p. 212). Despite this, theory development, or at least "big" theory development (see Figure 6.1), regarding regime change has hardly advanced (p. 212). There may be several good reasons for this, the most salient of which, perhaps, is simply that no general, all-inclusive explanation is possible. McFaul and others seem to agree, although this does not mean valuable "middle-range" theories on democratization are likewise impossible.

■ Democracy and the Three Research Traditions

The tension between general and middle-range theories, however, is not a central concern of this chapter. Instead, our main point of focus, as in our other chapters, is how the three research schools have sought to explain or help us understand the process of democratic transition.[3] As we shall see, al-

---

Figure 6.1   A Note on Method: Using Comparative Analysis to "Test" Big Claims

---

It is useful to take careful note of the contrasting conclusions of regional studies concerning the transition from communism, for they highlight a key point of comparative analysis discussed earlier in this book. To put the issue simply, even fairly broad comparative analysis provides a quick way to "test" or control for the bigger claims made by researchers who look primarily at democratization in a single region or even across several regions. At a minimum, the experiences of the postcommunist states force scholars to come to terms with evidence that, on the surface at least, does not conform to their theoretical claims.

though there is sharp disagreement among the various perspectives, there is also a great deal of overlap and, therefore, perhaps even greater potential for meaningful theoretical synthesis, especially compared to the other issues we have explored. This is a very important point to keep in mind as you proceed through the chapter. Before we examine the various explanations and accounts of democratic transition and consolidation, however, we need to define or at least discuss the meaning of the term "democracy." As we have learned, definitions are important. This is especially the case for a concept such as democracy that, despite its seemingly straightforward nature (for example, "majority rule" or "rule of the many"), is actually an extremely elusive and contested concept. Certainly the concept of democracy is far more problematic than the concepts of poverty and prosperity.

■ Defining Democracy

A Formal Definition

To begin this section, it would be useful to reiterate a reason why definitions of key concepts are important. To put it in very simple terms, unless we can adequately define (delimit and specify) what we are talking about, we cannot have a meaningful "scientific" conversation. Indeed, if we do not adequately define the main topic of our conversation, we may end up talking about something entirely different. If the main topic, moreover, is a key variable in one's analysis (as "democracy" in one form or another is), then it is even more important to provide a clear and specific definition. This said, in the academic literature, democracy is generally defined either formally (that is, narrowly) or substantively, or sometimes as a combination of the two. The formal definition of democracy *is* straightforward. Here is one definition offered by Anthony Giddens (2000), an eminent sociologist: "I would say democracy exists where you have a multiparty system with political parties competing with one another, free and non-corrupt voting procedures to elect political leaders, and an effective legal framework of civil liberties or human rights that underlie the mechanisms of voting processes" (n.p.). If we break this definition down, we have three readily discernible components of democracy: (1) a competitive multiparty system, (2) free and noncorrupt elections, and (3) an effective legal framework of civil liberties or human rights. To this list we might add a fourth component: universal and equal suffrage (suffrage is simply the right or privilege of voting). These four components constitute what many, but not all, scholars would consider the minimum requirements for democracy. But this raises an obvious question: are the "minimum requirements" enough? That is, is a country that has a competitive multiparty system, free and noncorrupt elections, an effective legal framework of civil liberties or human rights, and universal or near-universal suffrage a "real" democracy? Or is something else—something more substantive—required?

Formal vs. Substantive Conceptions of Democracy

Not surprisingly, the answer, at least to numerous scholars and ordinary citizens alike, is clear: much more is required. Michael Saward (1999), for example, proposed "that democracy be understood as a political system in which the citizens themselves have an *equal effective* input into the making of binding collective decisions. A non-democratic system is a system in which some individual or sub-group possesses superior power to make binding collective decisions without any formal accountability to citizens" (emphasis added; p. 15). Under this definition, many countries generally considered democracies today would not qualify as democracies at all, since it is almost unquestioningly clear that individuals and subgroups within these countries, especially large corporations and other special interests, possess the "superior power" of which Saward spoke. Saward, of course, is not alone. David Held, to cite just one more (and one very prominent) example, argued that a justifiable account of democracy must be premised on the principle of autonomy. As Held (1987) explained it, autonomy means that "individuals should be free and equal in the determination of the conditions of their own lives; that is, they should enjoy equal rights [and, accordingly, equal obligations] in the specification of the framework which generates and limits the opportunities available to them, so long as they do not deploy this framework to negate the rights of others" (p. 271). Democracy, in this view, implies a high level of accountability from all members of society and a limitation on the exercise of political power. It also calls upon, as Sørenson (1993) noted, "a bill of rights that goes beyond the right to cast a vote to include equal opportunity for participation and for discovering individual preferences as well as citizens' final control of the political agenda" (p. 10). This means that citizens in general must have the resources—ensured through social and economic rights—to exercise democratic autonomy. For, as Held argued, "without tough social and economic rights, rights with respect to the state could not be full enjoyed; and without state rights new forms of inequality of power, wealth and status could systematically disrupt the implementation of social and economic liberties" (cited in Sørenson 1993, p. 10).

The substantive definitions of democracy offered by Saward, Held, and others are certainly important, even essential. One reason is clear: their definitions tell us that formal conceptions provide, in general, only a minimal framework for democracy. Much is left out, albeit purposely, in order to establish a firm foundation for "scientific" analysis. In a more subtle vein, substantive definitions tell us that democracy is likely to be (and is) imperfect even in what many people might consider to be the most "advanced" of democratic societies. In this regard, substantive definitions are intentionally and explicitly normative, that is, they tell us that we must not be satisfied with nominally democratic systems (that is, democracy in name only). We must, instead, strive for the ideal. Substantive definitions likewise tell us that democracy is not necessarily the same everywhere, even when the outward trappings—that is, elections, competitive parties, protections of basic rights—are the same. In other words, it is not only possible but concretely obvious that real-world "democracies" take on a wide variety of different forms.

The Case for a Formal Definition of Democracy

Still, according to other scholars, this is a key reason why a substantive definition of democracy is not always helpful for researchers and comparativists intent on developing an explanation of democratic transitions and consolidation. Sørenson (1993) explained it this way: A substantive definition "does not give us much guidance in determining whether specific countries are democratic. For that purpose we need a precise concept that provides a clear identification of what democracy essentially is" (p. 11). It is necessary, therefore, "to cut through the debates in order to find a *tool* with which we can identify democracy by its *core features,* as a form of government in which the people rule. Most helpful would be a *narrow concept* that focuses on democracy as a specific type of political system" (emphasis added; p. 11).

Sørenson, to be clear, is not an apologist—he is not making the case for a narrow definition of democracy in order to justify the less-than-ideal democracies that exist throughout the world, including (or especially) the United States. Instead, he is asserting that, in studying the phenomenon of democratic transition and consolidation, we need to set forth minimal and clearly identifiable boundaries for what *is* and what *is not* a democracy. If we fail to do this, comparativists and other researchers will face serious analytical difficulties, not the least of which is that the dependent variable—the outcome we are most interested in understanding/explaining—ends up being anything we want it to be, or nothing at all. Still, some of you no doubt remain uncomfortable with and even hostile to Sørenson's position. This is especially true if you believe that a formal definition of democracy is nothing but a sham, nothing but a way to mollify the "masses" into believing they have political power when, in fact, they do not (a position held by many Marxist and progressive scholars). In this case, Sørenson's argument would be far less defensible, perhaps indefensible. The key question, therefore, is this: does a formal definition of democracy have any meaning beyond its "operational" precision?

To many scholars who study and think about democracy, the answer to this question is an unequivocal, albeit often implicit, "yes." One set of scholars who address this question explicitly is Rueschemeyer, Stephens, and Stephens (1992). In their book *Capitalist Development and Democracy*, these authors asked, "Why do we care about formal democracy if it considerably falls short of the actual rule of the many?" (p. 10). Their answer was simple: "We care about formal democracy because it tends to be more than merely formal. *It tends to be real to some extent"* (emphasis added, p. 10). In other words, Rueschemeyer, Stephens, and Stephens believe that formal democracy matters. It matters because, once the most basic institutions, practices, and components of democracy are established in a society, they almost invariably create a "promising basis for further progress in the distribution of power and other forms of substantive equality" (p. 10). Specifically, the authors contended, "the same factors which support the installation and consolidation of formal democracy, namely the growth in the strength of civil society in general and of the lower classes in particular, also *support progress towards greater equality in political participation and towards greater social and economic equality"* (emphasis added; pp. 10–11). Whether or not you fully agree with Rueschemeyer, Stephens, and Stephens, it is important to carefully consider their points and the questions they raise. Does the mere establishment of certain institutions of democracy create the basis for substantive change in society (for example, toward greater social and economic equality)? Do these institutions, no matter how weak they may be or become, ultimately give political power to ordinary citizens—power that citizens would otherwise not have? Are real-world democracies "better" than the nondemocratic systems that preceded them?

The answers to these questions are not necessarily obvious. Nonetheless, a strong case can be made that formal democracy can be and invariably is more than an empty shell—that it has substance and meaning, even if largely and often unrealized, imperfect, or transitory. If we accept this premise, however, we need to return to the starting point of this section, namely, offering a working or **operational definition** of democracy. For our purposes, the minimal definition provided by Giddens above might well suffice. But it would be useful to at least consider other "minimal requirements." In this regard, one standard point of reference is Robert A. Dahl's classic definition. Among the requirements for democracy, Dahl argued that eight institutional guarantees are required: (1) freedom to form and to join organizations, (2) freedom of expression, (3) the right to vote, (4) eligibility for public office, (5) the right of political leaders to compete for support and votes, (6) alternative sources of information, (7) free and fair elections, and (8) institutions for making government policies depend on votes and other expressions of preference (1971, pp. 1–3).[4] Other scholars, although agreeing with Dahl's basic list of guarantees, argue that it is insufficient because it lacks, for example, the requirement for a "constitution that itself is democratic in that it respects fundamental liberties and offers considerable protections for minority rights" (Stepan 2000, p. 39).

Based on our discussion above, a country can be said to be democratic (or nondemocratic) when its political system satisfies (or fails to satisfy) the eight conditions set forth by Dahl and when it has a constitution that guarantees fundamental liberties and protections for minority rights. Whichever formal definition you choose (or whichever definition researchers use in their analyses), it is important to remember the main purpose. To repeat, a *formal* definition of democracy is designed, first and foremost, to provide a clear-cut basis for analysis—for determining, at a minimum, the basic dividing line between (real-world) democracies and nondemocracies. If a researcher cannot or will not do this, then there is little reason to even attempt an analysis of how and why countries democratize *in a concrete sense,* which is the topic of this chapter. After all, if you do not define what democracy is, or if your definition essentially excludes all or mostly all real-world cases, then any analysis of "democracy" will be empirically (and perhaps even theoretically) empty. A formal definition of democracy is also a necessary starting point for differentiating between "strong" (or consolidated) democracies and weak or highly restricted democracies—and given the relatively large number of "failed democracies," this distinction is hardly trivial.

Explaining or accounting for changes in the democratization process, of course, is the main topic of this chapter and our next subject of discussion. Unlike the previous two chapters, however, we will begin with the structural school. The reason, although not immediately apparent, is straightforward: many, albeit not all, researchers and comparativists accept the premise that some level of structural changes—particularly in the balance of power within a given society—is essential to democratic transformation and consolidation. Even those who do not explicitly agree with this premise are unlikely to assert that democracy can happen in any context, at any time, without the balance of power's having first been affected in some manner.

■ Democracy, Power, and Class: A Structural Explanation

Democracy and Economic Development: A "Modernization" Reprise

It is virtually impossible to dispute, from an empirical perspective, the strong positive relationship between democratization and "economic development." (Here the concept of economic development is used in its narrowest sense—the accumulation of economic wealth as measured through increases in *per capita* income.) Almost everyone acknowledges, in other words, that economic development is related to, but not necessarily a direct cause of, greater democracy. Agreeing that there is a relationship between economic development and democracy, however, is not the same as agreeing on the reasons for or the exact nature of this relationship. Indeed, within comparative politics (and the social sciences more generally), sharp and even fundamental differences exist among researchers who have attempted to explain this relationship. One school of thought—which derives from early research made most famous by Seymour Lipset—argues that democratization is the final stage in a general process of social change brought about by **modernization** (modernization, in this reading, is largely synonymous with capitalist development).[5] As explained by Przeworski and Limongi (1997),

> Modernization consists of a gradual differentiation and specialization of social structures that culminates in a separation of political structures from other structures and makes democracy possible. The specific causal chains consist of sequences of industrialization, urbanization, education, communication, mobilization, and political incorporation, among innumerable others: a progressive accumulation of social changes that ready a society to proceed to its culmination, democratization. (pp. 156–157)

In (contemporary) modernization accounts, then, the relationship between economic development and democratization is not one-dimensional. It is not, to put it very simply, just a matter of a country reaching a certain level of wealth and then magically transforming into a democracy (although popular accounts, to some extent, are based on this simplistic premise); rather, the transition to democracy happens because modernization creates new economic, social, technological, and political *conditions* that "primitive" or premodern political systems (for example, dictatorships) are simply unable to handle over the long run. One less obvious but very important product of these conditions is a viable **civil society**—that is, the set of social institutions, organizations, and associations that stand apart from the state. In modernization theory, civil society invariably challenges the state and favors democracy. The transition to democracy, in sum, may not always be smooth and completely predictable, but it is largely *irresistible* once (capitalist) economic development gets under way.

As you should already have discerned, modernization theory offers a structural—and strongly deterministic—account of democratic transformation. From the perspective of other structuralists (especially historical structuralists), however, it is a very limited account. It is limited, in part, because many of its advocates presume that the key to understanding democratic transformation can be found in the inability of nondemocratic political systems to deal with rising social, economic, and technological complexity. But, as a few exceptional cases clearly show—Singapore is perhaps the best contemporary example—authoritarian regimes not only are concretely capable of maintaining control over complex, "modern" societies but also are capable of managing these complexities in an effective and efficient manner over relatively long periods of time. Even if Singapore's authoritarian regime were to democratize fully tomorrow, the point remains: nondemocratic regimes have proven to be functionally capable of dealing with the complexities of modernization. (It is debatable whether Singapore fulfills the requirements of a formal democracy. Although the country has regular elections, civil liberties are often curtailed, and a single party utterly dominates the electoral system.) Modernization theory, according to its critics, is also limited because it does not account for numerous, but significant, exceptions, of which India is perhaps the most salient example (we will discuss the case of India below).

But if modernization theory is limited, how do these other structuralists explain the relationship between economic development and democratization? There is, of course, no single answer to this question. But one thought-provoking argument is provided by a set of authors we mentioned above, namely, Dietrich Rueschemeyer, Evelyne Huber Stephens, and John D. Stephens in their book *Capitalist Development and Democracy* (1992). We will focus on their argument for the remainder of this section.

Capitalist Development and Democracy: A Historical-Structural Interpretation

In laying out their explanation of the relationship between economic development and democracy, Rueschemeyer, Stephens, and Stephens began with a simple but telling observation (an observation, by the way, that researchers in the rational choice school also generally accept): the people (or the social class) that have predominant control over economic resources in society are generally not friends of democracy. Indeed, for the dominant groups in society, genuine democracy represents a concrete threat to their own interests, since, by its very nature, democracy gives power to subordinate classes who constitute the large majority of any society's population. Think of it this way: if the majority of people in a society are poor and exploited (which is often the case), would they not be immediately tempted, in a democratic system, to use their newfound and overwhelming voting power to redistribute economic resources and, ultimately, to undermine permanently—if not destroy—the position and privileges of the wealthy (or political and economic elite)? More to the point, would not the elite be well aware of this potential threat and, therefore, do whatever they could to prevent democracy from taking hold? The answer to both questions is clear: of course they would. It is largely for this reason that Rueschemeyer, Stephens, and Stephens argued that political democracy "inevitably stands in tension with the system of social inequality" (p. 41).

Given the almost undeniable tension between democracy and social inequality, Rueschemeyer, Stephens, and Stephens made a basic assertion, one that undergirded their entire argument: *democracy is above all a matter of power* (p. 5). By this they meant that democracy is not the product of altruism or of morality. It is not a "gift" given to the masses. Neither, as we have already discussed, does democracy emerge merely because society has become "too complex" or modernized. Instead, it is almost always a product of *political struggle*—a result of one or (more likely) several hitherto excluded groups assiduously fighting to break down barriers to their more complete participation in the political process. The struggle for democracy, however, is also *highly conditioned*. Specifically, transitions to (and consolidations of) democracy are conditioned—that is, constrained and enabled—by broad *structural changes* that reorder the balance of power among different classes and class coalitions in society. These structural changes, in turn, are primarily—although not exclusively—an inexorable product of capitalist development. As the authors explained it:

> Capitalist development is associated with the rise of democracy primarily because of two *structural effects:* it strengthens the working class as well as other subordinate classes, and it weakens large landowners. The first of these must be further specified: capitalist development enlarges the urban working class at the expense of agricultural laborers and small farmers; it thus shifts members of the subordinate classes from an environment extremely unfavorable for collective action to one much more favorable, from geographical isolation and immobility to high concentrations of people with similar interests and far-flung communications. (emphasis added; p. 58)

It is worth emphasizing that Rueschemeyer, Stephens, and Stephens were not merely dressing up modernization's structural argument in new clothes. It is not a generic and uniformly prodemocratic civil society that creates the basis for democratic transformation. Instead, it is a historically shaped civil society, within which class interests can and do play out in very different ways. In other words, the concrete role of various classes in various societies—with regard to the issue of democracy or any other social issue—will differ according to the particular historical circumstances in which they emerge and develop. "History matters," therefore, even in the face of large-scale structural change. At the same time, the authors argued that a specific segment of civil society—the *urban* (that is, nonagricultural) *working class*—almost always stands at the center of the struggle for democracy. The centrality of the urban working class is, to reiterate, no accident. As suggested in the passage above, this class is not only a direct product of the capitalist process, but it also is the most consistently and most important prodemocratic force within capitalist societies.

Democracy and the working class. The foregoing discussion raises an important question: *why* does the urban working class support, and more important, *how* does it bring about democratic transformation? The answer to the first part of the question should already be clear, namely, the urban working class supports democratic transformation because it is this class that has the most to gain from democracy, both in the short and long run (Rueschemeyer, Stephens, and Stephens 1992, p. 57). These authors, however, were careful to assert that class interests, and working-class interests in particular, are not given or objectively determined. Interests, instead, are **socially constructed**. By this they meant that class interests are variable and subjective—they are shaped by a large number of factors, including leadership, organizational dynamics, race, ethnicity, "history," and so on. Still, according to Rueschemeyer, Stephens, and Stephens, for the most part (and from a concrete historical perspective), the urban working class consistently and systematically favors democracy because democratic change gives members of this class greater control of economic and other resources in society, which ultimately gives members of this class greater control over their own lives.

The answer to the second part of the question (how does the urban working class bring about democratic transformation?) is less clear, but it goes to the heart of the authors' argument. To begin, it is important to re-emphasize two points made earlier. First, the capacity of the urban working class to bring about democratic transformation is, to a significant extent, a function of a changing "balance of power" within society. Second, shifts in the balance of power are the product of capitalist development, which simultaneously erodes the (relative) power of some social groups/classes while fortifying the power of others. In this regard, and just to underscore the main point here, it is not "capitalism" (or wealth creation) per se that creates the basis for democracy but capitalism's largely unintended and unavoidable effect on class structure—or as Rueschemeyer, Stephens, and Stephens put it, "It was not the capitalist market nor capitalists as the new dominant force, but rather the *contradictions* of capitalism that advanced the cause of democracy" (emphasis added; p. 7).

The main contradiction, to be clear, is this: although capitalism as a system is not designed to empower ordinary workers (in fact, capitalists, for the most part, are positively hostile to this outcome), this is exactly what it does. And it does so because capitalist development *necessarily* creates subordinate classes with the capacity for *self-organization*. The basis of this self-organization is explained by the authors: "Capitalism brings the subordinate class or classes together in factories and cities where members of those classes can associate and organize more easily; it improves the means of communication and transportation facilitating worldwide organization; in these and other ways it strengthens civil society and facilitates subordinate class organization" (pp. 271–272). Still, this does not tell *how* the urban working class actually brings about democratic transformation.

How the working class brings democracy. Here is where the answer becomes particularly complicated. This is largely because—as I have suggested several times already—the working-class role in democratization is highly *contingent* or context dependent (that is, dependent on particular historical, social, and geopolitical circumstances). This is a crucial point, and one that must not be underestimated. For it means, in part, that there is, according to Rueschemeyer, Stephens, and Stephens, no single or homogenous pattern of causation in the process of democratic transformation (p. 284); instead, there are (potentially) innumerable and innumerably divergent paths to democracy. On the surface, this makes the process of democratization very messy, theoretically speaking (a bane to many social "scientists"). But, underlying this ostensible messiness is, to repeat, *a key similarity:* an overall balance of power between classes (and between civil society and the state) that gives the urban working class the potential strength to challenge the status quo. From a methodological or comparative perspective, I might note, the challenge is to find and demonstrate the importance of this "key similarity" across as many cases as possible. With this in mind, then, the very broad contours of how the urban working class brings about democratic transformation are as follows.

First, once the urban working class develops a sufficient level of organizational strength, pressures and demands for greater political inclusion are brought to bear on the dominant class. This pressure, not surprisingly, is manifested through a variety of forms: radical mass political parties, organized labor unions, and broader-based labor movements (a type of social movement) are the most common. Sometimes the demands of the working class are met through **co-optation**, whereby the state or dominant classes accommodate some working-class interests without opening up the political system in a meaningful way. One of the best examples of this is in Mexico (according to the authors), where the subordinate classes, including the urban working class, have been effectively co-opted into state-sponsored and elite-controlled organizations for a long time. At other times, demands by the working class are met with violence and repression—this is especially likely when the organizational strength and ideological radicalism of the working class are particularly high and, therefore, particularly threatening to the dominant classes. We can see evidence of this throughout the developing world. In most situations, however, even a well-organized urban working class is not strong enough to achieve an expansion of political and democratic rights *on its own*; this was generally the case in the countries that underwent capitalist industrialization early on (for example, in Western Europe, the United States, and Commonwealth countries) and is even more significant for the late industrializing countries of the twentieth century. For this reason, the working class has invariably had to rely on establishing *alliances* across class boundaries. This is the second, and more salient, part of the answer of how the working class, in concrete terms, brings about democratization.

These alliances, as with the interests of the working class itself, are not predetermined. That is, the allies of the working class are not always the same. Historically, for example, it was the urban and the rural **petty bourgeoisie** (merchants, craftsmen, farmers, and other self-employed groups) who were the most significant allies of the working class in Europe. In Latin America and East Asia, however, the most important ally has been the employed **middle classes** (and, in the case of South Korea in particular, college students). Because of the variable nature of class alliances—and because working-class power itself is a highly variable phenomenon—the specific role the working class plays in the process of democratization also varies across time and space. Sometimes (in fact, quite often) this role will be subtle and seemingly secondary and sometimes quite obvious and important. Nonetheless, in virtually all cases, the working class constitutes an essential *foundation* for democratic change. On this latter point, it is important to note that, even when the middle class (or other allies of the working class) plays the leading role in pushing for democratic rule, the middle class "commitment to democracy [has] tended to be instrumental and contingent, aimed at their own exclusion and subject to abandonment in the face of militant lower-class pressures for radical reforms which [might affect] . . . the material conditions of middle-class life" (Rueschemeyer, Stephens, and Stephens 1992, p. 282). To put it more bluntly, one can never count on the middle class (or any other potential class ally of the working class) to support democracy; indeed, absent an alliance with the working class, the middle class tends to be antidemocratic (or favors only a highly exclusionary form of democracy). If this is true, though, why does the middle class (or other social class) ally with the urban working class in the first place? The answer should be obvious, for, just as the working class is sometimes too weak to bring about political change on its own, other excluded social classes are also too weak to accomplish their goals on their own.

Alliances and the balance of power among social classes within a given society obviously play a central role in the framework put forth by Rueschemeyer, Stephens, and Stephens. It is not surprising, then, that balance of class power constitutes the first and main configuration of power in their analytical framework. It should also be noted, however, that the authors put strong weight on two other broad configurations of power (or, as the authors put it, "clusters of power"): (1) the structure, strength, and autonomy of the state apparatus and its interrelations with civil society and (2) the impact of transnational power relations. Both factors deserve in-depth discussion, but for sake of brevity (and because they are explicitly not the analytical focal point of Rueschemeyer, Stephens, and Stephens), I will not cover them here. Suffice it to say, however, that the three clusters of power—largely because they are inextricably interrelated—all play an integral role in the process of democratic transformation and consolidation. Even more, each is generally a product of or deeply affected by long-established social patterns. For this reason, according to Rueschemeyer, Stephens, and Stephens, we must, without exception, avoid "presentist" explanations of democracy (that is, explanations of democracy that ignore history) or, in a similar vein, any "mechanical account of the impact of class, state and transnational power on constitutional form" (p. 7). In sum, to understand the process of democratic transition (and consolidation), we must engage in "comparative *historical* analysis, which can take . . . persistencies into account and respond sensitively to alternative paths of causation" (emphasis in original; p. 7).

Structure, Agency, and Method in
Capitalist Development and Democracy

It is clear that Rueschemeyer, Stephens, and Stephens's structural account of democratization does not completely dismiss the importance of agency. If anything, just the opposite may seem to be the case, as the urban working class—which must make a series of purposeful decisions to achieve its goals, including, but not limited to, creating strategic alliances with other classes— is accorded primacy as an agent of democratization. It is equally clear, however, that structural factors are at the core of their analysis. For it is only through an inexorable process of structural change that the conditions for working-class strength can be realized. Thus, to understand the "prospects" for democracy in a particular society, any analysis must start with an examination of underlying structural conditions and processes (which, as the authors assert, must include comparative *historical* analysis as well). Ignoring these conditions and processes—believing that democracy is possible "anywhere, anytime" as long as people "want it"—is analytically foolish and extremely naive. To assert, for example, that democracy in present-day Iraq is possible *merely* because Saddam Hussein and his cronies have been chased away is a "presentist" argument that assumes the only real obstacle to democracy in Iraq was the power of a single man and his regime. Whether democracy can be established and prosper in Iraq *is* certainly open to debate, but from the historical-structuralist perspective of Rueschemeyer, Stephens, and

Stephens, to properly address this question requires that we look carefully at the structures that define and shape the Iraqi condition today. (As we will shortly see, however, this is not a position that all comparativists accept.)

Before concluding this section, one last point on the issue of method is in order. The structuralist account that we have just read is abstract and empirically limited. (This is not to imply, however, that the analysis by Rueschemeyer, Stephens, and Stephens is empirically limited; in fact, they go into great depth and detail in their book. It is my summary of their argument that lacks empirical depth.) The historical reality of democratization, of course, is, in empirical terms, "messy" and complex. Rueschemeyer and his coauthors not only recognized this but also carried out a methodological strategy—much of which was based on the specific comparative strategies we discussed in Chapter 2—designed to deal head-on with this complexity. Their strategy was based on the concept of analytical induction that we discussed in Chapter 2. To refresh your memory, analytical induction is based on the idea of discerning general theoretical principles from only a few cases (a process called **induction**) and then "testing" and retesting these general principles through other detailed case studies (in comparative perspective). In the authors' words, "analytical induction builds its arguments from the understanding of individual histories" (p. 37).

At the same time, as you should also recall, this sort of approach, no matter how meticulously carried out, has shortcomings. Rueschemeyer, Stephens, and Stephens acknowledged these shortcomings. As they put it, "the speculative element, and even arbitrariness, can never be fully eliminated from such case-based theory building" (p. 37). It is important to note, however, that the authors did not rely solely on individual case studies. Instead, they used *multiple and overlapping comparative strategies* (or a mixed research design), including inter- and intraregional comparisons of three or more units, across broad stretches of history. Each of these comparisons, in turn, involved analyses of "most similar systems" and "most different systems." We don't have the time or space to cover this ground, but it is important to understand that no matter how persuaded or, conversely, no matter how unconvinced you are by their theoretical argument (or any theoretical argument), you must pay careful attention to the quality, depth, and comprehensiveness of the researchers' methods and evidence. When authors use multiple and overlapping strategies and do so with great care, all of which Rueschemeyer, Stephens, and Stephens did, then you are well advised to take the argument seriously. Of course, it is important, from a methodological point of view, always to consider what is left out. In *Capitalist Development and Democracy,* the authors have very little empirical and no systematic analysis of Asia, Africa, the Middle East—or, most pertinent today—post-Soviet Russia, Eastern Europe, and Central Asia. Yet, as we will see below, leaving out these major regions from their comparative study might very well weaken, if not seriously undermine, the theoretical generalizations they put forth. This point is taken up in our next section, which looks at actor-centric and rational choice explanations of democratization.

■ Agents of Democratization: Rational Choice and Democratic Transition

For many comparativists and other researchers, the structural approach outlined above offers a compelling portrait of democratization. It is theoretically coherent, methodologically rigorous, and empirically rich. Still, for others, the idea that democracy—and, more to the point, that the people who live under oppressive political regimes—must somehow "wait" for the conditions to produce it is simply untenable. In reflecting on his discomfort with old-fashioned structuralists, this is exactly what Przeworski (1997) argued. As he put it, "We [want] . . . to know what movements in different countries could do to bring dictatorships down rather than simply wait" (p. 6).[6] McFaul (2002), in even blunter terms, stated, "Inert, invisible structures do not make democracies or dictatorships. *People do.* Structural factors such as economic development, cultural influences, and historical institutional arrangements influence the formation of actors' preferences and power, but ultimately these forces have causal significance only if translated into human action" (emphasis added; p. 214). It is significant that neither McFaul nor Przeworski discounted structural factors completely, just as Rueschemeyer, Stephens, and Stephens did not completely discount agency; instead, they suggested that such factors are contributory to, as opposed to determinative of, democracy. The issue, then, may be one not necessarily of choosing between a structure-based and agent-centric approach but of determining the relative importance of each in explaining democratic transition (and consolidation).

Elite-Centered Explanations

For researchers wedded to a rational choice perspective, of course, the overriding emphasis will always be on the role that political actors play in the democratization process. Even so, this does not mean that all rationality-based or actor-centric explanations are the same. At the risk of oversimplification, we might say that there are two main variants: (1) elite-centered explanations and (2) mass-based mobilization (democratization from below). Elite-centered explanations themselves compose a relatively broad and diverse category of rationality-based approaches. As the name implies, this school of thought focuses on the role that the ruling elite plays in the process of democratization. The basic position in this school is that the transition to democracy (from an authoritarian regime specifically) is primarily the product of divisions or splits among elites. O'Donnell and Schmitter (1986) made this point very clearly and unequivocally in *Transitions from Authoritarian Rule: Prospects for Democracy.* There is, they categorically asserted, "no transition whose beginning is not the consequence—direct or indirect—of important divisions within the authoritarian regime itself, principally along the fluctuating cleavage between hard-liners and soft-liners" (pt. 4, p. 19).

The reference to "hard-liners" and "soft-liners" among the ruling elite in this view needs to be highlighted, for transitologists (as they are sometimes called) argue that these are *the* key choice-making actors in the large majority of democratic transitions. It is their decisions, generally arrived at through strategic interaction (that is, a process of calculating the costs and benefits for certain decisions *in relation to* the actions and interests of other relevant actors), that either lead to democracy or stop it in its tracks; it is their decisions and actions that provide the basis for democratic consolidation or that lead to a breakdown and reversion to authoritarian or some other nondemocratic form of governance. It is also important to understand, however, that there is a third set of actors we need to consider: actors who exist *outside* the established elite—these are moderates or radicals who want or demand political change. Although nonelites are not the main agents of change, the role of such outsiders is important because it is their challenge to the regime that brings about pressure for political change to begin with. That is, without the existence of challengers, the elite generally have no incentive to even consider bringing about political change. Once demands for change arise, however, the established elite are forced to react. If the elite are united and surmise that the challengers have little power, they will simply crush the opposition. A concrete and salient example of this was the crackdown on prodemocracy protesters in Tiananmen Square in Beijing in 1989. If the elite are divided and the challengers have some power, then the prospects for a compromise arise—a democratic transition is most likely when soft-liners in the regime have relatively equal power to hard-liners *and* when opposition is moderate, as opposed to radical. The relative equality of power is an important feature of this argument, for when one side within the elite has preponderant power, it will use that power to impose its will on everyone else; it is only when both sides within the elite realize that they cannot prevail unilaterally that they settle for compromised solutions. Even in this case, however, the dominance of the elite means that democracy is not "taken" by, but "given" to, the masses in a manner designed to protect the interests of the elite.

Thus, in strong contrast to the position espoused by Rueschemeyer, Stephens, and Stephens, advocates of elite-centered explanations portray democracy as being imposed on society from above or, alternatively, as being created through **pacts**, that is, through *negotiated agreements and bargaining* among contending elites that establish formulas for power sharing. This difference—between structuralists and elite-centered transitologists—raises a simple but very interesting question: who is right? After all, Rueschemeyer,

Stephens, and Stephens and most transitologists are examining many of the same cases, yet their interpretations of the "facts" are quite different. Although I cannot definitively answer this question here (indeed, my intention is to let you decide based on your own analysis), I raise the question to underscore a point made much earlier in this book: different theoretical "lenses" can and do lead to very different interpretations of the same empirical evidence.

Democratization from Below: An Alternative Rational Choice Explanation

A second major variant, and one that has more recent origins, derives primarily from comparatively oriented regional studies of "postcommunist" countries (see Figure 6.2 for a map of this region), including both "successful" cases (for example, Estonia, the Czech Republic, Hungary, Latvia, Lithuania,

**Figure 6.2   Map of Eastern Europe and Central Asia:
The Postcommunist States**

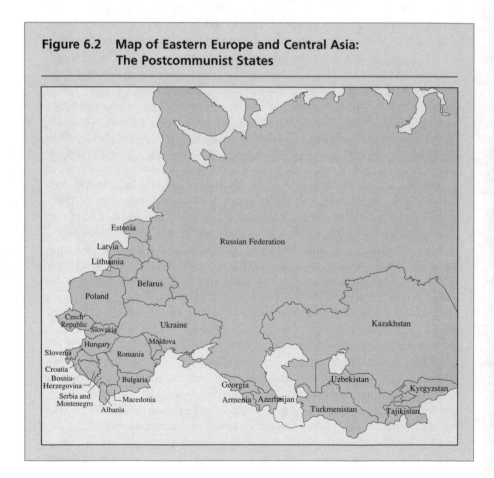

Poland, Bulgaria, Romania, Slovakia, and Slovenia) and "less successful" cases (for example, Tajikistan, Belarus, Kazakhstan, Kyrgyzstan, Turkmenistan, Uzbekistan, Armenia, Bosnia-Herzegovina, Moldova, Ukraine, Albania, and others). Figure 6.3 provides a summary of the various postcommunist cases. A number of researchers and comparativists who have examined the process of democratic transformation in these countries have concluded that democratic transformation is not primarily a "top-down process," or a product of divisions among contending elites. Instead, in almost all of these cases it is clear that *mass protests* played a key role in bringing about democratization (Bunce 2003, p. 172). "The people" (rather than the ruling elite or just the urban working class), in other words, are the key agents of change in this view. The experiences of postcommunist countries, moreover, have been buttressed by other studies of regime transitions in Africa. In a study of forty-

Figure 6.3   A Typology of Postcommunist Regimes: Dictatorships, Partial Democracies, and Democracies

	Dictatorships	Partial Democracies	Democracies
Balance of power in favor of challengers	—	Armenia Bosnia-Herzegovina Georgia	Croatia Czech Republic Estonia Hungary Latvia Lithuania Poland Slovakia Slovenia
Balance of power even or uncertain	Tajikistan	Moldova Russia Ukraine Albania Azerbaijan Macedonia	Bulgaria Mongolia
Balance of power in favor of ancien régime (or pre-existing elite)	Belarus Kazakhstan Kyrgyzstan Turkmenistan Uzbekistan	Yugoslavia/Serbia	Romania

Source: McFaul (2002).

two African countries, for example, Bratton and van de Walle (1997) concluded that "transitions in Africa seem to be occurring more commonly from below" (p. 83; cited in Geddes 1999, p. 120).

From a rational choice perspective, the significance of mass mobilization (as opposed to elite-centered strategic interaction) is not necessarily mysterious. As Bunce (2003) explained it, mass-based political protests signal a breakdown of authoritarian order; they create a widespread understanding of alternative political arrangements; they push authoritarian leaders to the bargaining table; they give opposition leaders a resource advantage when bargaining with authoritarian elites; and they create a mandate for radical change (p. 172). Mass-based protests, to put it simply (and perhaps a little simplistically), change the strategic environment of decisionmaking. It can be argued, as some scholars have done, that mass mobilization reduces "uncertainty" among those who both advocate and oppose political change (Bunce 2003, p. 172). When the strength of mass mobilization is unequivocally strong—even if only potentially—opponents of political change have little choice but to negotiate for an end to authoritarian or nondemocratic rule. Alternatively, they may accede to a "partial opening" or **liberalization** of the political system. If they fail to take either step, they face the dim prospect of a mass uprising that will forcefully remove them from office. Even with less certainty about the eventual outcome, mass mobilizations create a viable and all but impossible-to-ignore threat to the status quo, which opposition leaders can then exploit to their advantage. It is significant that this implies a situation quite different from what Rueschemeyer, Stephens, and Stephens posited, for it is not a *balance of power* per se that leads to change but a *highly unequal* distribution of power that produces political transformation—and one that is not necessarily the product of capitalist development. In the postcommunist cases, in particular, relatively equal distributions of power often "resulted in protracted confrontation, yielding unconsolidated, unstable partial democracies and autocracies" (McFaul 2002, p. 214).

Elites or Masses?

The division of rationality-based and actor-centric explanations into two categories is, of course, a simplification. It can also be an analytically dangerous one if taken to extremes. Przeworski (1991) argued along just these lines when he stated, "Short of a real revolution—a mass uprising that leads to the disintegration of the apparatus of repression—decisions to liberalize [which are precursors of democracy] *combine elements from above and from below*" (emphasis added; p. 56). From this perspective, a more reasonable or "realistic" rational choice approach *might* be to recognize and incorporate both mass-based mobilization and elite-centered strategic interaction into the same general framework. Intuitively, this makes sense. Empirically (and comparatively), however, the issue is far from clear. For although the experiences of postcommunist countries (and many countries in **sub-Saharan Africa**) underscore the importance of "mass power," as Geddes (1999) and others pointed out, there is little evidence of popular mobilization having played a major, still less causal, role in other places or regions, including, most prominently, much of Latin America (p. 120). A little comparative checking, in other words, tells us that the two major rationality-based explanations of democratic transition are both "right." Unfortunately, to rational choice comparativists, this is not necessarily a good thing, for if both sets of arguments are right, then two separate frameworks (as opposed to a combined one) seem to be required.

Differing Authoritarianisms and Transitions to Democracy

So where does this leave us? Can the rational choice approach provide a theoretically coherent and empirically comprehensive explanation of democratic transition? If so, how might this be possible? One potential solution is offered by Geddes (1999), to whom I have referred several times already. Geddes argued, in part, that a basic problem in much of the existing literature has been the tendency to treat authoritarianism as a generic concept—to portray all authoritarian political systems as basically alike. Although seemingly innocuous, this generally unacknowledged practice, Geddes suggested, is largely responsible for the inconsistent results among different rational choice/actor-centric models of democratic transition. Specifically, because "different kinds of authoritarianism differ from each other as much as they differ from democracy" (p. 121), it makes little sense to assume that transitions will all play out in the same general manner, even if all the relevant actors are acting strategically. As Geddes explained it: "Because comparativists have not studied these differences systematically, what theorizing exists about authoritarian regimes is posed at a highly abstract level, and few authors have considered how characteristics of dictatorship affect transitions. *These differences, however, cause authoritarian regimes to break down in systematically different ways, and they affect transition outcomes*" (emphasis added; p. 121). The necessary analytical step, therefore, is clear: develop a meaningful classification of different ("pure") types of authoritarian regimes. Geddes, of course, did this. In her research, she proposed three basic categories of authoritarian rule, plus a fourth "mixed" one: (1) personalist, (2) military, (3) single-party, and (4) "amalgams of pure types."

Each category reflects different institutional conditions and historical circumstances. In other words, each represents a different strategic environment or decisionmaking context. And, as any "good comparativist" knows, context matters—even to a rational choice comparativist. Within each category, according to Geddes, key actors define their interests and preferences in particular ways.

Military leaders and professional soldiers, for example, are primarily concerned with the survival and efficacy of the military itself and with preservation of national security. Other concerns—including, most significantly, holding political power (simply for the sake of holding power)—are secondary (p. 126). In this regard, authoritarianism is essentially a *means* toward an end or greater objective, which, to repeat, is ensuring the integrity of the armed forces. This, among a number of other factors, opens up the possibility for splits within the ruling military elite—and for voluntary reform—since, once political dominance is achieved, the incentive to cooperate diminishes. In fact, over time rivalries or policy differences within the military elite can threaten the cohesiveness, or integrity, of the military as a whole. When this happens, "a return to the barracks becomes an attractive option for most officers" (p. 17). After all, if ensuring the survival and efficacy of the military is paramount and if "returning to the barracks" (the traditional way of referring to the voluntary relinquishment of control of the civilian government by military leaders) will help prevent factional splits from further harming military cohesion, then this becomes the optimal choice. Moreover, as Geddes noted, "For officers, there is life after democracy, as all but the highest regime officials can usually return to the barracks with their status and careers untarnished" (p. 131).

By contrast, in personalist regimes, which are based on the dominance of a single individual and the cliques that form around him, the overriding interest of the ruling elite is the survival of the regime itself—and more specifically, of the dictator in power. Significantly, the cliques themselves are often based on family ties, which ties them even more strongly to the dictator-in-power. Of course, other forms of identity can also play a role—for example, clan, ethnicity, religion, region, or some combination thereof. But the key point is that "membership" in the ruling clique is severely circumscribed; that is, it is open to only a very small portion of the population, who must share some pre-existing relationship to the ruler. One of the most vivid examples of this type of system was the regime of Saddam Hussein, prior to his ignominious defeat and capture by US forces. In personalist regimes, voluntary reform or splits within the ruling elite are extremely unlikely—the potential costs are simply too high, as the loss of political power or position typically means personal calamity, imprisonment, and even death for the entire clique (or to anyone who unsuccessfully opposes the clique). The high costs are largely due to the relative narrowness of the support base and the violent repression typically used by such regimes. This means, however, that when change does come, it is typically violent and extreme (this point will be taken up again shortly).

Finally, in single-party authoritarian regimes, the preference of party leaders and **cadres** is quite simple: to stay in office. In this type of system, a little surprisingly perhaps, splits within the ruling elite are even less likely than in personalist regimes. As Geddes explained it, although "factions form in single-party regimes around policy differences and competition for leadership positions . . . everyone is better off if all factions remain united and in office" (p. 129). This is true even during periods of leadership struggles and succession crises, for the ordinary cadres understand that the best way to ensure their privileged positions within the regime is simply to support whoever wins. Another reason single-party systems remain highly cohesive is their capacity to co-opt potential opponents. For, quite unlike personalist regimes, single parties are "more likely to be open to all loyal citizens . . . and are less likely to limit their clientele to particular clan, regional or ethnic groups" (p. 134). Those who are excluded, however, have a great deal to lose, since the hegemony of single parties gives them near-total control over the allocation of educational opportunities, jobs, and positions in government (p. 134).

Explaining variations in democratic transition. Combined with the basic assumptions of rational choice analysis, this relatively simple schematic of different types of authoritarian regimes (see Figure 6.4), according to Geddes, provides a powerful way to explain democratic transitions across a wide range of cases. In transitions from military rule, as noted above, factional splits within the regime are relatively common, and, in an effort to preserve the integrity of the armed forces, military rulers are more likely to *negotiate* orderly—albeit top-down, elite-centered—transitions. This, in fact, is the modal (that is, the value or item occurring most frequently in a series of observations or statistical data) pattern of transition according to Geddes and was especially prevalent in Latin America. For a personalist regime, however, the situation is quite different: because it is far more resistant to endogenous instability—that is, instability located *within* the regime itself—*exogenous* (that is, external) factors are likely to play a stronger role in bringing about democratic transition. Exogenous factors may include such things as the oil crisis of the 1970s, the debt crisis, regionally centered financial crises, the collapse of the Soviet Union, and (as we have seen most recently with the US-led war against Iraq) a foreign invasion.

To put it in less formal terms: some outside "nudge" or, perhaps more accurately "shove," is usually necessary to bring about the breakdown of personalist regimes (a key but fairly obvious exception is the death of the leader). Exogenous shocks typically precipitate a particular event or process—for example, a coup, an insurgency, an assassination, a popular uprising—that directly brings down the regime. Some of these events or processes are "top-down" (coups and assassinations), and some are "bottom-up" (popular uprisings, insurgencies). Whatever the exact dynamics, breakdowns of personalist authoritarian regimes are usually *not* negotiated. Instead, they are forced and most often violent. And they are violent primarily because members of the personalist clique have, as was noted above, a lot to lose and almost nothing to gain once they no longer are in power. They will, therefore, generally fight to the bitter end. (This might help explain why—in the face of the overwhelming military power of the United States—Saddam Hussein refused to back down.)

Figure 6.4 Authoritarian Regime Types and Democratic Transition

Type of Authoritarian Regime	Likelihood of Democratic Transition	Primary Basis for Transition	Primary Mode of Transition	Examples
Personalist	Low	Exogenous shock (especially economic crisis); death of incumbent	Violent overthrow (coup, assassination, popular uprising)	Iraq/Hussein Uganda/Amin Argentina/Peron
Military	High	Factional split (among ruling elite)	Negotiated pact; top-down transition	Brazil (1964–1985) Argentina (1976–1983) El Salvador (1948–1984)
Single-party	Very low	Exogenous shock (often severe and multiple)	Mass-based pressure; negotiated "extrication"	China/CCP[a] Mexico/PRI[a] Tanzania/CCM[a]
Amalgam	(Depends on nature of amalgamation)	(Depends on nature of amalgamation)	(Depends on nature of amalgamation)	Indonesia/ Suharto Chile/Pinochet

Source: Adapted from Geddes (1999).
Note: a. CCP = Chinese Communist Party; PRI = Institutional Revolutionary Party; CCM = Revolutionary Party.

On first glance, one might assume that the logic of breakdowns in single-party regimes would be the same as in personalist regimes. But this is not necessarily the case because, as you should recall, single parties frequently try to co-opt their critics when faced with serious opposition or a crisis situation. This is possible, Geddes explained, because the institutional structures of single-party regimes make it relatively easy to allow for greater participation and popular influence on policy without giving up control of the political system (p. 135). For this reason, it is no surprise (at least to Geddes) that single-party authoritarian systems tend to survive the longest: of the single-party regimes that either existed in 1946 or were formed after that date, 50 percent still existed in 1998—by contrast, only 11.4 percent of military regimes and 15.7 percent of personalist regimes survived over this same period (p. 133). So, what brings an end to single-party regimes? Not surprisingly, the same thing that knocks down personalist regimes, namely, exogenous shocks. As in any authoritarian system, exogenous shocks undermine the regime by impeding the distribution of benefits to supporters and allies and, in some cases, destroying coercive capacity (pp. 138–139). Still, in single-party regimes, even long-lived, serious crises can be overcome. Indeed, as the statistics just cited demonstrate, single-party transitions are relatively uncommon; in fact, as Geddes and others have noted, most occurred as a direct result of the Soviet collapse—one of the most profound exogenous shocks of the twentieth century.

When exogenous shocks do lead to single-party breakdowns, moreover, it is often a combination of factors. The collapse of the Soviet empire, for example, not only caused widespread economic distress throughout the Soviet trading bloc but also destroyed coercive capacity in most of Eastern Europe (since most Eastern European regimes were dependent on Soviet power for domestic enforcement). On top of this double-barreled shock, postcommunist countries became more dependent on financial and technical support from major Western countries and Western-dominated institutions, which typically demanded a quid pro quo of aid for political reform (that is, democratization). In this situation, popular uprisings and bottom-up pressure—because they cannot be easily repressed or resisted—often play an important role in the breakdown of single-party authoritarian systems. Single-party regimes, in short, are faced with a clear choice: continue to resist or negotiate an "extrication" with *mass-based* opposition forces (as opposed to negotiating exclusively with other factions within the ruling elite). As Geddes noted, extrication through democratization is often the best alternative. This is so because single parties are almost always better off in a democracy than in some other form of authoritarianism. After all, "previous hegemonic parties have remained important in political life wherever countries have fully democratized, but they have been outlawed and repressed in several that did not. Consequently, they have good reason to negotiate an extrication rather than risking a more violent ouster" (p. 141).

Geddes's comparative strategy: A quantitative approach. Methodologically, Geddes provided empirical support through a broad-based comparison of a very large number of cases (to be precise, she included 163 regime *transitions* in her data set). Her basic methodological strategy, in this regard, was clearly more quantitative than qualitative; that is, rather than examining a few carefully selected individual cases in depth, she essentially fit all post-1946 authoritarian regimes into one of the three categories discussed above (plus amalgam-types). Through a fairly simple statistical analysis, Geddes then showed how the results—such as the survival rates of different types of authoritarian regimes, discussed above—confirmed her various hypotheses. When Geddes did compare or refer to individual cases, she did so at a very general level. For example, she noted that, of the fifty-one personalist regimes included in her data set, "only four survived more than a short time after the dictator's death or ouster: Salazar's in Portugal, Somoza's in Nicaragua, Tubman's in Liberia, and Duvalier's in Haiti" (p. 18). These cases, she argued, were exceptions that "underscore the importance of the elimination of able potential rivals as an explanation for why personalist regimes so seldom last longer than their founders" (p. 132). Except for a few brief words about each case, though, Geddes was content to let the cases largely speak for themselves. Although this approach is much too "thin" for many comparativists, it is important to recognize that behind her quick references to concrete cases lay not only a comprehensive statistical analysis but also a solid knowledge of important empirical details in dozens of individual cases.

Structure and Rationality: Competition or Synthesis?

In sum, Geddes provided a theoretically coherent and empirically comprehensive explanation of democratic transition based on rational choice principles. She seemed to account for a full range of variations in regime change dynamics (for example, in transitions to democracy) within a single and fairly parsimonious analytical framework. Does this mean that she offered a better explanation than the structural argument provided by Rueschemeyer, Stephens, and Stephens in *Capitalist Development and Democracy*? In considering this question, it is worth noting that Geddes had nothing to say about the role—pivotal or otherwise—of the urban working class and very little to say about the importance of a balance of *class* power as a *prerequisite* to democratic transition and transformation. Indeed, Geddes had very little to say—at least directly—about power at all, although the logic of her argument suggests that distributions of social power are at least relevant (for example, the stability of single-party regimes must be due, in part, to the power that comes from their capacity to limit serious factional splits; she also suggested that exogenous shocks are important only insofar as they undermine the power of authoritarian regimes). On the other hand, Rueschemeyer, Stephens, and Stephens did not say much about the *independent* causal power of different types of authoritarian regimes (or the strategic environment different types of authoritarianism entail). Yet to use their own standards for evaluating quantitatively oriented arguments, the strong correlation among different types of authoritarianism, regime survival, and democratic transition cannot be ignored.

The debate between structuralists and rational choice comparativists is clearly important, but not one that I intend to resolve here—even if this were possible. Suffice it to say that the arguments are not necessarily incompatible. They may, instead, be two sides of the same coin (as I suggested at the beginning of this chapter). Structuralists, for example, seem to provide a better account of the preconditions or prerequisites for democratic transformation, whereas rational choice scholars appear to offer a better explanation of how the structural *potential* for democracy is actually realized.[7] In this regard, a synthesis of the structural and rational choice models may be appropriate. Again, this is not an issue that can or really should be resolved here. It is, however, an issue that students of comparative politics would be well advised to contemplate. On this point, though, it is crucial to avoid overly simplistic remedies, which typically involve merely combining the two approaches in serial fashion—first one, then the other. As Gerardo Munck warned us, this is not enough. Instead: "What is needed is a theory of regime transition and formation that incorporates the simple yet theoretically complex notion that actors make choices but not in the circumstances of their choosing" (1994, p. 371). This requires us to consider how structure shapes "choices" and how choices influence structures (or more generally, how structure and choices interact), how the same choices may lead to different outcomes in different structural contexts, and so on. This is not easy, but it is necessary if we want to develop a fuller understanding of the complexities of democratic transition.

This said, we already know that structural and rational choice explanations are not the only games in town. Culturally oriented studies of democratic transition, although far less prominent (even marginalized), provide yet another set of variables to consider. The more recent culturally oriented studies, however, do not purport to provide a generalized, still less universal (and parsimonious), account of democratic transition and transformation (as structural and rational choice models do). Nor do most of these studies even claim that certain sets of cultural values and practices are necessary "preconditions" for the initiation of democracy, which many early culture-based studies did (Diamond 1994, p. 239). Instead, as I noted in Chapter 3, cultural theorists have tended to focus on how cultural factors *intersect* with political, social, and economic forces to produce specific outcomes in specific places and time periods. With this general point in mind, we will shortly proceed to the last major section of this chapter, which examines the relationship between culture and democratization.

Before we do, however, it is worthwhile noting at least one other significant approach in studies of democratization, namely, an institutional approach that posits a difference between presidential systems and parliamentary systems. This approach, made most famous by Juan Linz (1990), is discussed in Figure 6.5. The gist of the argument is that parliamentary systems are more conducive to democracy than presidential ones. In other words, Linz asserts that institutional variables have at least some, if not a great deal of, causal relevance. Like all the approaches discussed in the chapter, Linz's institutional argument should not be dismissed, much less ignored; moreover, like the structural and main rational choice arguments already discussed and like the cultural argument discussed below, the institutional perspective can likely complement and add to existing accounts of democratization. This is a crucial point to keep in mind as we proceed.

Figure 6.5 Presidentialism, Parliamentary System, and Democracy: An Institutional Perspective

In Juan Linz's highly influential paper (Linz 1990 is an abbreviated version), he argued that the institutional arrangements and practices that underlie presidential systems of government tend to weaken the chances for democracy to survive. He listed four main institutionally based problems. *First,* presidential systems create competing claims to legitimacy, since the president and the assembly are elected independently of each other. This is an inherently destabilizing condition in that serious disagreements between the elected legislature and the executive branch can lead to intractable conflicts that, ultimately, may only be resolved nondemocratically. *Second,* fixed electoral terms for presidents make it difficult to get rid of unpopular, corrupt, or incompetent leaders through democratic means. This, too, encourages behavior that may ultimately lead to a reversal or breakdown of democracy. Conversely, effective presidents are limited from exercising full power and authority when their terms are limited. In contrast, **parliamentary systems** allow the chief executive to stay in office based on an ongoing "vote of confidence" by the assembly. Moreover, in a parliamentary system, the chief executive can bolster his or her authority—especially in the face of a recalcitrant or reluctant assembly—simply by calling new elections. *Third,* the winner-take-all logic of **presidentialism** is unfavorable to democratic stability, since it encourage polarization in the political sphere and within society. And *fourth,* Linz asserted that the "style of presidential politics" is problematic in that it forces the president to be both head of the government and head of state.

From an empirical perspective, Linz's argument seems to have a good deal of support. On the basis of a statistical analysis of 135 countries observed annually between 1950 and 1990, for example, Przeworski and three associates concluded that "parliamentary regimes last longer, much longer, than presidential ones" (Przeworski et al. 1996, p. 47). Moreover, as Mainwaring and Shugart (1997) pointed out, "Of the thirty-three long established democracies, only six are presidential despite the prevalence of presidentialism in many parts of the globe. Twenty-two are parliamentary, and five fall into the 'other' category" (p. 456). A deeper examination of the evidence, however, reveals that the correlation between presidentialism and democracy may be spurious rather than causal. Most of the successful parliamentary systems exist among the most economically advanced countries, whereas most of the presidential systems—the United States being one major exception—exist within the developing world (p. 456). For this reason, it is not unlikely that another variable may be responsible for the stability of parliamentary democracies. In addition, Mainwaring and Shugart described other substantive flaws in Linz's argument, which we will not cover here. Suffice it to say that even critics of Linz's argument do not discount institutional factors. If anything, critics argue that much greater attention should be paid to the specific types of institutional arrangements and rules, which can vary to a considerable degree even within a basic framework, such as a presidential or parliamentary system.

■ A Missing Link? Culture and Democracy

On the surface, structural and rational choice models of democratic change account for a wide variety of cases. For this reason alone, it would be foolish to discount the dozens (if not hundreds) of well-supported, well-argued, and meticulously analyzed studies done by scholars in both research schools. And certainly few cultural theorists are willing to discount this vast body of literature. Still, for all the theoretical power of structural and rationality-based models, important questions remain largely unanswered (at least to the satisfaction of many). Why, for example, do some areas of the world seem so resistant to democracy? Was Samuel Huntington (1996)—one of the most outspoken observers of democracy—right when he suggested that the principles of democracy are simply, and forever, incompatible with the culture of many societies in the world? Conversely, how have some places in which the foundation for democracy seems especially bleak (theoretically speaking) been able to effectively break away from authoritarian rule? Do these "exceptional" places—for example, India, Mauritius, Costa Rica[8]—possess special societal attributes, derived from unique historical or cultural experiences, that set them apart? To most cultural theorists, the answers to these questions cannot be found strictly by peering through a cultural lens; at the same time, they believe the concept of culture cannot be divorced, much less extirpated, from studies of democratization. Culture, in short, does matter in the democratic process and not only in "exceptional" cases. The question, then, is how?

How Culture Matters in the Democratization Process

To understand the relationship between culture and democracy, it is important to first dispense with the naive (and ignorant) notion that certain "cultures" possess deeply rooted traits, characteristics, and practices that *automatically* lead to or, conversely, *permanently* block the democratization process. Empirically (and comparatively), this view is easily refuted. Many political leaders, commentators, religious leaders, and even professors, for example, have argued that the teachings, values, and practices of **Islam** are antithetical to democracy. But, as Alfred Stepan pointed out, this is empirically unsupportable. According to his calculation, in fact, upward of half of all the world's Muslims, 435 million people (or more than 600 million, if Indonesia is included), live in democracies, near-democracies, or intermittent democracies (2000, p. 48). In a similar vein, many observers used to argue that "Confucian cultures" (which might include South Korea, Taiwan, China, and Singapore) were also inherently inhospitable to democracy. This argument, too, turned out wrong, as the fairly recent democratic transformations of South Korea and Taiwan unequivocally demonstrate. One of the basic problems in these ostensibly culture-based arguments, to repeat a point made earlier, is clear: they all

AP/Wide World Photos

A lone protester standing in front of a column of tanks during the 1989 Tiananmen Square protests in Beijing.

portray "culture" as univocal, essentially fixed (or, at least, extremely resistant to change), and unidirectional with regard to causation. But, as many culturalists today argue, such assumptions are irredeemably flawed.

With this in mind, a starting point for understanding how culture matters in the democratic process is recognition that the ideas, beliefs, values, and identities societies embrace and by which they define themselves—among both the "leaders" and the "masses"—have power. These ideas, beliefs, values, and identities have power at both the individual and collective levels: they can compel individuals and whole peoples to act and behave in certain ways, to make profound sacrifices, and even to give up their very lives for the sake of a larger good. Consider, for example, the famous image of a lone protester standing in front of a column of tanks during the 1989 Tiananmen Square protests in Beijing. Certainly, that still-unidentified individual was putting his life on the line, and equally certainly his motivation for doing so was based on the power of an idea and of his beliefs and values. More important, he was not alone. At least 100,000 Chinese citizens also risked their lives and livelihoods for the same reasons. "Culture," however, is an unavoidably fluid system of meaning, which further means that it is subject to continuous "negotiation" and competing interpretations. Significantly, then, the power of an ostensibly single culture can be harnessed to achieve conflicting, even antithetical, goals. Culture, in this sense, is profoundly political. To see this, consider the foregoing example of the relationship between Islam and democracy. In Islamic societies, it is certainly true, as Robert Hefner noted, that many political leaders and activists frequently invoke the idea of Islam as "religion and state" to justify and make possible harshly coercive and decidedly nondemocratic polities—that is, they advocate a fusion of state and society into an unchecked and all-powerful monolith they call an "Islamic" state. Yet, asserted Hefner, the **Quran** (also spelled **Koran**) abhors compulsion and includes no such concept of an "Islamic" state, "least of all one with the coercive powers of a modern leviathan" (2000, p. 12).

The fluidity of Islamic culture (and of *any* culture), however, allows this reshaping of meaning to occur. It is equally important to recognize, in this regard, that Islam is "rich with other, pluralistic possibilities" (p. 12)—that is, possibilities that are perfectly compatible with democracy. Indeed, as Hefner and other scholars have argued, large numbers of Muslims are actively engaged in defining a civil pluralist Islam or, more simply, an Islamic democracy.[9] These Muslims believe, according to Esposito and Voll (1996), "that the processes of religious resurgence and democratization can be, and, in the case of the Muslim world, are, complementary" (p. 21). A basic problem, unfortunately, is that Muslim democrats, especially in the Arab world, face a daunting challenge. For it is not only a struggle of "interpretation"—made more complex in a global environment defined, in part, by deepening dissonance between the "West" and other parts of the world—but also a struggle against the entrenched material and institutional power of authoritarian regimes. In this mélange of competing forces (institutional, material, structural, and ideological), "culture" is clearly not the only important source of power, but it *is* significant. If it were not, one might ask, why do those seeking political power devote so much time and energy to controlling, manipulating, and otherwise expropriating culture for their own purposes? The answer, to repeat, is clear: those who are able to appropriate cultural symbols have the capacity to reshape the decisionmaking environment; to mold political, social, and economic institutions; and to legitimize (or delegitimize) specific practices that serve either to maintain or undermine the status quo.

Not coincidentally, an almost identical argument has occurred with regard to the relationship between Confucianism and democracy. In this debate, a number of Asian political leaders—most notably Lee Kuan Yew (note: in Asia, surnames, or family names, typically precede given names; thus, for Lee Kuan Yew, "Lee" is the family name; for Kim Dae Jung, mentioned below, "Kim" is the family name), the former prime minister of Singapore (1959–1990)—have asserted that cultural differences make the "Western concept" of democracy essentially incongruent with the "Confucian" societies of East Asia.[10] Other Asian leaders, however, have challenged this view. The most prominent was Kim Dae Jung, the former president of South Korea (1998–2003) and winner of the Nobel Peace Prize (2000), who criticized Lee specifically for using so-called Asian (cultural) values as a self-serving, but ultimately unsupportable, pretext for justifying Singapore's authoritarian system. More broadly, Kim argued that

democratic ideals and institutions have long been embedded in Confucian principles; indeed, Kim asserted that Asians developed the "fundamental ideas and
traditions necessary for democracy" long before the Europeans did, although
Europeans obviously formalized a comprehensive and effective electoral
democracy first (Kim 1997, p. 238). The fact that Kim not only espoused these
views, but that large segments of South Korea's population—including other
elites, the urban working class, students, and a large middle class—tightly embrace similar values and ideas underscores a potentially important cultural distinction between South Korea and Singapore. This distinction may also help us
understand why, despite broad similarities with regard to economic structure
and development, institutional arrangements, and even type of authoritarian
rule, South Korean democratization has progressed strongly (since 1987),
whereas democracy in Singapore remains, according to many critics, largely if
not completely a sham.

The debates regarding democracy in Islamic and Confucian societies
highlight the multivocal, variable, and multidirectional effects of culture. They
also hint at the underlying power of culture as a system of meaning—and as a
source of democratic change (and stability). Admittedly, though, our discussion so far has been extremely general and largely abstract. To get a better, or
more concrete, understanding of the power and significance of culture, it
would be useful to examine a specific case in comparative perspective (you
should recall that case studies are a particularly appropriate, if not indispensable, methodological strategy for culture-based comparative research). One of
the more interesting and instructive cases to examine is India (see Figure 6.6
for a map of India), which is only one of a very small handful of states in Asia
and Africa that made a successful and long-lived, if shaky and imperfect, transition from colonial rule to democracy following the collapse of the European
colonial system.

Explaining India's Transition to
Democracy: A Cultural Perspective

To begin, it is important to understand that India is *not*—from the standpoint
of most theories of democratic transition and consolidation—a "good" candidate for democracy even today, much less almost sixty years ago, when independence from colonial rule was first achieved (in 1947). Economically, for
example, India is relatively poor, with an estimated per capita gross domestic
product (GDP) of $2,540 in 2002 (placing India 156th out of 231 countries
and territories). Between 1983 and 2000, moreover, fully 86 percent of the
country's more than one *billion* people earned less than the equivalent of $2 a
day (United Nations Development Programme 2003), not only giving India
one of the highest poverty rates in the world but also making it an extraordinarily unequal society. Socially, India is strongly divided along linguistic and

Figure 6.6   Map of India and Surrounding Countries

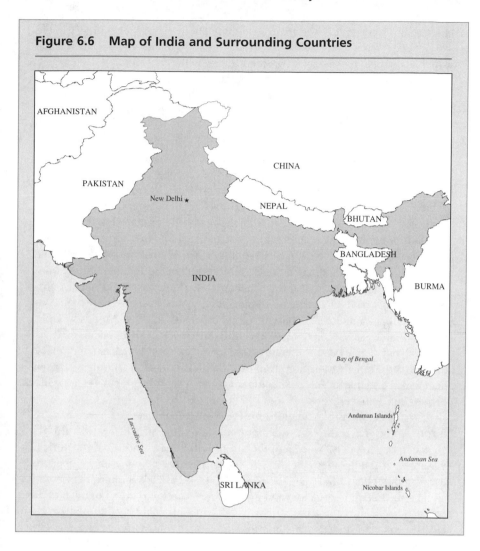

religious lines (although 80 percent of the population is Hindi); these divisions, in turn, are matched by even stronger vertical divisions, best exemplified by India's age-old and repressive **caste system**. Not surprisingly, the deep social divisions within India have resulted in decades of entrenched and violent conflict, sometimes bordering on internal war (Sisson 1994). Structurally and demographically, India remains a primarily rural society: in 2001, almost three-quarters of the country's population still lived in rural areas (Office of the Registrar General India 2001), and in 1991, the rural workforce accounted for 249 million or 79 percent of the total workforce. Within the much smaller urban labor force, moreover, there were only about 7.3 million workers in the "organized" manufacturing sector (the core of the urban working class), which accounted for just over 2 percent of the entire workforce (Office of the Registrar General India 2002). Stark as these figures are, if we extrapolate back to 1947, it is hard to imagine, from a structural perspective, many countries less prepared for democracy than India. (Figure 6.7 provides a summary of basic facts about India.)

Yet, India *is* a democracy—at least by the criteria we laid out earlier in the chapter. That is, India has had regular, free, and competitive elections (at the local, state, and national levels) consistently since independence. Fundamental freedoms of expression and association as well as the protection of individual rights against arbitrary state action (with the exception of a two-year period) have been guaranteed, albeit not always fully protected, by the Indian constitution; and the state apparatus—including the armed forces—has generally been responsive to the elected representatives. In substantive terms, the quality of Indian democracy is much more problematic. As many critics, including several members of the US Congress and international human rights organizations, have charged, the Indian government has engaged in or condoned serious violations of human rights, especially against "minority" religious populations. Corruption and intimidation of political opponents are also rampant and deep-seated. Although these are serious issues (and should not be disregarded), India's transition from quasi-authoritarian British rule to formal democracy still marks, for most comparativists, a significant, but theoretically perplexing, achievement.

Of course, many explanations for India's "exceptionalism" have been put forth. Some of these are ad hoc revisions of structural or rational choice–based models, whereas others explicitly draw on cultural/historical variables. It is the latter category of arguments that is our primary concern here—although, as I have suggested several times already, culturally oriented arguments do not, in principle and in practice, reject outright all or even most points made in structural and rational choice models. This said, culturally oriented accounts of India's transition to democracy typically focus on a number of key historical processes. One of the most salient of these is the "tutelary legacy" of British rule (1757–1947), which, despite its authoritarian and repressive nature, established bureaucratic structures, the rule of law, "representative" institutions, and even periodic elections (Weiner 1987). The basic argument is simple: exposure to and experience with these "liberal" traditions and institutions helped local elites not only learn but also internalize the norms, values, and practices of democratic procedure. After British rule ended, Indian elites essentially continued along the path set for them. There *is* something to be said about this argument, but the correlational, still less causal, relationship between countries experiencing British rule and subsequent democratization remains weak (Rueschemeyer, Stephens, and Stephens

Figure 6.7   A Summary of Basic Facts About India

Basic Information

Total area (sq. km.)	3,287,590[a]
Total population (millions), 2002	1,049.5
Projected population (millions), 2015	1,246.4
Annual population growth rate, 1975–2002	1.9%
Urban population (% of total), 1975	21.3
Urban population (% of total), 2002	28.1
Adult literacy rate (% of ages 15 and above), 1990	49.3
Adult literacy rate (% of ages 15 and above), 2002	61.3

Economic Statistics

GDP[b] (PPP[b] US$ billions), 2002	2,799.6
GDP per capita (PPP US$), 2002	2,670
Share of consumption—richest 10% (1999/2000)	27.4%
Share of consumption—poorest 10% (1999/2000)	3.9%
Gini index[b] (1999/2000)	32.5

Human Development and Poverty

Human Development Index (HDI) rank	127 (of 171)
Population living below $1 a day, 1990–2002	34.7%
Population living below $2 a day, 1990–2002	79.9%
Undernourished people (% of total), 1999/2001	21
Children underweight for age (% under age 5, 1995–2002	47

Other Information

Religions: Hindu 81.3%; Muslim 12%; Christian 2.3%; Sikh 1.9%. Other groups—including Buddhist, Jain, Parsi—2.5%

Languages: English is widely spoken and is the most important language for national, political, and commercial communication. Hindi, however, is the national language and primary tongue of 30% of the people. There are 14 other official languages: Bengali, Telugu, Marathi, Tamil, Urdu, Gujarati, Malayalam, Kannada, Oriya, Punjabi, Assamese, Kashmiri, Sindhi, and Sanskrit. Hindustani is a popular variant of Hindi/Urdu spoken widely throughout northern India but is not an official language.

Source: United Nations Development Programme, *Human Development Reports, Indicators: India,* http://hdr.undp.org/statistics/data/cty/cty_f_IND.html; *World Factbook 2003, India,* http://www.bartleby.com/151/in.html.

Notes: a. India is a little more than a third of the size of the United States.

b. GDP = gross domestic product; PPP = purchasing power parity; the Gini index is a measure of economic inequality (a lower figure represents less inequality).

1992, p. 228). Further, simple "comparative checking" quickly tells us that the argument is problematic. The best comparative example is Pakistan (a "most similar system"), which achieved independence at exactly the same time and under largely the same set of conditions, externally and internally. Pakistan, however, has been unable to *sustain* the minimal requirements of democracy. From 1947 to 1999, the military took over the government five times; six times democratically elected governments were dismissed on charges of misrule and corruption; twice military rulers were forced to relinquish the power. Not once did an elected government in Pakistan manage to complete its tenure and transfer power democratically. It remains to be seen whether the present government of Perez Musharraf (who seized power by force in 1999 but held a widely criticized referendum in 2002 to legitimize his rule) will be able to break the cycle. Even if he does, however, the fact remains: compared to India, Pakistani "democracy" has been problematic and extremely unstable.

Explaining India's Exceptionalism: Creating an "Indian Identity"

Still, the question remains: what explains the success of India's transition to democracy? Part of the answer, at least from a culturalist perspective, lies in the ability of India's preindependence leaders, including Mohandas Gandhi (1869–1948) and Jawaharlal Nehru (1889–1964), to *construct* a strong and cohesive *national identity* among India's huge and disparate population, at both the elite and mass levels. Forging a sense of national unity in a polity as (potentially) fragmented as India's was not only a monumental but also an essential task. To appreciate the significance of a shared national identity, one need only consider the severe instability and oftentimes brutal violence experienced by societies sharply divided by "conflicting" (but socially constructed) identities of race, ethnicity, religion, region, and so on. Yugoslavia and Rwanda are two of the most recent and unfortunate examples. In India, however, Gandhi ameliorated (although never fully resolved) this problem through his "ingenious ability," as Sisson described it, "to act as both agitator and arbiter during the quarter century before independence" (1994, p. 40). Continuing, Sisson noted that

> Gandhi acted in an historic tradition of reform movements in India, but he expanded and changed them. There had been a long tradition of movements of religious and social reform in medieval as well as early modern Hindi and Muslim society in India. The change introduced by Gandhi was not only that of raising mass society to new levels of consciousness and collective pride and of encouraging new attitudes toward traditional status groups and social behavior, but of asserting the idea that government must be responsible, that the state must be held accountable for India's myriad social ills, and that it be held accountable as a matter of right. (p. 40)

Gandhi, in short, helped create the basis for a democratically oriented collective identity at the mass level through an effective strategy of mass-based movements based on appeals to "historic traditions." These movements, it is important to recognize, both mobilized and profoundly *politicized* large segments of India's peasantry and dispossessed. It is in these movements, too, that the power of culture was unequivocally manifested.

At the elite level, Gandhi's role was equally crucial. Most important, perhaps, is the fact that Gandhi played a key role in transforming the Indian National Congress, which was founded in 1885 as a "native parliament." In its formative years, the Indian National Congress "did not entertain explicit notions of popular sovereignty and extensive democratic franchise. Instead it was a quintessentially reformist organization pursuing ameliorative goals" (Ganguly 1999, p. 221). Moreover, the congress was initially composed of traditional—but often Westernized—elite who largely supported the Raj (that is, British rule over India) and were, not surprisingly, largely disconnected from the bulk of India's population. Although the congress went through a number of hard-fought internal struggles over its direction and basic identity, it was Gandhi who, according to a number of scholars, brought about the most significant change. Simply put, Gandhi was able to effectively unify and democratize the Indian National Congress. He did this, in part, by skillfully merging the objectives of the "moderates" and "radicals" within the congress (the "moderates" wanted to continue working with the Raj, whereas "radicals" advocated "non-constitutional" means to achieve self-rule) (Sisson 1994). At the same time, he linked the Indian National Congress with the mass-based and decidedly nonviolent civil disobedience movements discussed above. As a result, by the 1930s, the congress "had largely shed its elitist orientation and was beginning to strike deep roots in the Indian soil" (p. 222).

Although Gandhi's work was clearly essential, particularly in democratizing the Indian National Congress, a great part of the effort in forging a broader sense of national unity fell to one of Gandhi's most trusted lieutenants, Jawaharlal Nehru.[11] Nehru, according to Ganguly, literally wrote a usable past for India's democratic future. More specifically, Nehru directly challenged—through copious writings and speeches—British colonial historiography, which portrayed the Indian state as a product of British colonialism. In contrast to this version, Nehru asserted that an Indian civilizational entity had long preceded the arrival of the British and had, moreover, a deep, underlying sense of unity. Nehru was persuasive. As Ganguly put it, he wielded his "argument with considerable force in bringing together what must be the largest concentration of human diversity within a fixed geographic space" (p. 222). This was, a culturalist might argue, an absolutely essential element of India's subsequent transition to democracy, for without some substantiation of India's underlying precolonial unity, the postindependence Indian polity could easily, and most likely would, have disintegrated into ethnic, religious, linguistic, and socioeconomic (class-based) fragments. In fact, the British attempted to rule through such a "divide-and-conquer" strategy—this was practically the only way the British could effectively govern such a huge country; that is, British power rested on a policy that "constructed" a fragmented and divided Indian polity. Nehru's efforts can therefore be seen as an attempt to construct an alternative reality—that is, a unified India via appeals to historical and cultural symbols. To a considerable extent he succeeded; Nehru's efforts not only countered the British strategy but helped to create an important and essentially nonmaterial—that is, cultural—foundation for democracy.

By itself, however, a nationalist myth is not sufficient to ensure national unity, nor is it sufficient as a basis for effective governance. Nehru and others realized this and also realized or believed "that the only way India could be effectively governed was through some form of a democratic dispensation" (p. 223). Of course, democracy was not the *only* possibility, but to India's political elite, it may have seemed to be the only viable choice *given the historical and sociocultural context* created during the colonial period and in which the Indian polity was deeply embedded. In this sense, culture helped determine the choices India's political leaders made. These choices, moreover, led to the creation of concrete institutions, which, from the very beginning, were imbued with the same democratic values and norms that had taken hold during the preindependence period. One of the most salient of these institutions was the Congress Party, an offshoot of the Indian National Congress. Unlike many political parties in developing countries, the Congress Party, even though dominated by traditional elites, from the very beginning sought "to represent all Indians regardless of religious affiliation, regional loyalty, or ethnic background" (p. 223). Although representation was far from perfect in that many Muslims and even an important segment of the majority Hindu population refused to join, the Congress Party was generally successful in achieving its goals. One other major exception was the potentates of the 500-odd "princely states," which comprised the territory of the subcontinent. Significantly, though, most were peacefully "integrated" into the state structure in postcolonial India (Sisson 1994, p. 42). The key point in this discussion, to be clear, is that the success of the Congress Party was due, at least partly and perhaps largely, to the broader political culture and environment that had been created in India during the colonial period. It was a culture that colored virtually all political decisions leading up to and following independence, and it was, therefore, a culture that almost assuredly had a meaningful impact on India's subsequent transition to democracy.

The Congress Party, of course, was not the only important institution in postcolonial India. Another crucial institution was the military. As suggested above, the military played an instrumental role in hindering the development of democracy in Pakistan—as it has in many nascent democracies throughout the world—both directly (through coups) and indirectly (through threat of intervention). In India, however, the situation has been quite different. Although it would be too much to ascribe the difference between Pakistan and India primarily, much less entirely, to political culture, it is reasonable to assume that culture was a key factor. It was a factor, moreover, that likely had an autonomous impact on the development of the military in India. As Ganguly explained it, establishing civilian supremacy over the military was in the minds of India's new civilian leaders from the very beginning. Nehru, in particular, understood the inherent danger of allowing the military to develop even limited autonomy from civilian authority, especially in the early stages of democratic transition. A significant part of this understanding was no doubt practical, but it is also clear that Nehru's attitude (as well as the attitude of many other political elites) reflected his adherence to and embrace of democratic norms and practices. Even more important, these norms and practices were inculcated into the military itself. Even in recent years, deference to the idea of civilian supremacy remains strong. For example, in response to increasing involvement in quelling outbreaks of civil violence in the 1980s and early 1990s (primarily in the states of Assam, Jammu, Kashmir, and Punjab), upper-echelon army officers warned that excessive use of the army to restore civil order might have a number of corrosive effects, including, most significantly, politicizing the army. The outgoing chief of army staff, General Sunith Francis Rodrigues, in fact, publicly articulated his misgivings on this subject in 1993 ("Public Order and Internal Security" 1995).

Culture and Democracy: Concluding Remarks

The foregoing discussion is far from sufficient to "prove" the significance of culture as a key variable in India's transition to democracy. Indeed, even an extremely detailed and in-depth analysis would likely be insufficient (on this point, remember the limitations of single-unit case studies and small-N analysis). Nonetheless, incorporating "culture" into an analysis of democratic transition in the case of India seems to fill significant gaps in the theoretical literature dominated by structural and rational choice models. At the same time—as I have repeatedly stressed—accepting a cultural interpretation of democratic transition in India (or anywhere else) does not mean you must reject other arguments. That is to say, accepting culture as an independent variable does not mean that it is the only independent variable. As I noted above, cultural theorists have tended to focus on how cultural factors *intersect* with political, social, and economic forces to produce specific outcomes in specific places and time periods. This is probably the best approach.

Before concluding this section, it would be worthwhile saying just a few words about the subsequent development of democracy in India. As many observers have pointed out, India has been and is experiencing a range of serious difficulties. In addition to the problems I noted above, these include the shrinking electoral base of the Congress Party; the concomitant entry of new social groups into Indian politics; the fragmentation of the electoral base along religious, regional, and class lines (Ganguly 1999, p. 230); rising violence and civil unrest; and a general "crisis of governability" (Kohli 1990). All of these issues call for serious study. Yet no matter how democracy develops in India, the importance of "culture" will likely remain strong, if not central, to any analysis. The key, however, is *not* to treat culture as a univocal, static, and unidirectional "variable." As I hope you have seen, doing so will lead to, at best, a crude and simplistic conclusion; at worst, your analysis will likely result in fatal distortions and misunderstandings.

■ Conclusion: Taking the Next Step

The study of democratization from a comparative perspective is complex and, in some respects, confusing. Indeed, despite the huge amount of research and writing on the subject, no definitive explanation of democratization exists. Nonetheless, a lot of immensely valuable work has been done, the best of which relies on a strong and sophisticated melding of theory, method, and evidence. Students who wish to better understand or explain the process of democratization are well advised to keep this basic lesson in mind. By this point in the text, however, you should have moved beyond simply understanding the importance of bringing theory, method, and evidence together; you should, instead, be ready to conduct your own analysis, that is, to *do* comparative politics. The issue of democracy is, in this respect, a particularly appropriate subject on which to focus your efforts, for there are a number of extremely interesting and relevant real-world cases, some of which we've already discussed, and some of which we have only mentioned. Russia is an interesting and important case, for despite great hopes and even assumptions, the country's path to democracy has been anything but smooth. Can Russia become a strong democracy, or will it revert back to dictatorship? China is another monumentally important case. Is the country destined to become democratic after years of rapid and sustained capitalist growth, or can the Communist Party hold on to political power indefinitely? On the other hand, what explains the fairly recent democratic transitions in Mexico, South Africa, South Korea, and Taiwan? And what of the Arab countries in the Middle East? What has been the primary impediment to political change among these countries? Is it "culture," as many have claimed? Or is the explanation based on underlying economic arrangements and processes, as a structuralist might argue? Or is it that Arab countries in the Middle East are dominated by firmly entrenched personalist or single-party systems in which the leaderships have no (endogenous) incentive to change?

In speaking of the Arab world and democracy, one country immediately comes to mind: Iraq. *Will Iraq become the first successful democracy in the*

Arab world? There is, of course, no easy answer to this question. Nor do I intend to answer this, or any of the questions I raised in the previous paragraph, here. Rather, these are questions *you* need to try answering. In so doing, though, it is crucial that you remember to think comparatively, theoretically, and critically. *Thinking comparatively,* to repeat, means doing as much comparative checking as possible before settling on a particular response. It also means setting up a comparative research design, using specific comparative strategies, and carefully considering what cases, and how many, to compare. *Thinking theoretically* means identifying the key forces or dynamics—whether political, economic, cultural, or institutional—that shape the social world. It also means carefully considering the relationship between agency and structure and the interaction between the "external" and "internal" environments. *Thinking critically* means taking seriously competing or potentially contradictory arguments, looking for and following the evidence where it leads, relying on reason rather than emotion, being aware of and self-reflective about one's own prejudices and biases, and maintaining an open-minded attitude. None of these can be done easily, but all are a necessary part of doing comparative politics.

Admittedly, these guidelines are very general and, therefore, difficult to apply. To provide you with more concrete assistance, then, I have included a table (see Figure 6.8) designed to guide you through some of the specific issues you might need to consider in assessing the prospects for democracy in Iraq. The table, though long, is by no means complete or comprehensive; at the same time, it is not meant to be followed in every detail. Instead, it is merely meant to give you a broad sense of what a comparative analysis of the prospects for democracy in Iraq would likely involve. A good comparativist will certainly expand upon, revise, and even reject some of my suggestions and tips. I hope you find yourself in this category.

■ Notes

1. McFaul (2002) argued that a number of cases—namely, Armenia, Bosnia-Herzegovina, Georgia, Moldova, Russia, Ukraine, Albania, Azerbaijan, Macedonia, Yugoslavia/Serbia—fall somewhere between democracy and dictatorship. He called these "partial democracies."

2. According to some scholars, there have been two major "waves" of democratization since the early 1970s. The first of these—commonly referred to as the third wave (the two previous "waves" of democracy occurred prior to 1970)—is generally agreed to have started in southern Europe but is most closely associated with democratization in Latin America and parts of Asia and Africa. Many scholars also include the former Soviet Union and its republics in the third wave (see, for example, Diamond 1999), but at least one prominent scholar, Michael McFaul (2002), has argued that we should consider the expansion of democracy among these countries to be a "fourth wave."

3. In this chapter, the focus will be on democratic transition, which is the initial stage in the process of democratization. A second important stage is democratic con-

Figure 6.8 A Few Tips on Assessing the Prospects for Democracy in Iraq—Thinking Comparatively, Theoretically, and Critically

	Type of Comparison	Examples/Possible Cases	General Questions/Issues
Thinking Comparatively *What sorts of comparisons make sense?*	Comparing Iraq to other nondemocratic Arab countries in the Middle East (MSS[a] design)	Bahrain, Jordan, Kuwait, Lebanon, Oman, Qatar, Saudi Arabia, Syria, United Arab Emirates, Yemen	What can be learned from this type of comparison? What are the limitations of comparing "most similar systems" with no variance on the dependent variable? Do "regional factors" help explain the lack of democracy in Iraq and the Middle East more generally?
Remember to *constantly engage in "comparative checking"*	Comparing Iraq to nondemocratic Arab countries in other parts of the world (MDS[b] design?)	Algeria, Comoros, Djibouti, Egypt, Libya, Mauritania, Morocco, Somalia, Sudan, Tunisia	What can cross- or interregional comparisons tell us that an intraregional comparison does not? What are the key similarities, if any, among all cases?
	Comparing Iraq to non-Arab Muslim democracies or "partial democracies" (MDS design?)	Turkey, Indonesia	Can this type of comparison shed light on the relationship of culture/religion and democracy?
	Comparing Iraq to other nondemocracies (MDS design)	Iran, North Korea, Cuba (Note: historical cases can also be used.)	On what basis should case selection be made? What can be learned from comparing Iraq to other long-lived dictatorships? (Hint: Geddes's framework could be very useful in this regard.)

(continues)

Figure 6.8 continued

	Type of Comparison	Examples/Possible Cases	General Questions/Issues
	Comparing Iraq to democracies in which "outside intervention" played a key role (MDS design)	South Korea (following liberation from Japan in 1945, the United States helped impose democracy in this country), Japan, Germany	Was "outside intervention" a *sufficient* factor to bring about stable democracy in all cases?

	Research Tradition	General Factors to Consider	Sample Questions/Issues
Thinking Theoretically *What theoretical approach will you use? Which theoretical approach makes the most sense?*	Structural approach	Structure and dynamics of the domestic economy; class relations and balance of class power; nature of state-society relations; structure and dynamics of the global economy; relationships of dependency; economic interests of major capitalist powers in Iraq/Middle East, especially of the United States	How strong is the urban working class in Iraq? What is the distribution of power within Iraqi society? Is the fact that wealth and wealth production are highly concentrated in a single industry—e.g., oil—important? Does the geostrategic significance of the Middle East affect class relations and state-society relations? Would a democratic Iraq be in the interests of dominant capitalists in major Western countries?
	Rational choice/actor-centric model	Interaction between/among elites; type of political system (e.g., single-party, personalistic, military); strength of opposition forces, including mass-based opposition; role of exogenous "shocks"	How did the ouster of Hussein impact the balance of power between/among elites in Iraq and between the elite and the Iraqi population? What are the prospects for political and economic stability? Can US and outside intervention provide a long-term incentive for democratic governance?

(continues)

Figure 6.8 continued

Research Tradition	General Factors to Consider	Sample Questions/Issues
Cultural approach	The struggle over national versus separate, subnational identities; the impact of transnational norms on domestic societies; the interaction of cultural, political, economic, and social forces	Will a single, democratically oriented identity emerge in Iraq? Will economic and political inequalities exacerbate pre-existing ethnic and religious cleavages, or will the ouster of Hussein create a general basis for equality among different groups within Iraq? Will conflict between the "West" and the Muslim world continue to worsen?
Thinking Critically	*Remember these general rules:* (1) Consider seriously competing or potentially contradictory arguments; do not assume your argument is right; this means you have to be familiar with the scholarly "literature." (2) Look for a wide range of evidence from all the relevant cases included in your analysis; this evidence can be historical, qualitative, and quantitative. (3) Do not dismiss or hide evidence that does not agree with your interpretation or argument; if the evidence is not consistent with your argument, you must revise your position. (4) Maintain an open-minded but critical attitude.	

Notes: a. MSS = most similar system.
b. MDS = most different system.

solidation. Although the two stages are obviously connected, the key factors or variables in each stage are not necessarily the same. In other words, analyses of democratic transition and consolidation can be regarded as two separate endeavors.

4. Dahl himself was hesitant to classify any real-world political system as a democracy. Instead, he used the term "polyarchy" for concrete systems and reserved "democracy" for the nonexistent, ideal-type. Few scholars today, however, stick to the distinction made by Dahl.

5. In Chapter 3, we placed modernization theory into the cultural camp, whereas in this chapter, modernization is placed in the structural camp. Although confusing, the discrepancy lies primarily in the fact that modernization theory treats culture as an exogenous variable. In this regard, culture helps explain why the modernization process takes time to develop in some areas, but once the process gets under way, culture is subject to the same structural imperatives as all other aspects of society.

6. Elsewhere Przeworski has expanded on this point. In a coauthored article, Przeworski and Limongi (1997) wrote, "The emergence of democracy is not a byproduct of economic development. Democracy is or is not established by political actors pursuing their goals, and it can be initiated at any level of development. Only once it is established do economic constraints play a role: the chances for the survival of a democracy are greater when the country is richer" (p. 177).

7. Geraldo Munck (1994) made basically the same observation in his review of the literature on democratic transitions. As he put it, "there can be no question that the study of democratic transitions has benefited from the emphasis put on choice. . . . But it is probably also fair to say that the shift from 'prerequisites' to 'process' or from structural determinants to strategic choices, has gone too far" (p. 370).

8. For a discussion of democracy in Mauritius, see Laville (2000), Srebrnik (2002), and Miles (1999). For a discussion of democracy in Costa Rica, see Wilson (1998) and Booth (1998). Wilson offered a primarily institutional argument, whereas Booth argued that Costa Rican democratization was best explained by structuralist and elite settlement approaches (p. 197).

9. Schmid (2003) provided a good example of this in Iran. As he noted, a leading Iranian philosopher, Abdolkarim Soroush, put forth a powerful argument that Islam, secularism, and democracy are fully compatible and even complementary.

10. For a reasonably thoughtful example of an argument along these lines, see Kausikan (1997).

11. The ideas and information expressed in the remainder of this section come primarily from the article by Samit Ganguly (1999), to which I have referred several times already. For convenience, I will only provide additional references to the Ganguly article when using direct quotes. I will reference other sources as usual.

7

What Makes a Terrorist?

Explaining Political Violence

Since September 11, 2001, terrorism has emerged as one of the most significant subjects of interest and inquiry, both within and outside the academic community. Of course, the academic study of terrorism long preceded the events of September 11. It is interesting, however, that it has not typically been a focus of study by comparativists; instead, terrorism as an academic subject has been dominated by scholars in other fields, including psychology, international relations, law, and terrorism or counterterrorism studies.[1] This does not mean that comparativists have been totally silent on the subject, much less that they do not have anything useful and important to say about "terrorism" or political violence. Indeed, one of the underlying points I wish to emphasize in this chapter is that the methods and theories of comparative politics can shed considerable light on the issue of terrorism. Even more, I believe that an *adequate* understanding of terrorists and terrorism depends on the systematic use of comparative strategies of analysis. Why this should be the case will become clearer as we proceed. For now, though, suffice it to say that comparative analysis serves as a necessary and effective check on many of the claims made by those who write about terrorism.

This chapter is organized in much the same fashion as the preceding chapters. After beginning with a brief discussion of the concept of terrorism, we will cover, in order, rational choice, cultural, and structural accounts of terrorism. Compared to the previous chapters, moreover, we will spend a little more time directly discussing questions of method.

■ What Is Terrorism?

This is a basic yet extremely complicated question. Despite a great deal of discussion and debate, there is no universally agreed-upon definition of terrorism.

This is regrettable but understandable. It is regrettable because the lack of a clear and harmonized definition means, as you should already know, that scholars and others who write and talk about "terrorism" may not always be referring to the same thing. Or they may be referring to the same thing but using entirely different labels. This is evident in the oft-used and now trite expression that "one man's terrorist is another man's freedom fighter." Although trite, the distinction, if one exists, should not be glossed over. Is a freedom fighter the same as a terrorist? Were, for example, the black South Africans terrorists who violently or not so violently opposed apartheid? Are ordinary criminals—including serial and mass killers—terrorists? Are soldiers who burn and destroy villages, who kill dozens if not hundreds or thousands of innocent civilians, terrorists? Does it make a difference if they do so on behalf of a **sovereign** state during a time of "war"? If not, what is the key distinction between all these other actors and a terrorist? And what about states themselves or state leaders? Are George Bush and others within his administration terrorists, as many have claimed?[2] The questions do not stop here. What about "insurgents" in post-Hussein Iraq, who attack both military and civilian targets (Iraqi and American)? Are these examples of terrorism or of something else? To repeat an oft-made point in this book, it is important to understand that debates over definitions are not mere quibbles: if you intend to say something meaningful about a subject, then you had better be able to define that subject, which means being able to differentiate or separate it from other, especially very similar, phenomena.

The lack of agreement about the proper way to define terrorism, on the other hand, is understandable in that the term is politically and ideologically loaded. Terrorism, in the minds of most people, is an illegitimate, even evil thing. To be labeled a terrorist is to be summarily condemned and debased. In this view, terrorists have no justifiable or conceivable foundation for their actions. Moreover, national governments of all stripes use the term "terrorist" as a rhetorical weapon that, once successfully deployed, can serve to mobilize, accumulate, and justify the use of vast resources in an ostensible effort to wipe out the terrorist threat. Indeed, a cultural theorist might argue that the **discourse** of terrorism is used by states not only to delegitimize others (or "**the Other**") but also to construct and reproduce specific identities designed to ensure the continuing power and legitimacy of the state. Unfortunately, there is no way to avoid the political and profoundly subjective understanding of the term. Still, this does not mean that we should not or cannot attempt, as Crenshaw (1995) argued, to transform the concept of terrorism "into a useful analytical term rather than a polemical tool" (cited in Whittaker 2001, p. 10).

So, how should terrorism be defined? I will not pretend to be an authoritative source on this question; indeed, even among the so-called terrorism experts, debates over the best way to define terrorism have resulted in a stalemate that, as Brannan, Esler, and Strindberg (2001) observed, has "led to a rather perverse situation where a great number of scholars are studying a phenomenon, the essence of which they have (by now) simply agreed to disagree upon" (p. 11). By one reckoning in the early 1980s, in fact, there were at least 109 different definitions of terrorism used in the scholarly literature (Schmid and Jongman 1983, pp. 5–6). Today, no doubt, there are probably dozens more definitions. Nonetheless, a definition provided by Bruce Hoffman (1998) strikes me as reasonable. Hoffman defined terrorism as

> the deliberate creation and exploitation of fear through violence or the threat of violence in the pursuit of political change. All terrorist acts involve violence or the threat of violence. Terrorism is specifically designed to have far-reaching psychological effects beyond the immediate victim or object of the terrorist attack. It is meant to instill fear within, and thereby intimidate, a wider "target audience" that might include a rival ethnic or religious group, an entire country, a national government or political party, or public opinion in general. Terrorism is designed to create power where there is none or to consolidate power where there is very little. Through the publicity generated by their violence, terrorists seek to obtain the leverage, influence and power they otherwise lack to effect political change on either a local or international scale. (cited in Whitaker 2001, pp. 9–10)

In his definition of terrorism, Hoffman also limited terrorists to subnational or nonstate actors. This may seem to be a politically motivated move because it automatically eliminates states and their governments from the definition of terrorism. Yet there is justification for doing so, since states, by virtue of their status as sovereign or semisovereign entities, are generally considered meaningfully different from any other actor. Even more, states can be considered different from other types of actors since they typically operate from a position of strength. To many who study terrorism, this is a significant difference in that terrorism is often seen as the "weapon of the weak." (A compromise, then, might be to differentiate state terrorism from other forms of terrorism.) Granted, both points are debatable. But if you look carefully at Hoffman's definition, it did not suggest that terrorism is automatically either a reprehensible or, conversely, a justifiable act. Instead, he defined it in largely neutral and amoral terms (in contrast to other definitions, some of which I list in Figure 7.1).

No doubt Hoffman's definition is not perfect. Still, it provides a useful and relatively neutral way of conceptualizing terrorism.[3] In this respect, though, Brannan, Esler, and Strindberg (2001) suggested that we should dispense with the word "terrorism" altogether and replace it with an even more neutral term: *violent substate activism*. The term "violent substate activism," I think, is useful, but it runs the risk of further confusing an already confusing concept. Thus, for the remainder of this chapter, I will generally use the term "terrorism" as defined by Hoffman. With this in mind, let's begin our examination of terrorism from a rational choice perspective.

Figure 7.1   Some Definitions of Terrorism

1. The unlawful use of force or violence against persons or property to intimidate or coerce a government, the civilian population, or any segment thereof, in furtherance of political and social objectives (Federal Bureau of Investigation).
2. The calculated use of violence or the threat of violence to inculcate fear, intended to coerce or intimidate governments or societies as to the pursuit of goals that are generally political, religious or ideological (US Department of Defense).
3. Premeditated, politically motivated violence perpetuated against noncombatant targets by subnational groups or clandestine agents, usually intended to influence an audience (US State Department).
4. The use or threat, for the purpose of advancing a political, religious or ideological cause, of action which involves serious violence against any person or property (United Kingdom government).
5. Contributes the illegitimate use of force to achieve a political objective when innocent people are targeted (Walter Laqueur).
6. A strategy of violence designed to promote desired outcomes by instilling fear in the public at large (Walter Reich).
7. The use or threatened use of force designed to bring about political change (Brian Jenkins).
8. The deliberate, systematic murder, maiming, and menacing of the innocent to inspire fear in order to gain political ends. . . . Terrorism . . . is intrinsically evil, necessarily evil, and wholly evil (Paul Johnson).
9. Terrorism is a political label given to people who are perceived to be planning or carrying out acts of violence for political objectives. The violence may be directed against individuals and sometimes property. The violence may not always be that of individuals or groups. A government's armed forces may be labeled terrorist, as they often are, by the party at the receiving end of that violence.

Sources: Definitions 1–8 are from Whittaker 2001, pp. 3–4; item 9 is from Nassar 2004, p. 17.

■ The Logic of Terrorism: Terrorist Behavior as a Product of Strategic Choice

The title of this section comes directly from the title of an article written by Martha Crenshaw (1998a). Although many scholars have attempted to analyze terrorists and terrorism using a rational choice framework, Crenshaw provided one of the clearest and most influential explanations. For this reason, my presentation of the rational choice perspective on terrorism will draw heavily from Crenshaw's argument. This said, as with any good rational choice explanation, Crenshaw began with a fundamental premise, namely, *terrorism is a rational act*. More specifically, Crenshaw argued that those organizations or people who engage in acts of terrorist violence do so with the intention of achieving a realistic political or strategic goal. As she put it: "Efficacy is the primary standard by which terrorism is compared with other methods of achieving political goals. Reasonably regularized decision-making procedures are employed to make an intentional choice, in conscious anticipation of the consequences of various courses of action or inaction" (p. 8). In this regard, I might note, terrorist activity is not, in principle, different from other types of organized political activism; it is "simply" a more extreme version.

Rational Choice, Psychology, and Suicide Terrorists

Crenshaw's position, it is worthwhile noting, contrasts quite strongly with that of a large number of researchers studying terrorism—many with a background in psychology or psychiatry—who argue that terrorists and terrorist violence are the product of a psychological pathology. To put it bluntly (and a little simplistically), these scholars argue that terrorists are not quite "right in the head." Jerrold Post (1998), for instance, argued that terrorists are, by and large, "aggressive and action-oriented," primarily as a result of failures in their personal, educational, and vocational lives (p. 31). It is significant that Post also asserted that, although terrorists may *believe* that they are acting rationally, their rationality is based on "special" psycho-logic that *only* terrorists possess. Part of this logic, according to Post, is based on a highly polarized and absolutist way of thinking. To terrorists, the world is divided into good and evil, us and them, black and white, and so on. With this framework of thinking, any actions undertaken by terrorists are, by definition, good and moral. This is the logic of which Post speaks. The key point, to repeat, is this: although terrorists act in a "logical" manner, their logic does not flow from a psychologically well-balanced or healthy mind but from a narcissistic and borderline personality disorder.

Psychology-based arguments are, in a roundabout way, buttressed by the recent rise of suicide terrorism, a phenomenon that seems to support the assumption that terrorists are not psychologically healthy. Certainly, from a rational choice perspective, it is hard to argue that committing suicide to achieve a political goal is an individually rational act. In this regard, suicide terrorism presents a logical quandary, since an individual committing the act of suicide terrorism *cannot* benefit from the outcome of the act yet seems to commit the act in the absence of coercion. Of course, we can argue that the individual is acting on the basis of religious beliefs or on the basis of benefiting his or her family, but these explanations do not easily fit into a rational choice framework (although, I should emphasize, they could easily fit into a cultural framework). So, how does Crenshaw overcome this obstacle? The solution is quite simple, albeit unconventional from the standpoint of mainstream rational choice theory. Briefly put, Crenshaw argued that terrorism is best conceived of as a product of *collective rationality*.[4] This means that when people identify with an organization's goals, they understand that their individually rational actions may *prevent* the group from achieving its broader, collective goals. Thus, they are willing to subordinate their individual preferences when doing so is collectively rational (note the difference between this argument and our earlier discussion of poverty, in which individually rational action oftentimes resulted in collectively irrational outcomes; the situation here is reversed: individually irrational behavior results in collectively rational outcomes).

This is a controversial position, which I will not attempt to resolve here. In fact, it may not even be necessary to accept the premise of collective rationality. Instead, in evaluating the phenomenon of terrorism, one can simply shift the focus to the *leadership* within an (ongoing) terrorist organization. The key question, therefore, is whether the leadership is acting rationally, and not whether every individual associated with the organization—or with a particular terrorist act—is rational. This position allows us to explain, with little difficulty, the hard-to-dismiss irrationality of suicide bombing. For even though such behavior makes little or no sense from the perspective of the individual bomber (more on this below), it makes very good sense from the perspective of an organization's leadership. Consider the 1983 suicide attacks launched by Lebanon's **Hizballah** (literally, "the party of God") against the US and French military contingents stationed in Beirut. Unlike the more recent spate of suicide attacks around the world (which have become an almost daily occurrence), the attacks launched by Hizballah met with "astonishing success" (Kramer 1998, p. 141), not in terms of the number of people killed but rather in terms of achieving a political objective—that is, the withdrawal of foreign forces from Lebanon. (See Figure 7.2 for a brief discussion of this incident.) The individuals who carried out the attacks, of course, died. So the "success" of the attacks meant nothing to them. The organization, however, not only survived but achieved its primary objective. In this view, we can say with confidence that the organization's leadership acted in a rational manner.

Still, how do we explain the behavior of the individuals who carried out the attacks? Herein lies much of the beauty of the rationalist argument. We can assume that the individual acted irrationally. We can assume the individual suffered from severe psychological problems. We can assume the individual was acting on the basis of religious fanaticism or blind hatred; we can assume the individual was "brainwashed," duped, or otherwise fooled into doing something against his or her interests. Yet, it does not matter what the motivation of the individual was, because we are concerned only with the *rationality of the*

**Figure 7.2   The Suicide Terrorist Attack Against US Forces
in Lebanon**

On October 23, 1983, around 6:20 A.M., a Mercedes delivery truck drove to Beirut International Airport, where the United States Marines had their head-quarters. The driver turned onto a road leading to the compound and circled a parking lot; he then gunned his engine, crashed through a barbed-wire fence, passed between two sentry posts, crashed through a gate, and barreled into the lobby of the Marine headquarters building. The suicide bomber detonated his truck, which contained 12,000 pounds of TNT. The force of the explosion collapsed the four-story cinder-block building into rubble, ultimately killing 241 US Marines and naval personnel (and injuring 60 others). At almost the same moment a similar explosion blew up the French military barracks a few kilometers away, killing 56 French troops.

The Marines were originally in Beirut as part of a Multinational Force (MNF) composed of 800 French, 800 US, and 400 Italian troops (the United Kingdom also joined a few months later). The MNF was an integral part of a cease-fire agreement designed to end the conflict between Israel and Lebanon, and also involving the Palestinian Liberation Organization (PLO) (who were using Lebanon as a base for attacks against Israel). The first deployment of the MNF was generally successful, but later incidents brought the MNF back to Beirut. The second deployment turned out to be much more politically complicated, as US forces, in particular, were involved in a number of incidences that made it appear as if the United States had taken a side in what had now become a largely internal struggle within Lebanon. Rather than a neutral arbiter, therefore, the United States became identified as a key player on the side of the Christian-dominated central government, which also had a friendly relationship with Israel. This made the MNF, in the eyes of those who opposed Israel, an unequivocal enemy. The attack against US forces, which was meant to drive the United States out of the country, achieved its goal: US Marines were moved offshore in February 1984, and the MNF operation essentially came to an end. All of this took place, moreover, despite a pledge by then-president Ronald Reagan that the United States would stay in Lebanon. Vice President George Bush was even clearer. After touring the bombing site on October 26, he said, "We will stay." He also asserted that the United States would not be cowed by terrorists.

Sources: "1983 Beirut Barracks Bombing," http://en.wikipedia.org/wiki/Marine_Barracks_
Bombing; and John H. Kelly, "Lebanon: 1982–1984," *Rand Conference Report: U.S. and Russian Policymaking with Respect to the Use of Force*, http://www.rand.org/publications/CF/CF129/
CF-129.chapter6.html.

organization and its leadership. We might even speculate that leaders of terrorist organizations purposefully recruit unbalanced or easily manipulated individuals to carry out the riskiest operations, largely because no one else will. Certainly, we rarely (never?) witness the leaders of terrorist organizations putting their own lives on the line, much less volunteering for suicide missions.[5]

What Makes a Terrorist? Calculating the Costs and Benefits

Keeping the foregoing discussion in mind, it becomes easier to answer the basic question of the chapter, namely, what makes a terrorist? The answer can be summed up as follows: *a terrorist is made when he or she believes that no other viable options exist to achieve a political goal (or a terrorist organization is made when the leadership does not believe any other viable options exist).* This is one reason terrorist organizations invariably begin from positions of relative weakness—if they were strong to begin with, they would not need to resort to terrorism in the first place. On this point, it is important to understand that terrorism is essentially a response to objective conditions, but it is rarely a *first* response. What this means is that terrorism grows out of conditions that lead some individuals to press for social, political, or economic change. The conditions are usually not pervasive enough to create a society-wide movement but are still strong enough to compel individuals to form groups/organizations designed to challenge the status quo. Once these organizations are formed, they will press for change through a variety of tactics but are likely to be continually frustrated. As a result, the group gradually turns toward more and more extreme measures, ultimately leading to terroristic violence. The decision to adopt terroristic tactics is, in this sense, a last resort. Indeed, most organizations that we associate with terrorism, whether today or in the past, began as nonviolent, albeit sometimes radical, but sometimes idealistic, political organizations. In many cases, in fact, the original participants were not terrorists but *peaceful* social or political activists. It is important to recognize this contextual aspect, for the turn toward terrorism is often part of a long-term process in which an organization—or individuals within an organization—seeking political or social change have consistently failed to achieve their goals.

If this argument is correct, we can more easily grasp a major advantage or benefit of terrorism, namely, its ability, as Crenshaw (1998a) argued, to "put the issue of political change on the public agenda" (p. 17). In other words, terrorist acts attract attention, and by "attracting attention it makes the claims of the resistance a salient issue in the public mind" (p. 17). This, in turn, may build or coalesce popular support, which would be *the* main ingredient for future success (on the other hand, a turn toward violence could lead to a loss of popular support). Ehud Sprinzak (1998), another prolific writer on terrorism, provided a useful case study to support this position—the emergence, in the 1960s, of the Weathermen, a small terrorist organization in the United States that developed as an offshoot of the much more broadly based and nonviolent Students for a Democratic Society (SDS). Although Sprinzak did not explicitly adopt a rationalist framework in his own analysis, his conclusions dovetail nicely with points made by Crenshaw. Specifically, he argued that the Weathermen organization—along with many other cases—was a "political phenomenon par excellence" (p. 78). That is, the group represented, as he put it,

> an extension of opposition politics in democracy, a special case of an ideological conflict of authority. It is, furthermore, the behavioral product of a prolonged process of delegitimation of the established society or the regime—a process whose beginning is, almost always, nonviolent and nonterroristic. In the main, the process does not involve isolated individuals. . . . Rather, it involves a group of true believers who challenge authority long before they become terrorists, recruit followers, clash with . . . law enforcement from a position of weakness . . . and, in time, radicalize within the organization to the point of become terroristic. (pp. 78–79)

The key point from the foregoing discussion is simple: *terrorism is a choice based on reason and logic* (but not a "special" logic). If we accept this argument, moreover, we must accept a clear implication, which is that terrorism is as much, if not much more, a *rational* (albeit not always fully justified) response to external forces and conditions as it is a product of internal "demons." This means, in part, that the choice of terrorism is made more likely under conditions where *not* turning to terrorism will virtually guarantee defeat. Thus, from a rational choice perspective, we would expect to see greater incidences and more intense levels of terrorism in those areas where other forms of political resistance are largely or completely ineffective. We would also expect to see more terrorism where the perception (reality?) of injustice, political and economic inequality, and oppression is high. Predictably, then, terrorism is most intense in places such as Palestine, Sri Lanka, and Chechnya and less intense in Western Europe, the United States, and Japan. At the same time, if the costs are *too high*—if any resistance is absolutely doomed to failure—then terrorism would not be anticipated. This perhaps explains why some of the most oppressed and weakest peoples do not engage in terrorism—that is, they simply have no chance of even the most marginal of victories. Certainly, we saw little terrorism in the former Soviet Union or in Iraq under Saddam Hussein and have seen little in North Korea since the end of World War II.

Rationality, Mistakes, and Constraints

Arguing that terrorist organizations act rationally does not mean that their decisions are always or even mostly effective or productive. Indeed, as Crenshaw (1998a) pointed out, terrorist organizations often make miscalculations and even huge blunders. But this is primarily (albeit not completely) a product of limited or imperfect information and not of an insufficient or distorted grasp of reality. As Crenshaw aptly put it, "Perfect knowledge of available alternatives and the consequences of each is not possible, and miscalculations are inevitable" (p. 9). In addition, and perhaps even more important, the decisions that terrorist organizations make are constrained by a lack of viable alternatives, a point that I have already made. In the case of the Hizballah's opposition to the United States, for example, suicide bombings represented one of the few means available to confront the overwhelming military advantage enjoyed by US (and Israeli) forces. As one Hizballah cleric put it, "If an oppressed people does not have the means to confront the United States and Israel with the weapons in which they are superior, then they possess unfamiliar weapons. . . . Oppression makes the oppressed discover new weapons and new strength every day" (quote by Sayyid Muhammad Husayn Fadallah; cited in Kramer 1998, p. 144). One might argue, moreover, that the success of the Beirut bombing has become a model for a range of terrorist organizations. The reasons are clear. As Hoffman (2003) explained it: "Suicide bombings are inexpensive and effective. They are less complicated and compromising than other kinds of terrorist operations. They guarantee media coverage. . . . Perhaps most importantly, coldly efficient bombings tear at the fabric of trust that holds societies together" (p. 40). This is why we have witnessed the spread of suicide terrorism from Lebanon and Palestine, to Sri Lanka and Turkey, to Argentina, Chechnya, Russia, and Algeria, and, finally, to the United States (p. 40). Hoffman's analysis also explains why terrorist organizations continue to use this tactic even when it does not seem to work particularly well. In most cases, suicide attacks represent the best of very limited choices: they are "cost effective," relatively easy to carry out, and terribly destructive in terms of the physical and, especially, psychological damage they can do.

Assessing the Rational Choice Argument: Some Tips on Method

As is typical in the rational choice approach, Crenshaw's argument began at a high level of generality or abstraction. That is, she began by making an overarching claim regarding the *rational* motivation of terrorist organizations and concluded by arguing that "terrorism can be considered a reasonable way of pursuing extreme interests in the political arena" (1998a, p. 24). As a caveat, though, Crenshaw did not claim that strategic calculation explains everything about terrorism or that it is always the most important factor in the decision-making process leading to terrorism. "But," as she put it, "it is critical to include strategic reasoning as a possible motivation, at a minimum as an antidote to stereotypes of 'terrorists' as irrational fanatics" (p. 24).

Despite her qualifications, such arguments have a certain appeal; after all, if correct, they cannot only tell us a lot about the phenomenon of terrorism generally, but they can also, as Crenshaw stated, make prediction of future terrorism possible. This raises an obvious question, namely, is strategic reasoning a key element of terrorism? Are terrorists, in fact, rational actors doing rational things? In my summary of Crenshaw's argument, I cite a few *illustrative examples*, but are these sufficient to confirm all that she says? Conversely, can you think of any cases that would (fatally?) *invalidate* her central, albeit qualified, claim? More generally, from a broader methodological perspective, has Crenshaw done everything necessary to establish a strong and compelling case? Asking these questions, I should emphasize, is not meant to imply that Crenshaw is wrong; rather I pose them to make a few important points:

1. In making a general argument about political, social, or economic phenomena, *illustrative examples* are never sufficient. (Unfortunately, students often rely entirely on such examples in their own papers. Just remember, illustrative examples are just that—they illustrate a point you are making, but by themselves, they provide only the barest level of empirical support.)
2. The consideration of (seemingly) contradictory cases, even with a qualified claim, should not be ignored or dismissed but dealt with in a serious manner. (That is, you need to explain why they do not discredit your entire argument.)
3. Strong and compelling arguments require the researcher to consider and incorporate into her analysis broader questions of method—for example, what sort of comparative strategy to use, how many cases to examine, what specific cases to compare, and why.

We cannot, in other words, accept *or* reject Crenshaw's argument on faith, on principle, or on the basis of personal biases. Instead, as students of comparative politics, our responsibility is to assess her theoretical argument on the basis of empirical "testing" or analysis. One way to do this is through the comparative method. If what Crenshaw says is correct, for example, we should find evidence of strategic reasoning in a wide range of cases, some of which she may have discussed in her own research, but some of which she has not. Of course, it is not always possible, at least from a practical standpoint, to conduct comparative analysis of dozens, if not hundreds, of cases. There is, however, one comparative strategy that is particularly useful for assessing rational choice arguments. Peters (1998) called this the "variable reduction strategy."

If a researcher begins with a clear and parsimonious theory—such as rational choice—then it is possible to test it with a limited number of cases. "This is especially true," Peters noted, "if the cases are selected to make *falsification* more likely, for example, if the researcher looks for the *hardest cases*" (emphasis added; p. 70). By "hardest cases," Peters meant those cases that appear least likely to confirm the theory or hypothesis being tested. Using Crenshaw's argument, for example, one such case could very well be the September 11 attack against the United States by Osama bin Laden's **Al-Qaida** organization. On the surface, at least, it is difficult to discern a rational motivation for the attack by Al-Qaida. Certainly, the organization—even with imperfect information—should have anticipated the heavy costs of such an attack—namely, the almost guaranteed reprisal against its bases in Afghanistan and around the world. The organization's leaders, then, could surmise that launching such an attack would threaten not only the survival of the organization but also their own survival. And what of the benefits? What could Al-Qaida have *reasonably* hoped to achieve? Although it is not possible to provide a definitive answer here, it is worthwhile noting that, as events have transpired since September 11, 2001, Al-Qaida remains a viable, dangerous, and arguably much more effective organization than it has ever been. Certainly it is more visible. One can even argue that Al-Qaida is moving toward the achievement of certain political goals. If, for example, we assume that one of Al-Qaida's goals has been to destabilize the Saudi Arabian regime and undermine US influence in that country (in the Middle East more generally), an assumption shared by many informed observers, then it is not unreasonable to conclude that the possibility is growing, rather than diminishing. (For another view of the motivation for the attack, one expressed by bin Laden himself, see Figure 7.3.)

Figure 7.3   Why Did Al-Qaida Attack the United States?

Three years after the September 11, 2001, attack, Osama bin Laden provided his rationale for the decision. According to tapes released to the Al-Jazeera television station in Doha, Qatar, bin Laden's main objective was to undermine the power of the United States by forcing the country to spend billions of dollars in a new fight against terrorism. Bin Laden's model was the holy war against Soviet forces in Afghanistan two decades earlier. The holy war, according to bin Laden, "bled Russia for 10 years, until it went bankrupt and was forced to withdraw in defeat." The attack against the United States, therefore, was a way of "bleeding America to the point of bankruptcy." Indeed, according to bin Laden's calculation, only $500,000 was spent to finance the September 11 attacks, yet the United States was forced to spend $500 billion in response.

Source: "Bin Laden's Target: U.S. Wallet," November 2, 2004, http://www.cbsnews.com/.

Demonstrating how this sort of "hard case"—*along with others*—clearly reflects strategic reasoning would strengthen the rational choice argument. Although, I must hasten to add, it would not necessarily "prove" the argument correct. For as Peters also pointed out, the variable reduction strategy is not foolproof (indeed, as we have already learned, no comparative strategy—especially a small-N comparative strategy—is foolproof). The problem, according to Peters, is the danger of "premature closure"; in other words, just "because a single hypothesis can be tested with a limited number of cases does not mean that there are not other possible explanations" (p. 70). Moreover, Peters noted, "a strong theory such as rational choice may contain a number of untested assumptions that are, in many ways, also hypotheses. Failure to test the assumptions empirically may lead the researcher to accept what is in essence a spurious relationship" (p. 70).

The main point of this discussion, to repeat, is to emphasize the necessity of *well-grounded empirical testing* when evaluating an argument, whether your own or someone else's. A second point, however, is to underscore the fact that a variety of comparative strategies exist to carry out such empirical testing. A third and last point is to help you remember that comparative analysis, although necessary, is complicated and imperfect. We will return to some of these same issues in other parts of this chapter. For now, though, let us see how we can use a cultural approach to better understand the issue of terrorism.

▣ Culture, Religion, and Terrorism

Does Culture "Make" a Terrorist?

Few culturalists would argue that terrorism is inextricably and always linked with certain cultural or religious values and beliefs. By the same token, few would deny that cultural and religious factors play a role, and sometimes a central role, in motivating individuals and organizations to undertake acts that, to an outsider, seem unreasonable and even irrational. With this in mind, cultural approaches to terrorism or ethnic conflict generally emphasize the significance of culture as a "meaning-making" medium that interacts with other forces (political, economic, and social) to influence or shape the behavior of individuals, communities, or even whole societies. In this sense, most culturalists would *not* argue that "culture makes a terrorist" but that cultural and religious values—which are often intentionally manipulated by charismatic leaders or strong organizations—can contribute to the making of terrorists. The distinction is critical. In the former statement, the implication is that certain cultures or religions essentially serve as breeding grounds for terrorists and terrorism. This claim, not surprisingly, has been leveled against Islam following the events of September 11. For example, after September 11, Robert A. Morey, a popular evangelical Christian leader, had this to say about the relationship between the Islamic faith and terrorism: "The blood lust of Islam is . . . rooted in a perverted religious impulse to kill and mutilate in the name of Allah. This is what makes it so insidious and wicked. The killing of innocent men, women, and children in the name of Islam becomes a thing of praise and a badge of honor. The more you kill, the more Allah is honored. The greater the destruction, the greater the glory of Islam" (Morey n.d.)

The latter claim (that is, that cultural and religious values can contribute to the making of terrorists), on the other hand, is quite different. To say that cultural and religious values can contribute to the making of terrorists implies that even ostensibly bedrock values are malleable. This is to say that cultural and religious values can be used in a variety of ways to serve a variety of different purposes. This does not mean, as I noted in Chapter 3, that cultures or systems of belief can be invented (and reinvented) out of whole cloth: There *is* an enduring substance to any culture or system of belief. But this is partly where the confusion lies. Those who accuse some religions or cultures (and not others) of creating hate, intolerance, or terrorism assume that what is true today must be true for all times and all places. Or that what is true of the part must be true of the whole. More concretely, these accusers believe that if Islam, or just an aspect of Islam, is responsible for terrorism in the contemporary world, then there must be something *inherently* aggressive, even evil, in Islam.

A moment's reflection, however, should be enough to undermine, if not completely dispel, this notion. For, as most of us know, "Christian anti-Semitism has a long and terrible history, as does Christian aggression against Islam during the Crusades and against fellow Christians during the Wars of Religion" (Beverly 2002). Was (or is) there something inherently aggressive or evil in Christianity? Almost certainly not. But, as the past history of Christianity clearly indicates, no religion is immune from being used to promote or contribute to hate, intolerance, aggression, and terrorism. Even today, various right-wing terrorist groups in the United States regularly, if not predictably, use their beliefs in Christianity to justify and motivate their behavior (as well as to appeal to potential recruits).

The Power of Culture and the Context of Terrorism

Such a use is not, many culturalists would argue, an accident. Those who use culture or religion to achieve their ends, to put it simply, understand its power. They understand that the use of cultural and religious symbols can evoke powerful emotions, can unify otherwise disparate followers, and can compel people to act in ways they would normally—and under most conditions—eschew. The effective use of such symbols, however, does not take place in a vacuum. There are, in other words, broader social, political, and economic forces that make the use of cultural and religious symbols more or less possible, more or less effective. At the same time, many culturalists would agree that culture and religion have an autonomous effect insofar as they sometimes provide a *necessary* or, at least, "authoritative" basis for *collective* (as opposed to individual) action. Put in different terms, one can say that *without* an appeal to cultural or religious symbols, certain collective undertakings would be difficult if not impossible to achieve, particularly on a sustained or long-term basis. This is probably truer with terrorism than with other types of collective endeavors, if only because becoming a terrorist requires an extraordinarily high level of commitment and risk.

Perhaps the best way to understand this point is through an analysis of terrorism in specific situations (that is, a case study). Given the nature of cultural analysis and the case study method (discussed in previous chapters), however, my intention is not to provide a definitive—or all-encompassing—discourse on the relationship between culture/religion and terrorism. This is not possible. Rather, my aim is to provide illustrative examples of how appeals to cultural and religious symbols have been used, not only to "make terrorists" but also to build and sustain a terrorist organization.

Before beginning, though, it is important to recognize that many terrorist organizations, even those now intimately associated with specific religions, have a secular basis for their establishment and emergence. In the case of Hizballah, for example, this secular basis is easy to find. A. A. Khalil (1991) provided a nice summary. As he put it, "Hizballah is the product of the tensions and conflicts within the **Shiite** community. The underlying causes for its emergence are deeply rooted in indigenous Lebanese conditions and in the aftermath of the Israeli invasion of Lebanon in 1982" (cited in Whittaker 2001, pp. 390–391). The "indigenous Lebanese conditions" about which Khalil speaks are complex (too complex to describe here). But one very important aspect of these conditions is the *unequal division of political and economic privileges* between **Muslims** and Christians in Lebanon. Indeed, it would be difficult to put forth any reasonable interpretation of terrorism in Lebanon without taking careful account of this quintessentially political issue. Nor, as Khalil also pointed out, is it an issue limited strictly to relations among Christians and Muslims. In Lebanon, relations within the Muslim faith are "far from harmonious"; thus, any redistribution of power in favor of Muslims in the past would likely have resulted in further tension and conflict among the various Islamic groups and would be likely to have the same result in the future.

Inequality and seriously unbalanced power relations, in fact, are an underlying factor in many, if not most, cases of terrorism. In Northern Ireland, Sri Lanka, South Africa, Algeria, Pakistan, and Palestine, to name a few, struggles for power have been clearly paramount. Yet conditions of inequality and political discrimination do not always lead to a significant level of terrorism or to the formation of terrorist groups. Conversely, in relatively equitable and democratic societies, incidences of (domestic) terrorism not only occur but also are sometimes quite serious—as in Italy, West Germany, Spain, and (to a lesser extent) Japan and the United States. Culturalists, for the most part, do not pretend to have an all-inclusive answer. Instead, to understand why terrorism occurs in some situations and not others, culturalists assert, or at least imply, that it is vital to consider the larger social, political, and historical context, both at the domestic and transnational levels. Similarly, to understand the specific role that culture and religion play in any situation of terrorism, it is necessary to take a close look at the same overall context.

Terrorism in Lebanon: A Cultural Interpretation

Returning to the situation in Lebanon (see Figure 7.4 for a map of the country's location), we can see that inequality and unbalanced power relations, although providing a catalyst for political struggle, did not immediately lead to terrorism. Indeed, Hizballah as a coherent and effective "terrorist" organization did not emerge until 1982—almost forty years after independence and after the time in which the basic division of power between Christians and Muslims had been created. Prior to 1982, civil or political violence was extremely serious but primarily defensive or reactive (Picard 1997; cited in Whittaker 2001); it had not yet been characterized by most observers as "terrorism." Moreover, until the 1970s, radicalism in Lebanon was primarily the domain of secular activists, as opposed to religious leaders (Khalil 1991). The turning point came in 1982, when Israel reinvaded southern Lebanon in an attempt to eliminate, once and for all, Palestinian bases in this area (the first invasion had taken place in 1978). The intrusion of Israel into Lebanese territory—and its long-standing alliance with Christian-dominated militias—created an obvious opportunity for hitherto disparate and factionalized groups to coalesce into a more unified (at least in purpose) anti-Israel force. But even this was not enough to ensure organizational success. Another key element in the Lebanese context was the role of Iran, which played a crucial role in financing and supporting terrorist organizations throughout the Islamic world beginning in the 1980s. Into this mix, we must add the religious/cultural element, which was obviously significant. Indeed, a culturalist might argue that, given the larger sociopolitical and economic context surrounding the conflict in Lebanon, religion was bound to play a pivotal and pervasive role in this conflict.

Co-opting Islam and the rise of terrorism. It was not, however, simply a matter of "pure" Islamic beliefs automatically and naturally fitting into a new program and structure of terrorism. Instead, Islam was, to a significant degree, co-opted and reshaped by the leaders of Lebanon's political struggle—and

Figure 7.4 Map of Lebanon and Surrounding Area

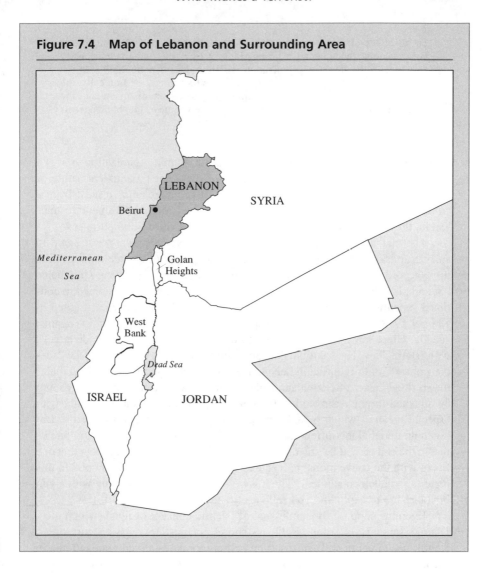

specifically by the leaders of Hizballah—as a way to enhance the possibilities for success. Or at least this is an argument a culturalist might make. Khalil, for example, argued that Hizballah, the "Party of God," used Islamist principles to justify the struggle against Israel and other "enemies of Islam" but also heavily borrowed from Marxist-Leninist principles to build and sustain the organization. According to Khalil, the reasons for this were fairly clear. As he put it:

> The model of Leninist party organization was convenient to all those groups
> in the Arab world who favoured one-party organization and who are based

on absolute self-righteousness and intolerance. Nasserism, Ba'thism, and some Islamic fundamentalist groups benefit from the undemocratic party structure of the Leninist organization which undermines the ability of the party members to bring about change and restructuring. . . . Ironically, the Party of God, which professes a strong enmity to communism emulates the Leninist model of party organization and borrows some of its political terms with some necessary modifications. (Khalil 1991, p. 394)

From this perspective, Hizballah is as much an Islamic organization as it is a Marxist-Leninist—and, therefore, atheistic—party. The paradoxical nature of this situation, however, is not all that difficult to understand, at least from a cultural perspective. To repeat: since cultural and religious values are malleable, they can be adapted to a wide variety of situations and purposes.

The malleability of Islamic values is particularly apparent with regard to suicide attacks. Indeed, the accepted theological view of suicide among Muslims, according to Franz Rosenthal (1946), is the same as among Christians: "Suicide is a grave sin, and the person who commits suicide is doomed to continual repetition in Hell of the action by which he killed himself" (quoted in Kramer 1998, pp. 142–143). Yet, in spite of the unequivocal prohibition against suicide, Hizballah's religious leaders found a way to reconcile suicide attacks with Islamic law. The solution, not surprisingly, relied on an appeal to the "special context" of the conflict in Lebanon. Sayyid Muhammed Husayn Fadlallah,[6] the spiritual leader of Hizballah, explained it this way: When an enemy cannot be attacked through conventional means, then the combatant must fight with "special means," which includes purposefully sacrificing one's own life. But "such an undertaking differs little from that of a soldier who fights and knows that in the end he will be killed. The two situations lead to death; except that one fits in with the conventional procedures of war, and the other does not." In this regard, Fadlallah concluded, "There is no difference between dying with a gun in your hand or exploding yourself" (quote in Kramer 1998, p. 145).

Even the supposedly quintessential Islamic concept of jihad (which most Islamic scholars interpret as the "striving for justice") has, according to Khalil, been intentionally misused by contemporary Islamic organizations. In particular, he argued that Hizballah has appropriated the concept for its own purposes. "Under the name Jihad," Khalil stated, "hostages were taken, battles have been fought, and suicide missions have been ordered. . . . The revolutionary ideology of Hizballah broadened the definition of jihad to include all facets of party activity" (p. 398). This broadening of the definition, of course, serves a clear purpose; namely, it is meant to legitimize and "Islamize" all the activities undertaken or sanctioned by Hizballah. The "Islamization" of its activities allows the organization to claim a divine or sanctified role, which, in turn, confers an obligation on the part of *all* Muslims to support, or at least not oppose, the actions taken by Hizballah (Whittaker 2001, p. 47). The more successful Hizballah's leaders are in convincing the Islamic community of its divine mission, the stronger the organization becomes.

A comparative aside: Comparing Pakistan and Lebanon. A similar situation, I might note, is said to exist in Pakistan where, according to Jessica Stern (2000), Islamic religious schools, called **madrasah**, have been set up to inculcate young Pakistanis. Originally these schools were designed to provide much-needed general education and basic services (food, housing, and clothing for the poor), but they have since become highly sectarian training centers. As Stern described them, "Most [madrasah] offer only religious instruction, ignoring math, science and other secular subjects. . . . Even worse, some extremist [madrasah] preach jihad without understanding the concept: They equate jihad . . . with guerilla warfare" (p. 119). Whether or not the leaders of these extremist schools fail to "understand" the concept of jihad is highly debatable. Indeed, it is likely they understand the concept very well; however, like the leaders of Hizballah, they choose to teach a special version of the concept in order to achieve their own purposes. For, as Stern also pointed out, these more extreme madrasah also "encourage their graduates . . . to fulfil their 'spiritual obligations' by fighting against Hindus in Kashmir or against Muslims of other sects in Pakistan" (p. 119).

Culture and the Making of Terrorists: Concluding Remarks

Despite the brevity of the foregoing discussion, it is easy to see (albeit still arguable to some) that terrorism is *not* a natural or inevitable by-product of Islamic culture. The specific culture of Lebanon or Pakistan (or dozens of other places we did not examine), in short, was not responsible for "making terrorists." Instead, it was a particular context and a particular set of political, economic, and historical dynamics (both domestic and international) that created an environment conducive, even highly receptive, to the emergence of "violent substate activism." In this environment, Islamic culture was already an important, if not integral, facet of social and political life. For this reason, its appropriation in support of terrorism was not at all surprising—even predictable, to some extent. The fact that Islamic culture now plays, and will likely continue to play, an important role in making and sustaining terrorism in Lebanon and other places throughout the world means not only that it has been *successfully* appropriated but also that it has been proven to be a valuable political resource. Culture, however, has a way of being constantly reinvented. And as power relations shift, we can expect the relationship between Islamic culture and terrorism to shift as well, perhaps dramatically so. If there is a general lesson to be found in the cultural approach to terrorism, this may be it.

■ Globalization and the Rise of Terrorism: A Structural View

Cultural explanations of terrorism, as we learned above, generally pay serious attention to the *context* in which terrorism emerges and develops. Understanding the context of terrorism is also important, if not central, to most structural explanations of terrorism. Unlike culturalists, however, scholars using a structural approach are much more interested in specifying and *theorizing* about the essential forces, relationships, and dynamics—or process— that create the basis for the conflict and violence that lead to terrorism. Put in different terms, they are concerned with identifying the underlying or root causes of terrorism as a generalized (as opposed to particularized) phenomenon. Not surprisingly, this is a complicated task. Part of the complication, however, is simply that not all structuralists agree. Indeed, in identifying the fundamental causes of terrorism, there are likely to be some very strong and intense disagreements among scholars using a structural approach. To make my task easier, then, this section will focus on a single but representative structural account of terrorism (and of political violence more generally), one that posits that (1) the homogenizing forces of *globalization* are giving rise to an increasingly strong, and sometimes extremely violent, backlash among groups, societies, and peoples who do not wish to be "globalized"; and (2) the increasing reach and deepening of economic globalization, in particular, are upsetting and even destroying traditional relationships and practices.

From a structural view, "globalization" is the *primary* causal force; it puts into play a particular dynamic that creates unavoidable tensions and pressures in every corner of the world. One particularly salient, but certainly not the only, manifestation of these "tensions and pressures" is profound political violence—whether in the form of "ethnic conflict," civil strife, interstate war, terrorism, or myriad other forms of death and destruction. I will return to a discussion of the relationship between globalization and political violence shortly; first, though, it is important to spend some time discussing the concept of globalization. In other words, when we talk about "globalization," just what do we mean?

Globalization: A Primer

Globalization, which I cover in more depth and detail in Chapter 9, is a nebulous and controversial concept. As with the concept of terrorism, however, it is important to have a clear—or at least explicit—definition of the term before going very far. This said, one useful, although not particularly concise, way of defining globalization is provided to us by Ulrich Beck (2000). Beck, a German sociologist, began by pointing out that globalization is *multidimensional*, by which he meant that globalization has many analytically separate but profoundly interrelated aspects: cultural, ecological, social, technological (or informational), economic, and so on. This multidimensionality is complicated by the fact that each dimension is itself merely a convenient label for a wide assortment of related processes. Consider, for example, the economic dimension of globalization, which, as Beck points out, is nearly always at the center of public debate. But what do we mean by economic globalization? Is it a question, Beck asks,

> of direct investment abroad by German firms, or of the international operations of large corporations? Is it *de*nationalization of the economy that is involved, and hence the fact that national brand-names are becoming as fictitious as national economies, so that the prosperity of a "national" industry no longer coincides with the prosperity of (national) citizens? Are we talking of that "virtual economy" of monetary and financial flows which appears detached from any material substratum or use-value production? Or is the real point the much more banal one that the German [or American or Japanese or Mexican] economy is under pressure from cheaper production elsewhere in the world? (emphasis in original; p. 19)

The simple answer to all the questions Beck poses above is "yes." Economic globalization refers to all the processes Beck mentions—and more. In addition, what is true of economic globalization is true of the other dimensions of globalization: each, to a significant degree, refers to a multitude of related processes, which are far too many to list here. My point is not to confuse you but to underscore the fact that "globalization" can mean many different things, in many different areas. Recognizing this, however, does not mean that the concept of globalization is completely amorphous (and therefore undefinable). From the various dimensions of globalization it is possible, Beck argued, "to extract a common denominator" (p. 20). So what is this? According to Beck, it is the gradual breakdown of both political borders and natural barriers around the world. Globalization, in other words, "means that borders become markedly less relevant to everyday behavior in the various dimensions of economics, information, ecology, technology, cross-cultural conflict and civil society" (p. 20). More concretely, globalization means that "money, technologies, commodities, information and toxins 'cross' frontiers as if they did not exist. Even things, people and ideas that governments would like to keep out . . . find their way into new territories. So does globalization *conjure away distance*" (emphasis added; p. 20). This may seem a good thing. But, as Beck also noted, when distance is "conjured away," people can be "thrown into transnational lifestyles that they often neither want nor understand" (p. 20).

More than changing lifestyles, however, globalization in all its various forms may sometimes *destroy* long-existing lifestyles, dense networks of social relationships, and all those things that have held many societies together for hundreds of years. This is because globalization is not just an abstract concept but a concrete process that imposes new structures, relationships, values, and practices everywhere it reaches. Globalization, and **neoliberal** economic globalization specifically, is, in this sense, akin to a tsunami. A tsunami, as the terrible events in December 2004 clearly demonstrated, travels through the ocean with unrelenting speed, and when it reaches the shore, rises up and crashes down on everything in its path. In its wake, whole villages or cities are destroyed, families and communities may be torn apart, hundreds of thousands of people perish, and others are left to struggle for survival. And, like the tsunami that hit Indonesia, Sri Lanka, India, and many other countries, there is often little that people can do to escape its destructive power. So too with economic globalization.

Globalization and Terrorism: An Unavoidable Connection?

Conflict and political violence have been around for a long, long time, certainly since long before the advent of globalization. Terrorism, too, is an age-old phenomenon. So the argument that globalization (a seemingly very new concept) is the causal force behind terrorism may seem, to many people, wrong-headed. The fact that violence and terrorism are not new, however, does not mean that globalization is irrelevant to understanding the nature of political violence and terrorism *today*. Most so-called terrorism experts would likely agree. For example, a prominent terrorism expert, Magnus Ranstorp (1996), pointed out that the current "wave of [terrorist] violence is unprecedented, not only in its scope and the selection of targets, but also in its lethality and indiscriminate character" (p. 43). Moreover, present-day terrorism has a distinctly fundamentalist tinge. This, too, is not new, but as Ranstorp also pointed out, the number of religion-based terrorist groups has exploded over the past few decades. Indeed, the association between fundamentalist religion and terrorist violence has become virtually inseparable in the minds of many people. This is particularly true, as we have seen, with regard to Islam (although it is clear that the resurgence of fundamentalism is by no means limited to Islam).

The Dialectics of Violence

To a structuralist, none of this is coincidental. Rather, the explosion of terrorist violence *and* its increasingly strong connection with fundamentalism are part and parcel of a larger pattern and process. The obvious question, then, is: what is the larger pattern or process about which structuralists speak? The answer, as I suggested above, can be partly found in the dynamic interrelationship between the forces of globalization, on the one hand, and the forces of "localization" on the other hand. The forces of globalization, as James Rosenau (1995) explained it, are "all those forces that impel individuals, groups, societies, and transnational organizations toward more encompassing and coherent forms of centralization and integration" (p. 49). These are the forces, in short, that are eroding or completely demolishing barriers. The forces of localization, by contrast, are "all those pressures that lead people, groups and transnational organizations to narrow their horizons and withdraw in *decentralizing* and possibly *disintegrating* directions" (emphasis added; p. 49). Globalization and localization, however, should not be viewed as strictly separate or independent forces; they especially should not be viewed as either strictly positive or negative forces. They are, instead, mutually constitutive. One leads to the other, and vice versa. More significantly, both are part of a unified whole. Both have positive *and* negative impacts on human society (as well as the natural world), and both are an integral part of the human condition.

At the same time, it is essential to recognize that the forces or dynamics of globalization and localization are not simply linked together in a primarily contingent and, therefore, random manner; rather, they are, as Rosenau argued, "founded on underlying tendencies that infuse direction into the course of events . . ." (p. 51). To see this, we need, first, to adopt a long-term perspective. Second, and more important, we need to adopt a position "as to whether in a broader context of time the dynamics of globalization occur prior to, and underlie, those of localization" (p. 52). That is, we need to attribute "primary causal power to globalization," which, Rosenau claimed, is not difficult to do. As he put it:

> For a broad array of reasons, recorded human experience is a history of expanding horizons, of individuals, families, tribes and societies driven by technology and industrialization to move into increasingly coherent and encompassing forms of social, economic and political organization. No less historically conspicuous than the movement along these lines have been the resistances to the globalizing dynamics, counter-reactions driven by the need for identity and the psychic comforts of shared territory and culture to retreat into narrower forms of social, economic and political organization, all of which can be seen as localizing processes that infuse further fragmentation into the course of events. Considered across long stretches of time, in short, the interactive dynamics consist of globalizing *theses* that give rise to localizing *antitheses* which foster new globalizing *syntheses*. (emphasis added; p. 52)

The words "thesis," "antithesis," and "synthesis" in Rosenau's passage highlight the presumption that globalization is the driving force of history. The words also highlight Rosenau's understanding of history as a *dialectical* process; that is, as a *cumulative* but inherently *conflictual* and seemingly *contradictory* process of change. For the purposes of this chapter (and at the risk of oversimplifying a complex argument), this means that the process of globalization itself is a key source of conflict in the world today. And as the process of globalization accelerates, which it has been doing, the prospects for more conflict and more intense forms of conflict—and violence—also increase. If true, exactly why is this the case?

The answer, as I have already suggested, is very clear. Globalization is often a highly disruptive process. It not only breaks down borders and barriers among peoples, but in so doing, it threatens traditional or long-standing relations of power, patterns of behavior, and social arrangements. Globalization, moreover, is not merely some generalized process that affects all societies and all peoples equally. It is, instead, a deeply *politicized* and profoundly *uneven* process. Some places and people benefit more (much more) than others, and some places and people have far greater influence over the nature, pace, and direction of globalization than others. All of this is well understood by those who "resist" or contest globalization—or, to put it in a more positive light, by those who attempt to "preserve" their way of life and maintain a greater balance in their world or the world at large. Resistance, of course, does not always entail violence; indeed, much (if not most) resistance to globalization is nonviolent. Terrible violence, however, is sometimes difficult to avoid because the stakes are so high and the changes—at times—are so rapid, disruptive, and far-reaching, whether at a local, national, or global level. When whole communities or societies are seriously threatened by change, or when the opportunities for peaceful contestation are limited (or nonexistent), moreover, the turn toward violence may be practically inevitable (or, at least, *highly probable*).

Globalization and Terrorism: An Example

A good example of how globalization disrupts lives at the local level and leads to violence is provided by Helena Norberg-Hodge (2001/2002). For centuries, she noted, the relationship between the Buddhist majority and Muslim minority in Ladakh, or "Little Tibet," in the state of Kashmir, was extremely amicable and peaceful: *in 600 years, there was not one recorded instance of conflict.* "But within a decade of the imposition of western-style 'development' [that is, economic globalization], Buddhists and Muslims were engaged in pitched battles—including the bombing of each other's homes. Even mild-mannered grandmothers, who a decade earlier had been drinking tea with their Muslim neighbors, told me, 'We have to kill all the Muslims or they will finish us off'" (p. 37). The transformation from tranquillity to terrorism, contended Norberg-Hodge, was the direct product of globalization. Specifically, it was the result of Ladakh's integration into the global economy, which began in 1975. Before 1975, the local economy had been largely self-sufficient; villages produced food, energy, medicine, and all those products necessary for a comfortable life. Once opened up to the outside world, however, local producers were overwhelmed, and the traditional culture was displaced by a global monoculture.

In addition, wrote Norberg-Hodge, "A new form of competition began to separate the Ladakhis from one another [although all Ladakhis were becoming 'closer' to the rest of world]. As the 'cheap' subsidised goods from outside destroyed the local economy, Ladakhis were forced to fight for the scarce jobs of the new money economy" (p. 37). But this was not all. New competitive pressures also replaced the local materials and resources upon which the Ladakhis had relied for centuries. Instead of cheap and plentiful stone and wool, the local economy became increasingly dependent on expensive and scarce imported materials: concrete, steel, cotton, and polyester. "The result was artificial scarcity: people who had managed well for centuries on local materials were now, in effect, in fierce competition with everyone else on the planet" (p. 37). Of course, not everyone suffered—or suffered equally—in this changed environment. Some Ladakhis, no doubt, fared quite well. Not coincidentally, those who did fare well were primarily Muslim. This was because the breaking down of boundaries between Ladakh and Kashmir meant a dramatic change in (local) *relations of power:* where power was once dispersed throughout the villages, it became concentrated in bureaucracies controlled by the Muslim-dominated state of Kashmir. This concentration of power in Muslim hands led to discrimination against the Buddhists living in Ladakh. In this way, Norberg-Hodge argued, "ethnic and religious differences—once largely ignored—began to take on a political dimension, causing bitterness and enmity on a scale previously unknown" (p. 38).

The division of power based on religious lines, a structuralist would point out, is not preordained. What is important is the fact that religion often serves as the most convenient—and powerful—*symbol of difference* among peoples. In times of relative peace and stability, this is not of great concern. In times of significant change and instability, by contrast, symbols of difference can play a central role in, for example, justifying or legitimizing new relations of power, or an uneven distribution of resources, or social injustice, or any other situation of inequality and oppression. When this is done, moreover, the differences begin to take on a life of their own. Differences—be they religious, ethnic, racial, socioeconomic, tribal, or something else—are exaggerated and *essentialized.* In this situation, one's own identification becomes the standard by which all differences are judged or, more accurately, *prejudged* as dangerous, inferior, or debased. This, in short, is fundamentalism. And it is this type of fundamentalism that, in the contemporary period, has sparked (*but* not caused) a global outbreak of hatred, political violence, and terrorism.

Some Methodological Considerations

In the example of Ladakh, it is evident that the underlying cause of violence (and terrorism) was the inequality and seriously unbalanced power relations brought about by globalizing forces. It was *not* religion or religious differences. It was *not* fundamentalism per se. It was *not* blind hatred of others. Nor was it a psychological trauma or mental defect suffered by a few (thousand) unbalanced individuals. Or at least this is what a structuralist might argue. But this raises an important question (the same sort of question I raised following the discussion of the rational choice perspective): how do we *know* if the structural argument is correct? To many of you, the argument above may sound persuasive. Still, as a good comparativist (and as a good reader), you should have already asked yourself: is one example—one case, no matter how compelling and seemingly relevant—enough?

The clear answer is "no." To accept, even tentatively, the structural argument about the relationship between globalization and political violence (and terrorism), it is necessary to engage in much more extensive comparative analysis. But how much more extensive does our comparative analysis need to be? Certainly, a two-unit comparison would be equally inadequate. In large part, this is because the argument above makes a big claim about the general (and causal) impact that a particular, albeit complex, phenomenon (that is, globalization) has on a wide range of units or countries. In other words, because the argument above purports to make a comprehensive theoretical claim (as opposed to a very limited or narrowly focused one), it is necessary to provide as broad an empirical base as possible—that is, to include a very large number of units or countries. Unfortunately, this is much, much easier said than done, especially for a student with limited knowledge, resources, and time. Even for a full-time researcher, this would be extremely difficult. In addition, it is important to remember that the greater the number of cases, the less likely that each individual case will be examined in sufficient depth and with sufficient care. This unavoidable trade-off means that the structural argument above would be, for all intents and purposes, impossible to "prove." This does not, however, mean that we should simply give up. Rather, it means that we should exercise caution and humility with regard to making "big" causal claims.

This said, a *practical approach* would be to incorporate at least four, five, or six *carefully chosen* cases into our analysis using a mixed design, including within-case comparisons (as Norberg-Hodge did in her analysis of the Ladakh case). There is, however, no "magic number." But four to six cases do allow us to do better what Guy Peters (1998) argued is a strength of small-N comparative analysis, namely, to *eliminate* possible causes. It is far easier— and quite valuable—to argue that X does not cause Y than it is to establish that X causes Y. Thus, if we want to eliminate "religion" and "ethnicity" (or, even more specifically, "Islamic culture") as a cause or *the* cause of political violence or terrorism, we can try to choose cases in which religion or ethnicity clearly play an important role *and* cases in which they do not. Moreover, if we want to show that it is not strictly "poverty," "inequality," or "oppression" per se that results in political violence or terrorism, then we need to include additional cases focusing on these variables. Eliminating a range of possible causes, however, does not automatically strengthen a structural argument focused on globalization. Accordingly, our research would also need to examine cases, such as the Ladakh case, in which the impact of "globalization" can be clearly established and the consequences clearly delineated. Of course, in all those cases in which our point is to eliminate other causes, we also need to demonstrate the causal significance of "globalization." From this brief discussion, it is easy to see why it is necessary to examine more than one or two cases. We can also see, however, that as the number of cases expands, the sheer effort required to carry out a *meaningful* and *substantive* comparative analysis also expands at an even greater pace.

■ Conclusion: The (Methodological) Dangers of Studying Terrorism

"Terrorism" is not only a complex term but also an extremely emotional one. One might even say that the concept of terrorism is inherently arbitrary. For this reason alone, the study of "terrorism"—that is, the attempts to discern its reasons, motivations, and causes—is fraught with dangers. But the study of terrorism is also difficult because the phenomenon itself (no matter how we choose to define it) is extremely diverse and complex. As Crenshaw wrote, "Terrorism is often presented as an undifferentiated phenomenon, yet its conduct takes a variety of complex forms. Terrorism differs in level of violence, innovativeness, and choice of targets. The actors who use it are different. Its effectiveness varies" (1998b, p. 248). Indeed, the contexts of terrorism are sometimes so different as to make meaningful comparisons extremely problematic. Consider, for example, the case of Sri Lanka, in which terrorism is endemic and protracted: the violence began in the 1950s and still continues; since 1972, according to Whittaker (2001, p. 84), some 58,000 civilians and military people have died as a result of terroristic violence (with two-thirds of these deaths occurring in the years 1984–1997). Now, compare this with the former West Germany, in which the infamous Red Army Faction (once known as the Baader-Meinhof Gang) attacked several banks, burned a department store or two, and killed a number of bankers, industrialists, and judges over the span of seven years or so. Is it worthwhile comparing these two cases? Or are these two situations of terrorism so different that completely separate theories or explanatory accounts are required?

There is a good reason to think about this question. In much of the earlier literature on terrorism—especially the literature dominated by psychological explanations—there was a strong tendency by researchers to make blanket statements that, as Reich (1998) put it, "attributed certain characteristics to 'terrorists' with the implication that all terrorists, of whatever variety, possess them" (p. 262). This sort of overgeneralization, Reich continued, "is a product of loose and weak thinking . . ." (p. 262). I agree. *But it is also a product,*

I might emphasize, of a lack of serious comparative thinking. On this point, it is worth noting that many, if not most, psychological explanations of terrorism focused on terrorism in the Western world: Europe (Germany, Italy, Spain) and the United States. In this regard, comparisons were definitely made, but they were made among a relatively circumscribed group of "most similar countries." This sort of comparison is certainly reasonable (as I discussed in Chapter 2), but the claims that derive from such comparisons must be appropriately qualified. For example, in his study of "terrorist psychologic" (which I referenced earlier in this chapter), Jerrold Post (1998) claimed that *"individuals become terrorists in order to join terrorist groups and commit acts of terrorism"* (emphasis in original; p. 35). Post made no effort to qualify this argument. It is simply *the* truth about terrorists and terrorism. As he put it, "That is surely an extreme statement, but since we are discussing political extremism, perhaps that excess can be forgiven" (p. 35). He is wrong. That is, his excess *cannot* be forgiven, because he has not taken the minimal methodological steps to support such a bold claim. Even if he is right about the German or Basque terrorists on whom he focused, his disregard for well-thought-out comparative analysis makes his whole argument suspect.[7]

In addition, as Brannan, Esler, and Strindberg (2001) pointed out in their aptly titled article, "Talking to Terrorists," many studies of terrorism contain another serious methodological flaw that, although not directly related to comparative analysis, is certainly worth highlighting. Specifically, despite an emphasis on qualitative, context-rich, and historically based analysis, there is an almost complete absence of the most critical type of empirical data, namely, in-depth interviews with the terrorists themselves (that is, "talking to terrorists"). Although such firsthand evidence is not always required, it is extremely pertinent for research that claims to know about the psychological attributes and motivations of "terrorists." As the authors asked, "How is it possible to make psychoanalytical pronouncements about individuals one has never had contact with? What is the validity of statements about the morality of individuals with whom one has never communicated? How is one able to gauge the human dimensions that underpin the embrace of violence without having, quite simply, ever made an effort to find out?" (p. 8). The answers are obvious. Even more, because so much of the research on terrorism is systematically biased in that researchers generally approach terrorism and terrorists as an enemy to be defeated, rather than as a social phenomenon to be understood and explained, the unwillingness to "talk to terrorists" tends to create distorted, "unscientific," and deeply flawed analysis. The problem is exacerbated when researchers only rely on studies (that is, secondary sources) done by other researchers following the basic practice. Although not everyone would agree with this position, the methodological point is sound.[8]

The lessons here are clear. First, good, solid arguments require you to think carefully about method. Second, thinking carefully about method specifically allows you to avoid making simple mistakes, overstatements, or unsupportable claims. Third, thinking carefully about method often involves thinking comparatively. Last, a strong methodological approach is useless if you ignore relevant and important evidence and if your analysis is systematically distorted by hidden or not-so-hidden biases. The subject of "terrorism" is particularly prone to this sort of problem, but no matter what subject or issue you study, the lessons, pitfalls, and dangers are likely to be the same or quite similar.

■ Notes

1. For some representative examples from psychology, see Post (1998), Bandura (1999), and Charlesworth (2003). In international relations, a few prominent examples include Pillar (2001), Abrams and Johnson (1998), and Richardson (1998); in law, see Evans and Murphy (1978); and in counterterrorism studies, see Hoffman (1998), Laqueur (1999), and Betts (2002). To give a sense of the number of legally based analyses of terrorism, consider that the American Society of International Law (ASIL) lists nearly 200 articles on the "Legal Aspects of Terrorism" (1990–2001) on its Web site (http://www.asil.org/terrorism.htm).

2. Many scholars have argued that states have been among the main perpetrators of terrorist violence. For a few examples, see Sluka (1999) and Corradi (1992). Nassar (2004), to cite another example, argued that the modern era, especially since the beginning of World War II, has been largely defined by state-sanctioned terrorism: the Holocaust, Stalin's reign of terror in the former Soviet Union, the US decision to drop atomic bombs on Hiroshima and Nagasaki, the Soviet invasion of Afghanistan, and the US attack on Indochina, among many others (pp. 30–31).

3. For a more in-depth discussion on defining terrorism, see Howard and Sawyer (2003), chap. 1.

4. The concept of collective rationality is based on the work of Edward Muller and Karl-Dieter Opp (1986), who wrote that "average citizens may adopt a collectivist conception of rationality because they recognize that what is individually rational is collectively irrational" (cited in Crenshaw 1998a, p. 9).

5. For other discussions of suicide terrorism, see Sprinzak (2000) and Hoffman (2003).

6. A profile of Sheik Muhammed Husayn Fadlallah can be found on the Internet at http://almashriq.hiof.no/lebanon/300/320/324/324.2/hizballah/Fadlallah-Muhammad.html.

7. Significantly, Post (1998) explicitly included Shiite and Palestinian terrorists in his analysis but admitted that "comparable data are not available . . . , but specialists who have closely followed Middle Eastern terrorist groups share the *impression* that many of their members come from the margins of society and that belonging to these fundamentalist or nationalist groups powerfully contributes to consolidating psychosocial identity at a time of great societal instability and flux" (emphasis added; p. 31).

8. For another slightly different perspective on methodological issues in terrorism studies, see Silke (2001).

8

What Makes a Social Movement?

Understanding the Rise and Success of Social Movements

Atsuko Sato

The study of social movements has generated a large liter-
ature in sociology, history, political science, and comparative politics. In the ear-
liest literature (prior to the 1970s), social movements were largely portrayed as
anomalous, "irrational," sometimes "hysterical," and invariably threatening political phenomena.[1] In this respect, social movements were typically described
as the organized end of a spectrum, whose opposite, disorganized pole was characterized by anomic (that is, socially unstable and alienated) crowds and riots
(Blumer 1939; cited in Roth and Horan 2005). Over time, the image and understanding of social movements changed, a reflection, in part, of changes in social movements themselves. Many participants in social movements from the
1960s on, for example, could hardly be described as "socially unstable and
alienated" malcontents—for example, those pressing for the expansion of civil
rights, social justice, and political equality in the civil rights and women's
movements in the United States were often highly educated and economically
well off. Equally important were theoretical developments. The growing influence of rationalist approaches and rational choice theory, for example, led many
scholars to reject completely the idea that any significant social, political, or
economic phenomenon could be driven primarily, if not purely, by collective
"irrationality." In other words, many researchers believed that there *had* to be a
rational basis for explaining the phenomenon of social movements.

From a different perspective, developments in structural and cultural approaches, too, encouraged a rethinking of traditional explanations. It is significant that one of the most prominent new approaches emerged from comparatively based research in Western Europe, the new social movement (NSM)
approach. This approach rejected old-fashioned structural theories (that is,
Marxism) for being "reductionist"; that is, for attempting to reduce everything

to economics and class. A good part of this criticism derived from close empirical analysis of the Western European cases, which seemed to show that contemporary social movements were being dominated by a new type of collective actor. The identity of this new actor was not, as a Marxist would assert, fundamentally based on his place in the system of production but instead was defined in relation to ostensibly nonclass issues, such as gender, ethnicity, age, neighborhood, the environment, and peace (Canel 1997). The NSM approach, in this regard, argued that a full understanding of social movements—in particular, the passage from the (structural) *conditions* for change to *mobilization* and *action*—could only be achieved by accounting for the effects of culture, politics, and ideology (Canel 1997).

In sum, there has been a sea change in studies of social movements. This chapter, of course, will discuss a number of these changes. As in the other chapters, we will discuss the issue of social movements from a rationalist, structural, and cultural perspective. As we will see, however, the separation among these three approaches is not as strong as in some of our other chapters. In this sense, there is clear space for theoretical synthesis or integration. Indeed, many researchers argue that there is a *need* for synthesis (for example, McAdam, Tarrow, and Tilly 1997; Canel 1997).

■ Defining Social Movements

Before going any farther, it is important to clarify what is meant by the term "social movement." Unfortunately, as with many concepts in the social sciences, we can find a number of competing and not always compatible definitions. One reason for the lack of a strong consensus is clear: namely, researchers using different theoretical approaches do not always share the same assumptions and goals. Of course, this is not always an insurmountable obstacle—for example, in studies of democracy, as we have seen, there is a considerable degree of consensus among scholars from all three research schools. Still, it is not unusual for definitions within different research schools to emphasize different properties, aspects, and characteristics of key concepts. This is the case with social movements. For instance, Sidney Tarrow, deeply influenced by works on **collective action** by Charles Tilly,[2] defined social movements as *"collective challenges by people with common purposes and solidarity in sustained interaction with elites, opponents and authorities"* (emphasis in original; Tarrow 1994, pp. 3–4). Tarrow also specified that the concepts of "collective challenge," "common purpose," "solidarity," and "sustained interaction" were the four key empirical properties of social movements (pp. 3–4). By defining social movements in this manner, it is important to note, the causes of and the efficacy of these movements are essentially embedded in the definition itself. That is, the main cause of a social movement is a collective challenge, and efficacy is measured by the commonality of purpose, solidarity, and sustainability of interaction (sustained interaction suggests that social movements are always more than a single protest).

A similar definition is given to us by Jenkins and Klandermans (1995), who have also been influenced by Tilly's pathbreaking work. Specifically, Jenkins and Klandermans defined a social movement as "a sustained series of interactions between the state and challenging groups" (p. 5). The authors asserted, moreover, that social movements themselves were, in effect, collective agents capable of restructuring the relationship between the state and civil society. Like Tarrow, Jenkins and Klandermans highlighted the empirical—that is, observable and measurable—aspects of social movements in their definition. The authors, therefore, presented us with an operational definition that we can use to analyze social movements in a wide range of contexts and places.

In contrast to empirically based definitions, scholars who adopt a cultural framework tend to focus on the cognitive and ideational dimensions of social movements. That is, they tend to define social movements in terms of ideology and identity. For instance, Kaase defined social movements as "eventual manifestations of latent sociospatial networks with culturally derived identities" (1990, p. 98). This admittedly dense and difficult-to-decipher definition tells us that culture shapes and influences social movements by defining how people see and think about themselves. At the same time, cultural theorists recognize, as we have already learned, that social movements are not just an "effect" of culture but also a "cause," which is to say that once social movements emerge they may produce or alter dominant cultural patterns (Johnston and Klandermans 1995, pp. 14–16). The focus on cognitive and ideational factors, it is important to note, has an important methodological implication, one that contrasts quite sharply with an empirically based definition—namely, cultural analysis of social movements is much more likely to be deeply qualitative, interpretative, and holistic.

Despite the obvious gulf between the two sets of definitions discussed above (for more definitions, see Figure 8.1), some basic agreement is possible. Indeed, there are at least two essential characteristics of social movements about which most scholars agree. One of these is the understanding that all social movements reflect *collective action* usually manifested through organized protest, and the second is the understanding that social movements are meant to influence or effect some change in society (the change, however, does not need to be progressive). With these two points in mind, social movements can be defined most simply as *any broad social alliance of people who are associated in seeking to influence an aspect of political or social change* (Jary and Jary 1991, p. 456). Concretely, there are many examples of social movements:

- the 2003 antiwar movement in the United States and other countries protesting the Bush administration's preemptive attack against Iraq;
- the 1989 student-led democracy movement in China (symbolized most powerfully by the massive demonstrations in Tiananmen Square in Beijing);

Figure 8.1 Selected Definitions of Social Movements

Social movements can be viewed as collective enterprises to establish a new order of life. They have their inception in the condition of unrest, and derive their motive power on one hand from dissatisfaction with the current form of life, and on the other hand, from wishes and hopes for a new scheme or system of living.

Source: Herbert Blumer, "Collective Behavior," in Robert E. Park, ed., *An Outline of the Principles of Sociology* (New York: Barnes and Noble, 1939), p. 199.

Mass movements mobilize people who are alienated from the going system, who do not believe in the legitimacy of the established order, and who therefore are ready to engage in efforts to destroy it. The greatest number of people available to mass movements will be found in those sections of society that have the fewest ties to the social order.

Source: William Kornhauser, *The Politics of Mass Society* (New York: The Free Press, 1959), p. 212.

[Social movements are] those organized efforts, on the part of excluded groups, to promote or resist changes in the structure of society that involve recourse to noninstitutional forms of political participation.

Source: Doug McAdam, *Political Process and the Development of Black Insurgency 1930–1970* (Chicago: University of Chicago Press, 1982), p. 25.

A social movement is a collectivity acting with some continuity to promote or resist a change in the society or organization of which it is a part. As a collectivity a movement is a group with indefinite and shifting membership and with leadership whose position is determined more by informal response of the members than by formal procedures for legitimating authority.

Source: Ralph H. Turner and Lewis M. Killian, *Collective Behavior* (Englewood Cliffs, NJ: Prentice Hall, [1972] 1987), p. 223.

[A social movement is a] set of opinions and beliefs in a population which represents preferences for changing some elements of the social structure and/or reward distribution of a society.

Source: John McCarthy and Mayer Zald, "Resource Mobilization and Social Movements: A Partial Theory," *American Journal of Sociology* 82 (May 1977): 1217–1218.

Based on a list of definitions compiled by Benita Roth, http://womhist.binghamton.edu/socm/definitions.htm.

- the civil rights movements of 1955–1965 in the United States;
- ecological or environmental movements concerned with limiting or reversing environmental degradation both at the local/national level and the international/global level;
- the "prolife" and "prochoice" movements, both of which seek to influence public policy on abortion;
- the "antiglobalization" movement, an extraordinarily disparate movement designed to challenge **neoliberal** reforms, reshape the agenda of major international institutions and organizations (such as the International Monetary Fund, World Bank, and **World Trade Organization**), and influence national-level regulations and laws governing economic activity;
- the neo-Nazi or "white power" movement in the United States and Europe.

From this very short and admittedly selective list, it should be apparent that social movements can be and are quite diverse. It should also be clear that social movements are not inherently "progressive" and peaceful but, instead, can be profoundly reactionary and aggressive, as in the case of the neo-Nazi movement. Some movements, moreover, are essentially local, whereas others have morphed into broad-based transnational or global movements. Finally, some movements have been extremely "successful" (see Figure 8.2 for a discussion of this deceptively complex concept), whereas others have achieved little or only transitory success in "influencing" political or social change. For "good comparativists"—and for any concerned citizen, really—such observations should raise a plethora of questions about the nature and dynamics of social movements, for social movements are clearly an important and relevant part of our world; indeed, social movements likely come closer to our everyday lives than any other subject discussed in this book. It would not be surprising, in fact, if you, your friends, or your family have participated in a social movement. Fortunately, the three research schools all provide useful frameworks and valuable conceptual tools for understanding social movements. With this in mind, let us begin by examining social movements from a rationalist perspective.

■ Collective Action, Social Movements, and Rationality

How do social movements emerge, develop, and change? Why do some social movements, but not others, result in successful political or social outcomes? To answer these questions from a rationalist perspective, we must, as usual, begin with the basic assumptions of rationality, one of which is a focus

Figure 8.2   What Is a "Successful" Social Movement?

The *American Heritage Dictionary* defines *successful* as "having obtained something desired or intended." In assessing the success of social movements and other forms of political protest, many scholars have adopted the same basic meaning. Gamson (1990), for example, argued that social movements can be considered successful when they fall into two basic clusters: (1) acceptance of a "challenging group" (for example, a social movement) by its antagonists as "a valid spokesman for a legitimate set of interests" and (2) the gain of new advantages by the group's beneficiaries during the challenge and its aftermath (pp. 28–29). Although this basic definition has been accepted by many researchers in their work on social movements, it is actually a bit more complicated than it appears. Specifically, Gamson's two clusters create four possible outcomes, which are represented in the figure below:

	New Advantages	No New Advantages
Acceptance	Full success (partial success)	Co-optation
Nonacceptance	Preemption (partial success)	Collapse (failure)

Source: Adapted from Gamson (1990), p. 29.

(continues)

on individual-level action. That is, from a rationalist perspective it is important to remember that social movements—even if they are defined in terms of *collective* action—must still be understood as the product of decisions made by individual actors. After all, there can be no movement without people (Dixon and Roscigno 2003, p. 1297). Understanding how social movements arise, therefore, requires that we identify the determinants of individual participation. A key question in this regard is whether or not individuals gain new advantages or benefits from a decision to participate in or join a social movement (Gamson 1990, p. 29). For rationalists, in short, individual motivation and strategic calculation are the *basic* keys to explaining the emergence, development, and success or failure of social movements.

Figure 8.2   continued

According to Giugni (1998), this typology has not been fully exploited by most researchers in their analyses of social movement; instead, social movements have been judged in essentially binary terms, that is, full success or full failure. This is regrettable, but it is not the only problem. At a more fundamental level, Giugni asserted that the concepts of success and failure themselves are problematic for three reasons. First, there is a tendency to apply the terms to whole movements, when, in fact, social movements are rarely homogenous. For example, within movements, there is often little agreement among the leaders and participants regarding which goal to pursue, and if we cannot identify a common goal, how can we judge its success or failure? Second, the concept of success itself is subjective. Movement participants and external observers, in particular, may have very different perceptions of what counts as success. Third, "the notion of success is problematic because it overstates the intention of participants" (p. 383).

Despite these problems, most researchers continue to use the concept of success (and failure) in their analyses, and Giugni himself saw this as a legitimate endeavor. The key, however, is to remember that, "like all kinds of action, the effects of social movements are often indirect, unintended, and sometimes even in contradiction to their goals" (p. 386). Moreover, many effects of social movements (unintended and intended) may not be fully recognized for years. It is critical to keep these points in mind.

Unlike the collective goods problem discussed in Chapters 4 and 5, however, participation in social movements does *not* ultimately hinge on the capacity of political or social institutions to coerce or otherwise compel participation from reluctant free riders. Indeed, a distinguishing aspect of social movements is that participation is largely voluntary. In this regard, many rationalists understand social movements as a form of cooperative or collective self-help designed to achieve material gains (or other individual benefits) that would be difficult, if not impossible, to achieve through individual action alone. It is easy to see, for example, that individuals who are not happy with their working conditions will join a labor movement to pursue material advantages, such as higher wages, increased health benefits, greater job security, and reduced workloads. More generally, some researchers argue that given situations of deprivation, people are more likely to develop grievances and, therefore, more likely to participate in social movements to address their grievances. Moreover, for individuals experiencing severe economic deprivation, doing nothing (that is, nonparticipation) is already very costly; therefore, joining a social movement that promises to improve their situation is rational, even if the rewards are relatively diffuse and uncertain. Deprivation and grievances, it is important to understand, are not necessarily based on economic or material considerations alone. The gay pride movement, the civil rights movement, the feminist (or women's) movement (including, for example, the political struggle for the Equal Rights Amendment or ERA) all revolved or revolve around questions of social alienation and political marginalization, although, even here, economic concerns may be an underlying factor.

On the surface, then, a rationality-based approach seems to offer an exceedingly simple yet compelling explanation for the emergence of social movements. Yet if we delve only slightly below the surface, it is clearly a very limited explanation, as many critics have pointed out. To understand why, it is important to re-emphasize a point made above: social movements, in general, are geared toward achieving collective, as opposed to private, goods. That is, social movements (especially contemporary social movements) typically produce broad political, economic, and social changes that, by their very nature, are nonexclusive. The success of the civil rights movement in the United States or the antiapartheid movement in South Africa, for example, brought essentially the same expansion of rights to every member of black society in both countries whether or not they participated in the struggle. It is worth noting, too, that participating in the struggle for civil rights or against apartheid entailed huge potential costs—for example, imprisonment, extreme harassment, torture, and even death. As I suggested earlier, we are therefore faced with a serious collective goods problem, which is significantly different from the collective goods problem we discussed in Chapters 4 and 5. To repeat: without the existence of a political or social institution that can coerce or compel participation in the creation of a public good, how can the free-rider problem be overcome?

Social Movements and the Collective Goods Problem

This issue, not surprisingly, has not gone unnoticed by rationalist scholars. It is ironic, though, that many seem only to offer an explanation for why people do *not* participate in social movements. Mancur Olson (1932–1998), one of the leading figures in the field of public choice and an eminent economist, for example, came right to the point in his seminal work, *The Logic of Collective Action* (1965). As Olson put it, "unless the number of individuals is quite small, or unless there is coercion or some other special device to make individuals act in their common interest, *rational self-interested individuals will not act to achieve their common or group interests*" (emphasis in original; p. 2). Writing much earlier, Eric Hoffer, another prominent scholar working under the collective behavior tradition, described the seemingly irrational human behavior of participation in mass movements in much more colorful terms: "For men to plunge headlong into an undertaking of vast change, they must be intensely discontented yet not destitute. . . . They must also have an extravagant conception of [or be] wholly ignorant of the difficulties involved in their vast undertaking. Experience is a handicap" (Hoffer 1951, 7).

The basic assumption of rationality, in short, leads to a paradox: guided by self-interest, participation in collective action based on voluntary, cooperative group behavior is seemingly irrational; yet there are hundreds of significant, dynamic, and successful social movements throughout the world. Indeed, given the singular logic of self-interest, many social movements should not even exist, still less develop the collective force necessary to bring about significant political or social change. Without resolving the free-rider puzzle, therefore, rationalist theories might very well have little or nothing meaningful to say about social movements.[3]

The problem is made even more serious in the case of so-called new social movements (see Figure 8.3 for a definition), which tend to be more "al-

---

Figure 8.3   New Social Movements

Most simply, *new social movements* can be defined as those that have arisen since the late 1960s; they include the ecology, gay rights, animal rights, anti–nuclear energy, New Age, peace, and women's movements (Kriesi et al. 1995). What separates "new" social movements (NSMs) from "old" social movements, according to Johnston, Laraña, and Gusfield (1994, pp. 6–9), are eight basic characteristics:

- NSMs are not generally class-based; instead, the "structural roots" of these movements tend to be based on a diffuse social status, such as gender, sexual orientation, or profession.
- NSMs are characterized by a pluralism of ideas and values rather than a clear-cut ideological position.
- NSMs often involve the emergence of new or formerly weak dimensions of identity, often ethnically or historically based.
- In NSMs, the distinction between the collective and the individual is blurred.
- NSMs are concerned with a range of ostensibly noneconomic issues: abortion, alternative medicine, opposition to smoking, sexual behavior, and so on.
- NSMs tend to use "radical" mobilization strategies of disruption and resistance.
- NSMs reflect, to some degree, skepticism toward conventional channels for democratic participation.
- NSMs tend to be segmented, diffuse, and decentralized.

truistic" (that is, less materially motivated) than traditional social movements. To appreciate the significance of this point, consider environmental movements. In these movements, the effort by participants to protect the ozone layer, combat climate change, save endangered species, or preserve tropical rain forests is based on achieving an unequivocal collective good. Even more, since "successful" environmental movements may actually raise the economic costs for individuals living in the most industrialized societies (from which many of the most vocal and active participants in environmental movement come), the rational basis for participation is undermined even further. Other types of new social movements, such as animal rights, are even more problematic from a rationalist perspective, since it appears that individuals in such movements are motivated exclusively by nonmaterial and normative considerations. Moreover, new social movements present at least one additional and no less important complication: namely, many of the participants come from "high-status" as opposed to "low-status" groups. We will discuss why this is important below.

Resource Mobilization Theory

Despite or even because of these difficulties, a great deal of valuable and insightful research on social movements has been done using a rationalist framework. One of the most important efforts in this regard is what has come to be called the *resource mobilization model* (RSM) of political action, which is primarily a product of US scholars. As Dalton, Kuechler, and Bürklin (1990) explained it, "Resource mobilization theorists presume that political dissatisfaction and social conflicts are inherent in every society; thus the formation of social movements depends not on the existence of these interests but on the creation of organizations to mobilize this potential" (pp. 8–9). In this way, researchers adopting a rationalist framework are able to address the collective goods problem by shifting the analytical focus to the social movements themselves or rather to the organizational basis for social movements. At first glance, this may appear to be little more than intellectual sleight of hand, for a "social movement," or even a "social movement organization," is obviously not an individual actor. It is important to understand, however, that social movements or social movement organizations (SMOs)[4] *are* peopled by individual actors. This is a simple yet key aspect of RSM theory, which asserts that a relatively small group of individual actors—the leadership in particular (McCarthy and Zald 1973)—is most responsible, and sometimes entirely responsible, for ensuring the success of social movements. It is the leadership, for example, acting through the SMO, that mobilizes people, money, and other resources in pursuit of a cause (Dalton, Kuechler, and Bürklin 1990, p. 9). Leaders, moreover, identify and define grievances, develop a group sense, devise strategies, and facilitate mobilization by reducing its costs and taking advantage of opportunities for collective action (Canel 1997). It is the leadership, in short, that is the rational core of social movements.

With respect to this last point, it is also important to emphasize that leaders (and other key members of the SMO) *are* rational actors. That is, their decisions are based on a cost-benefit assessment of the chances of success and on a conscious calculation of how best to advance the organization's goals. Even more important, perhaps, leaders of SMOs are frequently motivated by wholly self-interested goals. RSM scholars, for example, point to the increasing professionalization of contemporary SMOs. This means that *the leaders'* participation in SMOs is not necessarily based on creating a collective good for all to enjoy but on enhancing their own careers and professional status. From this perspective, it is no surprise that the strategies and actions of SMOs are not always those of the social movements as a whole (Canel 1997). Indeed, some scholars have found that, once a social movement organization is formed, the implementation of policies desired by the "rank-and-file" membership often has to compete with the desire of the organization's leadership to maintain itself (Dalton, Kuechler, and Bürklin 1990, p. 9).

Social Networks and Participation in Social Movements

Although the foregoing discussion is quite general (and, admittedly, oversimplified), it is fair to say that RSM theory has made strong contributions to our understanding of social movements and social movement organizations, especially with regard to their internal and organizational dynamics. Still, as presented, the RSM model of political action fails to account for the ostensibly irrational behavior of ordinary citizens who participate in social movements—a phenomenon that cannot be overlooked. After all, even a strong, rationally motivated SMO requires some sort of mass base to be successful. Not surprisingly, there are many studies that address this issue, too. If you recall, we already suggested one simple explanation above, namely, that individuals with little or nothing to lose may have a rational basis for joining social movements. Indeed, as Dixon and Roscigno (2003) noted, this is the basic position in a large body of literature grounded in rationality that holds, in very general terms, "that individuals of markedly low status or those with greater autonomy from institutional or political constraint will be more likely to participate, since the costs of involvement (be they social, political or economic) will be lower and rewards arguably higher" (p. 1294). But, as we also noted, it is not only individuals from "low-status" groups that join new social movements; instead, there is increasing participation from members of "high-status" groups—for example, highly educated, upper-middle-class whites. This is clearly evident in women's movements, environmental movements, and peace movements (p. 1294), especially in the United States and other well-off countries. The reason why this is a concern is simple: high-status individuals have much less to gain from participation (at least in material terms), and the "costs" of participation (even if only "opportunity costs") are generally higher. In short, their participation has a weaker rational basis.

To account for the participation of individuals from high-status groups in particular (but for all individual actors in general), some rationalists have focused on the idea of "social ties" or "social networks" (concepts, it is important to note, that are also used by structuralists). The basic argument here is that social networks, which are generally based on friendships or community relationships, serve to "condition" the decisions individuals make. More specifically, rationalists argue that individuals are more likely to join social movements when they have social ties to other joiners (Gould 2003, 240). But why is this rational behavior? Gould explained it this way: "people who expect *future interaction* with movement participants should be more likely, all else [being] equal (in particular, holding constant sympathy with movement goals and tactics) to join." "Such people," Gould continued, "are more likely to view joining as *beneficial to themselves* because their 'ties' to other joiners give the latter an opportunity to reward (or punish) their decision to join (or not to join)" (emphasis added; p. 241). This account, moreover, helps explain why social movements that are directed to the benefit of a third party (for example, child workers in foreign countries, endangered animals, young women subject to female circumcision in Africa) are still able to attract participants; to repeat, so long as the other joiners can reward us with their continued "friendship" or other benefits of an ongoing social relationship, our participation is rational (p. 241).

The process just described is, in more formal terms, similar to reciprocity in the logic of a reiterated or repeated game.[5] In a repeated game, the behavior of actors is dependent on or conditioned by the prospect of continued interaction. Put simply, since all actors understand that they will meet again, all have an incentive to be "nice" to each other: if you are nice to me, I'll be nice to you, because I know that, if I'm not nice today, you'll "punish" me tomorrow and thereafter (Gould 2003, p. 240; Axelrod 1984). Thus, if my friend wants me to join a social movement, I will cooperate ("be nice") by joining the movement, but I will expect a sustained friendship (my reward). Of course, my friend also realizes a (reciprocal) gain. This is a key point, for, as Axelrod argued, "once cooperation based on reciprocity is established in a population, it can protect itself from invasion by uncooperative strategies" (1984, p. 173). In other words, the free-rider problem is overcome in a repeated game.

What Makes a Social Movement Successful?

So, from a rationalist perspective, what makes a movement successful? Based on the foregoing discussion, we can identify several key factors. Perhaps the most important is a capable, strategically oriented leadership. Leaders are indispensable for generating a movement and providing the necessary impetus to move it forward. Successful movements also require a second factor, however: an organizational structure or a social movement organization. SMOs allow a movement to maintain itself over time, in part because they provide the frame-work for an institutionalized flow of people and money to support the "cause" (Dobson 2003) A third important factor is simply people. Successful social movements require an active membership, but as we have learned, this is eas-ier said than done. In particular, the free-rider problem creates a tremendous obstacle to broad-based participation. Thus, a successful movement will tap into social networks as a way to build membership. Often this takes the form of "micromobilization" (Dobson 2003)—that is, the mobilization of small, in-formal groups connected to a broader but very loose network. Micromobiliza-tion, as many rationalist studies predict, takes place among friends and coworkers or sometimes within a subgroup of a larger group, such as a church or a labor union (Dobson 2003). Finally, successful social movements require achievable goals. This may sound obvious, but many movements fail precisely because their goals are not achievable given their resources and the political context within which their action takes place. There are, no doubt, other im-portant factors. The four key factors listed here, however, provide the minimal foundation for a successful social movement.

Conclusion: Limitations of the Rationalist Approach

Do rationalist accounts explain all we need to know about social movements? The short answer is "probably not," but we do not have the space here to pro-vide an in-depth critique. One main criticism, however, is that rationalist expla-nations "do not fully account for the passage from condition to action" (Canel 1997). That is, rationalist accounts, such as resource mobilization theory, "can-not explain the processes of group formation and the origins of the organiza-tional forms it presupposes" (Canel 1997). They fail, moreover, "to explain how a social category—an aggregate of people with shared characteristics—devel-ops a sense of identity and becomes a social group" (Canel 1997). Repeated games may explain some of this, but almost certainly many social movements are more than groups of "friends." Moreover, as Gould pointed out, even if we accept that social movements are largely the product of social networks and ties, "we still have to account for the first movers" (2003, p. 255). That is, we need to answer the question, "If people are converted or recruited by others to whom they are tied, who recruited the first recruiters?" (p. 255).

Finally, it is useful to note that, from a methodological point of view, much (but by no means all) of the research coming from a rationalist per-spective focuses disproportionately on cases located in the United States. Every argument we have discussed in this section (at least those that are not strictly deductive), for example, is based on data or evidence (both qualitative and quantitative) from US-based social movements. When comparative research is done, moreover, Western Europe is the main alternative source of cases. In this sense, the research design adopted by many rationalists, albeit often only implicitly, is the most similar systems (MSS) design. On this point, it is worth asking, would the incorporation of cases from very *different* systems—say, from Africa or Asia—likely confirm or undermine the conclusions rationalists make? In other words, would a most different systems design contribute to our understanding of social movements? Would incorporation of these cases likely support or undermine rationalist claims? We ask these question rhetorically, but they are questions requiring serious attention.

■ Structural Accounts of Social Movements

Rationalists, as we have seen, tend to focus almost exclusively on microlevel or individual-level factors to explain social movements. The underlying social, political, or economic *sources* of the movements are not dismissed, but it is clear that rationalists do not consider these nearly sufficient to account for the rise, development, and (especially) the success of social movements. Structuralists, on the other hand, argue that microlevel factors, even though relevant, are unequivocally secondary in the sense that individual action necessarily takes place under conditions that cannot be molded to the actors' preferences (McAdam, Tarrow, and Tilly 1997, p. 145). In simpler terms, this means that the rise, development, and success (or failure) of social movements are conditioned—constrained and enabled—by forces or structures largely beyond the control of even the most capable leaders and individual activists. It is important to point out, though, that structural accounts of social movements are generally based on a "soft" structuralism; that is, a structuralism that is contingent, rather than strictly determined, and one that is sensitive to the "nuances of the political process" (p. 145). This makes sense, especially for those scholars who focus most of their intellectual energy on the study of social movements. For embedded in the very concept of social movements is an understanding that agency matters. Social movements, after all, are *agents of change;* they are the manifestation of people working collectively and with purpose to bring about change within societies.

Political Opportunity Structure: Mobilizing Social Movements

This position is certainly evident in one of the main structural approaches to the study of social movements, which is based on a concept known as *political opportunity structure* (POS). As with resource mobilization theory, the political opportunity approach emerged first among US scholars studying social movements in the United States. Indeed, it is worth noting that the political opportunity approach arose partly in response to shortcomings in microlevel analyses of social movements, which, as we discussed above, had trouble accounting for the willingness of "rational actors" to join social movements on a large scale. Thus, recognizing the problem of collective action, social movement scholars developed the concept of the "political opportunity structure." Sidney Tarrow (1994) explained this term in the following manner: "By political opportunity structure, I refer to consistent—but not necessarily formal, permanent or national—dimensions of the political environment which either encourage or discourage people from using collective action. The concept of political opportunity emphasizes resources *external* to the group—unlike money or power—that can be taken advantage of even by weak or disorganized challengers" (emphasis in original; p. 18).

According to Tarrow, *it is the political opportunity structure itself, or rather changes in the structure, that create the impetus for social movements.* As he put it, "Social movements form when ordinary citizens, sometimes encouraged by leaders, respond to changes in opportunities that lower the costs of collective action, reveal potential allies and show where elites and authorities are vulnerable" (p. 18). In other words, Tarrow and others posit that changes in the underlying political process (or structure) create "openings" that enable the mobilization of resource-poor actors into new movements.

In this view, then, the analytical focus clearly shifts away from the individual. But rather than shifting to a largely abstract structure like the capitalist system or to a concrete entity like the social movement organization, the POS approach identifies the *political system* and particularly the state as the key structures. The political system, according to Kriesi (1995), is composed of three broad properties: (1) a *formal* institutional structure, (2) *informal procedures* and *prevailing strategies* with regard to challengers, and (3) the *configuration of power* relevant for a confrontation with the challengers (p. 168). On the surface, this makes the POS approach very similar to an institutional approach (or institutionalism). Yet with a stronger deterministic element, there is, arguably, a reasonable basis for classifying POS as a structural approach. The deterministic bias of POS is readily apparent in Tarrow's conceptualization above. But he is not alone: other proponents speak of the manner in which the timing and fate of movements are largely *dependent* upon the opportunities afforded to activists by changes in the broader political system or structure (see, for example, Lipsky 1970, Jenkins and Perrow 1977, and McAdam 1982; cited in McAdam, Tarrow, and Tilly 1997, p. 152). Subsequent studies have continued along the same general track, although there have been efforts to incorporate rationalist assumptions into the political opportunity framework (for example, McAdam 1982).

The Political Opportunity Structure and
"New" Social Movements in Western Europe

With this point in mind, it would be useful to turn to a more concrete discussion of the POS approach. In this regard, a comparative study done by Kriesi, Koopmans, Duyvendak, and Giugni (1995) offered an instructive, although by no means definitive, illustration. Their study is particularly helpful for our purposes, however, because the authors are intent on "specifying the mechanisms that link the *macrostructural* level of the POS to the collective action of movement actors" (emphasis added; p. xv). It is also helpful because Kriesi et al. adopted, as they put it, a "resolutely comparative perspective" for their analysis (p. xxii), one that is explicitly based on a most similar systems design using France, Germany, the Netherlands, and Switzerland in a multiunit study. Thus, they argued that France, Germany, the Netherlands, and Switzerland were quite similar with respect to the level and type of their economic and social development—that is, the control variables—but that they differed with regard to the "political contexts for the mobilization of the new social movements" (p. xxii). The "political context" or structure, in other words, is the key independent variable, whereas the dependent variables in their study are the "mobilization patterns" and the effectiveness of social movements. To the extent that mobilization patterns and effectiveness differ, there is variance on the dependent variable, which, you remember, is an important consideration in an MSS design. Indeed, one of the inspirations for their study is the peace movement of 1983, in which there was a dramatic variation among the Western European countries with regard to mobilization patterns. In Germany, Italy, Britain, Spain, the Netherlands, and Switzerland, the peace movement generated a huge response, but in France there was (relatively speaking) barely a ripple. From the authors' comparative perspective, this raised an obvious question: what set France apart? That is, what were the factors that limited the success of the movement in France?

The authors, of course, have an answer. But before we get to this, it would be useful to summarize the logic of their comparative research design. (See Figure 8.4 for a summary of their basic research strategy.) First, by selecting countries that share a wide range of similar economic and social traits, the authors can (with proper analysis, of course) eliminate these as explanatory or independent variables. Second, by focusing on significant *variations* or differences among the four countries—that is, the political context or political structure—the authors are able to "test" the claims they have derived from their theoretical framework, which, to repeat, is based on the political opportunity structure. Third, by ensuring variance on the dependent variable, Kriesi et al. provided a firmer (although by no means foolproof) methodological basis for their conclusions, since doing so reduced the likelihood of identify-

Figure 8.4   Summary of Research Strategy for Kriesi, Koopmans, Duyvendak, and Giugni, *New Social Movements in Western Europe* (1995)

Comparative Strategy:	Most similar systems, multiunit
Units (4):	France, Germany, the Netherlands, and Switzerland
Control Variables:	Level and nature of economic and social development
Independent Variable(s):	"Political context"
Dependent Variable(s):	Patterns of mobilization, effectiveness of social movements

Source: Adapted from Kriesi et al., *New Social Movements in Western Europe: A Comparative Analysis* (Minneapolis: University of Minnesota Press, 1995).

ing only a spurious correlation between the presumed independent and dependent variables. In sum, the authors laid out a solid, logically consistent, but still fairly simple comparative research design, one that could certainly be replicated by any beginning comparativist.

Empirically, the authors also employed a basic, but useful, strategy, one based primarily on an analysis of newspaper sources. Indeed, the use of "protest-event data" derived from newspapers is a popular method among scholars who study social movements, largely because of the accessibility and consistency of news reports (p. 253). As Kriesi et al. explained it, "Compared to other quantitative sources such as official statistics, yearbooks, or archives, the most important advantages of daily newspapers for the study of the mobilization of social movements are perhaps that they provide a continuous, easily accessible source that includes the whole range of protest events produced in a given country" (p. xxiii). At the same time, reliance on news sources has a number of potential pitfalls: biased or inaccurate reporting and a lack of consistency or comprehensiveness in coverage are the most obvious. In addition, the coding process is a difficult task, since coding of newspaper reports requires transforming qualitative data into quantitative data. This type of problem, however, can be solved by creating specific, systematic coding instructions (p. 255). (The authors provided an extended discussion of the advantages and pitfalls of newspaper analysis in their book on pp. 253–273.)

Theoretically, Kriesi et al. identified four determinants of new social movements in the political opportunity structure: national cleavage structures, institutional structures, prevailing strategies, and alliance structures. Each of these component represents a key part of the political context/structure mentioned above, and each is "more or less systematically linked to each other" (p. xiv). We do not have the space here to provide a full discussion of these components and their interrelationship (the authors devote a full chapter to each one), so a few words will have to suffice.

- *National cleavage structures* refer to "established political conflicts," which have traditionally been divided into four basic categories: center-periphery, religious, urban-rural, and class. The nature and strength of these cleavages will vary depending on particular historical and cultural contexts. In addition, each has a different "mobilization potential," which is a key element of the authors' argument. Kriesi et al. argued, for example, that "salient traditional cleavages," which are evident in the French case, "can be quite constraining for the mobilization of new social movements" (p. 25). On the other hand, "where traditional cleavages are no longer closed and have been pacified, the new social movements seem . . . to find more 'space' to mobilize" (p. 25).

- *Institutional structures* are composed of formal institutional structures of the political system (that is, the state) and the informal procedures and *prevailing strategies* of political elites in dealing with challenges. Both are "deeply embedded in the political heritage of a given political system and, from the point of view of the mobilizing social movements, are essentially fixed and given" (p. 26). More specifically, the authors focused on the "strength" of the state (measured as weak, intermediate, and strong) and the nature of prevailing elite strategies, which they categorized as exclusive (repressive, confrontational, polarizing) or inclusive (facilitative, cooperative, assimilative). It is the combination of the formal institutional structures and the informal procedures, the authors argued, that helps determine the level of movement mobilization, although not always in direct and obvious ways.

- *Alliance structures* refer to specific configurations of power in the political system that are less stable than the other components and include the opening up of access to participation, shifts in ruling alignments, the availability of influential allies, and cleavages within and among elites (p. 53). With respect to Western European social movements, the authors argued that the two most important aspects of the alliance structure were the configuration of power on the left and presence or absence of the Left in government (p. xiv).

Using the methodological and theoretical framework outlined above, the authors set out to systematically "test" their political process model. Not surprisingly, the general results are positive. In relation to the national cleavage structure, for example, their study found that the persistent class cleavage in

France significantly constrained the mobilization of new social movements compared to the other three cases, where traditional cleavages had been "pacified." Indeed, their analysis showed a "zero-sum relationship" between traditional political cleavages and the corresponding capacity of the new social movements to articulate new issues (p. 25). According to the authors, this was because traditional but multilayered structures, which unevenly distribute resources and power, serve to divide people in a society. As a result, if traditional cleavages are not pacified, preoccupation with traditional struggles prevents new social movements from entering the dominant political arena.

Their examination of institutional structures similarly supported their basic argument: in Switzerland, which they characterized as weak and inclusive, there was a very high aggregate level of mobilization and a moderate "action repertoire"; in France, which was characterized as strong and exclusive, there was lower mobilization and unconventional forms of participation; in moderately strong, highly inclusive Netherlands, there was higher mobilization and a relatively strong reliance on conventional forms of mobilization; and, finally, in weak, exclusive Germany, there was a moderate level of mobilization (except for a strong labor movement) and higher unconventional forms of mobilization. In sum, their analysis showed that countries with (1) weak institutional structures but relatively open access to the democratic arena (for example, popular initiatives) and (2) a facilitative, cooperative, and assimilative political culture provided the greatest potential for a successful social movement.

The examination of the alliance structure showed similar results. In all four cases, the success of social movements depended on support from organizations of the Left, although the distinction between the "old" and "new" Left proved to be an important factor. Specifically, when a long-standing polarization between the old Left and the old Right remained strong in the main political arena, the effectiveness of new social movements was limited (as in France); if the old Left had been "pacified," however, new social movements had a much better chance to impact policy through an alliance with a reinvigorated Left. This was true in Germany, the Netherlands, and Switzerland.

The political opportunity structure, however, does not explain everything about the emergence, development, and success of social movements. As the authors themselves pointed out, there are at least three considerations that limit the reach of the impact of the POS. First, it is important to recognize that there are different types of movements and different issues raised by social movements. These differences create specific dynamics between the movement and other political actors and within the movement itself. Second, "once a mobilizing process has been set in motion, the strategies adopted by the social movements will have a feedback effect on the strategies adopted by the authorities," thus creating a unique dynamic (p. xv). Third, larger and more significant social movements have the potential to modify the POS itself, most likely on the level of the alliance structures but possibly on the level of institutional structures, prevailing strategies, and cleavage structures.

Political Opportunity Structure and Rationalist Approaches: A Quick Comparison

Although the authors dealt at length in their study with the three considerations mentioned above, we will not say anything more here. Suffice it to say that Kriesi et al. provided a theoretically coherent, empirically rich, and comparatively sound argument. It is an argument, moreover, that differs substantially from the rationalist approaches we examined earlier in the chapter. Resource mobilization and social network theories, you should recall, are based on the assumption that social movements can be explained largely in terms of individual action and decisions. In principle, then, the basic dynamics of social movements should not differ fundamentally from one country to another. The key elements, in this view, are the existence of strategically oriented leadership and a strong SMO. The POS approach, however, tells us that such microlevel factors, although not necessarily insignificant, do not tell us all we need to know. Instead, as we have seen, understanding the emergence, development, and success of social movements requires an understanding of the political context/structure in which they take place. In this way, the POS approach provides a much more "natural" basis for comparative analysis, since political structures are likely to differ—sometimes dramatically—from country to country. Indeed, to many comparativists, this is a particularly appealing and valuable aspect of the POS approach, which helps explain why it has been adopted by so many comparativists studying social movements (Goodwin and Jasper 1999). It certainly provides food for thought when assessing the strength of rationalist approaches.

Criticisms and Disadvantages of the Political Opportunity Approach

Despite its many strengths, the political opportunity approach is not free from criticism. Critics point to five main problems. The most basic problem, perhaps, is the tendency to oversimplify a complex sociopolitical and cultural reality (although you should recall from Chapter 3 that simplification is not necessarily a bad thing). For instance, in the study by Kriesi et al., informal institutional structures are classified as *either* exclusive *or* inclusive and formal institutional structures as *either* weak, intermediate, *or* strong; critics note, however, that this broad classificatory scheme likely obscures potentially significant institutional differences between countries. In this regard, too, despite its nod to history, the POS approach shies away from in-depth qualitative comparisons. Institutional structures, in other words, are largely dehistoricized in the POS approach. Second, because of its strong focus on state structures, the political opportunity approach excludes social movements (for example, literary, musical, and other artistic movements) that do not directly challenge existing state policies or political representations. In this way, the POS approach divides social movements into those that are "political" and those that are not. Yet, as Goodwin and Jasper (1999) argued, ostensibly nonpolitical movements are significant—and profoundly political—in that they challenge dominant beliefs and symbols (p. 34).

Third, the political opportunity approach and other mainstream approaches more generally (for example, resource mobilization, social networks, new social movements) tend to focus on Western Europe and North America. By itself this is not a problem, but it becomes a problem when it is presumed that the experiences of the West are a theoretical template for all regions of the world. Indeed, comparativists studying Latin America and other regions tend to be deeply skeptical about theories built on "Western" assumptions that ignore the historical specificity of other places (Davis 1999). The basic issue is this: the specific context of mobilization in Latin America (and other regions) is so different from that of the West that theories based solely or primarily on empirical studies of North American and Western European countries are bound to be dangerously biased and ethnocentric, even if only unintentionally. To frame the issue in the context of this book, the political opportunity approach, although often comparative, is simply *not comparative enough*. This is particularly the case when proponents make "big" theoretical claims as opposed to more limited, "middle-range" claims.

Fourth, although much of the POS research has focused almost exclusively on the relationship between movements within a country and national institutional traits, the movements themselves are becoming increasingly transnational. This means, in part, that the scope of investigation must also go beyond national boundaries. In fact, this point is well taken by Kriesi et al., who argued that "internationalization will doubtless substantially alter the role of nation-states and the context of social movement mobilization" (p. 249).[6] Fortunately, this trend is already well under way.[7] In Chapter 9 we discuss the significance of globalization and its relationship to domestic political processes, such as social movements, in some depth.

Finally, like resource mobilization theory, the POS approach does a poor job of demonstrating the passage from condition to action. As one social movement researcher put it, "expanding political opportunities . . . do not, in any simple sense, produce a social movement. . . . [Instead] they only offer insurgents a certain objective 'structural potential' for collective action. Mediating between opportunity and action are people and the subjective meanings they attach to their situations" (McAdam 1982, p. 48). In sum, "structural" approaches to the study of social movements, although undoubtedly valuable, appear not to give us all the answers. To fill in the gaps, it may be necessary to again turn to culture, which we will do in the next section.

■ Culture and Social Movements: Two Contrasting Approaches

For most scholars, it is difficult to dismiss completely the idea that culture and cultural factors "matter" in the study of social movements. After all, members of any movement, at some level, subscribe to a set of values and beliefs that are distinct from the population at large. Furthermore, as Crossley (2002) put it, "those who subscribe to those beliefs must feel some degree of affinity with others [that is, solidarity] . . . at least if they hold those beliefs with any degree of passion" (p. 6). Many cultural theorists, however, argue that culture does not just "matter" but is a crucial element to understanding why and how people mobilize. Yet as you know, "culture" is a problematic concept, defined or conceptualized in very different ways by different people. We have discussed many of these differences already in other chapters, so I will not cover the same ground here. Suffice it to say that, in research on social movements, there are generally two broad views of culture that, although not necessarily irreconcilable, have moved off in very different directions.

The Inside-Out Approach

The first, more traditional view might be called the "inside-out" approach (Swidler 1995). This approach, according to Swidler, focuses on the powerful, but essentially internalized, beliefs and values held by individual actors. Based on the ideas of Max Weber, the inside-out approach argues that our internalized views of the world (that is, the "inside") come to have an independent—and therefore explanatory—influence on social action. In other words, people find themselves constrained, or enabled, by the very ideas they use to describe the world. Thus, as Swidler put it, "culture shapes action by defining what people want and how they imagine they can get it" (p. 25). In this view, social movements are presumed to be a product, at least in part, of cultural processes located entirely within the movement itself; the focus is on how the pre-existing "stock" of cultural symbols—already internalized by activists and others—is used to accomplish key processes in mobilization (Johnston and Klandermans 1995, p. 14). Culture's influence, therefore, is presented in fairly unproblematic terms; that is, it either is an obstacle to or a resource (or "tool kit") for mobilization depending on the nature of values and beliefs individual actors in a society already hold. This actor-based understanding of culture is well illustrated by Weber's concept of the "Protestant ethic," which we discussed in

Chapter 4. Weber, you may recall, argued that the deeply held values of Protestantism constituted an essential foundation for capitalist development in the West.

The Outside-In or Global Approach

The second view largely rejects the Weberian, inside-out image of culture and, according to Swidler (1995), rightly so. The problem is not that inside-out treatments of culture are all wrong but that they are incomplete. Instead, Swidler and others (for example, Wuthnow 1987; Sewell 1985; and Melucci 1995) have suggested that social movement researchers need to adopt a "global approach" to the study of culture and its relationship to social movements. This entails a number of basic but fundamental changes that Swidler distilled into four concrete suggestions.

- First, it is critical to "entertain the possibility that culture's power is independent of whether or not people believe in it" (p. 39). This may not make much sense on the surface, but consider how we often do things we don't "believe in"—for instance, giving Christmas presents even though we may deplore the commercialization and secularization of Christmas (p. 32). In understanding social movements, this means, for example, we need to dispense with the idea that culture only matters insofar as individual actors believe in the values of the movement or even in the value of activism.
- Second, it is equally important to understand that the influence of culture is not dependent on shaping or reshaping the beliefs of individuals per se; instead, culture's influence is premised on shaping their knowledge of how others will interpret their actions. The example of Christmas gift giving works here, too: we give gifts, in part, because of our knowledge of how others interpret this action (pp. 32–33). In this regard, the success of a social movement should not be judged purely in terms of its "success" in influencing public policy but also in terms of its ability to transform aspects of the prevailing culture and dominant public discourse.
- Third, she suggested "that students of culture in general, and social movement scholars in particular, need to pay close attention to the public contexts in which cultural understandings are brought to bear" (p. 39). In other words, it is essential to recognize that culture influences action much more powerfully in some contexts and historical moments than in others.
- Fourth, Swidler reminded us to recognize that cultures of social movements are shaped by the institutions the movements confront. As she explained it, "Different regime types and different forms of repression

> generate different kinds of social movements with differing tactics and
> internal cultures. Dominant institutions also shape the movements'
> deepest values." (p. 37)

Admittedly, this is a lot to digest. But you should already be familiar with most
of the ideas expressed by Swidler, since we have discussed them, in one form
or another, throughout this book. The task, then, is to see how we might use the
suggestions given to us by Swidler (as well as other modes of cultural analysis) to make sense of social movements in a concrete and meaningful manner.
Unfortunately, this is easier said than done. It is difficult, in part, because the
social movement literature that might, in one way or another, be classified as
culturalist is extremely diverse and often more conceptual than empirical.[8]
This is particularly apparent in NSM theory, which draws from the ideas of
prominent European intellectuals, including Jurgen Habermas (1981), Claus
Offe (1985), Alberto Melucci (1995), and Alain Torraine (1981). In addition, it
is not always clear where some approaches fit. McAdam, Tarrow, and Tilly
(1997), for instance, asserted that NSM theory, like the political opportunities
approach, is "resolutely structural" (p. 145). Yet as Williams (2004) noted,
there is general consensus that NSM theory represents a "cultural turn" in
studies of social movements. To simplify our task, therefore, we will not attempt to summarize whole literatures, including the NSM literature,[9] nor will
we refer to dozens of different studies. Instead, as in other chapters, we will
focus on a representative, but by no means definitive or comprehensive, argument (chosen as much for its instructional value as for its intellectual
power).

Collective Identity, Names, and Social Movements— A Case Study of Nationalist Movements in "Canada"

Culturalist approaches to social movements typically stress the **social construction** of *collective identity* as an essential part of collective action. At the
most basic level, collective identity can be defined as a shared sense of "we-
ness." Polletta and Jasper (2001, p. 284) explained it this way: "It is a perception of a shared status or relation, which may be *imagined* rather than experienced directly, and it is distinct from personal identities, although it may
form part of a personal identity" (emphasis added). In addition, although a
collective identity is often self-defined, it may, the authors noted, "have been
first constructed by outsiders (for example, as in the case of 'Hispanics')" in
the United States. When imposed by outsiders, a collective identity is often
meant as a basis for discrimination, marginalization, or subordination.
Whether imposed from the outside or self-defined, collective identities are
usually based on and expressed through "cultural material," which may include narratives, symbols, verbal styles, rituals, clothing, and so on. A collec-

tive identity, therefore, is not preformed or objectively determined (in the way a classical Marxist understands **class** identity) but arises through an interactive, intersubjective, and largely purposeful process that, however, sometimes develops in unintended ways.

Oftentimes, as Jane Jenson (1995) argued, a collective identity—and the social movements it defines—hinge on a *name* (a type of "cultural material"); "movements," as she put it, "struggle over names and seek recognition of the one they prefer, both within and outside the community" (p. 107). More broadly, this can be seen as a competition for "discursive space," the construction of which allows social movements to demarcate their *boundaries*—that is, the line between their collective self and a collective other; or more simply, the line between "us" and "them" (Hunt and Benford 2004). The (culture-based) demarcation of boundaries, therefore, is a critical step in the formation, maintenance, and even "success" of a social movement. It is clear, however, that choices "are never unconstrained. . . . They are made in particular structural and institutional contexts, traversed by relations of power" (Jenson 1995, p. 108). This means that dominant groups and institutions invariably limit the ability of subordinate communities to define and name themselves, for a name is more than just a word; it is, instead, an exercise and expression of power.

Naming, to repeat, is more than just attaching a unique label for one's group or movement. It can provide a basis for mobilization, for the definition of interests, and for the elaboration of strategies, all of which have real, material consequences (p. 108). Consider, in this regard, the struggle over the representation of "Canada." For nearly a century, "Canada" was officially represented as a society with two distinct languages (English and French), two cultures, and equal rights of recognition and cultural expression for the two groups (p. 109). In the 1970s, however, the federal government began pursuing a "pan-Canadian" project based on redefining (or reimagining) "Canada" as a *liberal* and multicultural nation, where individual, as opposed to collective, rights would take center stage. The effort by the federal government to create a new collective and cultural identity for *all* Canadians, however, generated strong resistance among women, visible minorities, aboriginal peoples (a self-defined collective identity), and French-speaking nationalists within Quebec (p. 109). In particular, among many (but not all) groups within the province of Quebec, the effort reinvigorated a long-standing social movement based on nationalism that, despite a number of strong factional differences, coalesced around "Quebec" as a collective name. Indeed, as Jenson argued, "the imagery of the Quebec nation [has become] . . . hegemonic both in Quebec and in the rest of Canada" (p. 110). Moreover, the "pan-Canadian idea of a single country defined around a linguistic duality has virtually disappeared" (p. 110). Thus, although it may seem natural now to think of Quebec as distinct from the "rest of Canada," it is important to understand that this was not always the case. Indeed, prior to the 1960s, the name "Québécois" did not, strictly speaking, exist (p. 110; see 125n8).

It is significant that a great deal of meaning and a number of concrete implications are attached to the seemingly innocuous name "Quebec" (there is also a lot of dispute). Christopher Jones (2000) explained one implication: "The choice of Quebec as a collective name and territorial definition of francophone Canada . . . denies equal recognition to francophones living in Ontario, Manitoba and New Brunswick, while at the same time diminishing the rights of indigenous peoples and anglophones living within Quebec borders." In fact, Quebec was never a homogenous French-speaking province but was composed of at least fourteen ethnic groups with hundreds of thousands of residents who spoke only English (since the 1970s, according to some estimates, 100,000–400,000 English-speaking residents have left Quebec[10]). The name, in this regard, creates an *imagined* identity, where the Québécois share a common culture, history, and language. Even more, the name necessarily implied an other, which stood in direct opposition to the imagery of Quebec. The "other" is English (or anglophone) Canada. Yet, as Jones (2000) asserted, the "Anglo/French opposition represents a *necessary myth*—part of the foundation of contemporary Quebec nationalism—but the historical reality on which it is based is more complex" (emphasis added).

The "historical reality" is, indeed, complex and, for this reason, something we cannot delve into in this chapter. Suffice it to say, then, that the construction of an identity based on the collective name "Quebec" was designed to mobilize and give substance to a broad-based but focused social movement. As a movement defined by a particular language and culture, it is not surprising that language and culture became the primary basis by which the movement identified its collective interests. Thus, although the *political* goal of the movement was to assert francophone control of the economy in Quebec, one of the chief means used to accomplish this was a campaign to change public *and* private institutions through laws establishing the primacy of the French language (Jones 2000). This was certainly the most visible aspect of the Québécois social movement (or Quebec nationalism), at least to those of us living outside of Canada, but it was probably one of the most perplexing as well. After all, if the Québécois were primarily interested in changing their socioeconomic status, why did they not just attack the problem directly? To the Québécois, however, the problem was not just economic, but cultural. It was not just that Quebec had lagged behind all other Canadian provinces in terms of economic performance (and still does) but also that francophone residents were near the bottom of the economic ladder in Quebec. According to several studies, in fact, francophones ranked twelfth among fourteen ethnic groups in Quebec in terms of economic prosperity, and Canadian corporations systematically excluded French-speaking employees from the management ranks. Even bilingual French and English speakers suffered from wage discrimination. Culture, therefore, was *the* issue, which is why the Québécois were insistent on demanding that the sites of provincial social *and* commercial power become francophone (Jones 2000).

A focus on naming and the construction of a collective identity, however, does not explain everything about the Québécois movement (or Quebec nationalism). As we have learned throughout this book, most contemporary culturalists do not insist that a cultural approach tells us all or even most of the story. Jenson (1995), for example, suggested that we must avoid making a false choice between culture and structure, between culture and rationality, and so on. Indeed, she argued that an integrative approach is not only advisable but necessary. In her own analysis, she brought together "identity" and "opportunities." As she explained it, "the configuration of the political opportunity structure cannot be analyzed without first inquiring about who the actors are. The names with which movements represent themselves in seeking representation are one of the ways that opportunities can be made, and the names may contribute to a reconfiguration of the political opportunity structure" (p. 114). What Jenson was saying, in part, was that the very act of naming—of self-defining a collective identity—generates resources, solidarity, alliance possibilities (and opposition), and "routes to representation" (that is, institutional access). In other words, naming helps to "make opportunities" within the prevailing political opportunity structure. But it is not only a matter of "making opportunities," for Jenson also suggested that, although we cannot do whatever we want (that is, structural and institutional constraints—including structured relations of power—*do* exist), political structures and the larger social environment are not fixed entities "*into which* social movements must enter" (emphasis in original; p. 115). Instead, structures and institutions are dynamic and can themselves be "changed actors struggling in the universe of political discourse," a crucial dimension of which is the activity of self-naming (p. 115).

So, what does all this tell us about the Québécois movement? On the one hand, it tells us that culture was an integral, perhaps indispensable, element of the movement. It also tells us that culture, expressed through a self-defined collective identity, can create new openings in the political opportunity structure. On the other hand, it tells us that, although cultural politics can help "make" opportunities in the prevailing political structure, it can also, unintentionally, close off future opportunities. Jenson argued that this, in fact, happened to the Québécois movement. The success of the Québécois movement, for example, invited other groups to press their claims for representation and collective rights as well. Chief among these groups were the aboriginal peoples, who insisted that they be recognized as nations within Canada. Moreover, as Jenson explained it, "[t]hey learned from the nationalists in Quebec that claims to nation building and national identity were powerful tools in the Canadian universe of political discourse" (p. 119). In "naming" themselves, the aboriginal groups created their own opportunities in the political opportunity structure and were eventually included in constitutional negotiations over the distribution of political power in Canada. The expansion of the constitutional agenda, however, was a direct blow to the Québécois nationalists, who had always claimed that their needs took precedence over the concerns of any other group (p. 117). Ironically, though, it was their own success at transforming political discourse, which opened up the political opportunity structure, that led to a diminution of their power. In this regard, too, we can see how context matters.

The story, of course, is far more complex than this. But the basic point should be clear. To repeat, culture/identity and structure are part of an interrelated and dynamic whole. They should not be analyzed separately but in an integrative manner. This calls for in-depth, "whole" case analysis, which is always easier said than done. The example here lacked an explicit comparative perspective (although the author of the main study, Jane Jenson, did "compare" several cases within Canada); certainly, though, a well-thought-out and well-executed comparative strategy would strengthen any argument about the importance of culture/identity and about the relationship between culture and structure.

■ Conclusion

We have covered a lot of ground in this chapter, and we've done so in a speedy and admittedly superficial manner. But this is largely unavoidable when discussing, in a very limited space, a topic as theoretically and empirically diverse and complex as social movements. Our objective in this and all the other chapters, moreover, is *not* to provide a definitive and comprehensive treatment of the subject. This is not only impractical (if not impossible) but also ill advised for an introductory textbook on comparative politics. Our intention, instead, is to provide you with a very basic framework and understanding that you can use to develop your *own* analyses of social movements. *Minimally,* this means you should remember the significance of rationality, of structure, and of culture. You should also consider how all of these relate to one another (how you might "integrate" them) and how comparative analysis can strengthen your position. We believe this chapter provides the essentials for doing all of this.

■ Notes

1. The literature most identified with this view is known as the collective behavior approach, and the figure most closely connected with this approach is Herbert Blumer. For a critical, yet sympathetic, discussion of Blumer's argument, see Crossley (2002), chap. 2.

2. Charles Tilly is a renowned and highly influential US sociologist. His work on collective action has been particularly influential, but it is important to note that, although the concept of "collective action" ostensibly derives from the rational choice perspective, Tilly did not dismiss the importance of structure. As Lynn Hunt (1984)

noted, Tilly's research has two sides. One side is his concern for agency. Indeed, in his definition of collective action, according to Hunt, Tilly used the word "action" to emphasize the importance of agency—action implies that people *act* together, not simply as a response to changing (structural) conditions but also to bring about purposeful change (p. 248). The other side of Tilly's research emphasized the structural changes that have transformed the means and the ends of collective action (p. 246).

3. It should be noted, however, that rational choice theory does not, in principle, exclude altruistic behavior. This is because, as Levi (1997) explained it, rational choice does not require the assumption that individuals are self-interested or motivated solely by egoistic goals. The key is that people "act consistently in relation to their preferences" (p. 24). Thus, if the preference of an individual actor is a nonegoistic consideration such as "fairness" or some other ethical goal, this can be perfectly consistent with the rational choice model. Levi also noted, however, that "the addition of non-egoistic considerations or motivational norms . . . does increase the complexity and difficulty of analysis" (p. 24).

4. McCarthy and Zald (1973) made a strong distinction between a social movement and a social movement organization. According to these authors, the former is a "preference" for change, whereas the latter is "organized action for change." A social movement organization, as they explained it, is the "complex, or formal organization which identifies its goals with the preferences of a social movement . . . and attempts to implement these goals" (p. 1218). See Figure 8.1 for their definition of a social movement.

5. For a more in-depth discussion of reiterated or repeated games, see Morrow (1994), chap. 9.

6. According to Kriesi et al., "the POS concept is not tied to the national state, but can also . . . be applied at the international level" (p. 249). But other scholars are less sanguine about this possibility. Clifford Bob (2002), for example, warned us that we must be cautious in applying the POS concept to the transnational level. In his own research on the Movement for the Survival of the Ogoni People during the 1990s, Bob found that *leadership* and *political exchange*, which are neglected by POS, were crucial to understanding transnational movements in the Ogoni case. Keck and Sikkink (1998) argued along similar lines, although, like Bob, they did not discount the possibility of applying the POS concept to an understanding of transnational social movements.

7. Examples include Smith, Chatfield, and Pagnucco, *Transnational Social Movements and Global Politics: Solidarity Beyond the State* (1997); Keck and Sikkink, *Activists Beyond Borders: Advocacy Networks in International Politics* (1998); and Guidry, Kennedy, and Zald, *Globalization and Social Movements: Culture, Power, and the Transnational Public Sphere* (2000).

8. Hunt and Benford (2004) made this point specifically with regard to the social movement literature on collective identity, which we discuss later.

9. There are a number of fairly accessible introductions to the NSM literature. See, for example, Canel (1997); Crossley (2002), chap. 8; Laraña, Johnston, and Gusfield (1994), especially chap. 1.

10. Susan Taylor Martin, in an August 9, 1999, story for the *St. Petersburg Times* ("In Quebec, Some Take Law as Sign of Discrimination"), cited a high figure of 400,000 (between 1977 and 1999). Still another source, Alliance Quebec, cited a figure of 160,000 between 1971 and 1981, with no updated number for the following two decades (http://www.aq.qc.ca/English/ourcom.htm). The lowest estimates come from Jones (2000), who indicated that only 100,000 English-speaking citizens of Quebec had left the province by 1994 (citing Michael Ignatieff, *Blood and Belonging: Journeys into the New Nationalism* [New York: Farrar, Straus and Giroux, 1994]).

PART 3

The Future of Comparative Politics

9

Globalization and the Study
of Comparative Politics

Comparative politics, as we have seen throughout this book,
tends to pay close attention to specific times and places. There is, in other
words, a bias (albeit sometimes slight) toward particularity, or in-depth understanding, as opposed to generalization or explanation. Even in those approaches that ostensibly emphasize general theory over particularity (that is,
rational choice and structuralism), the tension between understanding and explanation is strong. Indeed, the ongoing tension between **understanding** and
explanation is one reason, and perhaps the most important one, why the concept of globalization is so important to the field. For "globalization" is typically portrayed as an economically, politically, socially, and culturally homogenizing force. This means that, as individual societies, cultures, and countries
are "exposed" to globalization—whether voluntarily or involuntarily—they
are compelled to act in a similar, if not identical, manner. Over time (and perhaps after a great deal of conflict, struggle, and violence), this will result, some
argue, in a world where every society, every country, and every person will be
basically the same. From a certain perspective, we can already see this happening: go to almost any major city in the world today, and you can find many
of the same shops, many of the same products, and many of the same services.
But globalization means much more than superficial changes in where we shop
and what we buy. As Benjamin Barber (1996) put it:

> Every demarcated national economy and every kind of public good is today
> vulnerable to the inroads of transnational commerce. Markets abhor frontiers
> as nature abhors a vacuum. . . . In Europe, Asia, and the Americas . . . mar-
> kets have already eroded national sovereignty and given birth to a new class
> of institutions—international banks, trade associations, transnational lobbies
> like OPEC [Organization of Petroleum Exporting Countries], world news
> services like CNN and the BBC, and multinational institutions that lack dis-
> tinctive national identities. (p. 13)

According to Barber, these trends will only intensify and broaden as time goes by. Moreover, the expansion of markets does not just mean far-reaching economic change but equally profound political, cultural, and social change as well: a global market creates a global culture based on "MTV, Macintosh, and McDonald's." In this new "McWorld," using Barber's now-famous term, the study of individual countries, societies, and cultures becomes largely irrelevant—or, at best, fodder for historians and anthropologists studying a defunct way of life. Although this is obviously an exaggeration, the basic point is clear: globalization portends a serious erosion of the raison d'être of comparative politics and comparative analysis. That is, if the world truly does become a big McWorld, then there will be very little left to compare and even less reason to compare, since studying one country or society will be pretty much like studying any other country or society. (Recall from Chapter 1 that comparison requires both similarities *and* differences between and among units.) In a world of no meaningful differences, politics and political science will still matter, although it will likely be a politics of the "whole" rather than of the "parts." (See Figure 9.1 for additional discussion of Barber's argument.)

Needless to say, most comparativists are not ready to throw in their towels. Indeed, even though most will concede that "globalization" is an important force in the world today, most also believe that "differences" will continue to matter a great deal. James Mittelman (1996b) put it this way: "Globalization is not flattening civil societies around the world but, rather, *combining with local conditions* in distinctive ways, *accentuating differences,*

Figure 9.1   Benjamin Barber's "McWorld"

Benjamin Barber, it is important to understand, is not an enthusiastic or uncritical proponent of "McWorld." Rather, he sees it as an unremitting and *undiscriminating* juggernaut: the logic of McWorld is simply too strong, too overwhelming to stand up to. Herein lies the danger. According to Barber (1998), McWorld displaces not only reactionary critics—the zealots and fundamentalists of the world—but democratic rivals as well, that is, those who dream of a genuinely internationalized civil society made up of free citizens from many different cultures. As he put it, "McWorld . . . does little for consumer autonomy, less for competition, and nothing at all for the kinds of liberty and pluralism essential to political freedom. But perhaps more dangerous to liberty, McWorld has encroached upon and helped push aside public space. Its greatest victory—and here it has been mightily assisted by the antigovernmental privatizing ideology that has dominated its politics in recent years—has been its contribution to the eradication of civic space" (p. 40).

and spurring a variety of social movements seeking protection from the disruptive and polarizing effects of economic liberalism [viz., globalization]" (emphasis added; cited in Crawford 2000, p. 69). This is a useful and reasonable perspective. The author is also almost certainly right. Still, the questions remain: How does (and how will) globalization impact the study of comparative politics? Will globalization, for example, require all comparativists to become hyperstructuralists? After all, as we saw in the preceding chapter, globalization fits into a structural framework quite nicely, even ideally. Or will globalization become simply another element in a broader context (and not necessarily the most important one) that needs to be factored into any analysis of domestic politics? Or does the answer depend on the particular circumstances of an individual case or issue?

This chapter will not endeavor to answer these and other pertinent questions in a definitive manner. Rather, like the general approach in this book, my intention is to get you thinking about the issue. To begin, though, it is important to take another look at the basic question, what is globalization? For, as we learned from Chapter 7, the concept is not at all clear-cut. At a minimum, therefore, we need to establish a common basis of understanding, or else we risk not talking about the same phenomenon. This does not mean that everyone must agree on a single definition, only that we have a common point of reference. Rather than merely repeat what was already covered, however, we will consider a few additional, but important, aspects of defining globalization.

▓ What Is Globalization? A Reprise

In Chapter 7, I argued (following Beck) that globalization is a multidimensional concept. The economic, social, cultural, and other dimensions of this process are, it is important to recognize, concrete processes "through which sovereign national states are criss-crossed and undermined by transnational actors with varying prospects of power, orientations, identities and networks" (Beck 2000, p. 11). It would be wrong to assume, however, that the various processes of globalization—no matter how much of their complexity we detail—are all there is to a comprehensive conceptualization of the term. For, as Beck pointed out, there are other analytically distinct aspects of "globalization" that are not adequately captured by these various dimensions alone. He identified two additional distinctions, which he called "globality" and "globalism." The first term, "globality," should already be familiar to you. It refers to the "conjuring away of distance" mentioned earlier. Or, as Beck put it, globality means "that *we have been living for a long time in a world society,* in the sense that the notion of closed spaces has become illusory" (emphasis in original; p. 10). Although this largely reiterates the definition of globalization introduced in Chapter 7, the point I want you to remember is this: globality and globalization are tightly related aspects of a larger whole, but they are *not* identical. There is a good reason why it is important, if not necessary, to maintain this analytical distinction. As Beck explained it, on one hand, globality is, for the most part, *here to stay.* That is, the gradual disappearance of closed-off spaces—time-space compression, as other scholars like to say—cannot be reversed, at least barring a catastrophic event that literally destroys most of the world as we know it. On the other hand, globalization (or, more accurately, the globalizing process) *is* reversible; at least, globalization is not an inexorable, impossible-to-manage, and overwhelming force majeure. Rather, it is a multitude of "various autonomous logics . . . the logics of ecology, culture, economics, politics and civil society [that] exist side by side and cannot be reduced or collapsed into one another" (p. 11). Each logic, moreover, can be independently "decoded" or understood, and through this understanding, Beck argued, it is possible to envision and create alternative paths or directions. What this means, in more understandable terms, is that the various globalizing processes are subject to human agency—or to political action. Indeed, Beck suggested that globalizing processes can move or unfold in very different ways, all depending on the (political) actions—or inactions—that people take or are *able* to take. Breaking "globalization" down into separate logics, moreover, provides a better way of seeing how it may not be as homogenizing a force as it is often portrayed to be.

The third analytical distinction that Beck made, and one that is more controversial than the other two, is "globalism." By this he meant "the view that the world market eliminates or supplants political action—that is, the *ideology* of rule by world market, the ideology of neoliberalism" (emphasis added; p. 9). This is a critical point, in large part, because most people, when they hear the word "globalization," do not think of it as an ideology at all—Marxism and even capitalism might be ideologies, but not "globalization." If you take a moment to reflect, however, Beck's point is not all that difficult to see. Consider, for example, the definition of **ideology** from the 1988 edition of the *Oxford Paperback Encyclopedia*:

> A political belief-system that both explains the world as it currently is and suggests how it should be changed. . . . Some have sought to reserve the term for political outlooks that are seen as rigid and extreme in contrast to those that are more pragmatic and moderate. It seems better, however, to recognize the pervasiveness of ideology as the means by which people order their perceptions of the social world, whether or not they consciously subscribe to a political creed.

Underlying most popular portrayals of globalization is the notion, although often only implied, that it is a technological/economic process leading toward the eventual creation of a global market, where people will be free not only to exchange goods and services but also to participate in an environment of unlimited individual choice, prosperity, and genuine democracy. Indeed, in this view, markets are *inherently* democratic, voluntary (that is, noncoercive), and apolitical. The unfolding of this process, moreover, is generally portrayed as a simple but hard "fact of life," where those who express any doubt, opposition, or resistance are seen as either naive or stupid or both.[1] Opponents of globalization are naive or "stupid" because they just "don't get it"—that is, they fail to understand that globalization is both inevitable *and* beneficial. In this way, then, the popular understanding of globalization clearly tells us how the world currently is and how it will be. But how is this a political belief-system? After all, isn't it possible that globalization *is* an inevitable and ultimately beneficial process? On this question, unfortunately, there is far less agreement. Suffice it to say, therefore, that Beck offered one of many competing perspectives (one that I support).

With this caveat in mind, Beck contended that globalism is a political belief-system in that it assiduously promotes a particular view of politics (recall from Chapter 1 what I mean by the term "politics") based on the idea that the market is essentially the solution to all our problems. We must, therefore, all put our faith in the market, because the "market knows best." This means, most tellingly, that nonmarket actors—states, churches, trade unions, nongovernmental organizations, and civil society more generally—either need to accept and adapt to this "new reality" or get out of the way. This is a political belief-system par excellence. The real keys to understanding globalization as an ideology, however, are to recognize, for one thing, that the market is not simply an abstraction where, if left alone (by "nonmarket" actors), the forces of supply and demand will *always* ensure an optimal (and socially acceptable) distribution of scarce economic resources. A second thing is that markets are populated not by millions of equally empowered individuals and companies but by some very large, extremely rich, and disproportionately powerful corporate actors. In this critical view, then, the "marketization of politics" means the empowerment of corporate actors in general and of large, rich, and transnational corporate actors in particular. In Chapter 1, I discussed an admittedly crude measurement of corporate power—the sheer economic size and muscle of Wal-Mart compared to a number of countries (Figure 1.5) and all of the individual actors that exist within their borders. Indeed, if Wal-Mart were a country, it would be the nineteenth largest economy in the world. Figure 9.2 provides figures for the twenty largest corporations in the world in 2001 (based on revenue) and a comparison with a range of countries, from some of the largest (in terms of nominal gross domestic product [GDP]) to some of the smallest. The key point is this: as an ideology, globalization is a political belief-system designed to build acceptance of a world where corporate decisionmaking and interests are given precedence over all other types of decisionmaking and all other interests. As an ideology, however, globalization is at least partly an intersubjective as opposed to a strictly objective phenomenon. This means, in

Figure 9.2 The Revenue of the World's Largest Corporations Compared to the Gross Domestic Product of Selected Countries in 2001

20 Largest Corporations by Revenue			GDP[a] (based on currency exchange rates, not on PPP[a])
Corporation Name	Revenues in US$ millions	Country	
Wal-Mart[b]	219,821	Japan	4,147,595
Exxon Mobil U.S.	191,581	Mexico	622,328
General Motors	177,280	South Korea	481,969
BP Britain	174,218	Russia	306,603
Ford Motor Company	162,412	Switzerland	245,839
Enron	138,718	Sweden[b]	219,439
Daimler-Chrysler	136,897	Austria	189,580
Royal Dutch/Shell	135,211	Turkey	145,244
General Electric	125,913	Indonesia	141,255
Toyota Motors	120,814	Saudi Arabia	182,257
Citigroup	112,022	Israel	112,714
Mitsubishi	105,813	Singapore[c]	84,871
Mitsui	102,205	Peru	53,639
Chevron-Texaco	99,699	Vietnam	32,685
Total FINA ELF	94,311	Guatemala	20,961
Nippon Telegraph and Telephone	93,424	Uzbekistan	11,401
Itocho	91,176	Ethiopia	6,510
Alianz	85,026	Haiti	3,651
IBM	85,866	Tajikistan	1,033
ING Group[c]	82,699	Kiribati[d]	47

Sources: Data for the twenty largest corporations are from *Fortune* magazine's annual "Global 500" report (vol. 146, no. 2, July 22, 2002). Data for GDP are from the World Development Indicators database (no longer available online), accessed from Irisdis Encyclopedia, http://www.iridis.com/glivar/List_of_countries_by_ gross_domestic_product.

Notes: a. GDP = gross domestic product; PPP = purchasing power parity.

b. Wal-Mart was the world's largest company in terms of revenue in 2001, and Sweden, with a nominal GDP roughly equivalent to Wal-Mart's sales, was the world's nineteenth largest economy in the same year. In other words, in 2001, Wal-Mart *by itself* would have been the world's nineteenth largest economy, and its total revenues would have exceeded the nominal GDPs of 168 countries.

c. The ING Group total revenues were roughly equivalent to the nominal GDP of Singapore, the world's thirty-seventh largest economy in 2001.

d. In 2001, Kiribati was one of smallest countries in the world in terms of nominal GDP.

turn, that globalization, or globalism, can unfold and develop in a number of divergent ways. Indeed, according to Beck, neoliberal globalization is only one form of globalism, albeit by far the most dominant form. There are also competing globalisms that confront, undermine, and interact in a variety of ways, all of which make globalization a more problematic process than it may appear to be on the surface.

To sum up: globalization is an important concept. It is important whether one agrees that it signifies a fundamental change in the world today or whether one believes that it is nothing new. For even if globalization is not entirely new—that is, if it reflects centuries-old processes of (uneven) integration, incorporation, or expansion—it is virtually undeniable that these processes (of integration, incorporation, and expansion) are taking place today and that they are having a meaningful impact on the world in which we live. In this sense, perhaps the one point on which almost everyone can agree is simply this: the world is more closely bound together—spatially and temporally—in more ways and in more areas (with both positive and negative results) than ever before. Moreover, most might also agree that the *pace* of change has been faster and the *scope* of change more extensive than at other times in history. Given all this, it is not difficult to understand why more and more observers—whether of a progressive, radical, or conservative persuasion—also agree that globalization is a dialectical process of homogenization *and* differentiation.

■ Implications of Globalization in Comparative Politics

The foregoing discussion of globalization is, I readily admit, clearly one designed to leave plenty of space for the "survival" of comparative politics as a distinct field of study. Still, we should not gloss over or simply dismiss the potentially profound impact that globalization may have on the study of comparative politics. *To repeat:* as time and space become more and more compressed and as globalizing processes create a more homogenized world—economically, politically, socially, and culturally—"differences" among countries and societies, on the surface at least, will become less pronounced and perhaps less meaningful. Consider, too, that in just the past several decades—a period of intense globalization—we have witnessed a worldwide breakdown in the legitimacy of authoritarianism, dictatorship, and political repression and a corresponding rise of a global and widely shared discourse on human rights, democracy, and individual freedom. In a similar vein, consider the massive movement away from centrally planned or socialist economies to economies based on the (universal?) principles of capitalism and "free markets." *If* all these trends continue, as Benjamin Barber and many others believe they will, we will see not only a continuing erosion of differences among countries, societies, and cultures but also the emergence of a single or "borderless" world, where spatial (and to a lesser extent, temporal) barriers to the cross-border movement of information, capital, ideas, values, people, and goods will have all but disappeared and where regions and individual countries will have shed their cultural parochialisms for more "global orientations." At this point, some might argue, the "dialectical process of homogenization and differentiation" will have reached its endpoint. Or, in the now immortal words of Francis Fukuyama ([1989] 1999), we will have reached "the end of history."

In the meantime, of course, differences will still matter, and they will matter a great deal. Indeed, it is possible, if not likely, that tens of thousands if not millions of lives will be lost as the forces of "differentiation" attempt to stave off the inevitable. But this is exactly the point to some: ultimately, the forces of differentiation are doomed to failure. To those who subscribe to this "story of globalization," then, comparative politics as a distinct field of study would also seem to be doomed (although it may be many decades before the field becomes completely irrelevant).

Globalization and Heterogeneity

As I have already suggested, however, this particular story is based on a one-dimensional and (probably) overdetermined conception of globalization. The more analytically distinct and multidimensional conception of globalization that we discussed above, on the other hand, allows us to see that comparative politics will likely remain a relevant and dynamic field for a long, long time. Not only is the world still quite heterogeneous, but in the interactive or dialectical process of homogenization and differentiation, *new forms* of heterogeneity or difference are likely to emerge. These, in turn, may be transformed into something else, and into something else again and again. The point is clear: *even as the world becomes more similar in some ways, it becomes different in other, often unanticipated, ways.* Even as the world becomes more democratic, for instance, democracy itself is likely to take more and more different forms. So, too, with capitalism, with nationalism, with environmentalism, or with any other symbol or force of homogeneity. On this point, consider this simple observation by Kopstein and Lichbach (2000): "The source of globalization, the West, is also frequently the source of the challenges to it: Liberalism, democracy, fascism, and socialism, for example, are all Western innovations" (pp. 7–8).

The Global Context

So what does all this mean? At a minimum, it means that comparative politics is clearly not dying as a field of study. But it also means that comparative politics, or comparativists, must pay increasingly serious attention to the "global context" within which all political, economic, social, and cultural change takes place. Comparativists, of course, have been doing this for a long time—long before the idea of globalization was even around. Still, a great deal of previous research in comparative politics had a tendency to take the global (and international) context for granted, which means that it was generally treated implicitly or as a part of the "background." Still other research has, in effect, treated domestic units as self-contained entities, where "outside" forces were considered largely, or at least analytically, separate. In future research, either type of approach will become less and less viable. From now on, in other words, comparativists—including students new to the study of comparative politics—will need to think explicitly, rigorously, and systematically about the *interrelationship* between the "global context" and "local conditions." This means, too, cultivating an understanding that globalization is not, as I have repeatedly stressed, a monolithic, primarily technological-economic force but a highly diverse and contradictory (or dialectical) force that includes nonmaterial (for example, ideological) as well as material processes.

This position, I should stress, would probably not be embraced by all comparativists. Still, as Martha Finnemore and Kathryn Sikkink (2001) put it, "the processes of globalization have made even the most passionate country specialists aware of the increasing influence of international factors, both material and ideational, on domestic politics around the globe. Comparativists are becoming increasingly attentive to the interpenetration of international affairs and domestic politics" (p. 411). One concrete example of this, the authors pointed out, is the tendency for researchers interested in social movements to be

> attentive not only to domestic social movements but also to transnational movements and to the linkages between domestic and transnational movements. Social movement theorists are increasingly aware that social movements operate in both a domestic and an international environment; they speak of "multi-layered" opportunity structures including a "supranational" layer, or a "multi-level polity," or highlight how international pressures influence domestic opportunity structures. (p. 411)

The main warning here, to repeat, is that comparativists be sensitive to and keenly aware of the potential significance of globalizing forces and processes in their analyses. This does *not* mean, however, that globalizing forces and processes will always or necessarily be at the center of the analysis. It is certainly possible that they may not be. In other words, how important globalization is in any situation will still depend on the circumstances of the individual case or issue under study. On some issues and in certain places, careful analysis may show that global and international forces have played, at best, a marginal role. On other issues and in different places (or sometimes on the same issue in different places), global and international forces may prove to be absolutely central. In all cases, however, it would be dangerous to simply assume that globalization is irrelevant.

■ Assessing Globalization's Impact on Comparative Politics: The Case of Immigrant Rights

The discussion thus far has been a little abstract. In this section, therefore, I will provide just one example of how a comparativist might examine the tension between certain aspects of globalization and domestic politics. Specifically, I will look at some recent research on migration control and immigrant rights. This is a useful issue on which to focus if only because migration control and immigrant rights have traditionally been—and even now are—treated as largely, even strictly, a domestic affair. The traditional argument can be stated simply: states, by virtue of their **sovereignty**, are assumed to have virtually complete discretion with regard to the rights that are bestowed upon foreign migrants and immigrants. In this view, many early studies of the development of immigrant rights naturally focused on domestic sources of control, regulation, and change—for example, on the institutional power of courts, on political activism and the role of social movements, on interest group politics, and so on. This domestically based approach has certainly not disappeared; indeed, there continue to be a number of strong arguments put forth by researchers who rely upon the same assumption of domestic or internal control.[2] More recent comparative studies, however, have begun to challenge the traditional view. Amy Gurowitz (2000), for instance, argued along just these lines. Gurowitz, like many comparativists, began with the claim that globalization—specifically, the globalization of international human rights norms and regimes—has undermined state sovereignty and had a meaningful impact on the development of immigrant/migrant rights within specific countries. To understand the impact of globalization on the domestic political process, however, Gurowitz adopted a nuanced view, which is based on the argument that "international norms have not played a direct role in recent policy-making toward immigrants" (p. 416). This said, Gurowitz believed,

> if we look for the influence of international norms in a less direct way, we find a somewhat different story. Policy toward migrants in Germany [for example] is in a sense self-limited, as opposed to externally limited. But to account for change in a particular state over time we often need to examine how that self is transformed, at times under the influence of international norms. For example, the "emergent moral consensus among the political elites to cope humanely with the consequences of guest-worker recruitment" noted by Joppke is partly due to a select few elites being influenced by international and regional standards, whether they appear in written treaties or simply are norms commonly practiced in Europe. These standards allow pro-immigrant actors to point out, for example, that Germany's policy of pure *jus sanguinis* is outdated. Yet . . . the impact of international norms is broad and diffuse. (pp. 416–417)

Gurowitz's main focus, however, was not Germany but Japan. In fact, Gurowitz argued that, in the case of Japan, there was much stronger evidence that international norms "matter." She was careful to point out, however, that they do not matter in "some mysterious or automatic way" (p. 443) but in a concrete and specific manner. As she put it, "International norms can matter only when they are used domestically and when they work their way into the political process. . . ." This means, moreover, that the impact of international norms is not uniform or predetermined but varies across time and place. The only way to understand the impact of international norms, therefore, is through "detailed process tracing" (p. 416). Finally, Gurowitz asserted that an understanding of the role international norms play cannot be achieved through an analysis that relies on the traditional dichotomy between international and domestic levels. Instead, it is necessary to examine the interaction and mutually constitutive nature of the relationship between domestic and international (or global) factors. Gurowitz, in short, was doing exactly what I prescribed above; namely, she was thinking explicitly, rigorously, and systematically about the *interplay* between the "global context" and "local conditions."

In the remainder of her analysis, Gurowitz did what she said she must do. That is, she looked closely at the ways in which international norms wound their way into the domestic political process. It was not, however, simply a matter of these norms being accepted or rejected, in which case there would be very little evidence that they did, indeed, matter. Rather, it was a case of international norms being very gradually integrated into the political process, such that, over time, the context in which immigrants and immigrant issues are discussed—from a perspective of domestic isolation to a more global and regional one—changed. This, in turn, "empowered new actors to contest and challenge state identity and policy with an arsenal of international norms that would not be useful if the government were not already highly sensitive to international criticism and if immigrant issues were seen as purely domestic matters" (p. 443). None of this, Gurowitz clearly pointed out, resulted in a rapid sea change in Japan's approach to immigrant integration; change, instead, has been slow and incremental.

There is, of course, much more depth and detail to Gurowitz's argument. My main objective, however, is not to provide a complete summary of her argument but to illustrate how some comparativists have begun to deal with the question of globalization. It is obviously not a cut-and-dried process—for example, it is not merely a matter of adding "globalization" to an analysis or of making vague references to the "importance of globalization." Conversely, it is not a matter of simply asserting that globalization does *not* matter. Whatever position you take, it is critical to consider, in a concrete and specific manner, how an issue or process unfolds, how it changes, or even how it stays the same, all within a global context. This is not easy, but it is necessary if one aspires to be a "good comparativist."

■ Globalization and the Three Research Traditions

Now that we have discussed the connection between globalization and the study of comparative politics in a more concrete manner, it would be useful to ask ourselves: how can a *beginning* comparativist think more explicitly, rigorously, and systematically about the interrelationship between the global context and local conditions? Not surprisingly, there is no simple, step-by-step way to answer this question. We can, however, use the same general framework we have been using throughout this book to help develop a useful approach. That is, in thinking about how "local conditions" both shape and are shaped by the global context, we need to consider this interrelationship from the perspective of rationality, culture, and structure.

Rational Choice in a Global Context

Globalization does not affect the basic premises of rational choice. Globalization can certainly have a profound impact, however, on the *environment* in which strategic calculations are made. At times, the impact of globalization on the environment of strategic calculation is obvious, but oftentimes the impact is likely to be quite subtle and complex. Consider, for example, how economic globalization—as many scholars argue—has fundamentally changed the strategic environment for a whole range of actors, from ordinary workers to entire nation-states. Certain aspects of this changed environment are easy enough to discern—for example, the transborder expansion of production and the increasing spatial and temporal mobility of capital. From the standpoint of rational choice, then, the question becomes how these processes or changes impact the strategic calculations made by certain actors. This is not difficult to discover. For example, beginning in the early 1990s, the American Federation of Labor–Congress of Industrial Organizations (AFL-CIO) and many smaller US labor unions put their support behind a project called the Coalition of Justice in the *Maquiladoras* (CJM). The idea behind this project was to improve working conditions (via a campaign for a corporate code of conduct) for Mexican workers employed in the **maquiladoras** (see Figure 9.3) along the United States–Mexico border.

On the surface, this would seem to be a strange event—after all, for decades, US unions had been, if anything, vehemently antiforeign and almost totally unconcerned with the conditions facing workers outside of the United States. Yet to a rational choice researcher, the source for this turnabout is quite simple: economic *constraints* created by economic globalization. More specifically, the ongoing—and seemingly irreversible—trend toward the internationalization of production, along with the coming of the **North American Free Trade Agreement** or NAFTA (see Figure 9.4), made it clear to US unions that it was in their economic interests to pursue cross-border alliances with foreign

Figure 9.3 *Maquiladora*

A *maquiladora* is a foreign-owned assembly plant located in Mexico, primarily along the United States–Mexico border in cities such as Ciudad Juárez, Tijuana, Reynosa, and Matamoros (originally, the *maquiladora* factories were restricted to border areas and the Baja California free trade zone, but today the factories may be set up anywhere in Mexico). The *maquiladoras* were set up primarily as a way for US companies to take advantage of lower production costs in Mexico (primarily wages). In 1990, according to one source, the average *maquiladora* wage in dollars per hour (operators and technicians), including benefits, was $1.85 at the border and $1.50 in nonborder locations. By 2000, the average had increased to $3.25 at the border and $2.00 elsewhere ("Maquiladora Labor Trends"). The other main advantage of the *maquiladora* is the ability to import in-bond and duty-free all the machinery, tools, equipment, and raw materials necessary to assemble and manufacture products for export. The finished product can then be re-exported to the United States, with additional assessments due only on the value-added portion of the product. The program originated in 1965, but since 1989, the *maquiladora* industry has been governed by the Mexican government's Decree for the Development and Operation of the Maquiladora Export Industry (the Maquiladora Decree). The Maquiladora Decree was amended effective January 1, 1994, to comply with certain provisions of the North American Free Trade Agreement.

Source: "Maquiladora Labor Trends," n.d., http://www.maquilaportal.com/editorial/editorial7.htm.

workers *and* with groups that support those workers. This also explains why, in supporting the CJM, the AFL-CIO and affiliated unions formed working relationships with dozens of religious and community based organizations, the Canadian Auto Workers, and even the radical and anti–AFL-CIO United Electrical Workers (which had long been a pariah in top AFL-CIO circles [Moody 1999, pp. 239–242]).

The same logic underlies the more recent series of protests—and broad-based social movements—against the World Trade Organization (WTO), the International Monetary Fund (IMF), the World Bank (see Figure 9.5 for a brief description), and other institutions of global neoliberalism. In these protests, the comingling of "strange bedfellows" (such as the Teamsters, Earth First!, the National Lawyers Guild, the Ruckus Society, and so on) is even more puzzling. But again, an understanding of the dramatically changed strategic environment provides us with a ready-made explanation.

As I said, however, the changes to the strategic environment wrought by globalizing processes are not always going to be obvious and easy to discern.

Figure 9.4   The North American Free Trade Agreement

In January 1994, Canada, the United States, and Mexico launched the North American Free Trade Agreement (NAFTA) and formed the world's largest free trade area. Designed to foster increased trade and investment among the partners, NAFTA contains an ambitious schedule for tariff elimination and reduction of nontariff barriers as well as comprehensive provisions on the conduct of business in the free trade area. These include disciplines on the regulation of investment, services, intellectual property, competition, and the temporary entry of businesspersons. Despite the seemingly technical nature of the agreement, NAFTA has been controversial since it was first proposed. Large corporations have tended to support NAFTA, in the belief that lower tariffs would increase trade and profits. Labor unions in the United States, on the other hand, have opposed NAFTA for fear that jobs would move out of the country owing to lower wage costs in Mexico. Farmers in Mexico have opposed NAFTA because the heavy agriculture subsidies for farmers in the United States have put a great deal of downward pressure on Mexican agricultural prices, forcing many farmers out of business. Opposition to NAFTA also comes from environmental, social justice, and other advocacy organizations that believe NAFTA has detrimental noneconomic impacts on health, environment, and so on.

Source: http://en.wikipedia.org/wiki/NAFTA.

Yet if the researcher stays sharply focused on the key tenet of rationalist approaches (that is, that individual actions are motivated by self-interested behavior or determined by a particular set of preferences), eventually she will be "rewarded." On this point, let us consider another real-world example: **anarchy** and brutal violence in the sub-Saharan countries of Angola, Sudan, Sierra Leone, Liberia, Somalia, and Rwanda (see Figure 9.6 for a map of this area). On the surface, it would seem hard to connect either rationality or globalization to the "anarchic violence" in what many people consider to be the least globalized region of the world. Looking a little below the surface, however, some possibilities become immediately apparent. William Reno (1995; cited in Hoogvelt 1997), for instance, argued that economic "globalization"—specifically, the imposition of neoliberal economic reforms on many weak states in Africa—has led to the disintegration of state-civil relations, which, in turn, has created the basis for anarchy and immense bloodshed in a number of countries. In particular, Reno argued that neoliberal reforms—pushed by the international financial institutions and leading Western governments—have seriously undermined, if

Figure 9.5   The International Monetary Fund, the World Bank, and the World Trade Organization

According to the Bretton Woods Web site, "the World Bank and the International Monetary Fund (IMF) are the so-called Bretton Woods Institutions. They were set up at a meeting of 43 countries in Bretton Woods, New Hampshire in July 1944. Their aims were to help rebuild the shattered postwar economy and to promote international economic cooperation. The original Bretton Woods agreement also included plans for an International Trade Organisation (ITO) but these lay dormant until the World Trade Organisation (WTO) was created in the early 1990s. The creation of the World Bank and the IMF came at the end of the Second World War. They were based on the ideas of a trio of key experts—US Treasury Secretary Henry Morgenthau, his chief economic advisor Harry Dexter White, and British economist John Maynard Keynes. They wanted to establish a postwar economic order based on notions of consensual decision-making and cooperation in the realm of trade and economic relations. It was felt by leaders of the Allied countries, particularly the US and Britain, that a multilateral framework was needed to overcome the destabilising effects of the previous global economic depression and trade battles."

The World Trade Organization Web site says that the "World Trade Organization (WTO) [created in 1995] is the only global international organization dealing with the rules of trade between nations. At its heart are the WTO agreements, negotiated and signed by the bulk of the world's trading nations and ratified in their parliaments. The goal is to help producers of goods and services, exporters, and importers conduct their business."

Sources: The Bretton Woods Project: http://www.brettonwoodsproject.org/about/background. html; the World Trade Organization: http://www.wto.org/english/thewto_e/whatis_e/whatis_e.htm.

not destroyed, the one basis for relative peace in these countries, namely, the patrimonial state.

In the patrimonial state, according to Reno, leaders use the state's resources to "buy off" the opposition. This is necessary because, following the end of colonialism, there were few other bases of authority or legitimacy. In addition, fledgling state leaders needed a way to counterbalance formidable coalitions of tribal-based "strongmen." (In this regard, the "patrimonial state" itself can be explained easily via a rational choice framework.) This particular state form, unfortunately, is inherently "corrupt" and inefficient, at least from an economic standpoint. Thus, when these African countries began to experience serious economic difficulties, the first "target" of neoliberal reformers (that is, the IMF and the World Bank) was the "corrupt" and ineffi-

Figure 9.6   Map of Sub-Saharan Africa

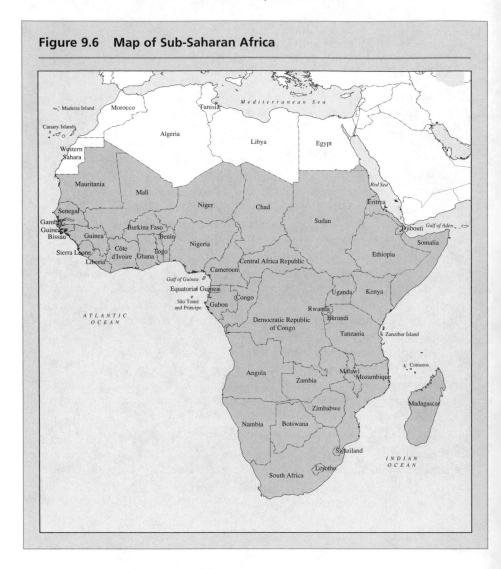

cient state apparatus. In attacking the patrimonial state, however, the IMF and World Bank did nothing to replace, much less institutionalize, an alternative form of centralized authority. As a result, any semblance of central authority collapsed in these countries.

With the collapse of a central authority, the strategic environment changes considerably. Moreover, the collapse of central authority in an economy with few prospects makes "anarchic violence" a far more understandable phenomenon. In Sierra Leone, Reno noted that "much recent fighting, especially its territorial spread, is directly related to the elimination of opportunities for powerful strongmen under 'reform' [imposed by the IMF] and the efforts of these strongmen to strike out on their own for *personal gain*" (emphasis added; p. 217; cited in Hoogvelt 1997, p. 176). And what of ordinary civilians? Why do they engage in brutal, seemingly senseless violence? According to Paul Richards (1999), the reason is clear: "They [primarily teenage fighters in Sierra Leone] see their violence not as anarchic bickering over scraps, but [as] a life-and-death struggle against a political elite pursuing global riches at the expense of domestic improvement. . . . If rebels burn the UN compound it is because the UN is full of successful educated West Africans who have abandoned their countries (so the fighters believe)." Or, in the words of one teenage fighter, "Everybody just has to fight for themselves" (p. 17). They need to fight for themselves, I might note, because fighting is one of the few ways to pursue their self-interests. As Richards pointed out, "Many young combatants report they took up arms as a substitute for non-existent schooling. It was better than nothing. Learning to service a heavy machine gun is access to modern technology of a sort. But they also know war is a zero-sum game" (p. 17).

It is important to underscore the point that this globally oriented, rationalist interpretation of the violence in sub-Saharan Africa does not emerge automatically. Instead, it derives from an analytical framework that is explicit with regard to assumptions (about rationality, for example), systematic with regard to tracing the process by which the global context shapes and is shaped by domestic forces, and rigorous with regard to the matching of theory with evidence. This is not to say that the rationalist perspective on violence in sub-Saharan Africa is necessarily right. Indeed, from my brief summary above, it would be impossible to say this with any certainty. But this is one reason why *comparative analysis* is so important. It is through comparative analysis that one can "test" one's theoretical claims and the assumptions upon which these claims are based.

Globalization and Culture

Culture, as we have learned, is understood from a variety of perspectives. Some comparativists see culture as an unchanging, or at least highly stable, system of beliefs, values, and practices that is passed on, more or less intact, from one generation to the next. Others see culture as a societal resource—which is one way of saying that some cultures are impoverished or backward, whereas others are rich or advanced; or that some cultures are weak or dysfunctional, whereas others are strong and highly adaptive. This second view of culture is often combined with the first to produce a *hierarchy of cultures*—for example, if some cultures are not only weak and dysfunctional but also unchanging, then those cultures are inherently inferior to others. It is possible, therefore, to rank cultures from the "best" to the "worst." In stark contrast to this view, still other comparativists see culture as merely a label for values and commitments generated in the process of making social life happen—that is, "We produce culture as we go" (Richards 1999, p. 17). The importance of this is that "cultures" are not only mutable—that is, capable or subject to change—but adaptive and highly porous.

Culture and globalization: The traditional view. In the first and second views, the relationship between "culture" and "globalization" is straightforward and could be characterized in the following (albeit simplistic) way. Cultures are like self-contained ships. Those cultures with enough passengers and an able crew will likely continue to survive for some time to come, but almost all are destined to disappear in an era of globalization. This is true because globalization is essentially a project of Western culture—the biggest, most powerful "ship" of them all. Thus, as the forces of globalization continue to expand and intensify, smaller ships (or cultures) will simply be overwhelmed. In this process, of course, some cultures will not go down easily—they may strike out at the dominant culture or retreat even further into themselves. That is, they may become ever more isolated and closed off from the rest of the world. In an era of *globality,* however, we know this is not possible. The forces of globalization will seep—or, more likely, flood—into these cultures no matter what they do to stop it. To some scholars—especially those who see cultures as part of a global hierarchy—this is both a positive and negative process. It is positive because, after the "flood" is over, only the "best" culture will survive. Not surprisingly, according to these scholars, the "West is the best" among all the world's cultures: not only will it survive, but it *should* survive (see, for example, Rothkopk 1997).

On the other hand, the process can be negative, as I have already suggested, because it will likely lead to pervasive conflict and violence between and among "cultures." This is a prediction made, for example, by Samuel Huntington, a Harvard University professor. In his provocative—and highly criticized—article (and subsequent book published in 1996), "The Clash of Civilizations?" (1993), Huntington asserted that cultures (he uses the term "civilization") are fundamentally different and that these differences "will not soon disappear" (p. 70). And although cultural differences do not have to lead to conflict, Huntington argued that globality and globalizing processes make the "clash of civilizations" increasingly likely. In particular, he argued, first, that because the world is "becoming a smaller place" (that is, globality), people are more likely to become aware of cultural differences, which, in turn, "invigorates differences and animosities stretching or thought to stretch back deep into history" (p. 70). Second, he contended that because economic globalization is weakening the nation-state as a source of identity, cultural (as opposed to national) identities will most likely fill the void. This reinforces the first factor and when combined with a number of other processes that Huntington identified—including Western dominance and increasing economic regionalism—means that a violent clash of civilizations is almost inevitable. Huntington and his supporters would probably point to the recent terror attacks against the World Trade Center and the Pentagon as significant "proof" of this thesis, for the attacks were carried out not simply by an isolated group of anti-American fanatics but by a group representing the civilization of Islam against the symbol of Western civilization.

Problems and issues with the traditional view. This is not the place to engage in a detailed critique of specific arguments, but it would be useful to note that those who subscribe to the views above tend to look at culture from an extreme distance. That is, they tend to make broad generalizations not only about cultures but also about how cultures shape people's thinking, sense of identity, and behavior—for example, Confucianism makes all Chinese think and act basically the same; it makes them all, in short, Chinese; Islam does the same to Muslims (no matter where they live); and so on. Looking at a culture from an extreme distance also encourages the observer to miss real and basic intracivilization differences. Not all Muslims, for example, are alike, and not all Muslims like each other; as Fouad Ajami succinctly put it, "The world of Islam divides and sub-divides" ([1993] 1999, p. 100). These divisions and subdivisions, Ajami and others might argue, are no less real and no less basic than the divisions between "civilizations." Finally, looking at a culture from a distance means that the subtler (but not always less important) aspects of the interplay between cultural values and identities, on the one hand, and globalizing processes and global identities, on the other hand, will likely be missed.

Needless to say, looking at culture from afar, especially while imputing to it causal powers, is not something I would recommend. I would not recommend it, if only because far-off observers of culture may only be observing what they *think* exists, rather than what actually does. They cannot be sure, because they never do the on-the-ground research necessary to find out. This is not to say, however, that observers who get "up-close and personal" are immune from making mistakes. They are not. On this point, let me return briefly to the issue of "anarchic violence," a subject about which one journalist, Robert Kaplan, has written a great deal. Looking at Sierra Leone, Kaplan argued that the cause of violence there is simple: a "weak" culture unable to withstand the pressures of rapid urbanization and population growth. Kaplan (1994) quoted approvingly from a West African "friend" (an unidentified government official):

> In the poor quarters of Arab North Africa, there is much less crime, because Islam provides a social anchor: of education and indoctrination. Here in West Africa we have a lot of superficial Islam and superficial Christianity. Western religion is undermined by animist beliefs not suitable to a moral society, because they are based on irrational spirit power. Here spirits are used to wreak vengeance by one person against another, or one group against another. (p. 46)

This all sounds fine until Kaplan finds a country that does not quite fit his (theoretical) vision of the world: Cambodia. Cambodia is neither overpopulated nor "culturally backward"; indeed, it has an ancient and long-admired cultural heritage. But, as Paul Richards (1999) noted, "it is uncannily like anarchic Sierra Leone." Kaplan not only recognized this but readily admitted: "I was light-headed. It was not the fear of crime that I felt or disease, but the deeper writer's fear of having oversimplified something—in this case, the idea of culture, which now seemed like a greater mystery to me than at the beginning of my journey in West Africa" (quoted in Richards, 1999, p. 17). Kaplan could have avoided this light-headedness, of course, if he had simply engaged in good comparative analysis from the very beginning.

Culture and globalization: A processual view. This brings us back to the third view of culture and its relationship to "globalization." Not surprisingly, in this view the relationship is less straightforward than in the others. One reason is clear: since culture is understood as "processual" (that is, culture is defined and redefined in the ongoing process of "making social life happen"), its relationship with globalization is likely to be more complex, interactive, and mutually constitutive. In other words, when culture and globalization "collide," it is not like two solid objects hitting one another (where the bigger and heavier object invariably smashes the other). Instead, it is more like two streams coming together. Even if one stream is larger and more powerful than the other, both not only survive but the quality of each is altered, sometimes subtly and sometimes dramatically. They may also combine together into a new stream or streams, which can move off in unanticipated directions. I do not want to take this imagery too far, for as James Rosenau (1995) usefully pointed out, "metaphoric analysis can extend understanding only so far. It can be suggestive but not incisive, hinting at relationships but not revealing their workings" (p. 48). So it is with the metaphor of two streams. Still, the basic point should be clear: when culture is understood as processual, its relationship and interaction with globalization will not be a simple matter of the latter destroying or completely absorbing the former.

A good way to illustrate this point is to focus on the issue of *identity,* which is not only a central part of cultural approaches but also an issue integrally related to globalization. We have already discussed (in Chapter 3) some reasons identity is central to cultural interpretations of politics, but a brief recap might be useful. As Kopstein and Lichbach (2000) explained it:

> Politics is . . . about identity. Although evidence shows that people all over the world often pursue common goals, and thus can be said to share certain interests, people also frequently define what is in their interests differently. Based on particular sets of beliefs and values that we often refer to as culture, they will even define their material interests differently. What people are willing to give

their life for, how much hardship they will bear during war, or how many hours on weekends people are willing to work varies across societies. Likewise, the kind of ideas, political language, and even physical demeanor that people expect from their politicians also varies across nations and states. (p. 12)

Identities, moreover, are not usually singular, but multiple: a person who lives in Northern Ireland is not just Irish, but Irish Catholic. A Muslim woman living in Iran is not just an Iranian Muslim, but also a Shiite woman. These multiple identities may exist side by side, but they are not always compatible, nor are they necessarily stable. This latter point is key. For although identities can be powerful forces in shaping human (and political) behavior, they can also be manipulated. Consider the case of Iran—that society's particular "Islamic" identity today is not merely a product of a centuries-old devotion to Islam but also very much a product of the late 1970s and 1980s, when a "revolutionary" Islamic regime "pursued an active program of Islamization of culture, media, education, and social conduct" (Tehranian 2000, pp. 362–363). In other words, the now-dominant identity of Iran was consciously created—socially constructed—by those who opposed the secularization of Iranian society. This was not an easy process, nor was it automatic; but once achieved, the Islamization of Iran gave the new fundamentalist leadership tremendous power and authority. (At the same time, we should not expect this newly fashioned cultural identity to stay the same; it, too, will change and is, in fact, in a constant state of change.) But what does this have to do with globalization? According to Lechner and Boli (2000), the connection is fairly clear:

While globalization was by no means the sole cause of Iranian fundamentalism, it helped *set the conditions for its mobilization* and provided targets for the Islamic program. Fundamentalists also took a stand on two questions raised by globalization as challenges for any society: What does it mean to live in world society? What is any one group's place in it? Globalization, in other words, challenges groups and societies to "identify" themselves. (emphasis added; p. 319)

It is important to understand, as Lechner and Boli also pointed out, that fundamentalism is but one of many possible responses to "globalization"— which means that the interaction between globalization and local cultures is not likely to lead to a single, undifferentiated "global culture" but to dozens, if not thousands, of "globalized local cultures." It is also important to understand, as I already suggested, that "globalization" in all its various dimensions is also affected by local cultures, which become part of an overall "global flow." Consider this admittedly trite but telling example: globalization was once almost completely defined in terms of a Westernization—even Americanization—of the entire world. Increasingly, however, globalization includes strong influences from Asia. Hello Kitty, feng shui, karaoke, Pokemon, anime, tai chi chuan, shiatsu, yoga, and so on have all become a significant portion of the global flow. The influences from local cultures, of course, can run much deeper than Hello Kitty. Much of the environmental movement today, for example, is based at least partly on "traditional" cultural understandings of the proper relationship between human society and "nature." (Environmentalism, I might note, is itself another type of identity.)

For a student researcher, it is critical to understand, first, the multidimensional and processual nature of culture and, second, the myriad and complex ways in which culture and globalization interact. For if we take seriously the idea that culture affects politics—that it "shapes what people want out of politics, what they are willing to do, and how they define their interests" (Kopstein and Lichbach 2000, p. 13)—then to do otherwise would invite gross oversimplification and misunderstanding. Unfortunately, it is not possible to provide a blueprint for how best to do this. Suffice it to say, therefore, that the methods and principles of comparative analysis provide a solid foundation for research incorporating culture and globalization.

Globalization and Structural Approaches

For many, but not all, historical structuralists the effects of globalization might be summed up in the following manner: "The more things change, the more they remain the same." By this, I mean that for historical structuralists—that is, Marxists and others who view capitalism as part of a still-unfolding historical process—globalization is simply the continuation of "trends that have long accompanied the expansion of capitalism" (Chase-Dunn 1994, p. 97). To be sure, as John Bellamy Foster (2002) succinctly put it, "capitalism has become more extreme." Still, this does not change the fundamental nature of the problem, which is that the capitalist system still "operates" as it always has. Perhaps the most significant novelty of economic globalization is that the expansion and deepening of capitalist integration are more widely recognized—by an increasingly diverse audience—than they have ever been. In this regard, too, concerns or questions about the structural effects and implications of the capitalist system have, in many ways, reached the mainstream, not only in academia but also in the mass media, in the popular consciousness, and even within the institutions of neoliberalism. In the opening pages of its *1996 World Development Report,* for example, the World Bank quoted approvingly from *The Communist Manifesto* by Marx and Engels: "Constant revolutionizing of production, uninterrupted disturbance of social conditions, everlasting uncertainty and agitation. . . . All fixed, fast frozen relations, with their train of ancient and venerable prejudices, and opinions, are swept away, all new-formed ones become antiquated before they can ossify. All that is solid melts into air . . ." (cited in Foster 2002). The quote was used by the World Bank to emphasize how the transition from planned to market economies, as well as the entire thrust of economic globalization, is an inescapable, elemental process, lacking any visible hand behind it (Foster 2002).

This does not mean, of course, that the World Bank has converted to Marxism. It definitely has not. Instead, it means that the World Bank—or rather the elites who ultimately control it—understand that the structural imperatives of globalization can no longer be ignored or hidden from plain view, so to speak. So, rather than cling to an obvious lie, the World Bank and others are attempting to co-opt Marxism and other historical structuralist perspectives. In other words, in recognizing that economic globalization is an ineluctable structural force, the World Bank and others implicitly reject the fundamental liberal view on the centrality of agency. In so doing, however, they are also implying that there is no discernible center of power behind economic globalization and that the processes of globalization are primarily progressive. This, in short, is the ideology of globalization, *globalism.*

Ironically, but not surprisingly, a notable exception to this trend toward greater recognition of the structural imperatives of globalization/global capitalism can be found in the so-called antiglobalization movement. Foster (2002) suggested that this is primarily a reaction (or perhaps overreaction) to the portrayal of globalization as an overwhelming structural force that erases any prospect of agency. As he put it, "the movement against the neoliberal global project has chosen to exaggerate the role of the visible instruments of globalization at the expense of any serious consideration of historical capitalism. Radical dissenters frequently single out the WTO, the IMF, the World Bank and multinational corporations—and even specific corporations like McDonald's—for criticism, while deemphasizing the system, and its seemingly inexorable forces." Both viewpoints, according to Foster, are wrong. The former is wrong because it presents a hyperstructural argument, and the latter is wrong because it overplays (or distorts) the role of agency.

This brings us back, albeit via a somewhat circuitous route, to the main question of this section, namely, how does globalization affect the study of comparative politics from a structural perspective? The basic answer should already be clear: very little. The reasoning is simple: because globalization is "nothing new" (or at least nothing fundamentally new), the study of comparative politics from a structural perspective can remain basically the same. The focus must still be on the structure and logic of global capitalism, on the importance of (structural) relationships, and on the continuing relevance of class.

This said, given the "extremeness" of the present era of capitalism and the efficacy of capitalism's new globalist ideology, it would still be useful to highlight a number of pertinent issues about which a beginning comparativist should take special heed. The first is the most obvious: the nature of the relationship between structure and agency. Not surprisingly, there is no agreement on just what the nature of this relationship is; nonetheless, there is widespread agreement on the need to "join structure and agency in a compelling manner" (Mittelman 1996a, p. 232). There are many ways to do this, but one of the most important is to understand that there actually *is* agency behind globalization. The key agents, however, are not a new breed of supranational organizations like the World Trade Organization, still less international institutions like the World Bank and the IMF, but instead the "usual suspects": globalized monopoly capital and "advanced" capitalist states. (With regard to states, there are many structuralists who argue that state power is on the decline, but the loss of sovereignty or control is primarily found among states in the periphery rather than among states in the "core.")

Understanding where power resides—or how power is configured—in the current capitalist system is crucial, especially for those who wish to understand the prospects for agency among subordinate actors—for example, social movements, peripheral states and their societies, labor unions, and so on. It is crucial, in part, because there is no way to pose a viable alternative—theoretical or practical—to neoliberal or economic globalization unless one knows how power is exercised in the system as a whole and from what sources. Recognizing that the state remains a center of power is particularly important in this regard, for despite its key role in the "international constitutionalization of neoliberalism . . . there is no prospect whatsoever of getting to more egalitarian, democratic, and cooperative world order beyond global competitiveness, without a fundamental struggle with domestic and global capitalists over the transformation of the state" (Panitch 1996, p. 109). In other words, the *system* of global capitalism cannot be effectively challenged if the political source of capitalist power is essentially left alone or ignored.

Another way to "join structure and agency in a compelling manner" is to understand that, despite its seemingly overwhelming nature, global capitalism is not a monolithic force but, instead, is permeated by unavoidable contradictions. Put more simply, this means that economic globalization, as it unfolds, creates not only strong tensions but also the conditions for its own destruction. It is the job of the historical-structuralist comparativist, in part, to identify and trace—in a concrete and historically specific manner—these tensions and contradictions. It is also the job of the comparativist to examine the impact of and response to the tensions/contradictions of global capitalism, whether at the local, regional, or transnational level(s). This, in fact, is an area in which a great deal of research has already been done. Comparativists, for example, have examined how the centralizing tendencies of globalization have given rise to an increase in religious or nationalist fundamentalism (an issue we discussed earlier) in Iran, India, Pakistan, Lebanon, Northern Ireland, and even the United States. For structuralists, it is important to reiterate, the rise of fundamentalism is not a "cultural" phenomenon per se but a reflection of structurally created tensions inherent in capitalist expansion.

Comparativists have also studied how the imperatives of global capitalism have created increased rivalry, conflict, and violence within states or political communities: throughout Africa, the Middle East, Eastern Europe, South and Southeast Asia, Latin America, and, really, the entire world. At the same time, an understanding of the logic and contradictions of capitalism has helped comparativists explain, for instance, the re-emergence of stronger—and reconstituted—labor movements in South Africa, South Korea, Venezuela, Brazil, Colombia, and so on (see Alder 1996; Moody 1997).

"Tensions" in the Structural Approach

All of this, I hope, gives you a good sense of the "issues about which a beginning comparativist should take special heed." Let me conclude this chapter, however, with one important methodological caveat regarding another "tension." This tension, as James Mittelman (1996a) pointed out, is the one between "top-down" and "bottom-up" approaches. As Mittelman explained it, "Although it would be wrong to present a dichotomy between top-down and bottom-up perspectives, or between macro- and microlevels of analysis, one cannot simply posit that in work on globalization there is room for views from both above and below." Instead, Mittelman continued, "the task is to determine how various aspects of globalization merge and interpenetrate under concrete and varied conditions. One way to do so is to examine a series of interactions that constitute the globalization process" (p. 234). This is a little abstruse, but Mittelman's basic point is clear: for a structural argument to hold water, a researcher must be able to connect seemingly discrete political, social, and economic phenomena into a single process.

■ Conclusion

This chapter has covered a lot of ground in only a limited amount of space. It is probably likely, then, that you still have many unanswered questions. But, for the most part, this is desirable. It is also unavoidable, for comparative politics remains an immensely diverse, immensely challenging field of study (notwithstanding the "homogenizing" effects of globalization). No matter how hard I try, moreover, I can only present a limited perspective. It is up to you, therefore, to take what I have written in this chapter—and in the entire book—and begin charting your own intellectual path. Indeed, this is my primary objective; that is, I wrote this book as a theoretical and methodological—but decidedly *not* empirical—primer to the study of comparative politics. On many topics of discussion, including globalization, you will no doubt need to consult other sources. This is not only good practice but also necessary to doing comparative politics.

■ Notes

1. Mittelman (2001) argued that we need to be very careful when we talk about those who "oppose" globalization, for opposition implies only two choices: for and against. Yet this twofold division is highly simplistic in that it obscures "the varied complaints about globalising trends that have emerged from different locales and diverse points on the political spectrum" (p. 214). Moreover, it suggests that "opponents" have nothing affirmative or positive to say; yet, as Mittelman nicely put it, many critics of globalization "oppose" it because "they are imagining possibilities for a more inclusive, participatory and democratic globalisation" (p. 214). Mittelman, therefore, suggested an alternative concept: resistance. This concept should not be considered a mere change in vocabulary but should, instead, be understood as a much more accurate and meaningful way to conceptualize the antithesis of (neoliberal) globalization. Resistance implies not opposition, but transformative potential, protection from "disease," and refusal to obey unjust and immoral conditions (as in the civil rights movement in the United States or resistance to the Nazi occupation in France).

2. In a comparative study of immigrant rights in the United States, Germany, and the European Union (EU), for example, Joppke (2001) argued that the sources of rights expansion in these polities (note that the EU is not a state but a "treaty-based functional regime") are mostly legal and domestic. "Rights expansion," he wrote, "originates in independent and activist courts, which mobilize domestic law (especially constitutional law) and domestic legitimatory discourses, often against restriction-minded, democratically accountable governments" (p. 339). He went on to show that, in each of the three polities, the legal empowerment of immigrants was primarily a product of an "expanding judicial domain" that was largely, if not completely, *unconnected* to broader developments in international human rights (which constitute an important aspect of globalization). Joppke, to make the point clear, rejected the assertion that politics of immigrant rights expansion in the United States, Germany, and the EU represented "the interplay of domestic and external forces on the politics of a given country, state, or society," to repeat a basic point made in Chapter 1 of this book.

Glossary

Many of the definitions in this glossary are adapted from three main sources: David Jary and Julia Jary, *The HarperCollins Dictionary of Sociology,* 2nd ed. (New York: HarperPerennial, 1991); "Wikipedia: The Free Encyclopedia," http://en.wikipedia.org/wiki/Main_Page; and Graham Evans and Jeffrey Newnham, *The Penguin Dictionary of International Relations* (London: Penguin Books, 1998). Items printed in SMALL CAPITALS are cross references to main glossary entries.

Administrative Guidance. Typically used in reference to DEVELOPMENTAL STATES, administrative guidance is an informal directive put forth by state agencies designed to give private firms "guidance" on certain economic issues and policies. These directives do not have the force of law, but they are not easily ignored.

Agency; Agent. Often contrasted with the concept of STRUCTURE, agency implies that actors, whether acting individually or collectively, have an ability to affect or shape the larger (social) environment in which they live. Although a seemingly commonsense assertion, many scholars argue that all human action is, to at least some degree, constrained or otherwise shaped by broader forces, which can derive from INSTITUTIONS, culture, the economic system, or other overarching structures.

Al-Qaida. Arabic for "the foundation." Al-Qaida, which can also be transliterated as **Al-Qaeda, Al-Quaida, El-Qaida**, or **Äl-Qaida**, is an Islamist paramilitary movement widely regarded as a terrorist organization, especially in the West. The organization, which is led by Osama bin Laden and Ayman al-Zawahri, was responsible for the attack against the World Trade Center buildings and the Pentagon on September 11, 2001.

Analytical Induction. A specific research strategy based on the case study. The basic idea behind analytical induction is to use individual case studies as a way to build a stronger theoretical EXPLANATION. Cases are used in a step-by-step manner, with each case contributing to the development of a general theory.

Anarchy; Anarchic. In INTERNATIONAL RELATIONS (IR), anarchy refers to the absence of a central or ultimate authority within a POLITICAL SYSTEM. In general, IR scholars consider the international system to be anarchic because there is no institution or political entity vested with the authority and capacity to resolve conflicts between individual states. In other words, there is no authority that exists beyond the level of the sovereign STATE.

Area Studies. In the HUMANITIES and SOCIAL SCIENCES, area studies refers to a type of research that focuses on a particular geographical region or country. Common area studies fields include Middle East studies, Asian studies (which can include East Asian, Southeast Asian, and South Asian studies), African studies, Latin American studies, and Caribbean studies. Although seemingly a "natural fit" for comparative politics, area studies research is a heterogeneous field, with no common methodological or theoretical approach.

Authoritarianism. A nondemocratic political regime in which decisionmaking authority is highly centralized and exclusionary. Typically, authoritarian regimes are ruled by a single dictator, or by a small elite, who makes decisions in top-down fashion. Authoritarian systems are characterized by limited individual freedoms, minimal civil liberties and rights, excessive reliance on violence and coercion (including imprisonment, torture, and murder) against political opponents, and limited accountability on the part of government officials.

Binary Analysis. In the context of comparative methodology, binary analysis refers to a comparison of two distinct units or CASES. For example, a researcher might compare the United States and Canada. See Chapter 2 for a more detailed discussion of this term.

Buddhist. A Buddhist is a follower of Buddhism, which is a major religion of Asia. There are an estimated 300 million followers worldwide. Buddhism is based on the teachings of Siddhartha Gautama, but there are many forms, including Theravada Buddhism (Way of the Elders), Mahayana Buddhism, Zen Buddhism, Pure Land Buddhism, Nichiren Buddhism (Lotus Sect), and Tibetan Buddhism (Lamaism).

Cadre. A cadre is an elite or select group—or a member of such a group—that forms the core of a larger organization.

Capital Flight. The term "capital flight" is ambiguous. The classic use of the term, according to Darryl McLeod (2002), "is to describe widespread currency speculation, especially when it leads to cross-border movements of private funds that are large enough to affect financial markets." In this view, capital flight is most closely associated with actions taken by *foreign* investors. Recently, though, capital flight "has been applied more broadly to capital outflow from residents of developing countries" (McLeod 2002). Some of these residents are domestic investors who are primarily interested in protecting their financial assets. Other "residents" are domestic political and economic elites who use their privileged positions to secretly and illegally send money out of their country strictly for personal gain.

Case; Case Study. These are frequently used, but vague, terms. In general, though, a case may be said to be based on (1) a specific issue or concern (for example, terrorism, industrialization, revolution), (2) a delimited geographic space (Japan, France, Italy), and (3) a certain period of time (although this is sometimes implicit). Thus, we may talk about the case of postwar Japanese industrialization or the case of the Russian Revolution of 1917. In addition, cases do not have to involve whole countries or societies but can focus on specific INSTITUTIONS, policies, events, or even people. A case study is simply research or analysis that focuses on a single case.

Caste System. A rigid organization of traditional Indian society defined in terms of hereditary occupation. Introduced in the second millennium BC, the caste system has been legally abolished, but remnants still exist today. There are four castes, in descending order: Brahmans (priests), Kshatriyas (warriors), Vaishyas (farm owners, merchants, artisans), and Shudras (menials, laborers, serfs). Below even the Shudras are the untouchables, a group considered so low that they are completely outside the caste system.

Causal Complexity. See COMPLEX CAUSALITY.

Causal Relationship. A relationship in which change in one or more factors or VARIABLES leads to, results in, or "forces" changes in one or more other factors or variables.

Causation. See CAUSAL RELATIONSHIP.

Civil Society. "Civil society" is an ambiguous term, but it is generally defined as the multitude of organizations in a *democratic* society that operate independently of the state. These include nonprofit organizations, nongovernmental organizations (NGOs), SOCIAL MOVEMENTS, trade unions, churches, policy institutions (for example, think tanks), the news media, universities, and so on. Many scholars also consider business firms to be separate from civil society, although the distinction is not always clear-cut (consider, for example, the mass media, which are all owned by large corporations).

Class. A hierarchical and relatively permanent division between individuals and groups within society, usually defined by occupation, income, or education. In Marxist thought, classes are economically determined and inherently conflictual divisions based on ownership and nonownership of property or the means of production.

Cold War (c. 1945–1990). A term used to describe the relationship between the United States and its noncommunist allies, on the one hand, and the Soviet Union and its satellites, allies, and other COMMUNIST regimes, on the other hand. In contrast to a "hot" war, the Cold War did not involve direct combat between the two superpowers, although the relationship itself was characterized by ongoing hostility, high levels of distrust, suspicion, and rivalry for influence throughout the world. The rivalry for influence often led to armed conflict in which the superpowers fought each other indirectly. The Cold War came to an end in 1989.

Collective Action. In the context of rational choice, collective action is concerned with the provision of COLLECTIVE GOODS through the cooperation or collaboration of two or more individuals. More generally, collective action or collective behavior refers to the nonroutine or out-of-the-ordinary actions of people in groups or crowds.

Collective Good (also Public Good). "Commodities" or services—for example, national defense, clean air and water, law enforcement, and highways—that, when made available to one person, are available to all. In short, a collective good is a *nonexclusive* commodity or service. The nonexclusive nature of collective or public goods leads to the FREE-RIDER PROBLEM in that "consumers" of the public good have no incentive to contribute to its cost.

Colonialism. A system in which one STATE claims SOVEREIGNTY over a territory and people outside its own established boundaries. The most common motivation for colonial expansion was to take control of the economic resources, labor, and often markets of the colonized territory. This was typically accomplished through military force. Historically, colonialism is most closely associated with the period from the fifteenth to nineteenth centuries, when the major European powers (Britain, France, Holland, Portugal, and Spain) steadily expanded their reach into Africa, Asia, and Latin America. The European powers were joined in the late nineteenth and early twentieth centuries by Belgium, Germany, Italy, the United States, Japan, and Russia. Colonialism, it is fair to say, has been a major force in shaping the political and economic character of the modern world.

Commodity Chain. Refers to a "network of labor and production processes whose end result is a finished commodity" (Hopkins and Wallerstein 1986, p. 159). More simply, a commodity chain includes all aspects of the production of a product, from the extraction and processing of raw materials (such as rawhide, leather, and rubber for shoes), to the fabrication and assembly of the constituent parts, to the exportation and importation of the finished product, to marketing, promotion, and sales in wholesale or retail outlets. Typically, a commodity chain for any product results in a highly uneven distribution of surplus value—those at the "lower" extractive and labor-intensive end receive very little, whereas those at the "upper" marketing and sales end receive a disproportionately large share. For further discussion, see Gereffi and Korzeniewicz (1990).

Communism. Communism is both a theory and a practice. As a theory, communism rests on the ideas of historical materialism proposed by KARL MARX and developed and implemented by V. I. Lenin. In Marxist theory, communism denotes the final stage of human historical development in which there is no STATE, and people rule both politically and economically. Ironically, as a practice, communism represented a totalitarian system of government in which a single party controlled state-owned means of production with the professed aim of establishing a stateless society (as in the former Soviet Union).

Communist. See COMMUNISM.

Complex Causality; Causal Complexity. This concept suggests that political, social, and economic phenomena are rarely the product of a single cause but, instead, are the product of combinations of conditions that intersect in various and interdependent ways (Ragin 1987). In addition, there are usually several different combinations of conditions that may produce the same change. For further discussion, see Ragin (1987), chapter 2.

Confucianism; Confucian. An East Asian ethical and philosophical system developed mostly upon the teachings of Confucius (traditionally 551 BC to 479 BC). Confucianism remained the mainstream Chinese orthodoxy for 2,000 years, until the beginning of the twentieth century, when the Chinese Communist Party (CCP) first began to exert influence in Chinese politics. Outside of China, Confucian ideas have influenced a variety of Asian societies, including Korea, Japan, Taiwan, Singapore, and Vietnam.

Contradiction. A key term in Marxist and other historical-structuralist analysis, contradictions are thought to be an inherent aspect of most social or economic processes. In capitalism, for example, the imperatives of competition and accumulation necessarily generate exploitation and oppression, which create conflict between workers and capitalists. Eventually, this conflict will lead to a revolutionary struggle that will destroy the system.

Control. In an experimental design, "to control" means to limit the factors influencing a variable under observation. In comparative politics, researchers use different forms of comparative analysis, such as the most similar systems (MSS) design or the most different systems (MDS) design, to loosely control for a wide range of variables.

Control Variable. Control variables are additional variables in a research design that might affect the relationship between the independent and dependent variables. When control variables are used, the researcher wants to ensure that these variables are not, in fact, responsible for variations observed in the dependent variable (Monroe 2000, p. 21).

Co-optation; Co-opt. A political strategy designed to neutralize or win over subordinate groups through accommodation. Unlike "power sharing," a policy of co-optation is fundamentally designed to limit or undermine the power of weaker, but potentially significant, groups by accommodating some demands for inclusion while deflecting more radical demands.

Correlation. Correlation describes a relationship between two different VARIABLES. If one increases when the other increases (or vice versa), then there is a correlation between them. For example, there is a well-established correlation between the per capita level of GROSS DOMESTIC PRODUCT (GDP) and democracy. The fact that there is a correlation, however, does not necessarily mean that one *causes* the other; a third (still unidentified) variable could be involved. In other words, correlation does not necessarily indicate a CAUSAL RELATIONSHIP.

Country. A country is a fixed geographical area that includes an independent political entity with its own GOVERNMENT, regulations and laws (generally codified in a constitution), judicial system, police/military force, and population. The terms "country" and "STATE" are generally interchangeable, but there are a few exceptions. Political entities that have a distinct history or culture, such as England, Scotland, and Wales, can be considered separate countries but part of a single state, namely, the United Kingdom.

Deductive Logic; Deduction. Deduction is a "top-down" approach. It begins with a general principle (for example, rational action) or theory, then draws conclusions about specific cases. Rational choice theory is based on deductive logic.

Dependence. When comparativists use the term "dependence," they are usually referring to the inability of poor and weak societies (or subordinate social classes) to control their own economic and political fates. They argue, instead, that the economic and political fate of poorer societies—primarily former colonies—is largely determined by exploitative and unequal relationships.

Dependency; Dependency Theory. Dependency theory—which was most influential in the 1970s—is a theory that attempts to explain the continuing poverty and political and social instability of many poor countries in the world. An explicitly structural theory, dependency focused on the exploitative relationship between advanced capitalist societies and the Third World. More specifically, dependency scholars argued that the nature of this relationship, rather than internal conditions, was the primary cause of poverty and "underdevelopment." There is a huge literature on dependency, but some of the leading figures are Fernando H. Cardoso and Enzo Faletto (1979), André Gunder Frank ([1966] 1988), and Theotonio Dos Santos ([1970] 1996).

Dependent Variable. In a causal or social scientific analysis, the dependent variable is that variable the researcher seeks to explain. It is the *result* or *effect* in a CAUSAL RELATIONSHIP. For example, if a researcher argues that economic deprivation causes an increase in violent crime, "violent crime" is the dependent variable. See INDEPENDENT VARIABLE below for further explanation and an additional example.

Developmental State. The developmental state is a particular type of STATE distinguished by its high capacity to promote and facilitate rapid industrial development. The concept has been around for several decades, and one of the most influential early works was Chalmer Johnson's *MITI and the Japanese Miracle* (1982). For a more recent discussion, see Woo-Cumings (1999).

Discourse. In academia, the term "discourse" is much more than a "conversation" or "words"; instead, discourse is considered to be an institutionalized way of thinking and understanding. Discourses, many scholars (especially REFLECTIVISTS) argue, shape our views of the world and provide a framework for action. Discourses, in this view, can have a profound impact on society.

Equilibrium. In rational choice theory, and especially game theory, equilibrium represents an optimum strategy for all players in a game, in the sense that no one player can benefit by changing his strategy while all other players keep theirs the same.

Ethnocentrism; Ethnocentric. The problem or tendency of assessing different cultures and societies by one's own standards, values, and expectations. Ethnocentrism can lead to misunderstanding and biased research.

European Union (EU). An international organization of twenty-five European STATES (as of July 2005), established by the Treaty on European Union (also known as the Maastricht Treaty). The European Union has many activities, the most important being a common single market, consisting of a customs union, a single currency called the euro (though some member states retain their own national currency), a Common Agricultural Policy, and a Common Fisheries Policy. Arguably, the EU is the most powerful regionally based international organization in the world today and represents, in an important respect, a completely new type of international organization.

Experimental Method. A research design in which the researcher has complete or near-complete control over the INDEPENDENT VARIABLE, the UNITS OF ANALYSIS, and the overall environment. Under experimental conditions, the researcher is able to manipulate one or more variables, while controlling other factors, to determine the effects on one or more other variables. In comparative politics, the experimental method is rarely used or used in only a very limited fashion.

Explanation. In the social sciences, explanation is generally concerned with identifying the cause or causes of a particular event or general phenomenon. Typically, explanations involve specifying the CAUSAL RELATIONSHIP between two or more VARIABLES—for example, "the existence of or a change in x causes y." In comparative politics, researchers often use case-based research to build a theoretical explanation in a step-by-step manner. This is also referred to as ANALYTICAL INDUCTION.

Export-Oriented Industrialization (EOI). As the term suggests, EOI is an industrialization strategy—typically associated with the East Asian NEWLY INDUSTRIALIZING COUNTRIES (NICS)—that gives priority to export-based growth. To encourage export-based growth, a government will typically provide domestic manufacturers with SUBSIDIES or other incentives to export their products. "EOI" and "export-led growth" are often used interchangeably.

Falsification. Falsification is a procedure used in science to test the validity of a hypothesis or theory by finding refuting evidence. For example, a single black swan refutes the general hypothesis that "all swans are white." For Karl Popper, a renowned philosopher, falsification provided the decisive criterion of demarcation between science and nonscience. Many scholars, however, reject this view, since a single refutation does not necessarily imply that theories are wrong; indeed, some commentators argue that the procedures suggested by Popper fail to fit the actual practice of science and, if used strictly, would likely cripple the scientific endeavor.

Fascism. A political philosophy or movement—most closely associated with Italy and Germany of the 1920s and 1930s—that places the nation or the race above the individual. Fascism is also premised on the need for a highly centralized government led by a dictator; belief in militarism, racism, and nationalism; and opposition to liberal capitalism and democracy.

Feudalism; Feudal. Although subject to a variety of definitions, feudalism can be generally thought of as a political, economic, and social system in which all the aspects of life were centered on "lordship." In feudal systems, lords (overlords and vassals) controlled the land. Serfs were required to work the central manorial farm and to provide the lord with produce and money payments in return for their own rights to land use. The lord was obligated to provide for the social welfare of peasants, however minimal that may have been.

Formalism/Legalism. In the context of comparative politics, the term "formalism" is generally used to denote the study of the formal political system, that is, the main IN-STITUTIONS and agencies of the state. These may include the legislature, the executive branch, the judiciary, and the bureaucracy. "Legalism" refers to the formal laws and lawmaking processes of the state.

Free-Rider Problem. A person who receives or benefits from a PUBLIC (or COLLEC-TIVE) GOOD, such as national defense or clean air, without contributing to its cost is a free rider. The "free-rider problem" is the question of how to prevent free riding from taking place, or at least limit its effects.

Globalization. "Globalization" is a complex term referring, very broadly, to the acceleration and deepening of processes of technological, economic, political, social, and cultural change throughout the world. See Chapters 7 and 9 for a more detailed discussion of this concept.

Government. A government is the agency or apparatus through which a body exercises authority and performs its functions. In this definition, governments need not be part of a STATE; moreover, multiple governments may exist within a single state. Indeed, we can find governments in all sorts of places—in a university or school (that is, the student government) or in sovereign "NATIONS" (for example, a Native American tribal council)—and at many levels. Cities, counties, provinces, and whole regions (for example, the EUROPEAN UNION), for example, can also have their own separate governments.

Gross Domestic Product (GDP). GDP is a measure of the total flow of goods and services produced by an economy over a specific period of time, normally one year. GDP is often used as a measure of an economy's overall size and prosperity, but it is only a very rough measure. Today, researchers prefer other measurements, including, more prominently, PURCHASING POWER PARITY (PPP) and the HUMAN DEVELOPMENT INDEX (HDI).

Hegemony; Hegemonic. "Hegemony" is used in a variety of ways, but the general meaning of the term is primacy or leadership. More specifically, hegemony implies complete dominance—politically, economically, militarily, and even culturally. An important aspect of hegemony is that the dominance of the leader (that is, the hegemon) is typically exercised without the use of force per se but instead is based on consent.

Hierarchy; Hierarchic. In general sociological terms, hierarchy refers to an asymmetrical relationship or a set of such relationships in which those "at the top" have power over those "at the bottom." In studies of formal political processes, however, hierarchy has a slightly different meaning: it refers to the existence of a state or governmental authority that has the legitimate power to impose public order. Domestically, most political systems are hierarchic, whereas the international system, according to many IR scholars (especially those who subscribe to REALISM), is considered to be anarchic.

Hizballah (alternate spelling: Hezbollah). A militant Shia (see SHIITE) political party in Lebanon. Hizballah—which means "Party of God"—began as a guerrilla group fighting against the Israeli occupation in southern Lebanon. It maintains an active militia, known as the Islamic Resistance.

Human Development Index (HDI). In 1990, the United Nations concluded that aggregate economic data, such as GROSS DOMESTIC PRODUCT (GDP), were inadequate to measure the concept of "development." In place of GDP, the HDI was developed. The HDI consists of three aspects of development: (1) standard of living (measured on the basis of per capita income in PURCHASING POWER PARITY (PPP), (2) knowledge (measured on the basis of adult literacy and combined enrollment ratio), and (3) longevity (that is, life expectancy at birth). The HDI varies between 0 and 1. The closer to 1 the score is, the higher the level of human development. Since its development in 1990, the HDI has been supplemented with a number of other measures, including the gender-related development index and the human poverty index. Additional information is available on the United Nations Development Programme's Human Development Report Web site (http://hdr.undp.org/).

Humanities. The branch of learning that connects the fine arts, literature, languages, philosophy, and cultural studies. Traditionally, the humanities have been distinguished from the SOCIAL SCIENCES (which include, among other disciplines, political science, economics, sociology, psychology, and anthropology).

Hypothesis. A statement proposing a relationship (usually a CAUSAL RELATIONSHIP) between two or more VARIABLES.

Ideology. An ideology is any system of ideas underlying and informing social and political action. Traditionally, ideology was clearly distinguished from THEORY; the latter was assumed to present an objective or scientifically based explanation of the world.

Import-Substitution Industrialization (ISI). An economic strategy premised on reducing the need for imports by expanding and increasing production of domestically produced goods. Typically, an ISI strategy involves heavy state involvement in the national economy. For example, to create the minimal foundation for ISI, the STATE must prohibit certain imports and provide financial assistance (for example, a SUBSIDY) to import-substituting firms and industries.

Independent Variable. An independent variable is one that influences another variable, called a DEPENDENT VARIABLE. In the statement "Poverty is responsible for an increase in violent homicides," "poverty" is the independent variable, and "increase in violent homicides" is the dependent variable—in other words, poverty is said to influence the rate of violent homicide.

Indirect Method of Difference. Based on the work of J. S. Mill, this method involves a comparison of at least three cases. The first two CASES should be compared on the basis of the METHOD OF DIFFERENCE; the third case should be similar to the first in a number of respects and to the second in a number of other respects.

Induction; Inductive Analysis. The process of reaching a conclusion by reasoning from specific premises (or observations) to form a general premise. In QUALITATIVE ANALYSIS, induction is frequently used to generalize from a single CASE STUDY or a series of case studies (this is also known as ANALYTICAL INDUCTION).

Industrial Organization. Industrial organization refers to the underlying characteristics of a national economy or specific market. The most important of these characteristics include (1) the size distribution of firms, (2) the degree of vertical and horizontal integration, (3) ownership patterns, and (4) barriers to entry of new firms.

Industrial Policy. Often associated with NEOMERCANTILISM and the DEVELOPMENTAL STATE, industrial policy involves state support of particular—or "targeted"—industries and firms. In Japan, for example, the Ministry of International Trade and Industry (MITI) has often taken an active hand in development of major industries, particularly electronics and software. All COUNTRIES, however, practice some form of industrial policy.

Infant Industry. In an already-established and internationally competitive industrial sector, an infant industry is one that emerges relatively late. As a newcomer, the infant industry normally cannot operate on the same scale and, therefore, at the same level of competitiveness and efficiency as its more established international competitors. Thus, some argue that states should be allowed to protect and nurture their infant industries until they have time to "grow up."

Institution. Traditionally, institutions were equated with concrete public and private organizations or agencies, such as a legislature, the presidency, the STATE as a whole, a university, and so on. The traditional definition is certainly still relevant and frequently used (including in this book), but recently scholars have adopted a more expansive definition. Specifically, the term "institution" is used to refer to "a stable, recurring pattern of behavior" (Goodin 1998), which may be either formalized/codified (for example, the institution of marriage) or informal/unwritten (for example, the "code of silence" among police officers can be considered an informal but powerful institutional practice). The key is the existence of "rules" that govern or influence, either directly or indirectly, the behavior of actors.

Institutionalism. A concept that includes a diverse and complex array of approaches (too many to discuss here). A common theme among the different approaches, however, is a focus on how INSTITUTIONS determine (enable or constrain), shape, or influence the behavior of actors. See Chapter 3 for a slightly more detailed discussion of institutionalism.

International Monetary Fund (IMF). An international financial institution established in 1946 to (1) provide international liquidity on a short- and medium-term basis and (2) encourage liberalization of exchange rates. The IMF has been subject to intense controversy in recent years, largely because of its policy of requiring debtor countries (mostly in the developing world) to implement sometimes painful NEOLIBERAL policy reforms.

International Relations (IR). The academic study of relations between and among states or nation-states. Although a diverse and heterogeneous field, IR has long been dominated by a particular theoretical perspective known as REALISM. Traditionally, comparative politics and IR have been considered separate fields of study, with the former focusing on domestic political, social, and economic dynamics. Recently, however, the separation between the two fields has begun to break down.

Intersubjectivity; Intersubjective. Most basically, intersubjectivity refers to the experiences, understanding, and knowledge *shared* among people and whole societies. REFLECTIVISTS and other POST-POSITIVISTS believe that intersubjectivity provides the basis for understanding how "reality" is socially constructed.

Islam. Arabic word meaning submission (to God) and the name for the religion founded under the leadership of the prophet Muhammad; it also denotes the MUSLIM community. There are an estimated 1.3 billion followers of Islam worldwide.

Koran. See QURAN.

Legalism. See FORMALISM/LEGALISM.

Level of Analysis. In studies of comparative politics and INTERNATIONAL RELATIONS (IR), the level of analysis is a shorthand way of describing the primary analytical focus of the researcher. The primary levels are the individual, society (or STATE), and the system.

Liberalization. Liberalization has several meanings, depending on the context. Political liberalization refers to the movement toward democracy, individual rights and liberties, and personal freedom. Economically, liberalization generally refers to increasing privatization, which is the economic process of transferring property from public ownership to private ownership. Another important element of economic liberalization is the promotion of a "freer" framework for market activity through deregulation.

Macrosocial. As a prefix, "macro-" means very large in scale, scope, or capability. Macrosocial, therefore, refers to large-scale social structures or to whole societies. For example, the United States is a macrosocial unit.

Madrasah (also madrassa). Madrasah means "school" in Arabic. Typically, it refers to an Islamic school for Muslims. It resembles a parochial school or a yeshiva, but with the purpose of teaching children about the religion of ISLAM.

Maquiladora. A specific type of assembly plant in Mexico, primarily located near the United States–Mexico border. Typically, in the *maquiladora*, foreign materials and parts are shipped in and assembled, and then the finished product is returned to the original market (usually in the United States). This allows US and other non-Mexican firms to take advantage of lower production costs in Mexico while avoiding duties and other taxes.

Marx, Karl (1818–1883). A German scholar of the nineteenth century and the founder of Marxism, the fundamental theory of COMMUNISM. Much of his work, including *Das Kapital* (volume 1 published in 1867, and volumes 2 and 3 published posthumously) and *The Communist Manifesto* (1848), was done with Friedrich Engels. Marx lived outside Germany most of his life, notably in London, where he wrote *Das Kapital.*

Method of Agreement. Based on the work of John Stuart Mill (1806–1873), this method is based on the idea that, when several observations of the same phenomenon (that is, the DEPENDENT VARIABLE) have only one of several VARIABLES in common, then the common variable is the cause of the phenomenon. The MOST DIFFERENT SYSTEMS design is based on this method.

Method of Difference. Also based on the work of J. S. Mill, this method involves studying two very similar cases that differ only with respect to the relationship between the INDEPENDENT and DEPENDENT VARIABLES. The MOST SIMILAR SYSTEMS design is based on this method.

Methodological Individualism. A theoretical/philosophical position holding that social phenomena can and must be explained strictly as outcomes of individual behaviors and decisions. It rejects structural, cultural, and even institutional theories and instead requires social sciences to ground theory strictly in individual action.

Middle Class. In "modern" capitalist societies, the middle class is composed of nonmanual occupational groups (small-business owners, "white-collar" professionals, managers, and so on). The middle class is considered important insofar as the interests of those who comprise this class differ from the interests of those in the upper and working classes.

Mixed Design. A mixed design combines a minimum of two comparative research strategies, such as the CASE STUDY (including a WITHIN-CASE COMPARISON), BINARY ANALYSIS, and multiunit analysis using three or more units. See Chapter 2 for a more detailed discussion.

Modernization Theory; Modernization Theorist. Theory based on a particular model of societal development in which the decisive factor in "modernization" is the overcoming and replacement of traditional values and practices considered antithetical to progressive social change and industrialization.

Most Different Systems (MDS). The MDS design is based on finding key *similarities* between or among very dissimilar units. See discussion in Chapter 2.

Most Similar Systems (MSS). The MSS design is based on finding key *differences* between or among very similar units. See discussion in Chapter 2.

Multiple Causation. Related to the idea of COMPLEX CAUSALITY, multiple causation implies that social phenomena are rarely the product of a single cause or condition but of multiple causes/conditions.

Muslim. A believer in or follower of Islam. The word *Muslim* means "one who submits" and implies complete submission to the will of God. Muslims believe that nature is itself Islamic, since it follows natural laws placed by God.

Nation. Although often confused with the concept of the STATE, nation refers to a social collectivity, the members of which share one or more of the following characteristics: a common identity (which may be based on ethnicity, race, religion, or a similar identifier) or a common history, culture, language, or economic life. Multiple nations, therefore, can exist within a given country or territory (for example, the Sioux nation) and can also cross borders (the Islamic nation).

Nation-State. The term "nation-state" or "nation state," although often used interchangeably with the term STATE, refers more properly to a state composed of a single NATION. By this definition, there are few, if any, nation-states in the world today. A looser definition of nation-state, however, is frequently used. Most scholars, for example, assert that a nation-state exists when a single nation is merely dominant. Yet even with this looser definition, places such as the United States, Canada, Belgium, Iraq, Spain, China, and Indonesia might not be considered nation-states. Typically, though, a common national identity has been constructed in most modern states to create a sense of unity. A better term than "nation-state," therefore, might simply be "national state."

Neoliberalism; Neoliberal. Loosely associated with neoclassical economics, neoliberalism is a school of economics based on the premise that GOVERNMENTS or STATES in general lack the capacity to manage complex industrial economies. Hence, except for core responsibilities of creating and maintaining an infrastructure, a system of justice and national defense, and a few other related COLLECTIVE GOODS, governments should shrink and privatize. Neoliberalism puts great emphasis on unregulated or "free" markets as the best way to build prosperity in any economy or society. The neoliberal doctrine, it is useful noting, is also a subset of the so-called Washington Consensus, a set of specific policy goals designed for Latin American countries to help them recover from the "lost decade" of the 1980s.

Neomercantilism. Neomercantilism is an economic strategy based on the idea that a country's prosperity and power require the STATE to exercise an active role in both protecting and promoting national economic development.

Neorealism. See REALISM.

Newly Industrializing Countries (NICs). NICs are countries that are not quite yet at the status of a first-ranked capitalist economy (for example, the United States, Japan, Germany, or Canada) but still more economically "advanced" than countries from the so-called Third World. The "classic" NICs include South Korea, Taiwan, Singapore, and Hong Kong. More recently, China, several countries in Southeast Asia (Malaysia, Thailand, and Indonesia), and a number of countries in Latin America have been said to have reached NIC status.

Norm. Any standard or rule, formal or informal, that regulates, shapes, or governs behavior in a social setting. A normative position is any position that holds certain rules, values, or practices as preferable to others.

Normative Theory. Any theory that attempts to prioritize specific values or NORMS. A normative theory, in other words, expresses a judgment about whether a situation is desirable or undesirable for a particular society or for societies in general. Many social "scientists" regard normative theory as anathema, since it adopts an explicitly subjective approach. Others, however, reject the distinction between normative and POSITIVIST social theories, arguing that all theories are inherently subjective and, therefore, normative.

North American Free Trade Agreement (NAFTA). A comprehensive, but controversial, trade agreement linking Canada, the United States, and Mexico in a "free trade" sphere. NAFTA went into effect on January 1, 1994. The agreement immediately ended tariffs on some goods; on other goods, tariffs were scheduled to be eliminated over a set period of time.

Objectivity; Objective. In the social sciences, objectivity implies that the existence of an entity, process, or structure does not depend on human awareness. The computer used to type this sentence exists "objectively," because it would still exist in exactly the same form whether or not I was aware of it. In studying the social world, however, objectivity is not as clear-cut. Do social CLASSES, for example, have a purely objective existence? Or are they partly a product of our awareness? Many scholars, especially REFLECTIVISTS, reject the idea that our accounts of the world can be purely objective. Instead, they argue that the world we perceive is INTERSUBJECTIVE.

Operational Definition. A process that involves defining a concept empirically so that it can be measured. In QUALITATIVE ANALYSIS, the emphasis on empirical specification is not strictly followed, but the key to operationalizing a concept is the ability to translate it into a consistent measurement of some kind.

Operationalize. See OPERATIONAL DEFINITION.

Other, the. This concept denotes the practice of portraying "outsiders" as not only different or alien but also inherently inferior. Outsiders become the Other—an ideological construct designed not only to legitimize and naturalize the subjugation and oppression of different peoples but also to reinforce and reproduce a unified self-identity. In this sense, the Other signifies the relationship between power and knowledge. Thus, it was the Western states that used their dominant military-economic power to create a world premised on a fundamental division between the forces of civilization and progress (that is, the West), on the one hand, and the forces of primitiveness, irrationality, and barbarism (that is, the Other), on the other hand.

Pact. In the context of research on democratization, a pact refers to a negotiated settlement (or agreement), typically among a country's elite, for limited political change toward democracy. Some scholars, especially rationalists, believe that such settlements are essential to democratic transition and consolidation.

Parliamentary System. Refers to a democratic form of government in which the executive branch (the cabinet or the privy council) is formally dependent on the parliament's (that is, the assembly's or legislature's) acceptance. The cabinet can be removed by the parliament through a vote of nonconfidence. The leader of the executive cabinet, the prime minister, is usually the head of government. Although parliamentary systems may have a president, the president's authority is limited and is subordinate to that of the prime minister. The parliamentary system is often contrasted with PRESIDENTIALISM.

Path Dependence. In rational choice analysis, path dependence refers to the view that no economic or social process progresses steadily toward some predetermined and unique equilibrium. Rather, initial conditions determine the path followed and the final result. If path dependence prevails, it implies that history is relevant to what occurs now and when or if equilibrium is achieved. One famous example of path dependence is the QWERTY layout on typewriters. This was a built-in "inefficiency" meant to prevent jamming if the keys were pressed too quickly in succession. Although this design was logical for early typewriters, most modern computers use the same layout even though jamming is no longer a concern.

Petty Bourgeoisie. The class of small-business owners, artisans, and (middle-class) professionals. KARL MARX originally coined this term to distinguish between large capitalists and small shopkeepers, on the one hand, and small shopkeepers and the proletariat (that is, workers), on the other hand.

Political System. The political system includes the sum total of organizations and INSTITUTIONS within a country that influence or are influenced by the political process. This is an inclusive concept that covers the agencies of the STATE and GOVERNMENT; political parties, interest and pressure groups; the media of communication (newspapers, radio, television, the Internet, and so on); and a host of ostensibly nonpolitical institutions, including the family, the community, schools, churches, corporations, foundations, think tanks, and the like.

Positivist. A positivist subscribes to the principles of positivism, which is a doctrine formulated by Auguste Comte (1798–1857). Comte asserted that the only true knowledge is scientific knowledge; that is, a knowledge based on empirical observation. Positivists generally hold two strong positions: (1) a belief in the (methodological) unity of all sciences, which is to say that the methods of physical sciences can be carried over into the social sciences; and (2) an assumption that the "objective" world exists independently of any perspectives of the researchers; a distinguishing feature of positivism, in other words, is the absence of any distinction between reality (as things that exist) and knowledge of reality (as things that are recognized).

Postmodernism; Postmodern. A theory of POST-POSITIVISM or REFLECTIVISM that is profoundly skeptical of any account of the social world that purports to have direct access to the "Truth."

Post-Positivism. The rejection of the idea that science and knowledge can be grounded in entirely objective observations of the social world, as suggested by those who are POSITIVISTS.

Power. There is no simple definition of power; it is an extremely complex and contested concept. Suffice it to say, therefore, that power has many dimensions and can both constrain (for example, through coercion) and enable action. It is also important to understand that power has both material and nonmaterial sources, neither of which necessarily has primacy.

Presidential System. See PRESIDENTIALISM.

Presidentialism; Presidential System. Refers to a type of democratic political regime in which the chief executive (that is, the president) is elected by popular vote and in which the terms of office for the president and the assembly are fixed. In addition, in a "pure" presidential system, the president has authority over the cabinet. The presidential system is often contrasted with the PARLIAMENTARY SYSTEM.

Public Choice. Public choice theory is a branch of economics that developed from the study of taxation and public spending. The key principles of public choice draw from rational choice theory, but unlike many of the arguments we have discussed in this book, public choice is focused on the conditions for "government failure" rather than "market failure." In this sense, public choice theory has a strong normative position, which is that government intervention be strictly limited. For further discussion, see Shaw (2002).

Public Goods. See COLLECTIVE GOODS.

Purchasing Power Parity (PPP). A method that attempts to more accurately compare incomes across countries than do traditional statistics, such as GROSS DOMESTIC PRODUCT (GDP). PPP converts income in each country from that country's domestic currency to US dollars. At the PPP rate, therefore, one dollar has the same purchasing power over domestic GDP that the US dollar has over US GDP. PPP rates are designed to allow a standard comparison of real price levels between countries, just as conventional price indexes allow comparison of real values over time; otherwise, normal exchange rates may over- or undervalue purchasing power.

Puritanism. The Puritans were a group of radical Protestants who emerged in England after the Reformation (around the sixteenth century). The central tenet of Puritanism was based on a belief in God's supreme authority over human affairs, and followers advocated strict religious discipline along with simplification of the ceremonies and creeds of the Church of England.

Qualitative Analysis. Qualitative research places strong emphasis on understanding and interpreting data or information that cannot be adequately or meaningfully quantified (or expressed in numbers). An interview of a high-ranking official or peasant farmer, for example, is generally nonquantifiable. An analysis of historical records, events, and documents, too, often cannot be meaningfully expressed in numbers. CASE STUDIES and comparative-historical approaches are generally based on qualitative analysis.

Quantitative Analysis. In the social sciences, quantitative analysis refers to the use of numerical data and statistical techniques rather than the analysis of qualitative material. In its simplest form, quantitative analysis includes the analysis, reporting, and summary of aggregate data; but in its more sophisticated form, it includes the use of contingency table analysis, analysis of variance, and correlation and regression analysis.

Quran (also Qur'an, Koran, Alcoran). The Islamic holy book of Allah (the Divine, that is, God). Believers in ISLAM believe that the Quran is the eternal, literal word of God, revealed to the Prophet Muhammad over a period of twenty-two years. The Quran consists of 114 *suras* (chapters) with a total of 6,236 *ayats* (verses).

Realism; Realist. Realism, in the most general terms, refers to a type of theoretical argument in INTERNATIONAL RELATIONS that portrays the STATE as the preeminent actor in world affairs. Realism also emphasizes the overriding importance of POWER, defined primarily in terms of military capacity, as the driving force behind international politics. Indeed, to realists, international politics is defined primarily as a "struggle for power" among self-interested states. Realism, it is important to note, is not a single coherent theory; instead, it is a diverse school with many important cleavages. The dominant version of realism, however, is neorealism, which is based on the assumption that international politics is essentially the product of an anarchic structure. ANARCHY—not to be confused with chaos—locks all states into a "self-help" system that requires all states to do whatever they can to achieve national security. For further discussion of realism, see Dunne and Schmidt (2001).

Reflectivism. A very broad concept, reflectivism refers to a broad range of POST-POSITIVIST approaches or theories. A very basic, and perhaps overly simplistic, way to define reflectivism is to say that it is premised on the idea that there is no clear-cut distinction between reality and our knowledge (or theories) of reality. To put it even more simply, reflectivists believe that our theories or knowledge actually help construct the world or reality in which we live.

Rent-Seeking. In economics, rent-seeking occurs when an actor seeks to extract uncompensated value (that is, rent) from others by nonmarket or political manipulation of the economic environment. The word "rent" stems from Adam Smith's division of incomes into profit, wage, and rent. Rent-seeking behavior is distinguished from *profit-seeking* behavior, in which economic actors seek to extract value by engaging in mutually beneficial transactions.

Reproduction. When it is applied to studies of culture or societies, reproduction refers to the process by which aspects of culture are passed on from person to person, from generation to generation, or from society to society. Reproducing culture, however, is not the same as reproducing a memo on a copy machine (Miraglia, Law, and Collins 1999). The reproduction of culture is, instead, a continuous, highly interactive, and often contested process. As culture is reproduced, therefore, it is subject to change.

Selection Bias. In QUALITATIVE ANALYSIS or comparative research, selection bias refers to the tendency of researchers to "focus on certain outcomes of exceptional interest." In other words, selection bias occurs when a researcher chooses only those cases that clearly illustrate or support the argument being made. Although oftentimes unavoidable in comparative, SMALL-N research, this practice can seriously distort a study's findings, especially if the researcher is unaware of the biases in his or her selection of CASES.

Shiite (also Shi'a; Shi'ite). The Shiite make up the second largest sect of believers in Islam, constituting about 10–15 percent of all Muslims worldwide. The largest sect, the Sunni Muslims, make up about 85 percent of all Muslims.

Small-N. Refers to a situation in which the researcher has only a small number of relevant cases to analyze or compare. In QUANTITATIVE or statistical ANALYSIS, a small-N represents a serious, even fundamental, problem because the small sample size may yield biased results. In comparative politics, however, researchers often have only two or three relevant cases; thus, the small-N problem represents a large and inherent obstacle to the development of general theories. Despite this problem, the comparative method allows for in-depth and systematic comparison that, if appropriately utilized, can contribute to the assessment of alternative explanations and THEORY development.

Social Class. See CLASS.

Social Construction. The concept of social construction suggests that the world in which we live reflects an ongoing and INTERSUBJECTIVE process, whereby reality is produced (that is, constructed) and reproduced by people and societies acting on their interpretation and their knowledge of it.

Social Movement. A broad-based alliance of people seeking to effect political or social change. Unlike political parties or other organized political interest groups, social movements typically begin as informal organizations but may, over time, develop a strong institutional basis. Social movements are most generally associated with such issues as democratization, labor rights, environmental protection, civil and human rights, and world peace.

Social Revolution. For KARL MARX, a social revolution involved the overthrow of one class by another, producing a qualitative change in society. Revolutionary change is not to be confused with a coup d'état (replacement of one leader by another) or with reform (change that does not challenge the position of the class that holds power in the existing system).

Social Sciences. The social sciences (which include, among other disciplines, political science, economics, sociology, psychology, and anthropology) emphasize the scientific method or other rigorous standards of evidence in the study of the social world. Traditionally, the social sciences have attempted to develop explanatory accounts of human behavior at both the individual and collective levels.

Society. In the broadest terms, society refers to any grouping of people living in a country or region and having a shared culture and a distinctive way of life (which may be defined through family relations, economic practices, and political institutions). Among scholars in comparative politics, society (or civil society) is often distinguished from the STATE.

Sovereignty. In international law, sovereignty suggests, first, that every state has *supreme* decisionmaking and enforcement authority over the population, resources, and territory it controls or is responsible to; and, second, that no higher authority exists to regulate relations among states. In practice, however, the concept of sovereignty is more problematic than it appears. Some scholars argue that sovereignty has become anachronistic as a result of increasing GLOBALIZATION and interdependence, and others argue that sovereignty is a SOCIAL CONSTRUCTION, designed to preserve the privileges of the most powerful actors in world politics.

Stalinism. A colloquial term for the totalitarian political and economic system implemented by Joseph Stalin (1879–1953) in the Soviet Union.

State. Perhaps the simplest definition of state is a political entity or INSTITUTION possessing SOVEREIGNTY (that is, not being subject to any higher political authority). Most scholars agree, moreover, that another fundamental characteristic of the state is its monopoly on legitimate violence in a particular geographic area. In casual usage, the terms STATE, COUNTRY, GOVERNMENT, and even NATION are often regarded as synonymous. Although such usage is understandable and sometimes permissible, it is important to recognize the difference in meanings, which can be quite substantial. For further discussion, see Figure 1.1 in Chapter 1.

Statistical Analysis. See QUANTITATIVE ANALYSIS.

Strategic Interaction. Refers to situations in which rational decisions made by two or more actors involve an assessment of the other actor's knowledge and also of what the other actor knows about the first actor's knowledge state.

Structure. The everyday meaning of structure is akin to the framework of a building or some other artifact. Structure also refers to the interrelation or arrangement of parts in a complex entity. In comparative politics, both meanings are reflected in the concept of social structure, which might be most easily defined as any relatively enduring pattern of social relationships. The existence of a social structure implies that human action (or agency) is at least partly constrained and enabled by the structure within which that action takes place.

Sub-Saharan Africa. The region of the continent of Africa south of the Sahara Desert, ranging west from Sierra Leone to Somalia and south to South Africa.

Subsidy. Financial support provided by a GOVERNMENT to producers. The objectives of subsidies are usually (1) to keep the prices of goods low or stable (this is most common with agricultural subsidies), (2) to serve as a transfer from taxpayers to producers of a particular good, and (3) to improve the international competitiveness of local goods. Among "late industrializing" countries, it is this last objective that has been particularly important and contentious.

Taoism; Taoist. A spiritual belief-system developed in ancient China, based on the harmonization of counterbalancing forces (that is, *yin* and *yang*), such as dark and light, male and female, strong and weak. The aim is to achieve the *tao* (or *dao*), which is comparable to the idea of enlightenment. Translated literally, Taoism means "the Teaching of the Way" or "Path."

Theory. There are many complex ways to define the term "theory." For the purposes of this book, the following definition will suffice: theory is a simplified representation of "reality" and a framework within which facts are not only selected, but also interpreted, organized, and fitted together so that they create a coherent whole. See discussion in Chapter 3.

Totalitarian. A totalitarian system is a nondemocratic political system in which citizens are almost completely subject to the control of a governing authority in all aspects of day-to-day life. It goes well beyond an authoritarian system and involves pervasive surveillance, control, and indoctrination. Perhaps the closest real-world example of a totalitarian system today is North Korea.

Understanding. In common usage, "understanding" and "EXPLANATION" are used interchangeably, but it is worth distinguishing between the two terms. The basic difference revolves around the question of causality. Researchers interested in explanation are most concerned with discerning specific CAUSAL RELATIONSHIPS that hold across time and space. Researchers interested in understanding (or interpretation), by contrast, prefer to investigate a particular event or state of affairs in its own right. The objective is to develop an account that is keenly sensitive to the particular historical, social, cultural, and political context of the event or state of affairs being examined. Not surprisingly, culturalists are generally more interested in understanding, whereas rational choice scholars and structuralists are more concerned with developing causal explanations. In practice, however, explanatory and interpretative accounts often overlap.

Unit of Analysis. The main actor—for example, individual, group, INSTITUTION, STATE, "system"—specified in a particular hypothesis or argument. The unit of analysis may be either "observational" or "explanatory."

Utility; Utility Maximization. In economics, utility is a measure of the happiness or satisfaction gained from a good or service. Utility can be assessed, in the most basic manner, by simply asking an individual how he ranks different options. As Jon Elster (1989) explained it, if he prefers three oranges to four apples, but chooses five apples over three oranges, we can use this list of pairwise comparisons to create a preference ordering. "Using a mathematical trick, [this] preference ordering can be converted to a utility function, which is a way of assigning numbers to options so that the more preferred options receive higher numbers. We can then say that the person acts so as to maximize utility" (p. 23).

Variable. A term used in statistics and other social scientific analysis to describe the factor that is to be studied.

Weber, Max (1864–1920). A German economist and sociologist, considered one of the founders of modern sociology and public administration. Weber is known for a wide range of intellectual contributions, including his development of the "ideal-type." He also wrote *The Protestant Ethic and the Spirit of Capitalism*. This was a seminal essay on the differences between religions and the relative wealth of their followers.

Within-Case Comparison. A type of comparative strategy in which the same CASE is examined over two different periods of time. The key difference between the two time periods is a change or variation in the DEPENDENT VARIABLE.

World Bank. Originally known as the International Bank for Reconstruction and Development (IBRD), the World Bank is a group of related international financial institutions designed to provide long-term developmental loans. The World Bank is considered a "sister" institution of the INTERNATIONAL MONETARY FUND (IMF), which provides short-term loans. Like the IMF, the World Bank has been subject to a great deal of criticism.

World Trade Organization (WTO). An international organization created to manage and oversee international trade agreements. The WTO was established in 1995 as an outgrowth of the General Agreement on Tariffs and Trade (GATT). Recently the WTO has been a main target of so-called antiglobalization protestors.

World-Systems Theory. A Marxist-influenced theory of global capitalism, world-systems theory is a holistic theory, not only of capitalism but of world history in toto. With respect to the *current* world-system, however, advocates of this theory argue that capitalism is its defining characteristic and that the logic of capitalism has created a particular spatial and temporal structure. Spatially, the capitalist world-system is divided into three zones, the core, the semiperiphery, and the periphery, which are linked together in an inherently exploitative relationship. Temporally, the system is characterized by three basic processes: cycles, CONTRADICTIONS, and crisis. World-systems scholars argue that analyses of any social, political, or economic phenomena must begin with an understanding of the spatial relationships and temporal dynamics of the system.

Selected Bibliography

Abegglen, James C., and George Stalk Jr. *Kaisha: The Japanese Corporation*. New York: Basic Books, 1985.

Abrams, Elliot, and James Turner Johnson, eds. *Close Calls: Intervention, Terrorism, Missile Defense, and "Just War" Today*. Washington, DC: Ethics and Public Policy Center, 1998.

Abrams, Philip. *Historical Sociology*. Ithaca, NY: Cornell University Press, 1982.

Ajami, Fouad. "The Summoning." In *The New Shape of World Politics: Contending Paradigms in International Relations*, edited by Foreign Affairs, 92–100. New York: Foreign Affairs, [1993] 1999.

Alder, Glenn. "Global Restructuring and Labor: The Case of the South African Trade Union Movement." In *Globalization: Critical Reflections*, edited by James H. Mittelman, 117–143. Boulder, CO: Lynne Rienner, 1996.

Alexander, Titus. *Unravelling Global Apartheid: An Overview of World Politics*. Cambridge: Polity Press, 1996.

Amsden, Alice H. *Asia's Next Giant: South Korea and Late Industrialization*. Oxford: Oxford University Press, 1989.

———. "Taiwan's Economic History: A Case of *Etatisme* and a Challenge to Dependency Theory." In *Toward a Political Economy of Development: A Rational Choice Perspective*, edited by Robert H. Bates, 142–175. Berkeley: University of California Press, 1988.

Axelrod, Robert. *The Evolution of Cooperation*. New York: Basic Books, 1984.

Bandura, Albert. "Moral Disengagement in the Perpetuation of Inhumanities." *Personality and Social Psychology Review* 3, no. 3 (1999): 193–209.

Baran, Paul. *The Political Economy of Growth*. New York: Monthly Review Press, 1957.

Barber, Benjamin. "Democracy at Risk: American Culture in a Global Culture." *World Policy Journal* 15, no. 2 (1998): 29–41.

———. *Jihad vs. Mcworld*. New York: Ballantine Books, 1996.

Barclay, Gordon, and Cynthia Tavares. *International Comparisons of Criminal Justice Statistics 2000,* issue 05/02. London: RDS Communications and Development Unit, Home Office (United Kingdom), 2002. http://www.homeoffice.gov.uk/rds/pdfs2/hosb502.pdf.

Bates, Robert H. "Governments and Agricultural Markets in Africa." In *Toward a Political Economy of Development: A Rational Choice Perspective*, edited by Robert H. Bates, 331–358. Berkeley: University of California Press, 1988a.

————. "Toward a Political Economy of Development." In *Toward a Political Economy of Development: A Rational Choice Perspective*, edited by Robert H. Bates, 239–244. Berkeley: University of California Press, 1988b.

Baylis, John, and Steve Smith. "Introduction." In *The Globalization of World Politics: An Introduction to International Relations*. 3rd ed. Oxford: Oxford University Press, 1997.

Beck, Ulrich. *What Is Globalization?* Cambridge: Polity Press, 2000.

Benedict, Ruth. *The Chrysanthemum and the Sword: Patterns of Japanese Culture*. Boston: Houghton Mifflin, 1946.

Berger, Peter L. "An East Asian Development Model?" In *In Search of an East Asian Development Model*, edited by Peter L. Berger and H.H.M. Hsiao, 3–11. New Brunswick, NJ: Transaction Books, 1998.

Betts, Richard. "The Soft Underbelly of American Primacy: Tactical Advantages of Terror." *Political Science Quarterly* 117, no. 1 (2002).

Beverly, James A. "Is Islam a Religion of Peace?" *Christianity Today* (online), January 7, 2002. http://www.christianitytoday.com/ct/2002/001/1.32.html.

Biggart, Nicole Woolsey. "Explaining Asian Economic Organization: Toward a Weberian Institutional Perspective." In *The Economic Organization of East Asian Capitalism*, edited by Gary G. Hamilton, Nicole Woolsey Biggart, and Marco Orrù, 3–32. Thousand Oaks, CA: Sage Publications, 1997.

Blumer, Herber. "Collective Behavior." In *An Outline of the Principles of Sociology*, edited by Robert E. Park, 219–280. New York: Barnes and Noble, 1939.

Bob, Clifford. "Political Process Theory and Transnational Movements: Dialectics of Protest Among Nigeria's Ogoni Minority." *Social Problems* 49, no. 3 (2002): 395–415.

Booth, John A. *Costa Rica: Quest for Democracy*. Boulder, CO: Westview Press, 1998.

Boyce, James K., and Léonce Ndikumana. *Is Africa a Net Creditor? New Estimates of Capital Flight from Severely Indebted Sub-Saharan African Countries, 1970–1996*. Political Economy Research Institute Working Paper Series, no. 5. Amherst: University of Massachusetts–Amherst, 2000. http://www.umass.edu/peri/pdfs/WP5.pdf.

Brams, Steven J. "The Study of Rational Politics." In *Approaches to the Study of Politics*, edited by Brian Susser, 312–317. New York: Macmillan, 1992.

Brannan, David W., Philip F. Esler, and N. T. Anders Strindberg. "Talking to 'Terrorists': Towards an Independent Analytical Framework for the Study of Violent Substate Activism." *Studies in Conflict and Terrorism* 24 (2001): 3–24.

Bratton, Michael, and Nicolas van der Walle. *Democratic Experiments in Africa: Regime Transitions in Comparative Perspective*. Cambridge: Cambridge University Press, 1997.

Braudel, Fernand. "History and Social Science." In *Economy and Society in Early Modern Europe: Essays from Annales*, edited by P. Burke. New York: Harper and Row, 1972.

Bunce, Valerie. "Rethinking Recent Democratization: Lessons from the Postcommunist Experience." *World Politics* 55 (2003): 192–197.

Burks, Ardath W. *Japan: Profile of a Postindustrial Power*. Boulder, CO: Westview Press, 1981.

Canel, Eduardo. "New Social Movement Theory and Resource Mobilization Theory: The Need for Integration." In *Community Power and Grassroots Democracy: The Transformation of Social Life*, edited by M. Kaufman and H. Dilla Alfonso. The International Development Research Centre, 1997. http://web.idrc.ca/en/ev-33847-201-1-DO_TOPIC.html.

Cardoso, Fernando H. "Asssociated-Dependent Development: Theoretical and Practical Implications." In *Authoritarian Brazil*, edited by Alfred Stepan, 142–176. New Haven, CT: Yale University Press, 1973.

Cardoso, Fernando H., and Enzo Faletto. *Dependency and Development in Latin America*. Berkeley: University of California Press, 1979.

Chan, Steve. *East Asian Dynamism: Growth, Order, and Security in the Pacific Region*. 2nd ed. Boulder, CO: Westview Press, 1993.

Charlesworth, William R. "Profiling Terrorists: A Taxonomy of Evolutionary, Developmental and Situational Causes of a Terrorist Act." *Defense and Security Analysis* 19, no. 3 (2003): 241–264.

Chase-Dunn, Christopher. "Technology and the Logic of World-Systems." In *Transcending the State-Global Divide: A Neostructuralist Agenda in International Relations*, edited by Ronen P. Palan and Barry Gills, 84–105. Boulder, CO: Lynne Rienner, 1994.

Chilcote, Ronald H. *Theories of Comparative Political Economy*. Boulder, CO: Westview Press, 2000.

———. *Theories of Comparative Politics: The Search for a Paradigm Reconsidered*. Boulder, CO: Westview Press, 1994.

Coleman, James S. "Modernization: Political Aspects." In *International Encyclopedia of the Social Sciences*, edited by David L. Sills, 395–402. New York: Macmillan, 1968.

Collier, David. "The Comparative Method." In *Theory, Case, and Method in Comparative Politics*, edited by Nikolaos Zahariadis, 35–46. New York: Harcourt Brace College Publishers, 1997.

Comte, A. "Modernization: Political Aspects." In *Social Change: Sources, Patterns, and Consequences*, edited by Amitai Etzioni and Eva Etzioni, 14–19. New York: Basic Books, 1964.

Corradi, Juan E., Patricia W. Fagen, and Manuel A. Garreton, eds. *Fear at the Edge: State Terror and Resistance in Latin America*. Berkeley: University of California Press, 1992.

Crawford, Darryl. "Chinese Capitalism: Cultures, the Southeast Asian Region and Economic Globalisation." *Third World Quarterly* 21, no. 1 (2000): 69–86.

Crenshaw, Martha. "The Logic of Terrorism: Terrorist Behavior as a Product of Strategic Choice." In *Origins of Terrorism: Psychologies, Ideologies, Theologies, States of Mind*, edited by Walter Reich, 7–24. Washington, DC: Woodrow Wilson Center Press, 1998a.

———. "Questions to Be Answered, Research to Be Done, Knowledge to Be Applied." In *Origins of Terrorism: Psychologies, Ideologies, Theologies, States of Mind*, edited by Walter Reich, 247–260. Washington, DC: Woodrow Wilson Center Press, 1998b.

———. "Thoughts on Relating Terrorism to Historical Contexts." In *Terrorism in Context*, edited by Martha Crenshaw, 3–26. University Park: Pennsylvania State University Press, 1995.

Crossley, Nick. *Making Sense of Social Movements*. Buckingham, UK: Open University Press, 2002.

Cukier, Wendy. "Firearms Regulations: Canada in the International Context." *Chronic Diseases in Canada* 19, no. 1 (1998). http://www.phacaspc.gc.ca/publicat/cdic-mcc19-1/d_e.html (accessed July 1, 2005).

Cumings, Bruce. "Boundary Displacement: Area Studies and International Studies During and After the Cold War" (Special Issue: Asia, Asian Studies, and the National Security State: A Symposium). *Bulletin of Concerned Asian Scholars* 29, no. 1 (January–March 1997).

———. "The Origins and Development of the Northeast Asian Political Economy: Industrial Sectors, Product Cycles, and Political Consequences." In *The Political Economy of the New Asian Industrialism*, edited by Frederic Deyo, 44–83. Ithaca, NY: Cornell University Press, 1987.

———. "Webs with No Spiders, Spiders with No Webs: The Genealogy of the Developmental State." In *The Developmental State*, edited by Meredith Woo-Cumings, 61–92. Ithaca, NY: Cornell University Press, 1999.

Dahl, Robert A. *Polyarchy: Participation and Opposition*. New Haven, CT: Yale University Press, 1971.

Dalton, Russell J., Manfred Kuechler, and Wilhelm Bürklin. "The Challenge of New Movements." In *Challenging the Political Order: New Social Movements and Political Movements in Western Democracies*, edited by Russell J. Dalton and Manfred Kuechler, 3–20. New York: Oxford University Press, 1990.

Davis, Diane E. "The Power of Distance: Re-Theorizing Social Movements in Latin America." *Theory and Society* 28, no. 4 (1999): 585–638.

Diamond, Larry. "Causes and Effects." In *Political Culture and Democracy in Developing Countries*, edited by Larry Diamond, 229–249. Boulder, CO: Lynne Rienner, 1994.

———. *Developing Democracy: Toward Consolidation*. Baltimore, MD: The Johns Hopkins University Press, 1999.

Dixon, Marc, and Vincent J. Roscigno. "Status, Networks, and Social Movement Participation: The Case of Striking Workers." *American Journal of Sociology* 108, no. 6 (2003): 1292–1327.

Dobson, Charles. "Social Movements: A Summary of What Works." In *The Citizen's Handbook*, edited by Charles Dobson. Vancouver: Vancouver Citizen's Committee, 2003. http://www.vcn.bc.ca.citizens-handbook.

Dogan, Mattei, and Ali Kazancigil. *Comparing Nations: Concepts, Strategies, Substance*. Oxford: Blackwell Publishers, 1994.

Dogan, Mattei, and Dominque Pelassy. *How to Compare Nations: Strategies in Comparative Politics*. 2nd ed. Chatham, NJ: Chatham House Publishers, 1990.

Dore, Ronald. *Taking Japan Seriously: A Confucian Perspective on Leading Economic Issues*. Stanford, CA: Stanford University Press, 1987.

Dos Santos, Theotonio. "The Structure of Dependence." In *International Political Economy: State-Market Relations in the Changing Global Order,* edited by C. Roe Goddard, John T. Passé-Smith, and John G. Conklin, 165–175. Boulder, CO: Lynne Rienner, [1970] 1996.

Dowding, Keith, and Andrew Hindmoor. "The Usual Suspects: Rational Choice, Socialism, and Political Theory." *New Political Economy* 2, no. 3 (1997): 451–463.

Doyle, Michael W. "On the Democratic Peace." *International Security* 19, no. 4 (1995).

Dunne, Tim, and Brian C. Schmidt. "Realism." In *The Globalization of World Politics: An Introduction to International Relations,* 2nd ed., edited by John Baylis and Steve Smith, 141–161. Oxford: Oxford University Press, 2001.

Durkheim, Emile. *The Elementary Forms of the Religious Life*. Reprint ed. New York: Collier, [1915] 1961.

Eley, Geoff, and Ronald Grigor Suny, eds. *Becoming National: A Reader.* Oxford: Oxford University Press, 1996.

Elster, Jon. *Nuts and Bolts for the Social Sciences.* New York: Cambridge University Press, 1989.

———. *Ulysses and the Sirens: Studies in Rationality and Irrationality.* Paris: Maison des Sciences de l'Homme, 1984.

Esposito, John L., and John O. Voll. *Islam and Democracy.* Oxford: Oxford University Press, 1996.

Evans, Alona E., and John Francis Murphy. *Legal Aspects of International Terrorism.* Lexington, MA: Lexington Books, 1978.

Evans, Graham, and Jeffrey Newnham. *Penguin Dictionary of International Relations.* London: Penguin Books, 1998.

Evans, Peter B., Dietrich Rueschemeyer, and Theda Skocpol, eds. *Bringing the State Back In.* Cambridge: Cambridge University Press, 1985.

Fields, Karl J. *Enterprise and the State in Korea and Taiwan.* Ithaca, NY: Cornell University Press, 1995.

Finnemore, Martheanne, and Kathryn Sikkink. "Taking Stock: The Constructivist Research Program in International Relations and Comparative Politics." *Annual Review of Political Science* 4, no. 1 (2001): 391–416.

Firearms Research Unit. "Firearms: Canada/United States Comparison," *Canada Firearms Centre* (June 1998). http://www.cfc-ccaf.ge.ca.pol-leg/res-eval/other_docs/notes/canus/default_e.asp (accessed July 1, 2005).

Foster, John Bellamy. "Monopoly Capital and the New Globalization." *Monthly Review* 53, no. 8 (2002). http: www://monthlyreview.org/0102jbf2.htm.

Fowler, Barbara. *Critical Thinking Definitions.* Critical Thinking Across the Curriculum/ Longview Community College, n.d. http://www.kcmetro.cc.mo.us/longview/ctac/definitions.htm (accessed July 15, 2000).

Frank, André Gunder. "The Development of Underdevelopment." In *The Political Economy of Development and Underdevelopment,* edited by Charles K. Wilber, 109–120. New York: Random House Business Division, [1966] 1988.

Friedman, Milton. *Essays in Positive Economics.* Chicago: University of Chicago Press, 1953.

Fukuyama, Francis. "The End of History?" In *The New Shape of World Politics: Contending Paradigms in International Relations,* rev. ed., 1–25. New York: Foreign Affairs, [1989] 1999.

———. "Social Capital, Civil Society and Development." *Third World Quarterly* 22, no. 1 (2001): 7–20.

Gamson, William. *The Strategy of Social Protest.* 2nd ed. Belmont, CA: Wadsworth Publishing, 1990.

Ganguly, Sumit. "Explaining India's Transition to Democracy." In *Transitions to Democracy,* edited by Lisa Anderson, 217–236. New York: Columbia University Press, 1999.

Geddes, Barbara. "What Do We Know About Democratization After Twenty Years?" *Annual Review of Political Science* 2 (1999): 115–144.

Geertz, Clifford. *The Interpretation of Culture: Selected Essays.* New York: Basic Books, 1973.

Gereffi, Gary, and Miquel Korzeniewicz. "Commodity Chains and Footwear Exports in the Semiperiphery." In *Semiperipheral States in the World-Economy,* edited by William Martin, 45–68. Westport, CT: Greenwood Press, 1990.

Giddens, Anthony. *Director's Lectures: Runaway World—The Reith Lectures Revisited* (Lecture 5), 2000. http://www.lse.ac.uk/Giddens/pdf/19Jan00.pdf (accessed May 21, 2004).

Giugni, Marco G. "Was It Worth the Effort? The Outcomes and Consequences of Social Movements." *Annual Review of Sociology* 98 (1998): 371–393.

Goodin, Robert E. "Institutions and Their Design." In *The Theory of Institutional Design*, edited by Robert E. Goodin, 1–53. Cambridge: Cambridge University Press, 1996.

Goodwin, Jeff, and James M. Jasper. "Caught in a Winding, Snarling Vine: The Structural Bias of Political Theory." *Sociological Forum* 14, no. 1 (1999): 27–54.

Gould, David. "Why Do Networks Matter? Rationalist and Structuralist Interpretations." In *Social Movements and Networks: Relational Approaches to Collective Action*, edited by Diani Mario and Doug McAdam, 233–258. Oxford: Oxford University Press, 2003.

Guidry, John, Michael D. Kennedy, and Mayer N. Zald, eds. *Globalization and Social Movements: Culture, Power, and the Transnational Public Sphere*. Ann Arbor: University of Michigan Press, 2000.

Gurowitz, Amy. "Migrant Rights and Activism in Malaysia: Opportunities and Constraints." *The Journal of Asian Studies* 59, no. 4 (2000): 863–888.

Habermas, Jurgen. "New Social Movements." *Telos* 49 (1981): 33–37.

Hamilton, Gary G., and Nicole Woolsey Biggart. "Market, Culture, and Authority: A Comparative Analysis of Management and Organization in the Far East." In *The Economic Organization of East Asian Capitalism*, edited by Gary G. Hamilton, Nicole Woolsey Biggart, and Marco Orrù, 111–150. Thousand Oaks, CA: Sage Publications, 1997.

Harrison, Lawrence. "Introduction: Why Culture Matters." In *Culture Matters: How Values Shape Human Progress,* edited by Lawrence E. Harrison and Samuel P. Huntington, xxii–xxxiv. New York: Basic Books, 2000.

Hatch, Walter, and Kozo Yamamura. *Asia in Japan's Embrace*. Cambridge: Cambridge University Press, 1996.

Hefner, Robert W. *Civil Islam: Muslims and Democratization in Indonesia*. Princeton, NJ: Princeton University Press, 2000.

Held, David. *Models of Democracy*. Cambridge: Polity, 1987.

Henderson, David. "Lessons of East Asia's Economic Growth: Fresh Perspectives on East Asia's Future." In *Stand! Global Issues*, edited by Timothy Lim, 74–83. Boulder, CO: Coursewise, 2000.

Hobden, Steve, and Richard Wyn Jones. "World-System Theory." In *The Globalization of World Politics: An Introduction to International Relations*, edited by Steve Smith and John Baylis, 125–163. Oxford: Oxford University Press, 1997.

Hoffer, Eric. *The True Believer: Thoughts on the Nature of Mass Movements*. New York: Harper and Row, 1951.

Hoffman, Bruce. *Inside Terrorism*. London: Indigo, 1998.

———. "The Logic of Suicide Terrorism." *Atlantic Monthly*, June 2003, 40–47.

Hoogvelt, Ankie. *Globalization and the Postcolonial World: The New Political Economy of Development*. Baltimore, MD: The Johns Hopkins University Press, 1997.

Hopkin, Jonathan. "Comparative Methods." In *Theory and Methods in Political Science*, edited by David Marsh and Gerry Stoker, 249–267. Basingstoke, UK: Palgrave Macmillan, 2002.

Hopkins, Terence K., and Immanuel Wallerstein. "Commodity Chains in the World-Economy Prior to 1800." *Review* 10, no. 1 (1986): 157–170.

Howard, Russell D., and Reid L. Sawyer, eds. *Terrorism and Counterterrorism: Understanding the New Security Environment.* Guilford, CT: McGraw-Hill/Dushkin, 2003.

Hunt, Lynn. "Charles Tilly's Collective Action." In *Vision and Method in Historical Sociology,* edited by Theda Skocpol, 244–275. Cambridge: Cambridge University Press, 1984.

Hunt, Scott A., and Robert D. Benford. "Collective Identity, Solidarity, and Commitment." In *The Blackwell Companion to Social Movements,* edited by David A. Snow, Sarah A. Soule, and Hanspeter Kriesi, 433–457. Malden, MA: Blackwell Publishing, 2004.

Huntington, Samuel P. "The Change to Change: Modernization, Development and Politics." *Comparative Politics* 3 (April 1971): 283–322.

———. "The Clash of Civilizations?" *Foreign Affairs* 72, no. 3 (1993): 22–49.

———. *The Clash of Civilizations and the Remaking of World Order.* New York: Simon and Schuster, 1996.

James, William E., Seiji Naya, and Gerald M. Meier. *Asian Development: Economic Success and Policy Lessons.* Madison: University of Wisconsin Press, 1989.

Jary, David, and Julia Jary. *The HarperCollins Dictionary of Sociology.* New York: HarperPerennial, 1991.

Jenkins, J. Craig, and Bert Klandermans. "The Politics of Social Protest." In *The Politics of Social Protest: Comparative Perspectives on States and Social Movements,* edited by J. Craig Jenkins and Bert Klandermans, 3–13. Minneapolis: University of Minnesota Press, 1995.

Jenkins, J. Craig, and Charles Perrow. "Insurgency of the Powerless: Farm Worker Movements 1946–1972." *American Sociological Review* 42 (1977): 429–468.

Jenson, Jane. "What's in a Name? National Movements and Public Discourse." In *Social Movements and Culture,* edited by Hank Johnston and Bert Klandermans, 107–126. Minneapolis: University of Minnesota Press, 1995.

Johnson, Chalmers. *MITI and the Japanese Miracle: The Growth of Industrial Policy, 1925–1975.* Stanford, CA: Stanford University Press, 1982.

Johnston, Hank, and Bert Klandermans. "The Cultural Analysis of Social Movements." In *Social Movements and Culture,* edited by Hank Johnston and Bert Klandermans, 3–24. Minneapolis: University of Minnesota Press, 1995.

Johnston, Hank, Enrique Laraña, and Joseph R. Gusfield. "Identities, Grievances, and New Social Movements." In *New Social Movements: From Ideology to Identity,* edited by Enrique Laraña, Hank Johnston, and Joseph R. Gusfield, 3–35. Philadelphia: Temple University Press, 1994.

Jones, Christopher. "Song and Nationalism in Quebec." *Contemporary French Civilization* 24, no. 1 (2000). http://ml.hss.cmu.edu/facpages/cjones/QuebecSong1.pdf.

Joppke, Christian. "The Legal-Domestic Sources of Immigrant Rights: The United States, Germany, and the European Union." *Comparative Political Studies* 34, no. 4 (2001): 339–365.

Kaase, Max. "Social Movements and Political Innovation." In *Challenging the Political Order: New Social Movements in Western Democracies,* edited by Russell J. Dalton and Manfred Kuechler, 84–101. New York: Oxford University Press, 1990.

Kaplan, Robert. "The Coming Anarchy." *Atlantic Monthly* 273, no. 2, February 1994, 44–76 passim.

Katzenstein, Peter J., and Takashi Shiraishi. *Network Power: Japan and Asia.* Ithaca, NY: Cornell University Press, 1997.

Kausikan, Bilahari. "Governance That Works." *Journal of Democracy* 8, no. 2 (1997): 24–34.

Keck, Margaret E., and Kathryn Sikkink. *Activists Beyond Borders: Advocacy Networks in International Politics.* Ithaca, NY: Cornell University Press, 1998.

Khalil, A. A. "Ideology and Practice of Hizballah in Lebanon: Islaminization of Leninist Organizational Principles." *Middle Eastern Studies* 27, no. 3 (1991): 390–403.

Kim, Dae Jung. "Is Culture Destiny? The Myth of Asia's Anti-Democratic Values." In *The New Shape of World Politics: Contending Paradigms in International Relations,* edited by Foreign Affairs, 234–241. New York: W. W. Norton, 1997.

Kohli, Atul. *Democracy and Discontent: India's Growing Crisis of Governability.* Cambridge: Cambridge University Press, 1990.

Kohli, Atul, Peter Evans, Peter J. Katzenstein, Adam Przeworski, Susanne Hoeber Rudolph, James C. Scott, and Theda Skocpol. "The Role of Theory in Comparative Politics: A Symposium." *World Politics* 48, no. 1 (October 1995): 1–49.

Kopstein, Jeffrey, and Mark Lichbach, eds. *Comparative Politics: Interests, Identities, and Institutions in a Changing Global Order.* Cambridge: Cambridge University Press, 2000.

Kramer, Martin. "The Moral Logic of Hizballah." In *Origins of Terrorism: Psychologies, Ideologies, Theologies, States of Mind,* edited by Walter Reich, 131–157. Washington, DC: Woodrow Wilson Center Press, 1998.

Kriesi, Hanspeter. "The Political Opportunity Structure of New Social Movements: Its Impact on Their Mobilization." In *The Politics of Social Protest: Comparative Perspectives on States and Social Movements,* edited by J. Craig Jenkins and Bert Klandermans, 167–198. Minneapolis: University of Minnesota Press, 1995.

Kriesi, Hanspeter, Ruud Koopmans, Jan Willem Duyvendak, and Marco G. Giugni. *New Social Movements in Western Europe: A Comparative Perspective.* Minneapolis: University of Minnesota Press, 1995.

Lam, Danny, and Jeremy T. Paltiel. "The Confucian Entrepreneur? Chinese Culture, Industrial Organization, and Intellectual Property Piracy in Taiwan." *Asian Affairs: An American Review* 20, no. 4 (1994): 205–227.

Landes, David. "Culture Makes Almost All the Difference." In *Culture Matters: How Values Shape Human Progress,* edited by Lawrence E. Harrison and Samuel P. Huntington, 2–13. New York: Basic Books, 2000.

Lane, Ruth. *The Art of Comparative Politics.* Boston: Allyn and Bacon, 1997.

Laqueur, Walter. *The New Terrorism.* Oxford: Oxford University Press, 1999.

Laraña, Enrique, Hank Johnston, and Joseph R. Gusfield, eds., *New Social Movements: From Ideology to Identity.* Philadelphia: Temple University Press, 1994.

Laville, Rosabelle. "In the Politics of the Rainbow: Creoles and Civil Society in Mauritius." *Journal of Contemporary African Studies* 18, no. 2 (2000): 277–294.

Lechner, Frank J., and John Boli. "Introduction (Part 8)." In *The Globalization Reader,* edited by Frank J. Lechner and John Boli, 319–321. Malden, MA: Blackwell, 2000.

Leftwich, Adrian. *Redefining Politics: People, Resources, and Power.* London: Methuen, 1983.

Levi, Margaret. "A Model, a Method, and a Map: Rational Choice in Comparative and Historical Analysis." In *Comparative Politics: Rationality, Culture, and Structure,* edited by Mark Irving Lichbach and Alan S. Zuckerman, 19–41. Cambridge: Cambridge University Press, 1997.

Lewis, Oscar. "A Study of Slum Culture: Backgrounds for *La Vida.*" In *From Modernization to Globalization: Perspectives on Development and Social Change,* edited by J. Timmons Roberts and Amy Hite, 110–118. London: Blackwell Publishers, [1968] 2000.

Lichbach, Mark I. "Social Theory and Comparative Politics." In *Comparative Politics: Rationality, Culture, and Structure*, edited by Mark I. Lichbach and Alan S. Zuckerman, 239–276. Cambridge: Cambridge University Press, 1997.

Lichbach, Mark Irving, and Alan S. Zuckerman, eds. *Comparative Politics: Rationality, Culture, and Structure*. Cambridge: Cambridge University Press, 1997.

Lijphart, A. "Comparative Politics and the Comparative Method." *American Political Science Review* 65, no. 3 (1971): 682–693.

Linz, Juan J. "The Perils of Presidentialism." *Journal of Democracy* 1, no. 1 (1990): 51–69.

Lipsky, Michael. *Protest in City Politics*. Chicago: Rand McNally, 1970.

Little, Daniel. *Varieties of Social Explanation*. Boulder, CO: Westview Press, 1991.

Little, I.M.D. "An Economic Reconnaissance." In *Economic Growth and Structural Change in Taiwan*, edited by W. Galenson, 448–507. Ithaca, NY: Cornell University Press, 1979.

Lowndes, Vivien. "Institutionalism." In *Theory and Methods in Political Science*, edited by Gerry Stoker and David Marsh, 90–108. Basingstoke, UK: Palgrave Macmillan, 2002.

Macridis, Roy. *The Study of Comparative Government*. New York: Random House, 1955.

Macridis, Roy C., and Richard Cox. "Research in Comparative Politics." *American Political Science Review* 47, no. June (1953): 641–657.

Mahler, Gregory S. *Comparative Politics: An Institutional and Cross-National Approach*. 3rd cd. Upper Saddle River, NJ: Prentice Hall, 2000.

Mainwaring, Scott, and Matthew Shugart. "Juan Linz, Presidentialism, and Democracy: A Critical Appraisal." *Comparative Politics* 29, no. 4 (1997): 449–471.

"Maquiladora Labor Trends." http://www.maquilaportal.com/editorial/editorial7.htm (accessed July 1, 2005).

March, James G., and Johan P. Olsen. "The New Institutionalism: Organizational Factors in Political Life." *American Political Science Review* 78 (1984): 734–749.

———. *Rediscovering Institutions: The Organizational Basis of Politics*. New York: Free Press, 1989.

Marx, Karl. *The Eighteenth Brumaire of Louis Bonaparte*. New York: International Publishers, [1869] 1994.

Mason, Edward S., Mahn Je Kim, Dwight H. Perkins, Kwang Suk Kim, and David C. Cole. *The Economic and Social Modernization of the Republic of Korea*, Studies in the Modernization of the Republic of Korea: 1945–1975. Cambridge, MA: Harvard University Press, 1980.

McAdam, Doug. *Political Process and the Development of Black Insurgency, 1930–1970*. Chicago: University of Chicago Press, 1982.

McAdam, Doug, Sidney Tarrow, and Charles Tilly. "Toward an Integrated Perspective on Social Movements and Revolution." In *Comparative Politics: Rationality, Culture, and Structure*, edited by Mark I. Lichbach and Alan S. Zuckerman, 142–173. Cambridge: Cambridge University Press, 1997.

McCarthy, John, and Mayer N. Zald. *The Trend of Social Movements in American Professionalization and Resource Mobilization*. Morristown, NJ: General Learning Corporation, 1973.

McCormick, Thomas J. *America's Half-Century: United States Foreign Policy in the Cold War*. Baltimore, MD: The Johns Hopkins University Press, 1989.

McFaul, Michael. "The Fourth Wave of Democracy and Dictatorship: Noncooperative Transitions in the Postcommunist World." *World Politics* 54 (2002): 212–244.

McLeod, Darryl. "Capital Flight." In *The Concise Encyclopedia of Economics,* edited by David R. Henderson. Indianapolis, IN: Liberty Fund, 2002. http://www.econlib.org/library/Enc/CapitalFlight.html.

Melucci, Alberto. "The Process of Collective Identity." In *Social Movements and Culture,* edited by Hank Johnston and Bert Klandermans, 41–63. Minneapolis: University of Minnesota Press, 1995.

Migdal, Joel S., Atul Kohli, and Vivienne Shue, eds. *State Power and Social Forces: Domination and Transformation in the Third World.* Cambridge: Cambridge University Press, 1994.

Miles, William F.S. "The Mauritius Enigma." *Journal of Democracy* 10, no. 2 (1999): 91–104.

Mill, John Stuart. *A System of Logic: Ratiocinative and Inductive.* Reprint ed. Toronto, ON: University of Toronto Press, [1843] 1967.

Miraglia, Eric, Richard Law, and Peg Collins. "What Is Culture." 1999. http://www.wsu.edu/gened/learn-modules/top_culture/culture-index.html#top.

Mittelman, James H. "How Does Globalization Really Work?" In *Globalization: Critical Reflections,* edited by James H. Mittelman, 229–242. Boulder, CO: Lynne Rienner, 1996a.

———. "Mapping Globalisation." *Singapore Journal of Tropical Geography* 22, no. 3 (2001): 212–218.

———. "Rethinking the 'New Regionalism' in the Context of Globalization." *Global Governance* 2 (1996b): 190–197.

Monroe, Alan D. *Essentials of Political Research.* Boulder, CO: Westview Press, 2000.

Moody, Kim. *Workers in a Lean World: Unions in the International Economy.* London: Verso, 1997.

Morey, Robert A. "Will Islam Cause WWIII?" n.d. http://www.ldolphin.org/morey islamd.

Morrow, James D. *Game Theory for Political Scientists.* Princeton, NJ: Princeton University Press, 1994.

Mueller, John. "The Banality of 'Ethnic War.'" *International Security* 25, no. 1 (2000): 42–70.

Muller, Edward N., and Karl-Dieter Opp. "Rational Choice and Rebellious Collective Action." *American Political Science Review* 80 (1986): 471–487.

Munck, Gerardo L. "Democratic Transitions in Comparative Perspective." *Comparative Politics* 26, no. 3 (1994): 355–375.

Nassar, Jamal R. *Globalization and Terrorism: The Migration of Dreams and Nightmares.* Lanham, MD: Rowman and Littlefield, 2004.

Norberg-Hodge, Helena. "Globalisation and Terror." *The Ecologist* 31, no. 10 (2001/2002): 36–39.

North, Douglass C. *Institutions, Institutional Change and Economic Performance.* Cambridge: Cambridge University Press, 1990.

O'Donnell, Guillermo, and Philippe C. Schmitter. "Tentative Conclusions About Uncertain Democracies (Part 4)." In *Transitions from Authoritarian Rule: Prospects for Democracy,* edited by Guillermo O'Donnell, Philippe C. Schmitter, and Lawrence Whitehead, 3–78. Baltimore, MD: The Johns Hopkins University Press, 1986.

Offe, Claus. "New Social Movements: Challenging the Boundaries of Institutional Politics." *Social Research* 52, no. 4 (1985): 817–868.

Office of the Registrar General India. "Data on Workers and Their Categories: An Insight." *eCensusIndia,* no. 7 (February 28, 2002). http://www.censusindia.net/results/eci7_page3.html.

————. "Rural-Urban Distribution of Population—India and States/Union Territories: 2001." In *Census of India 2001.* New Delhi: Office of the Registrar General India, 2001.

Okimoto, Daniel I. *Between MITI and the Market: Japanese Industrial Policy for High Technology.* Stanford, CA: Stanford University Press, 1989.

Olson, Mancur. *The Logic of Collective Action: Public Goods and the Theory of Groups.* Cambridge, MA: Harvard University Press, 1965.

Ornatowski, Greg K. "Confucian Ethics and Economic Development: A Study of the Adaptation of Confucian Values to Modern Japanese Economic Ideology and Institutions." *Journal of Socio-Economics* 25, no. 5 (1996): 571–590.

Ostrom, Elinor, ed. *Strategies of Political Inquiry.* Beverly Hills, CA: Sage Publications, 1982.

Panitch, Leo. "Rethinking the Role of the State." In *Globalization: Critical Reflections,* edited by James H. Mittelman, 83–113. Boulder, CO: Lynne Rienner, 1996.

Park, Tae-Kyu. "Confucian Values and Contemporary Economic Development in Korea." In *Culture and Economics: The Shaping of Capitalism in Eastern Asia,* edited by Timothy Brook and Hy V. Luong, 125–136. Ann Arbor: University of Michigan Press, 1999.

Pempel, T. J. *Policy and Politics in Japan: Creative Conservatism.* Philadelphia: Temple University Press, 1982.

Peters, B. Guy. *Comparative Politics: Theory and Methods.* New York: New York University Press, 1998.

————. *Institutional Theory in Political Science: The "New Institutionalism."* London: Pinter, 1999.

Picard, Elizabeth. "The Lebanese Shi'a and Political Violence in Lebanon." In *The Legitimization of Violence,* edited by David Apter, 189–233. New York: New York University Press, 1997.

Pillar, Paul R. *Terrorism and U.S. Foreign Policy.* Washington, DC: Brookings, 2001.

Pinkney, Robert. *Democracy in the Third World.* 2nd ed. Boulder, CO: Lynne Rienner, 2003.

Polletta, Francesca, and James M. Jasper. "Collective Identity and Social Movements." *Annual Review of Sociology* 27 (2001): 283–305.

Popkin, Samuel L. "Public Choice and Peasant Organization." In *Toward a Political Economy of Development: A Rational Choice Perspective,* edited by Robert H. Bates, 245–271. Berkeley: University of California Press, 1988.

Post, Jerrold. "Terrorist Psycho-Logic: Terrorist Behavior as a Product of Psychological Forces." In *Origins of Terrorism: Psychologies, Ideologies, Theologies, States of Mind,* edited by Walter Reich, 25–40. Washington, DC: Woodrow Wilson Center Press, 1998.

Przeworski, Adam. *Democracy and the Market.* Cambridge: Cambridge University Press, 1991.

————. "Democratization Revisited." *Items* (Social Science Research Council) 51, no. 1 (1997): 6–11.

Przeworski, Adam, Michael Alvarez, José Antonia Cheibub, and Fernando Limongi. "What Makes Democracies Endure?" *Journal of Democracy* 7, no. 1 (1996): 39–55.

Przeworski, Adam, and Fernando Limongi. "Modernization: Theories and Facts." *World Politics* 49, no. 2 (1997): 155–183.

Przeworski, Adam, and Henry Teune. *The Logic of Comparative Social Inquiry*. New York: Wiley-Interscience, 1970.

Public Order and Internal Security Military Role Expansion. September 1995. http://reference.allrefer.com/country-guide-study/india/india200.html (accessed May 20, 2004).

Ragin, Charles C. *The Comparative Method: Moving Beyond Qualitative and Quantitative Strategies*. Berkeley: University of California Press, 1987.

Ragin, Charles C., and Howard S. Becker, eds. *What Is a Case? Exploring the Foundations of Social Inquiry*. Cambridge: Cambridge University Press, 1992.

Ranstorp, Magnus. "Terrorism in the Name of Religion." *Journal of International Affairs* 50, no. 1 (1996): 41–62.

Ravallion, Martin. "The Debate on Globalization, Poverty, and Inequality: Why Measurement Matters," n.d. http://poverty.worldbank.org/files/13871_Why_measurement_matters.pdf.

Reich, Walter. "Understanding Terrorist Behavior: The Limits and Opportunities of Psychological Inquiry." In *Origins of Terrorism: Psychologies, Ideologies, Theologies, States of Mind*, edited by Walter Reich, 261–279. Washington, DC: Woodrow Wilson Center Press, 1998.

Reno, William. "Market, War and the Reconfiguration of Political Authority in Sierra Leone." *Canadian Journal of African Studies* 29, no. 2 (1995): 203–221.

Richards, Paul. "Out of the Wilderness? Escaping Robert Kaplan's Dystopia." *Anthropology Today* 15, no. 6 (1999): 16–18.

Richardson, Louise. "Global Rebels: Terrorist Organizations as Trans-National Actors." *Harvard International Review* 20, no. 4 (1998): 52–56.

Roberts, J. Timmons, and Amy Hite. "Editors' Introduction." In *From Modernization to Globalization: Perspectives on Development and Social Change*, edited by J. Timmons Roberts and Amy Hite, 1–24. London: Blackwell Publishers, 2000.

Rosenau, James N. "Distant Proximities: The Dynamics and Dialectics of Globalization." In *International Political Economy: Understanding Global Disorder*, edited by Björn Hettne, 46–64. London: Zed Books, 1995.

Rosenau, James N., and Mary Durfee. *Thinking Theory Thoroughly: Coherent Approaches to an Incoherent World*. 2nd ed. Boulder, CO: Westview Press, 2000.

Rosenthal, Franz. "On Suicide in Islam." *Journal of the American Oriental Society* 66 (1946): 239–259.

Ross, Mark Howard. "Culture and Identity in Comparative Political Analysis." In *Comparative Politics: Rationality, Culture, and Structure*, edited by Mark Irving Lichbach and Alan S. Zuckerman, 42–80. Cambridge: Cambridge University Press, 1997.

Rostow, W. W. *The Stages of Economic Growth: A Non-Communist Manifesto*. Cambridge: Cambridge University Press, 1960.

Roth, Benita, and Marian Horan. "What Are Social Movements and What Is Gendered About Women's Participation in Social Movements? A Sociological Perspective." http://womhist.binghamton.edu/socm/intro/htm (accessed July 1, 2005).

Rothkopf, David. "In Praise of Cultural Imperialism." *Foreign Policy*, no. 107 (Summer 1997): 38–53.

Rueschemeyer, Dietrich. "Different Methods—Contradictory Results? Research on Development and Democracy." *International Journal of Comparative Sociology* 32, nos. 1–2 (1991): 9–38.

Rueschemeyer, Dietrich, Evelyne Huber Stephens, and John D. Stephens. *Capitalist Development and Democracy*. Chicago: University of Chicago Press, 1992.

Sarel, Michael. *Growth in East Asia: What We Can and What We Cannot Infer.* International Monetary Fund, September 1996. http://www.imf.org/external/pubs/ft/issues1/ (accessed July 30, 2001).

Sartori, Giovanni. "Compare Why and How." In *Comparing Nations: Concepts, Strategies, Substance*, edited by Mattei Dogan and Ali Kazancigil, 14–34. Oxford: Blackwell Publishers, 1994.

Saward, Michael. *The Terms of Democracy.* Cambridge: Polity, 1999.

Schmid, Alex P., and Albert J. Jongman. *Political Terrorism: A Research Guide to Concepts, Theories, Databases and Literature.* Amsterdam: North Holland Publishing, 1983.

Schmid, Peter D. "Expect the Unexpected: A Religious Democracy in Iran." *The Brown Journal of World Affairs* 9, no. 2 (Winter/Spring 2003): 181–196.

Selden, Mark, ed. *Asia, Asian Studies and the National Security State: A Symposium* (Special Issue). *Bulletin of Concerned Asian Scholars* 29, no. 1 (1997).

Sewell, William H., Jr. "Ideologies and Social Revolutions: Reflections on the French Case." *Journal of Modern History* 57 (1985): 57–85.

Shaw, Jane S. "Public Choice Theory." In *The Concise Encyclopedia of Economics*, edited by David R. Henderson. Indianapolis, IN: Liberty Fund, 2002. http://www.econlib.org/library/Enc/PublicChoiceTheory.html.

Sigelman, Lee, and G. H. Gadbois. "Contemporary Comparative Politics: An Inventory and Assessment." *Comparative Political Studies* 16 (October 1983): 275–305.

Silke, Andrew. "The Devil You Know: Continuing Problems with Research on Terrorism." *Terrorism and Political Violence* 13, no. 4 (2001): 1–14.

Sisson, Richard. "Culture and Democratization in India." In *Political Culture and Democracy in Developing Countries*, edited by Larry Diamond, 29–58. Boulder, CO: Lynne Rienner, 1994.

Skocpol, Theda. *States and Social Revolutions.* Cambridge: Cambridge University Press, 1979.

Sluka, Jeffrey A., ed. *Death Squad: The Anthropology of State Terror.* Philadelphia: University of Pennsylvania Press, 1999.

Smith, Jackie, Charles Chatfield, and Ron Pagnucco, eds. *Transnational Social Movements and Global Politics: Solidarity Beyond the State.* Syracuse, NY: Syracuse University Press, 1997.

Smith, Steve, and John Baylis. "Introduction." In *The Globalization of World Politics: An Introduction to International Relations*, edited by John Baylis and Steve Smith, 1–12. New York: Oxford University Press, 1997.

So, Alvin. *Social Change and Development: Modernization, Dependency, and World-System Theory.* Sage Library of Social Research. Newbury Park, CA: Sage Publications, 1990.

So, Alvin Y., and Stephen W.K. Chiu. *East Asia and the World Economy.* Thousand Oaks, CA: Sage Publications, 1995.

Sørensen, Georg. *Democracy and Democratization.* Boulder, CO: Westview Press, 1993.

Sprinzak, Ehud. "The Psychopolitical Formation of Extreme Left Terrorism in a Democracy: The Case of the Weathermen." In *Origins of Terrorism: Psychologies, Ideologies, Theologies, States of Mind*, edited by Walter Reich, 65–85. Washington, DC: Woodrow Wilson Center Press, 1998.

———. "Rational Fanatics." *Foreign Policy* 120 (2000): 66–73.

Srebrnik, Henry. "'Full of Sound and Fury': Three Decades of Parliamentary Politics in Mauritius." *Journal of Southern African Studies* 28, no. 2 (2002): 277–289.

Steans, Jill, and Lloyd Pettiford. *International Relations: Perspectives and Themes.* Essex, UK: Pearson Education Limited, 2001.

Stepan, Alfred. "Religion, Democracy, and the 'Twin Tolerations.'" *Journal of Democracy* 11, no. 4 (2000): 37–57.

Stern, Jessica. "Pakistan's Jihad Culture." *Foreign Affairs* 79, no. 6 (2000): 115–126.

Stoker, Gerry, and David Marsh. "Introduction." In *Theory and Methods in Political Science*, edited by David Marsh and Gerry Stoker, 1–16. Basingstoke, UK: Palgrave Macmillan, 2002.

Swanson, Guy. "Frameworks for Comparative Research: Structural Anthropology and the Theory of Action." In *Comparative Methods in Sociology*, edited by Ivan Vallier, 141–202. Berkeley: University of California Press, 1971.

Swidler, Ann. "Cultural Power and Social Movements." In *Social Movements and Culture*, edited by Hank Johnston and Bert Klandermans, 25–40. Minneapolis: University of Minnesota Press, 1995.

Taras, Raymond C., and Rajat Ganguly. *Understanding Ethnic Conflict.* 2nd ed. New York: Longman, 2002.

Tarrow, Sidney. *Power in Movements: Social Movements, Collective Action and Politics.* Cambridge: Cambridge University Press, 1994.

Tehranian, Majid. "Islamic Fundamentalism in Iran and the Discourse of Development." In *The Globalization Reader*, edited by Frank J. Lechner and John Boli, 359–370. Malden, MA: Blackwell, 2000.

Tipps, Dean C. "Modernization Theory and the Comparative Study of Societies: Critical Perspectives." In *Comparative Modernization: A Reader*, edited by Cyril E. Black, 62–88. New York: Free Press, 1976.

Tocqueville, Alexis de. *Democracy in America.* Translated by George Lawrence. Edited by J. P. Mayer. 2 vols. New York: Perennial Library/Harper & Row, [1835] 1988.

Torraine, Alain. *The Voice and the Eye.* New York: Cambridge University Press, 1981.

United Nations Development Programme. *Human Development Report 2000.* New York: Oxford University Press, 2000.

———. *Human Development Report 2003.* New York: Oxford University Press, 2003.

Verba, Sidney. "Comparative Politics: Where Have We Been, Where Are We Going?" In *New Directions in Comparative Politics*, edited by Howard J. Wiarda, 31–44. Boulder, CO: Westview Press, 1991.

Wade, Robert. *Governing the Market: Economic Theory and the Role of Government in East Asian Industrialization.* Princeton, NJ: Princeton University Press, 1990.

"Wal-Mart 2004 Annual Report." http://www.walmartstores.com/Files/annualreport_ 2004.pdf.

Ward, Hugh. "Rational Choice." In *Theory and Methods in Political Science*, edited by David Marsh and Gerry Stoker, 65–89. Basingstoke, UK: Palgrave Macmillan, 2002.

Weber, Max. *The Protestant Ethic and the Spirit of Capitalism.* Translated by Talcott Parsons. New York: Scribner, [1930] 1958.

Weiner, Myron. "Political Change: Asia, Africa and the Middle East." In *Understanding Political Development*, edited by Myron Weiner and Samuel P. Huntington, 33–64. Boston: Little, Brown, 1987.

Whittaker, David J., ed. *The Terrorism Reader.* London: Routledge, 2001.

Wiarda, Howard J. "Comparative Politics Past and Present." In *New Directions in Comparative Politics*, edited by Howard J. Wiarda, 3–30. Boulder, CO: Westview Press, 1991.

————. *Introduction to Comparative Politics: Concepts and Processes.* 2nd ed. Fort Worth, TX: Harcourt College Publishers, 2000.

Willets, Peter. "Transnational Actors and International Organizations in Global Politics." In *The Globalization of World Politics*, edited by John Baylis and Steve Smith, 287–310. New York: Oxford University Press, 1997.

Williams, Rhys H. "The Cultural Contexts of Collective Action: Constraints, Opportunities, and the Symbolic Life of Social Movements." In *The Blackwell Companion to Social Movements*, edited by David A. Snow, Sarah A. Soule, and Hanspeter Kriesi, 91–114. Malden, MA: Blackwell Publishing, 2004.

Wilson, Bruce M. *Costa Rica: Politics, Economics, and Democracy.* Boulder, CO: Lynne Rienner, 1998.

Wilson, Frank L. *Concepts and Issues in Comparative Politics.* Upper Saddle River, NJ: Prentice Hall, 1996.

Woo, Jung-en. *Race to the Swift: State and Finance in Korean Industrialization.* New York: Columbia University Press, 1991.

Woo-Cumings, Meredith, ed. *The Developmental State.* Cornell Studies in Political Economy, ed. Peter J. Katzenstein. Ithaca, NY: Cornell University Press, 1999.

Woods, Ngaire. "The Uses of Theory in the Study of International Relations." In *Explaining International Relations Since 1945*, edited by Ngaire Woods, 9–31. Oxford: Oxford University Press, 1996.

World Bank. "The Global Poverty Numbers Debate," n.d. http://web.worldbank.org.

Wuthnow, Robert. *Meaning and Moral Order: Explanations in Cultural Analysis.* Berkeley: University of California Press, 1987.

Zahariadis, Nikolaos. *Theory, Case, and Method in Comparative Politics.* New York: Harcourt Brace College Publishers, 1997.

Zuckerman, Alan S. *Doing Political Science: An Introduction to Political Analysis.* Boulder, CO: Westview Press, 1991.

Index

About the Book

Systematic, coherent, and user-friendly, this decidedly nontraditional introduction to comparative politics is designed to teach students how to think comparatively and theoretically about the world they live in.

The core of the book is organized around a set of critical questions—why are poor countries poor? why is East Asia rich? what makes a democracy? what makes a terrorist? what makes a social movement?—each the topic of a full chapter. These issue chapters are based on the solid methodological and theoretical foundation laid out in the first part of the book. Graphics and definition boxes enhance the text.

Doing Comparative Politics will stimulate students to critically engage with both the content and the methods of the field.

Timothy C. Lim is associate professor of political science at California State University, Los Angeles.